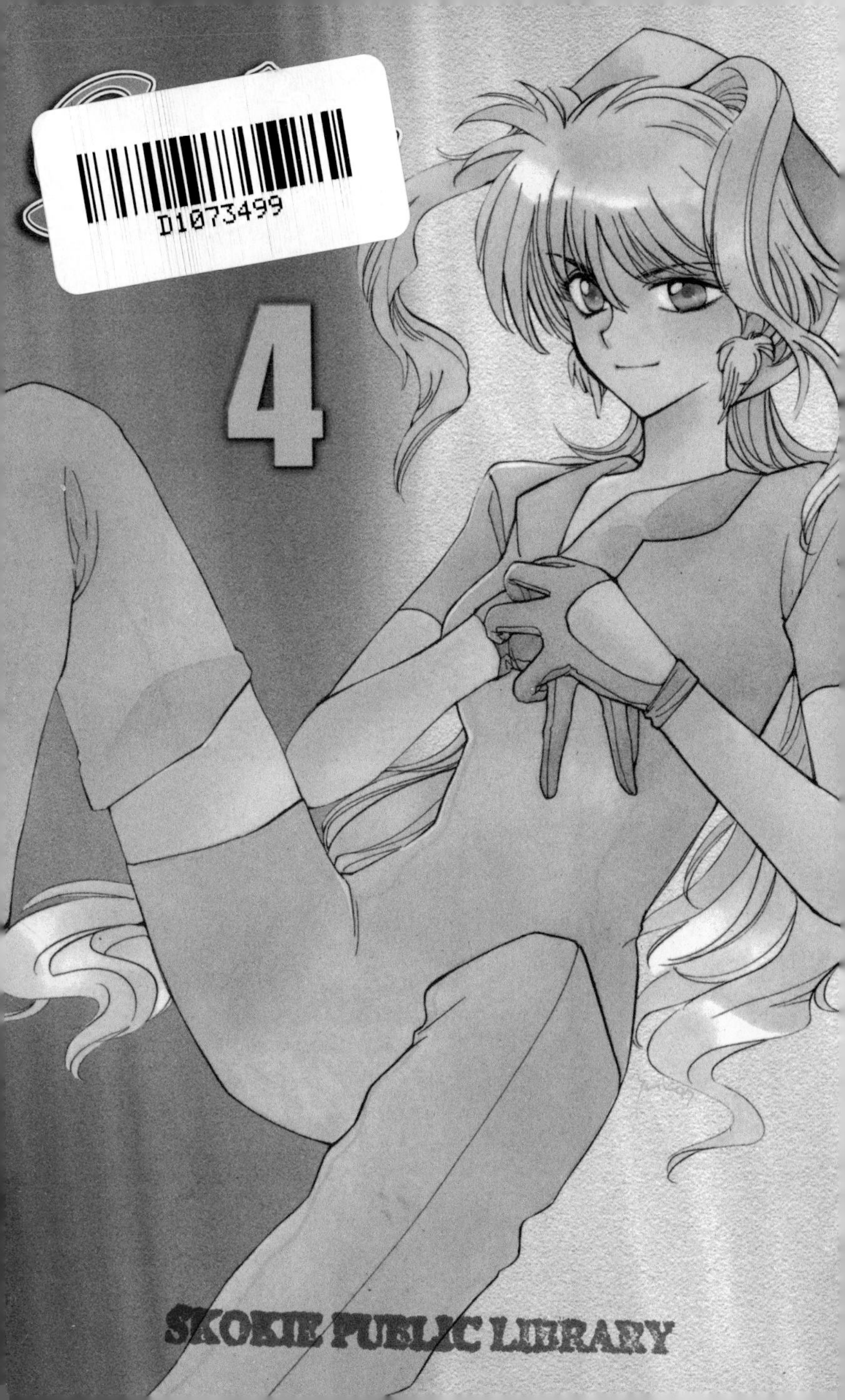
4

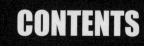

CONTENTS

4

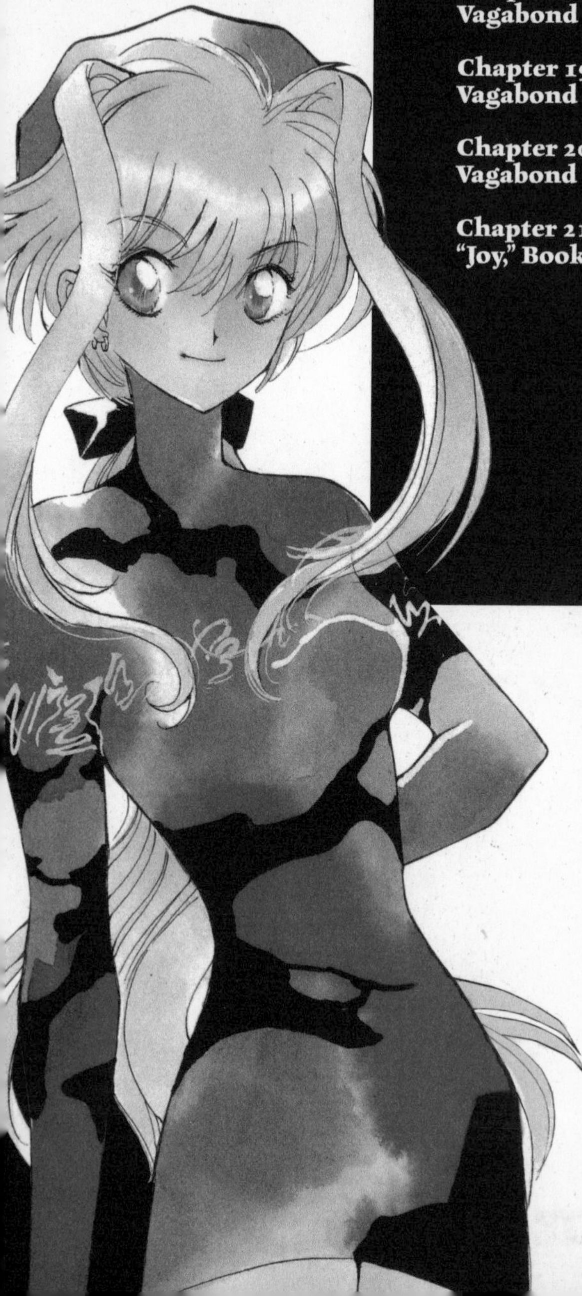

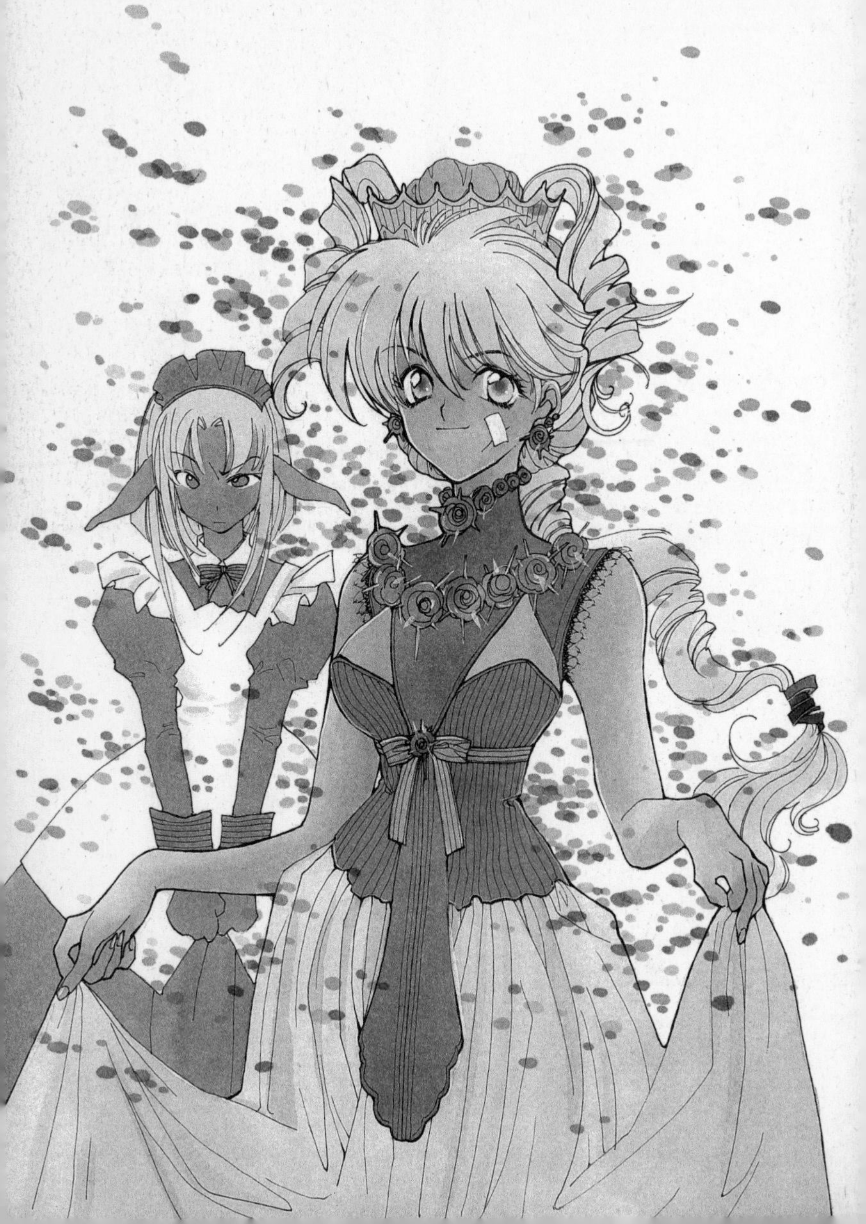

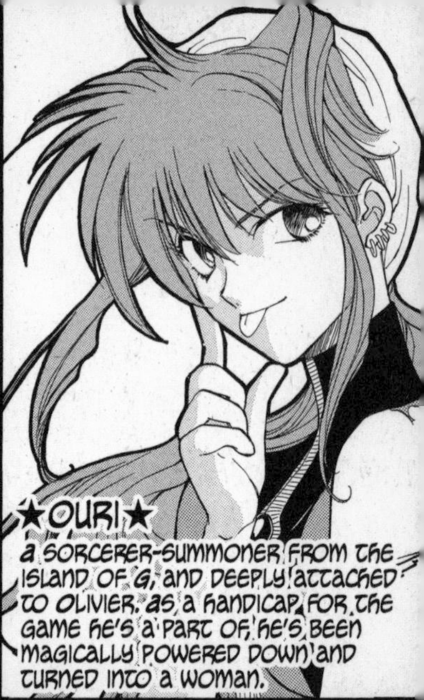
★OURI★
A SORCERER-SUMMONER FROM THE ISLAND OF G, AND DEEPLY ATTACHED TO OLIVIER. AS A HANDICAP FOR THE GAME HE'S A PART OF, HE'S BEEN MAGICALLY POWERED DOWN AND TURNED INTO A WOMAN.

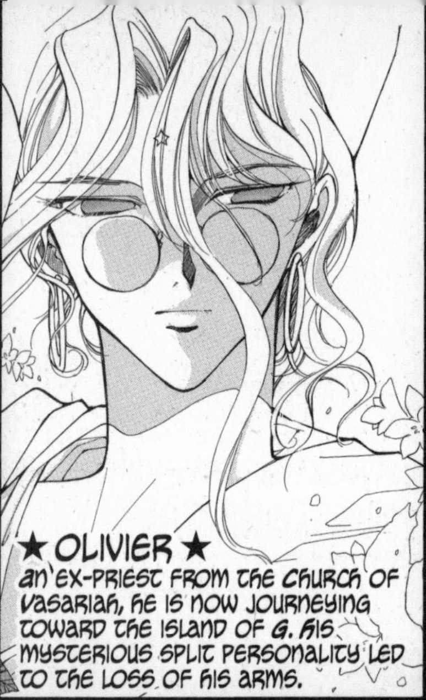
★OLIVIER★
AN EX-PRIEST FROM THE CHURCH OF VASARIAH, HE IS NOW JOURNEYING TOWARD THE ISLAND OF G. HIS MYSTERIOUS SPLIT PERSONALITY LED TO THE LOSS OF HIS ARMS.

CHARACTERS

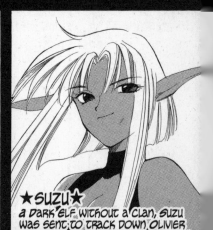

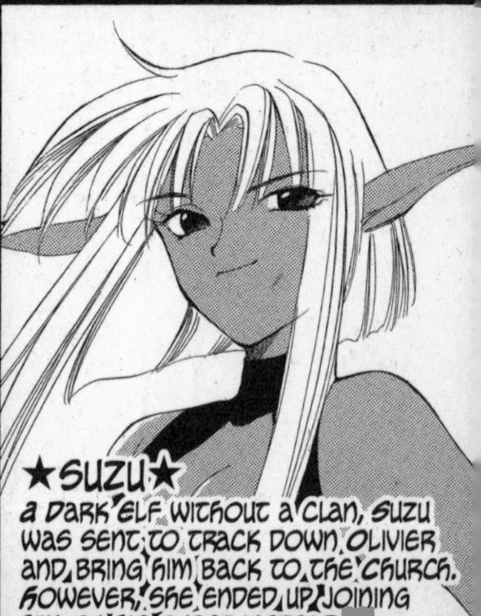
★SUZU★
A DARK ELF WITHOUT A CLAN, SUZU WAS SENT TO TRACK DOWN OLIVIER AND BRING HIM BACK TO THE CHURCH. HOWEVER, SHE ENDED UP JOINING HIM ON HIS QUEST INSTEAD.

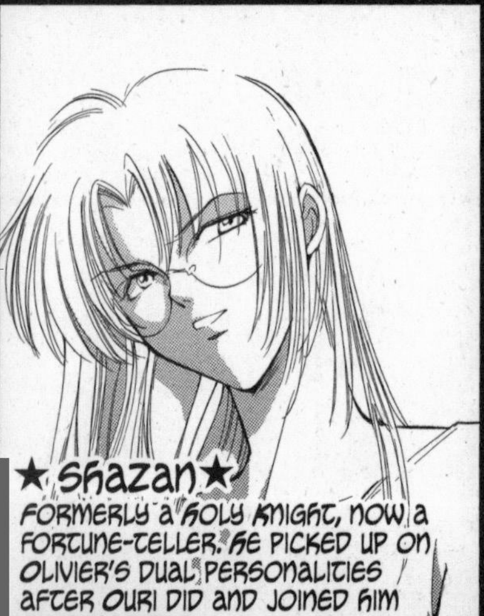
★SHAZAN★
FORMERLY A HOLY KNIGHT, NOW A FORTUNE-TELLER. HE PICKED UP ON OLIVIER'S DUAL PERSONALITIES AFTER OURI DID AND JOINED HIM ON HIS JOURNEY.

Legend of the Great Beast

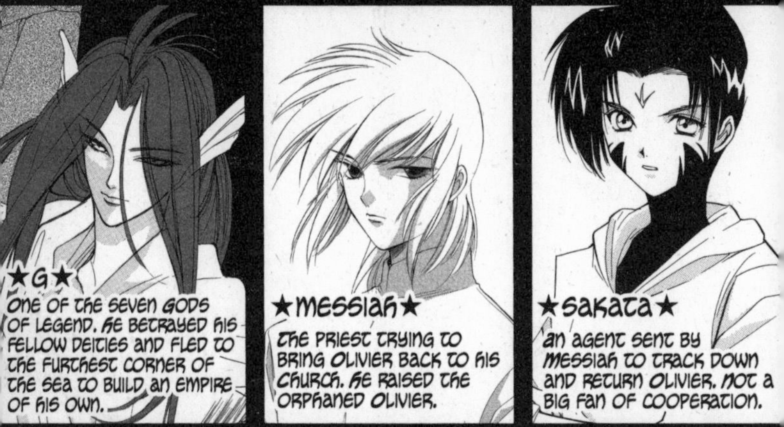
★SAKATA★
AN AGENT SENT BY MESSIAH TO TRACK DOWN AND RETURN OLIVIER. NOT A BIG FAN OF COOPERATION.
★MESSIAH★
THE PRIEST TRYING TO BRING OLIVIER BACK TO HIS CHURCH. HE RAISED THE ORPHANED OLIVIER.
★G★
ONE OF THE SEVEN GODS OF LEGEND. HE BETRAYED HIS FELLOW DEITIES AND FLED TO THE FURTHEST CORNER OF THE SEA TO BUILD AN EMPIRE OF HIS OWN.

OURI'S SIBLINGS

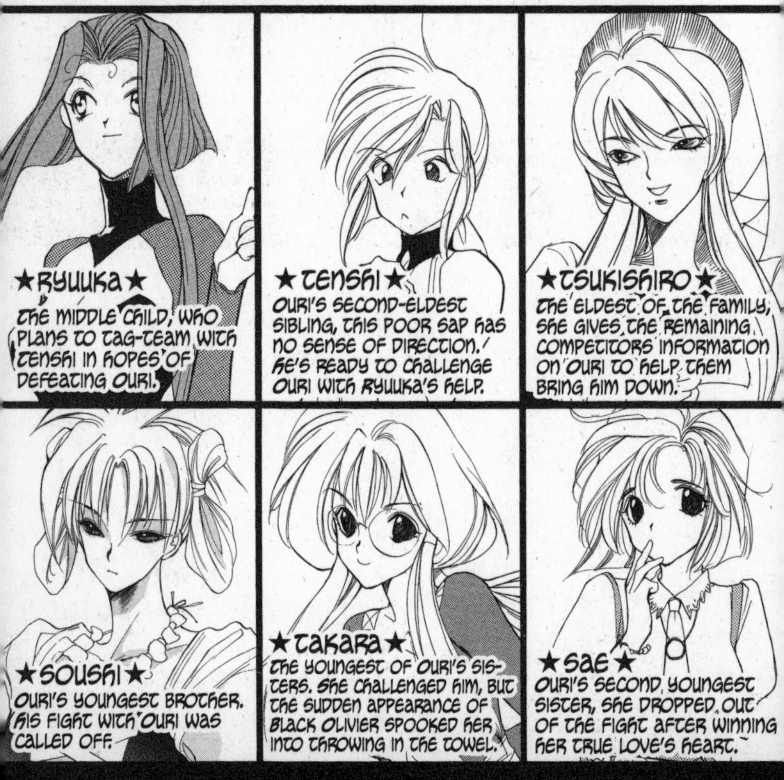
★TSUKISHIRO★
THE ELDEST OF THE FAMILY, SHE GIVES THE REMAINING COMPETITORS INFORMATION ON OURI TO HELP THEM BRING HIM DOWN.
★TENSHI★
OURI'S SECOND-ELDEST SIBLING, THIS POOR SAP HAS NO SENSE OF DIRECTION. HE'S READY TO CHALLENGE OURI WITH RYUUKA'S HELP.
★RYUUKA★
THE MIDDLE CHILD, WHO PLANS TO TAG-TEAM WITH TENSHI IN HOPES OF DEFEATING OURI.
★SAE★
OURI'S SECOND YOUNGEST SISTER, SHE DROPPED OUT OF THE FIGHT AFTER WINNING HER TRUE LOVE'S HEART.
★TAKARA★
THE YOUNGEST OF OURI'S SISTERS. SHE CHALLENGED HIM, BUT THE SUDDEN APPEARANCE OF BLACK OLIVIER SPOOKED HER INTO THROWING IN THE TOWEL.
★SOUSHI★
OURI'S YOUNGEST BROTHER. HIS FIGHT WITH OURI WAS CALLED OFF.

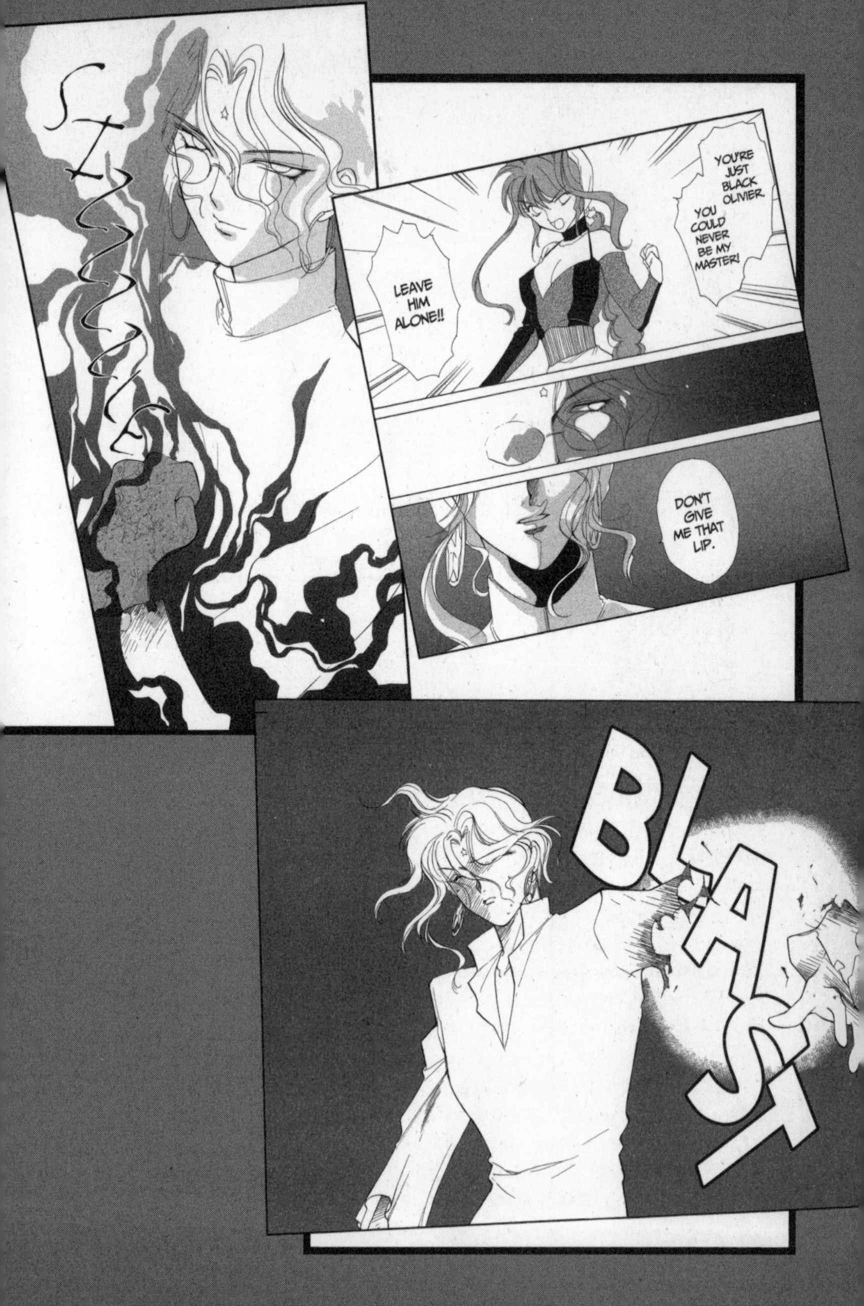
YOU'RE JUST BLACK OLIVIER.
YOU COULD NEVER BE MY MASTER!
LEAVE HIM ALONE!!
DON'T GIVE ME THAT LIP.
BLAST

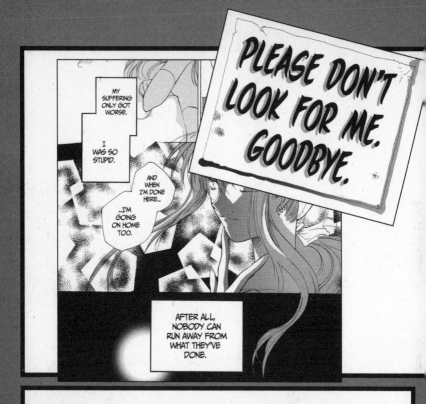

PLEASE DON'T LOOK FOR ME. GOODBYE.
MY SUFFERING ONLY GOT WORSE.
I WAS SO STUPID.
AND WHEN I'M DONE HERE...
...I'M GOING ON HOME TOO.
AFTER ALL, NOBODY CAN RUN AWAY FROM WHAT THEY'VE DONE.

Olivier was a priest of the Church of Vasariah until the day he fled his order to discover the forbidden island of G. On his journey, he meets a girl named Ouri who claims to hail from G. As it turns out, "she" is playing a dangerous "game" of magical combat against her siblings, and was handicapped with limited powers and a male-to-female sex change.
The two team up and are soon joined by Suzu—who was originally sent by the Church to take back Olivier—and the ex-Holy Knight Shazan, all making their way to G.
However, the ominous being hidden within Olivier surfaces. This "Black Olivier" tests Ouri's love for him by infecting the poor priest's arms with incurable poison. Our heroes are initially shocked by the atrocity, but in order to save Olivier's life, Ouri takes the drastic step of severing the infected arms with magic. Though he had no other choice, Ouri can't live with himself after what he's done and disappears.
After a stint as a bodyguard for a band of thieves, he finally realizes that he can't run away from himself forever and resolves to return to Olivier.
Meanwhile, Shazan splits up with the group to search for Ouri on his own, while Olivier goes to a stay at a mysterious manor with Suzu and Sakata.

THE STORY SO FAR

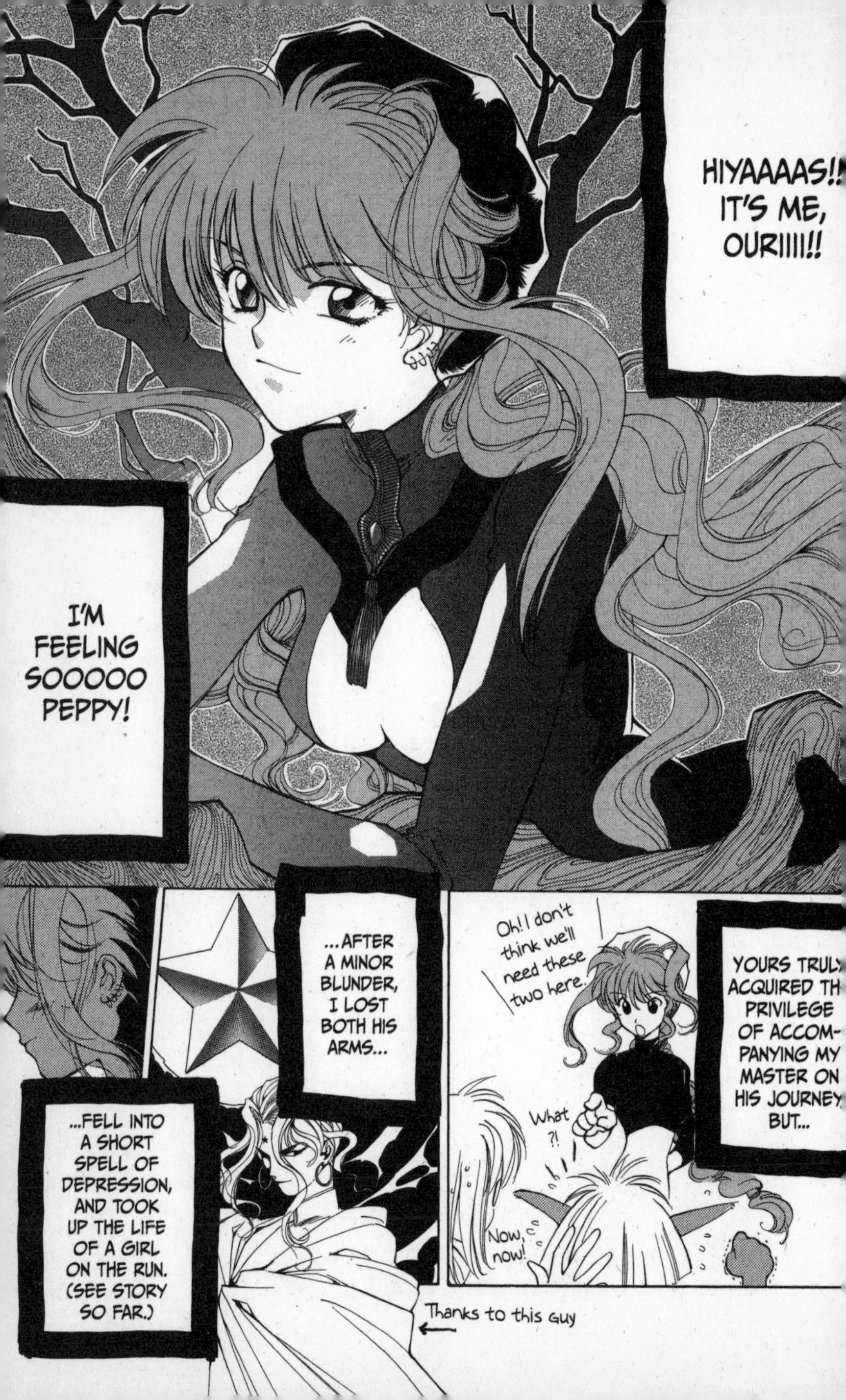
HIYAAAAS!! IT'S ME, OURIIIII!!
I'M FEELING SOOOOO PEPPY!
YOURS TRULY ACQUIRED TH PRIVILEGE OF ACCOM-PANYING MY MASTER ON HIS JOURNEY, BUT...
Oh! I don't think we'll need these two here.
What ?!
Now, now!
...AFTER A MINOR BLUNDER, I LOST BOTH HIS ARMS...
...FELL INTO A SHORT SPELL OF DEPRESSION, AND TOOK UP THE LIFE OF A GIRL ON THE RUN. (SEE STORY SO FAR.)
Thanks to this guy

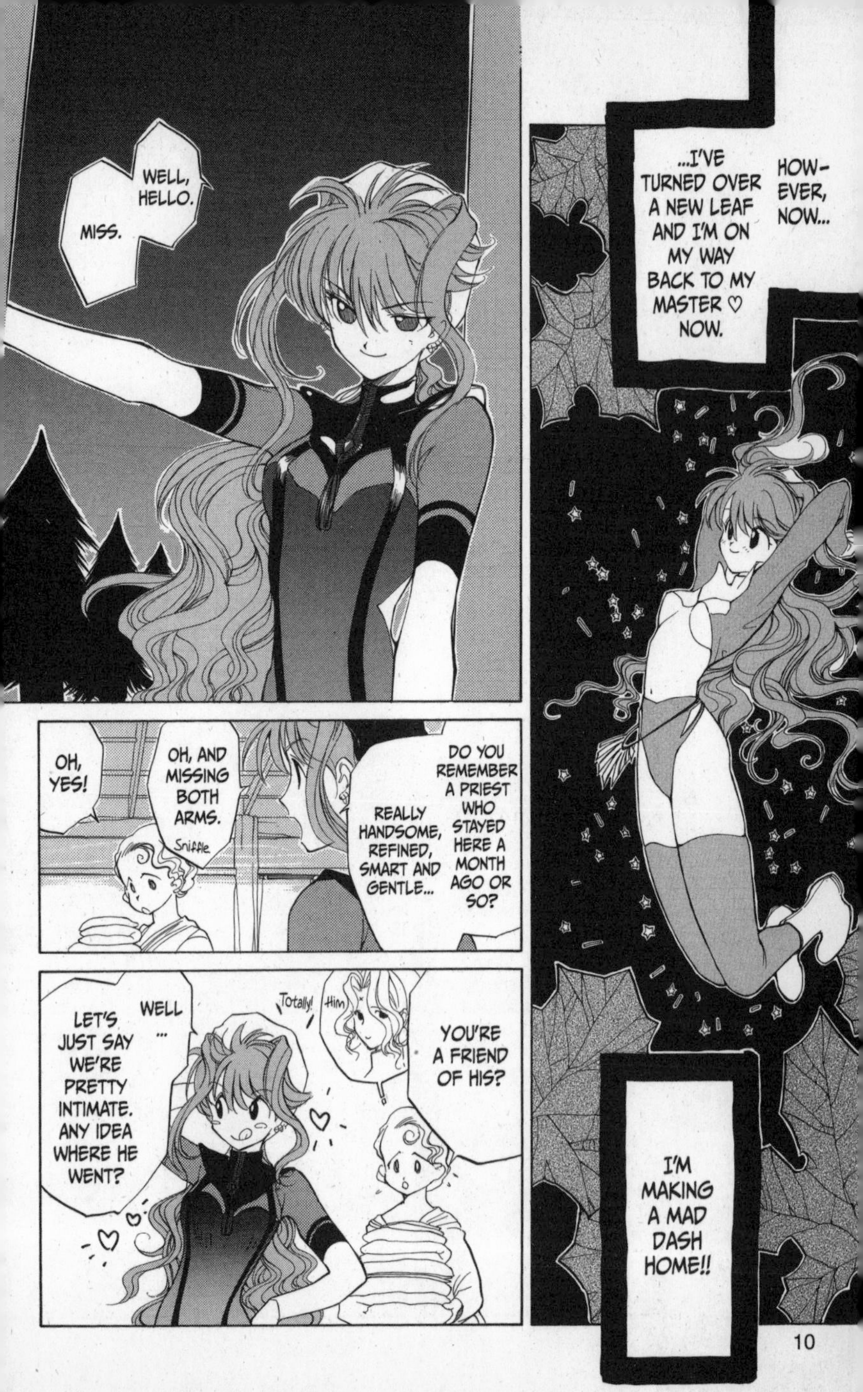
HOW-EVER, NOW...
...I'VE TURNED OVER A NEW LEAF AND I'M ON MY WAY BACK TO MY MASTER ♡ NOW.
I'M MAKING A MAD DASH HOME!!
WELL, HELLO.
MISS.
DO YOU REMEMBER A PRIEST WHO STAYED HERE A MONTH AGO OR SO?
REALLY HANDSOME, REFINED, SMART AND GENTLE...
OH, AND MISSING BOTH ARMS.
Sniffle
OH, YES!
YOU'RE A FRIEND OF HIS?
Him
Totally!
WELL ...
LET'S JUST SAY WE'RE PRETTY INTIMATE. ANY IDEA WHERE HE WENT?

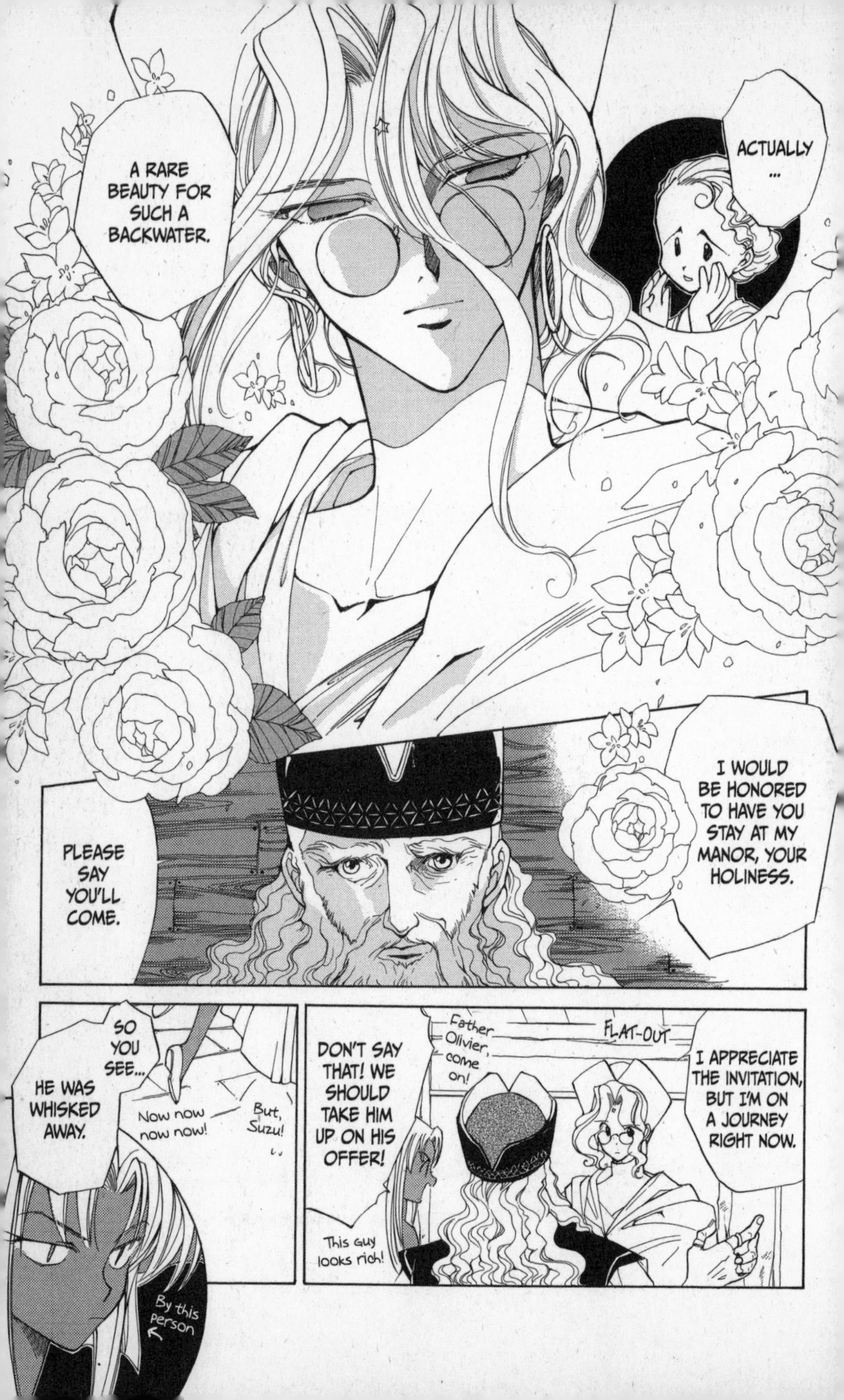
ACTUALLY ...
A RARE BEAUTY FOR SUCH A BACKWATER.
I WOULD BE HONORED TO HAVE YOU STAY AT MY MANOR, YOUR HOLINESS.
PLEASE SAY YOU'LL COME.
I APPRECIATE THE INVITATION, BUT I'M ON A JOURNEY RIGHT NOW.
FLAT-OUT
Father Olivier, come on!
DON'T SAY THAT! WE SHOULD TAKE HIM UP ON HIS OFFER!
This guy looks rich!
SO YOU SEE...
But, Suzu!
Now now now now!
HE WAS WHISKED AWAY.
By this person

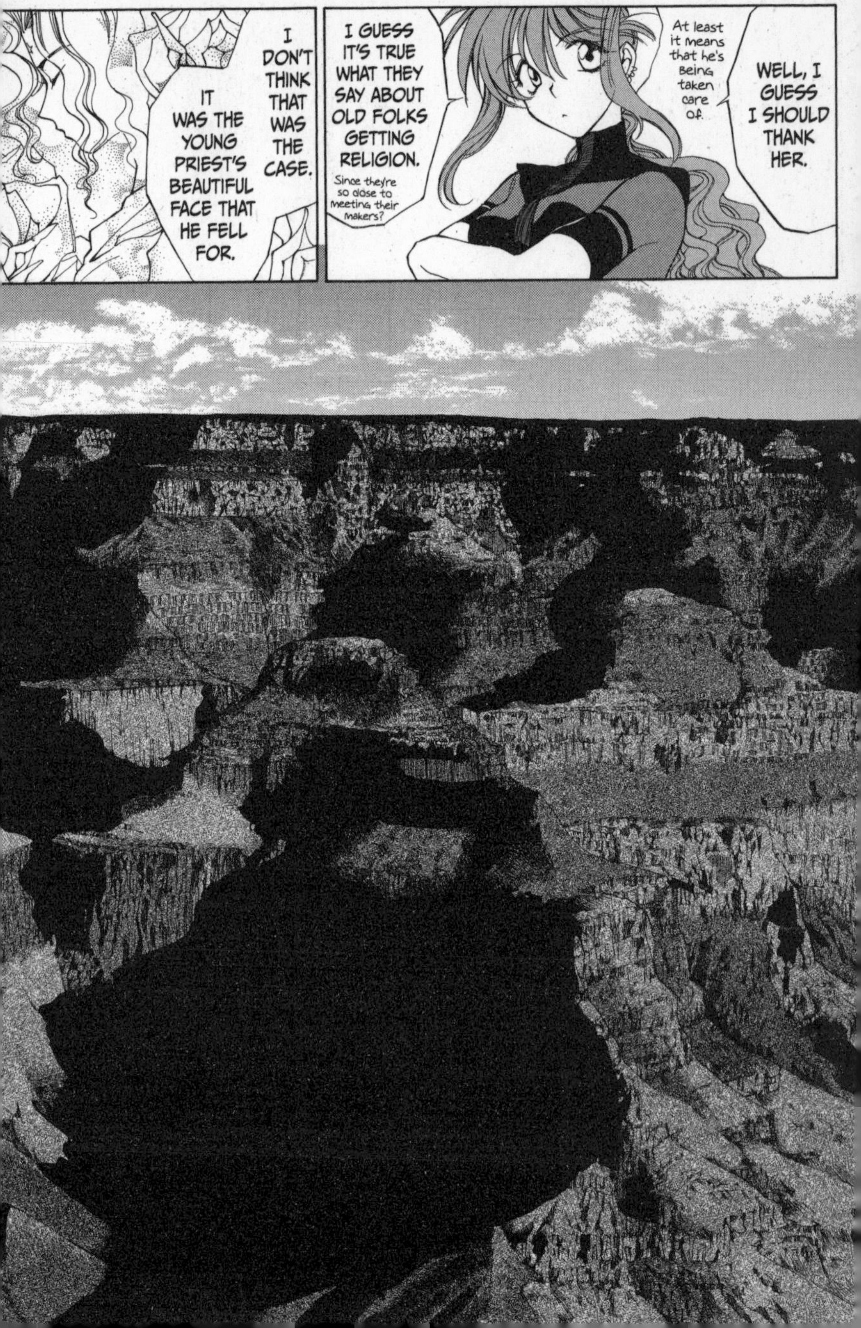
WELL, I GUESS I SHOULD THANK HER.
At least it means that he's being taken care of.
I GUESS IT'S TRUE WHAT THEY SAY ABOUT OLD FOLKS GETTING RELIGION.
Since they're so close to meeting their makers?
I DON'T THINK THAT WAS THE CASE.
IT WAS THE YOUNG PRIEST'S BEAUTIFUL FACE THAT HE FELL FOR.

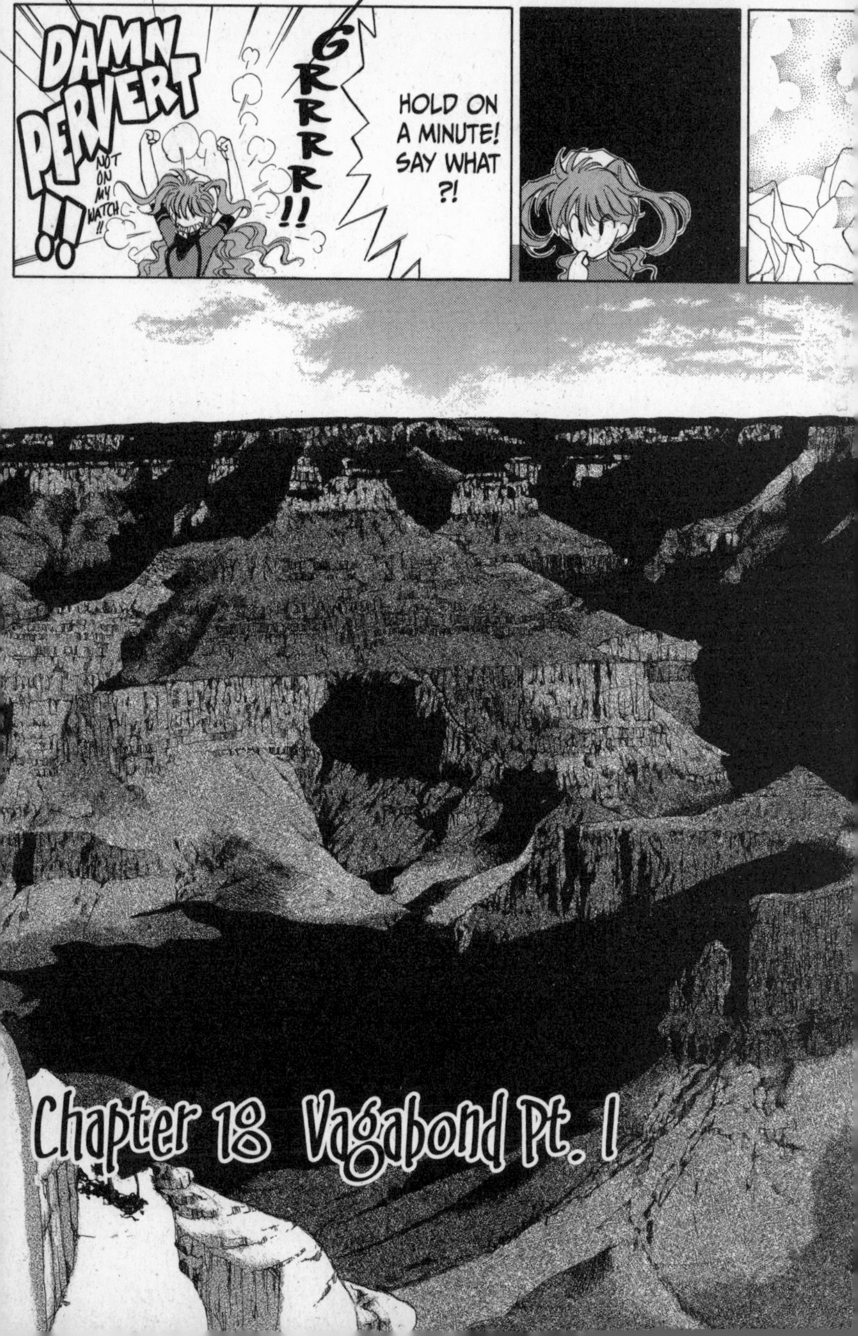
HOLD ON A MINUTE! SAY WHAT ?!
GRRRR!!
DAMN PERVERT!!
NOT ON MY WATCH!!
Chapter 18 Vagabond Pt. 1

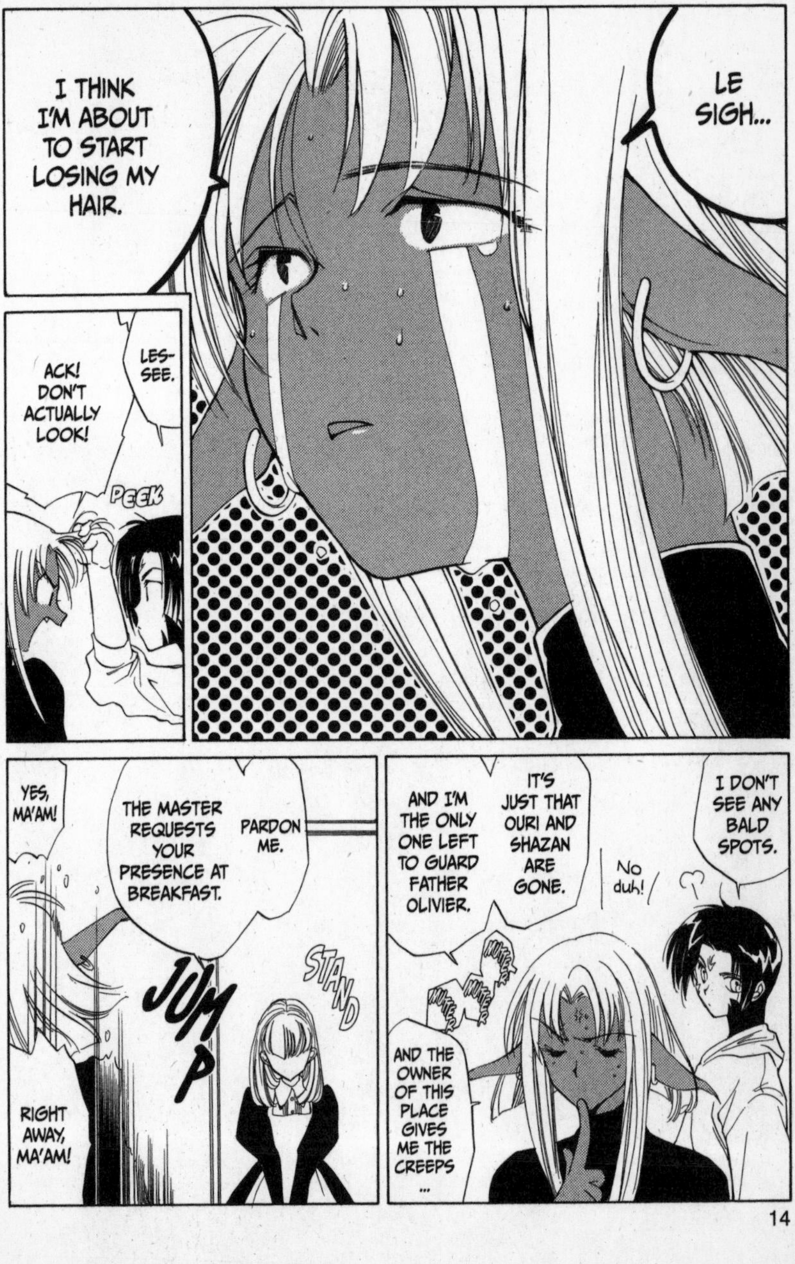
LE SIGH...
I THINK I'M ABOUT TO START LOSING MY HAIR.
LES-SEE.
ACK! DON'T ACTUALLY LOOK!
PEEK
I DON'T SEE ANY BALD SPOTS.
No duh!
IT'S JUST THAT OURI AND SHAZAN ARE GONE.
AND I'M THE ONLY ONE LEFT TO GUARD FATHER OLIVIER.
MUTTER
MUTTER
MUTTER
AND THE OWNER OF THIS PLACE GIVES ME THE CREEPS ...
PARDON ME.
THE MASTER REQUESTS YOUR PRESENCE AT BREAKFAST.
STAND
YES, MA'AM!
JUMP
RIGHT AWAY, MA'AM!

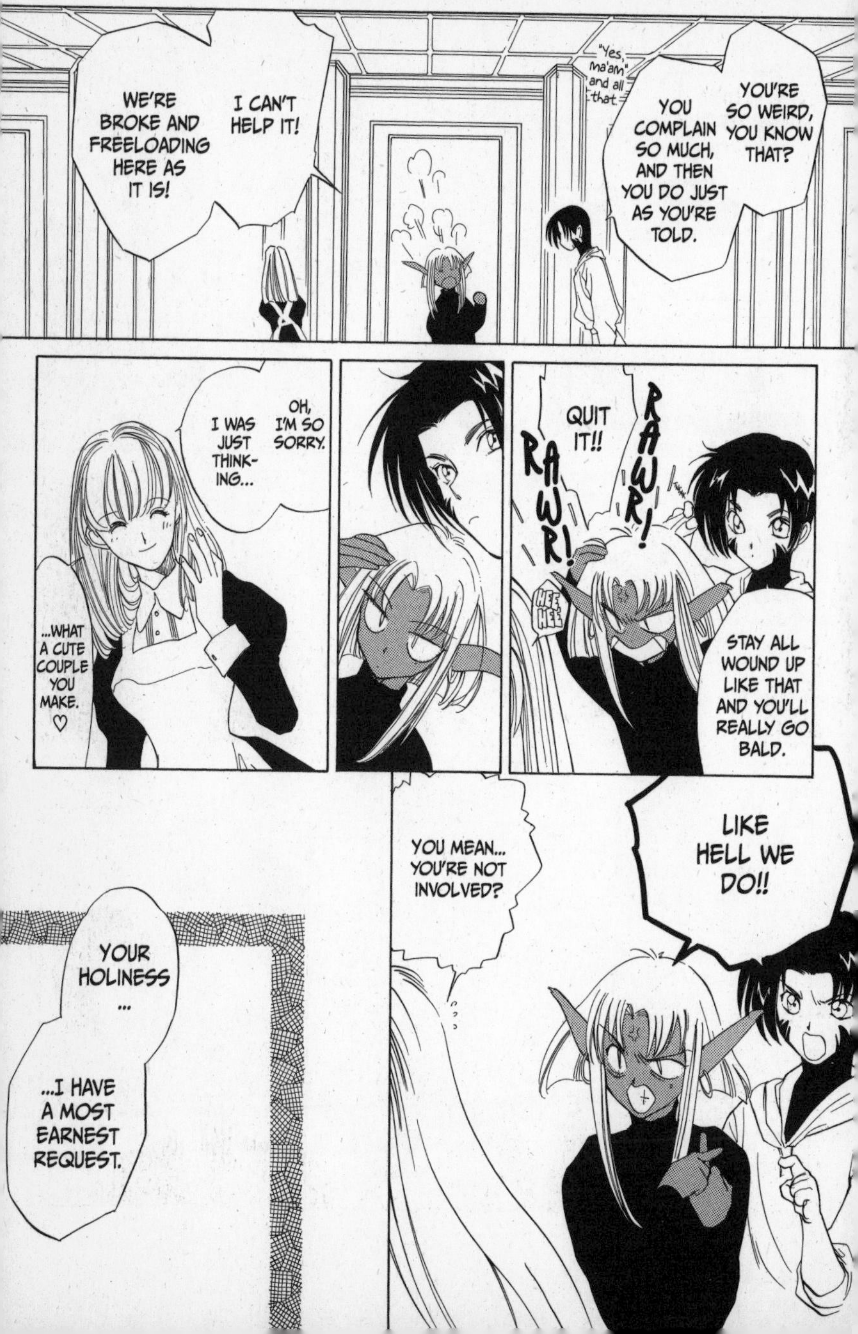
YOU'RE SO WEIRD, YOU KNOW THAT?
YOU COMPLAIN SO MUCH, AND THEN YOU DO JUST AS YOU'RE TOLD.
"Yes, ma'am" and all that.
I CAN'T HELP IT!
WE'RE BROKE AND FREELOADING HERE AS IT IS!
RAWR!
QUIT IT!!
RAWR!
HEE, HEE
STAY ALL WOUND UP LIKE THAT AND YOU'LL REALLY GO BALD.
OH, I'M SO SORRY.
I WAS JUST THINKING...
...WHAT A CUTE COUPLE YOU MAKE. ♡
LIKE HELL WE DO!!
YOU MEAN... YOU'RE NOT INVOLVED?
YOUR HOLINESS...
...I HAVE A MOST EARNEST REQUEST.

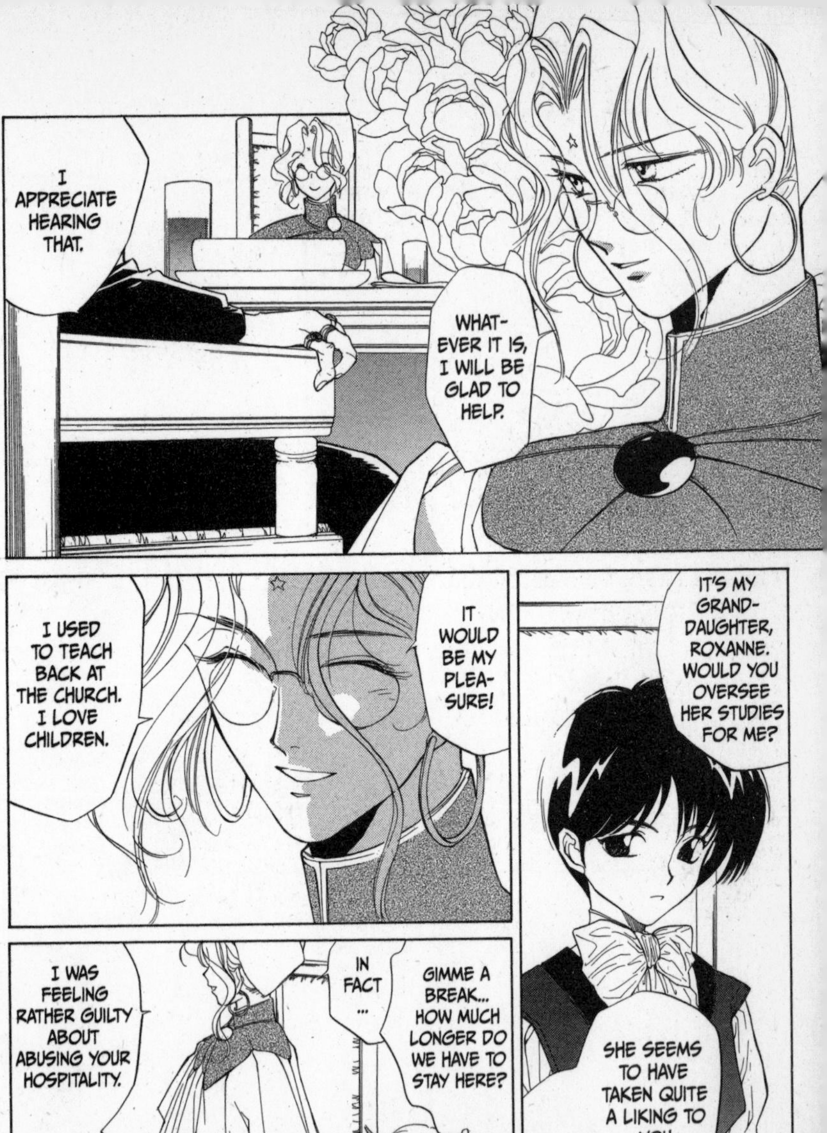
WHAT-EVER IT IS, I WILL BE GLAD TO HELP.
I APPRECIATE HEARING THAT.
IT'S MY GRAND-DAUGHTER, ROXANNE. WOULD YOU OVERSEE HER STUDIES FOR ME?
SHE SEEMS TO HAVE TAKEN QUITE A LIKING TO YOU.
THE POOR CHILD IS MUTE BUT AS BRIGHT AS THEY COME.
IT WOULD BE MY PLEA-SURE!
I USED TO TEACH BACK AT THE CHURCH. I LOVE CHILDREN.
IN FACT ...
GIMME A BREAK... HOW MUCH LONGER DO WE HAVE TO STAY HERE?
I WAS FEELING RATHER GUILTY ABOUT ABUSING YOUR HOSPITALITY.
I'D LOVE TO HELP OUT IN ANY WAY I CAN.

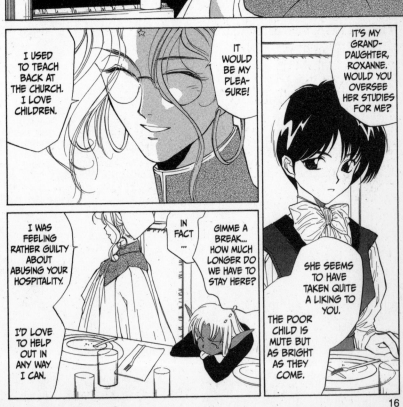

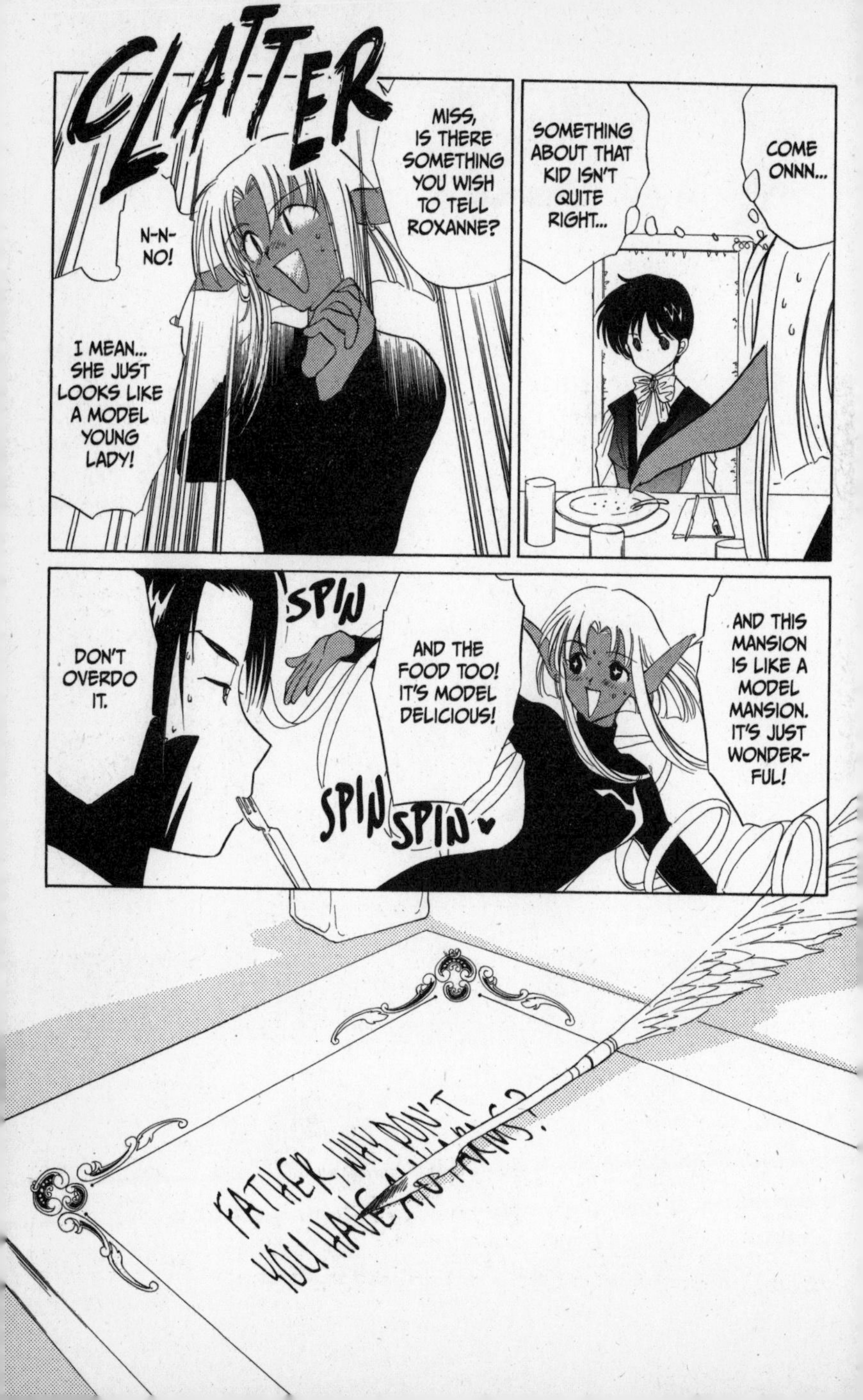
COME ONNN...
SOMETHING ABOUT THAT KID ISN'T QUITE RIGHT...
MISS, IS THERE SOMETHING YOU WISH TO TELL ROXANNE?
CLATTER
N-N-NO!
I MEAN... SHE JUST LOOKS LIKE A MODEL YOUNG LADY!
AND THIS MANSION IS LIKE A MODEL MANSION. IT'S JUST WONDERFUL!
AND THE FOOD TOO! IT'S MODEL DELICIOUS!
SPIN
DON'T OVERDO IT.
SPIN SPIN
FATHER, WHY DON'T
YOU HAVE

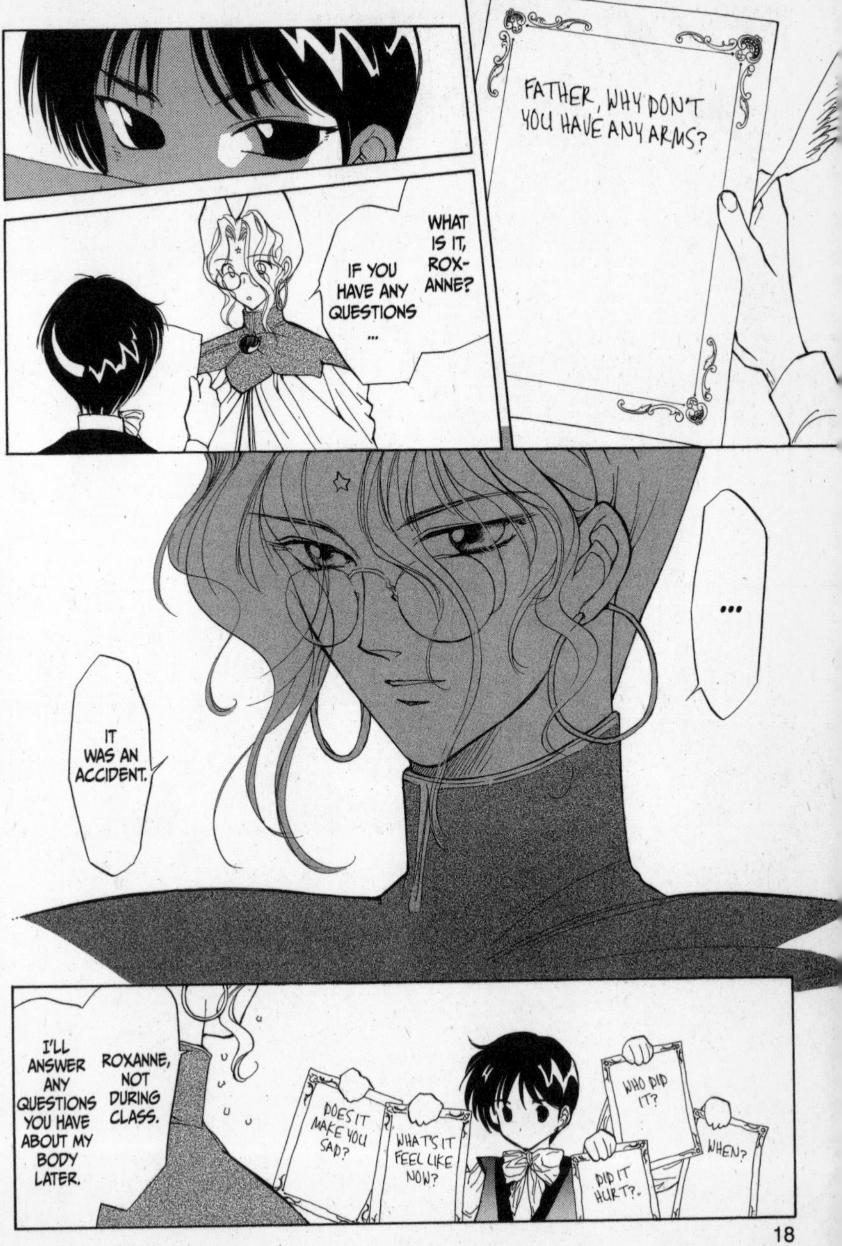

FATHER, WHY DON'T YOU HAVE ANY ARMS?
WHAT IS IT, ROXANNE?
IF YOU HAVE ANY QUESTIONS ...
...
IT WAS AN ACCIDENT.
WHO DID IT?
WHEN?
DID IT HURT?
WHAT'S IT FEEL LIKE NOW?
DOES IT MAKE YOU SAD?
ROXANNE, NOT DURING CLASS.
I'LL ANSWER ANY QUESTIONS YOU HAVE ABOUT MY BODY LATER.

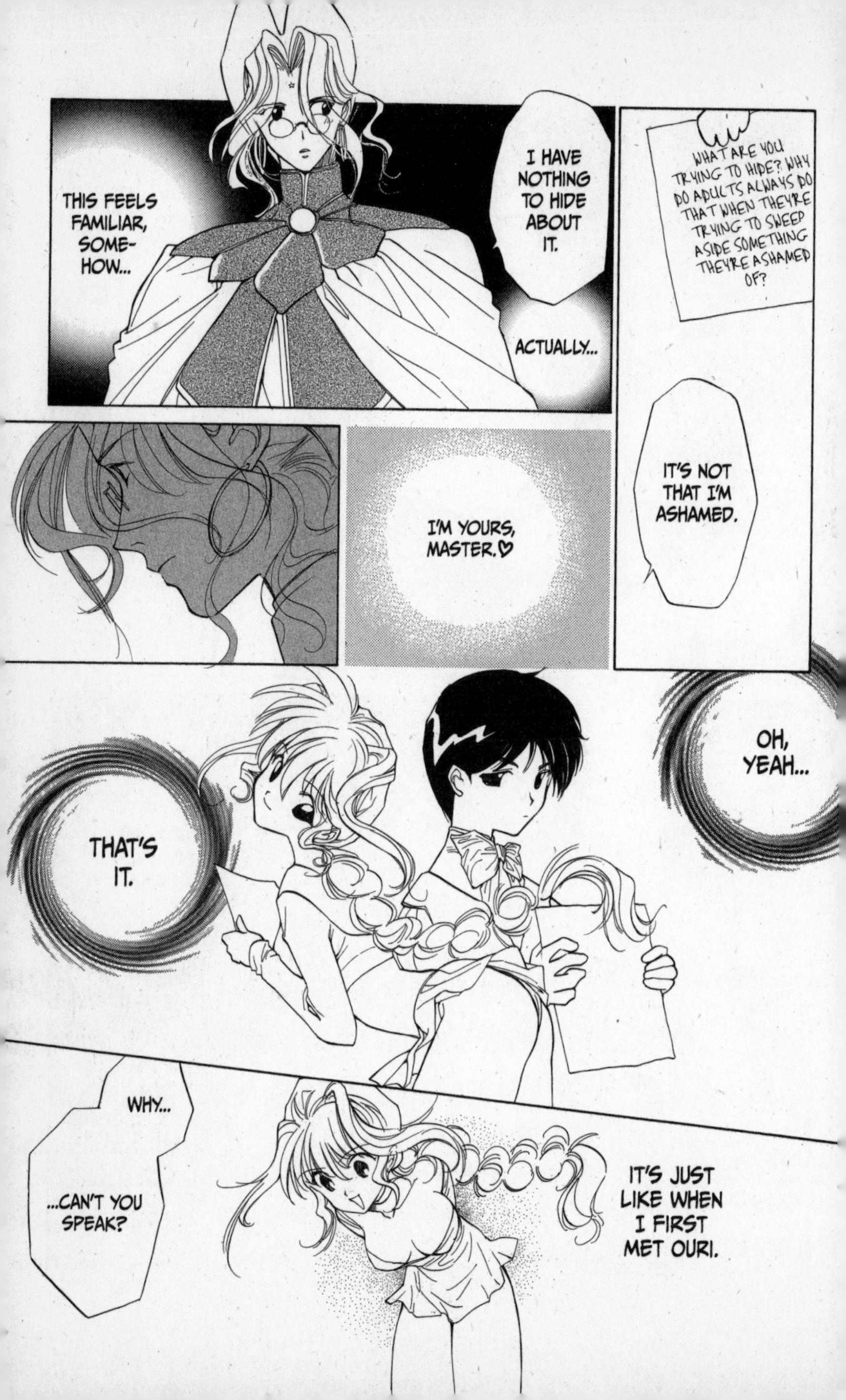
WHAT ARE YOU TRYING TO HIDE? WHY DO ADULTS ALWAYS DO THAT WHEN THEY'RE TRYING TO SWEEP ASIDE SOMETHING THEY'RE ASHAMED OF?
IT'S NOT THAT I'M ASHAMED.
I HAVE NOTHING TO HIDE ABOUT IT.
ACTUALLY...
THIS FEELS FAMILIAR, SOME-HOW...
I'M YOURS, MASTER.♡
OH, YEAH...
THAT'S IT.
IT'S JUST LIKE WHEN I FIRST MET OURI.
WHY...
...CAN'T YOU SPEAK?

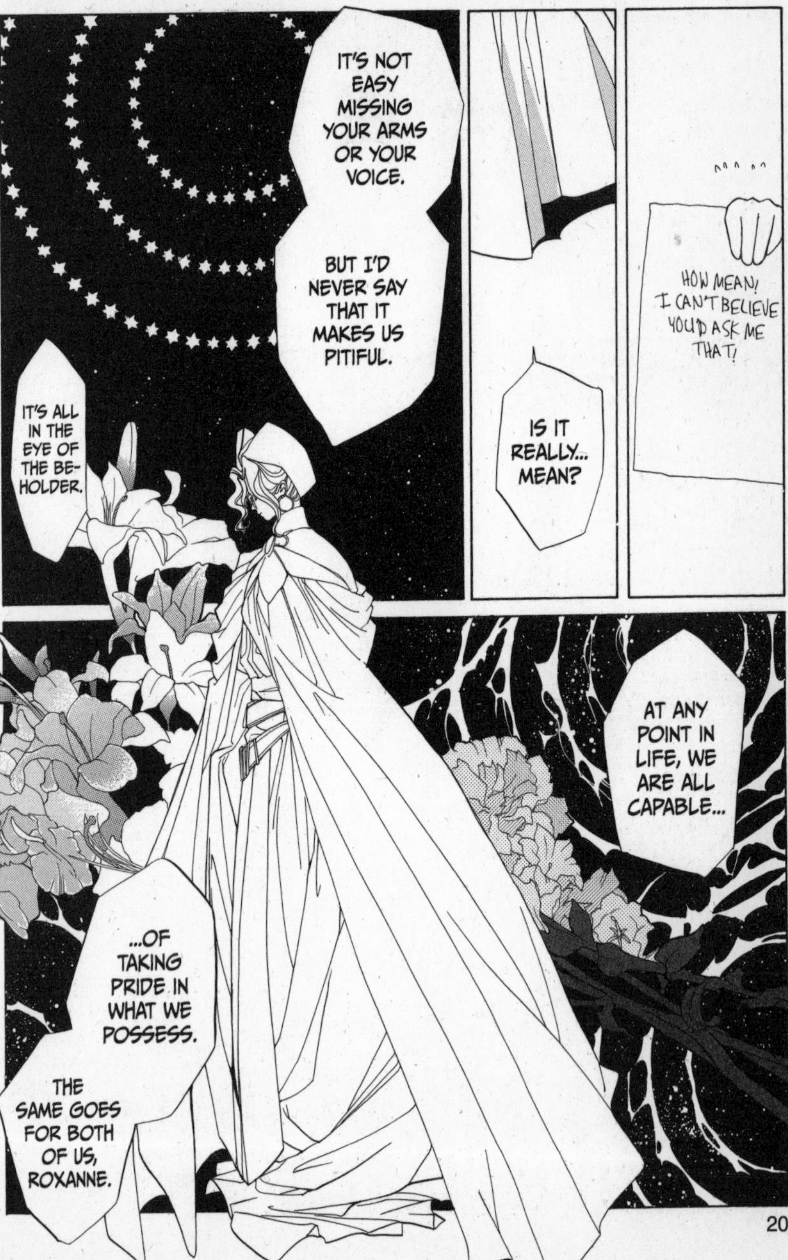
HOW MEAN! I CAN'T BELIEVE YOU'D ASK ME THAT!
IS IT REALLY... MEAN?
IT'S NOT EASY MISSING YOUR ARMS OR YOUR VOICE.
BUT I'D NEVER SAY THAT IT MAKES US PITIFUL.
IT'S ALL IN THE EYE OF THE BE-HOLDER.
AT ANY POINT IN LIFE, WE ARE ALL CAPABLE...
...OF TAKING PRIDE IN WHAT WE POSSESS.
THE SAME GOES FOR BOTH OF US, ROXANNE.

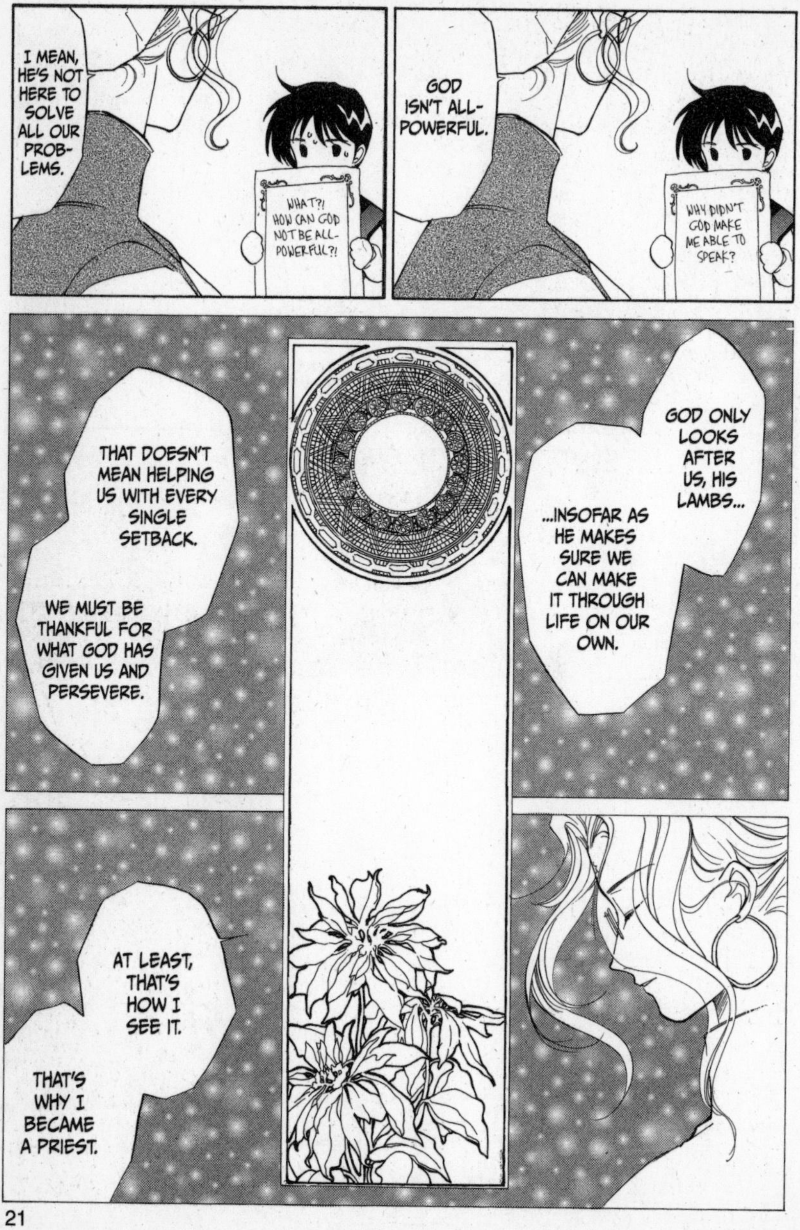
GOD ISN'T ALL-POWERFUL.
WHY DIDN'T GOD MAKE ME ABLE TO SPEAK?
I MEAN, HE'S NOT HERE TO SOLVE ALL OUR PROBLEMS.
WHAT?! HOW CAN GOD NOT BE ALL-POWERFUL?!
GOD ONLY LOOKS AFTER US, HIS LAMBS...
...INSOFAR AS HE MAKES SURE WE CAN MAKE IT THROUGH LIFE ON OUR OWN.
THAT DOESN'T MEAN HELPING US WITH EVERY SINGLE SETBACK.
WE MUST BE THANKFUL FOR WHAT GOD HAS GIVEN US AND PERSEVERE.
AT LEAST, THAT'S HOW I SEE IT.
THAT'S WHY I BECAME A PRIEST.

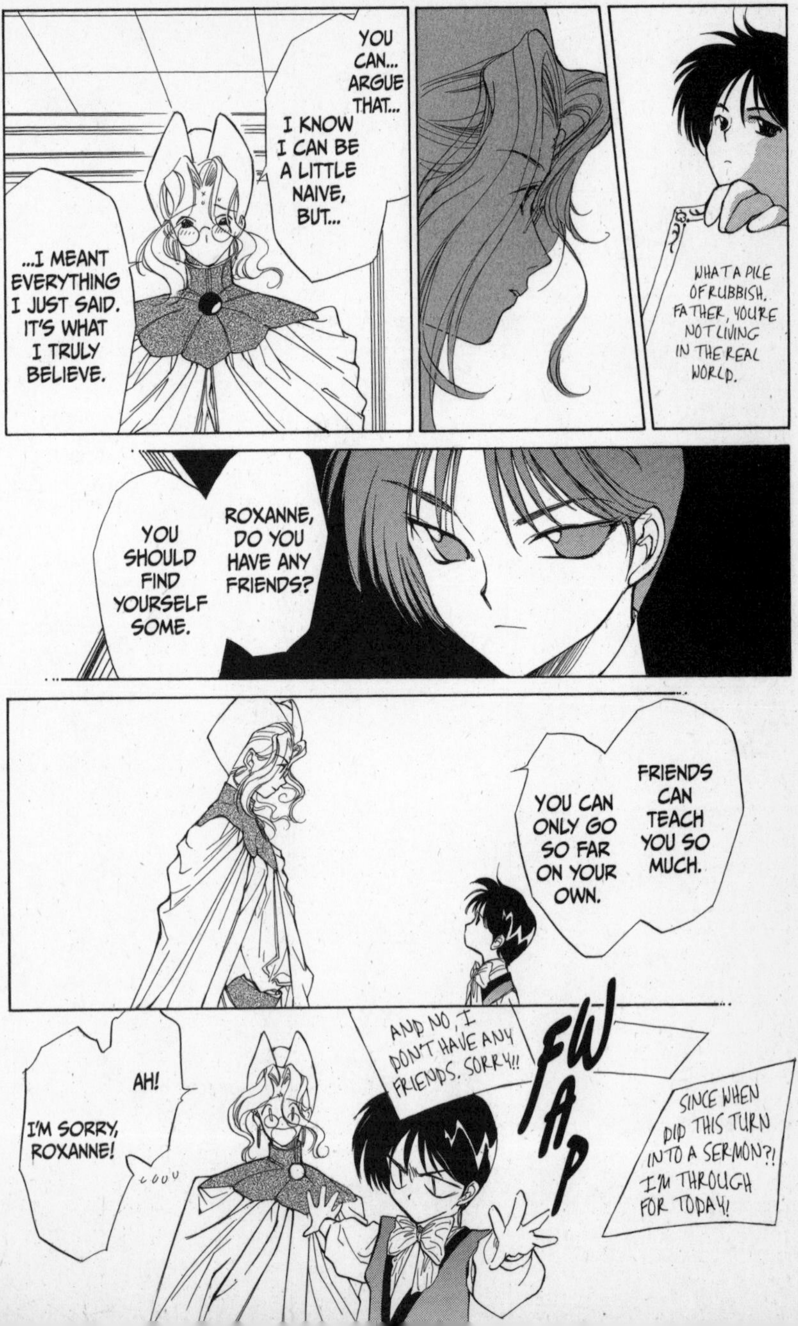
WHAT A PILE OF RUBBISH. FATHER, YOU'RE NOT LIVING IN THE REAL WORLD.
YOU CAN... ARGUE THAT...
I KNOW I CAN BE A LITTLE NAIVE, BUT...
...I MEANT EVERYTHING I JUST SAID. IT'S WHAT I TRULY BELIEVE.
ROXANNE, DO YOU HAVE ANY FRIENDS?
YOU SHOULD FIND YOURSELF SOME.
FRIENDS CAN TEACH YOU SO MUCH.
YOU CAN ONLY GO SO FAR ON YOUR OWN.
SINCE WHEN DID THIS TURN INTO A SERMON?! I'M THROUGH FOR TODAY!
FWAP
AND NO, I DON'T HAVE ANY FRIENDS. SORRY!!
AH!
I'M SORRY, ROXANNE!

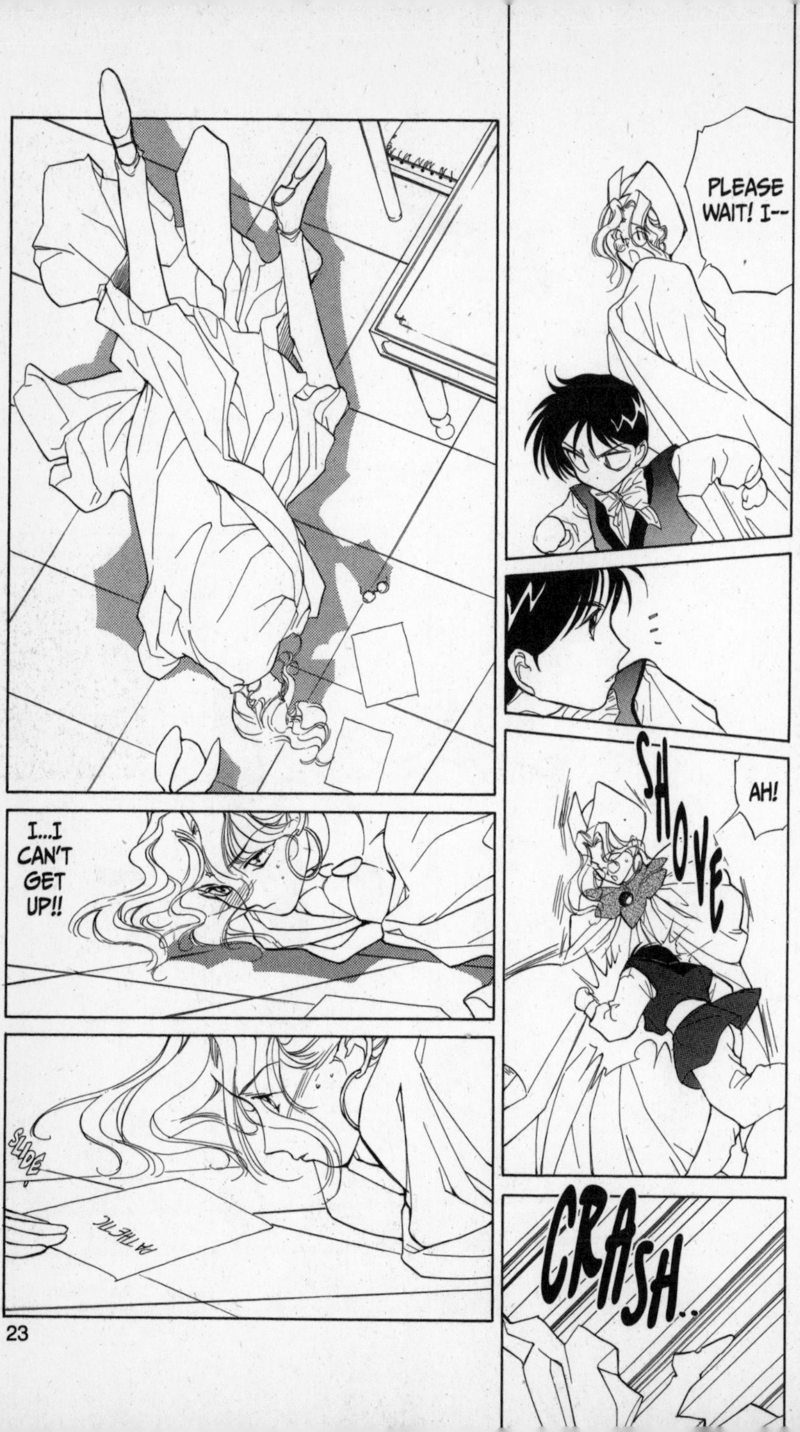
PLEASE WAIT! I--
AH!
SHOVE
CRASH..
I...I CAN'T GET UP!!
SLIDE
PATHETIC

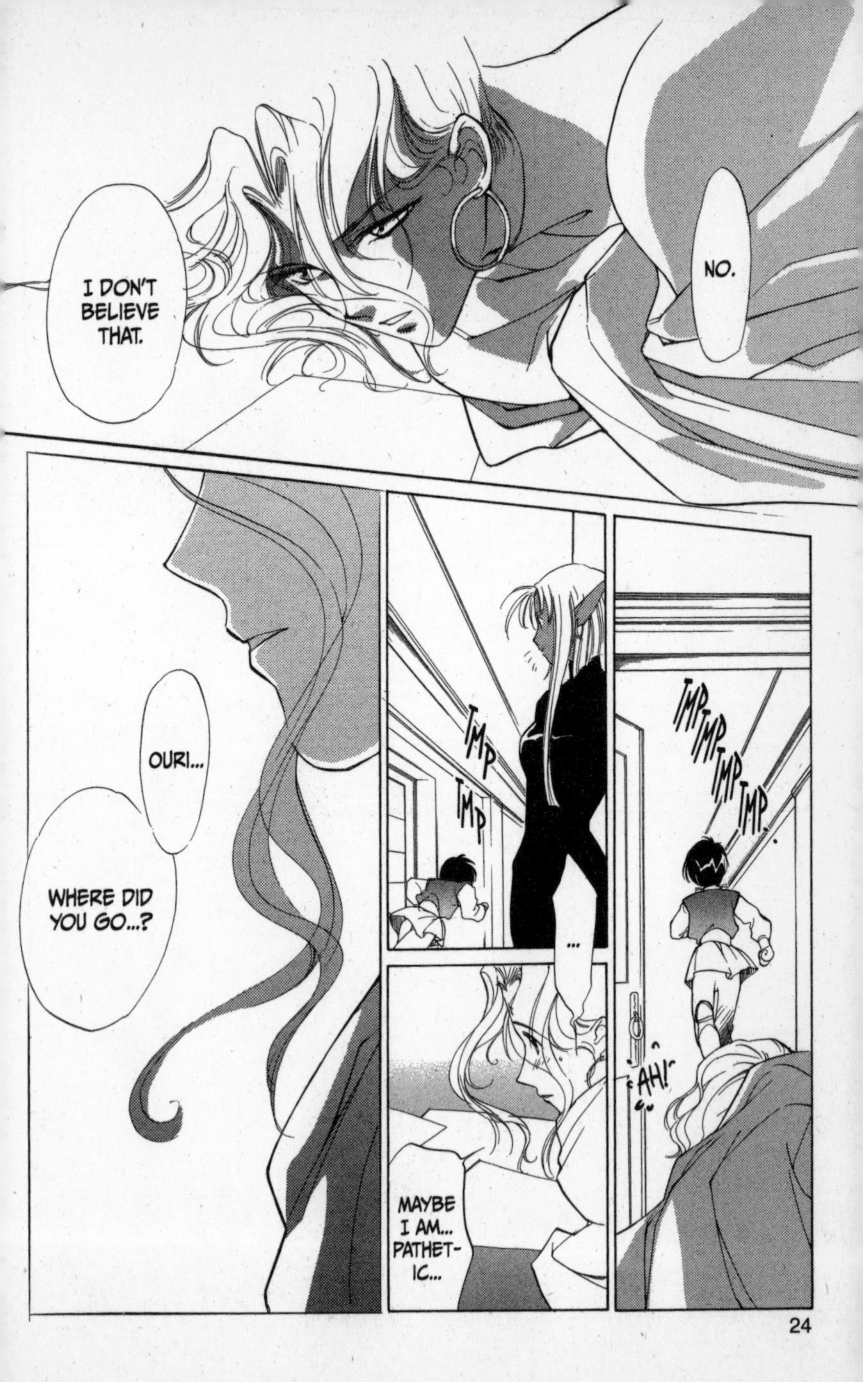
NO.
I DON'T BELIEVE THAT.
TMPTMPTMPTMP.
AH!
TMP TMP
...
MAYBE I AM... PATHET-IC...
OURI...
WHERE DID YOU GO...?

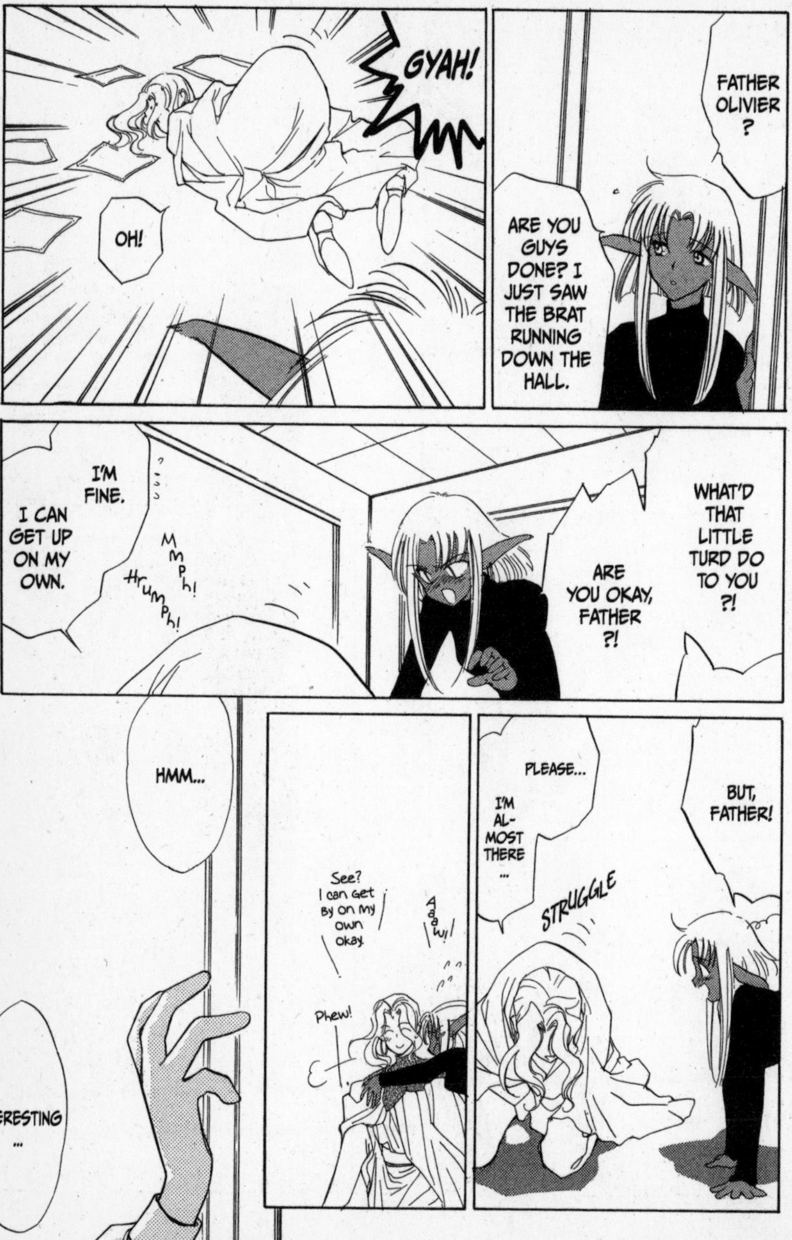
FATHER OLIVIER ?
ARE YOU GUYS DONE? I JUST SAW THE BRAT RUNNING DOWN THE HALL.
GYAH!
OH!
WHAT'D THAT LITTLE TURD DO TO YOU ?!
ARE YOU OKAY, FATHER ?!
Mmph!
Hrumph!
I'M FINE.
I CAN GET UP ON MY OWN.
BUT, FATHER!
PLEASE...
I'M AL-MOST THERE ...
STRUGGLE
Aaaw!
See? I can get by on my own okay.
Phew!
HMM...
INTERESTING ...

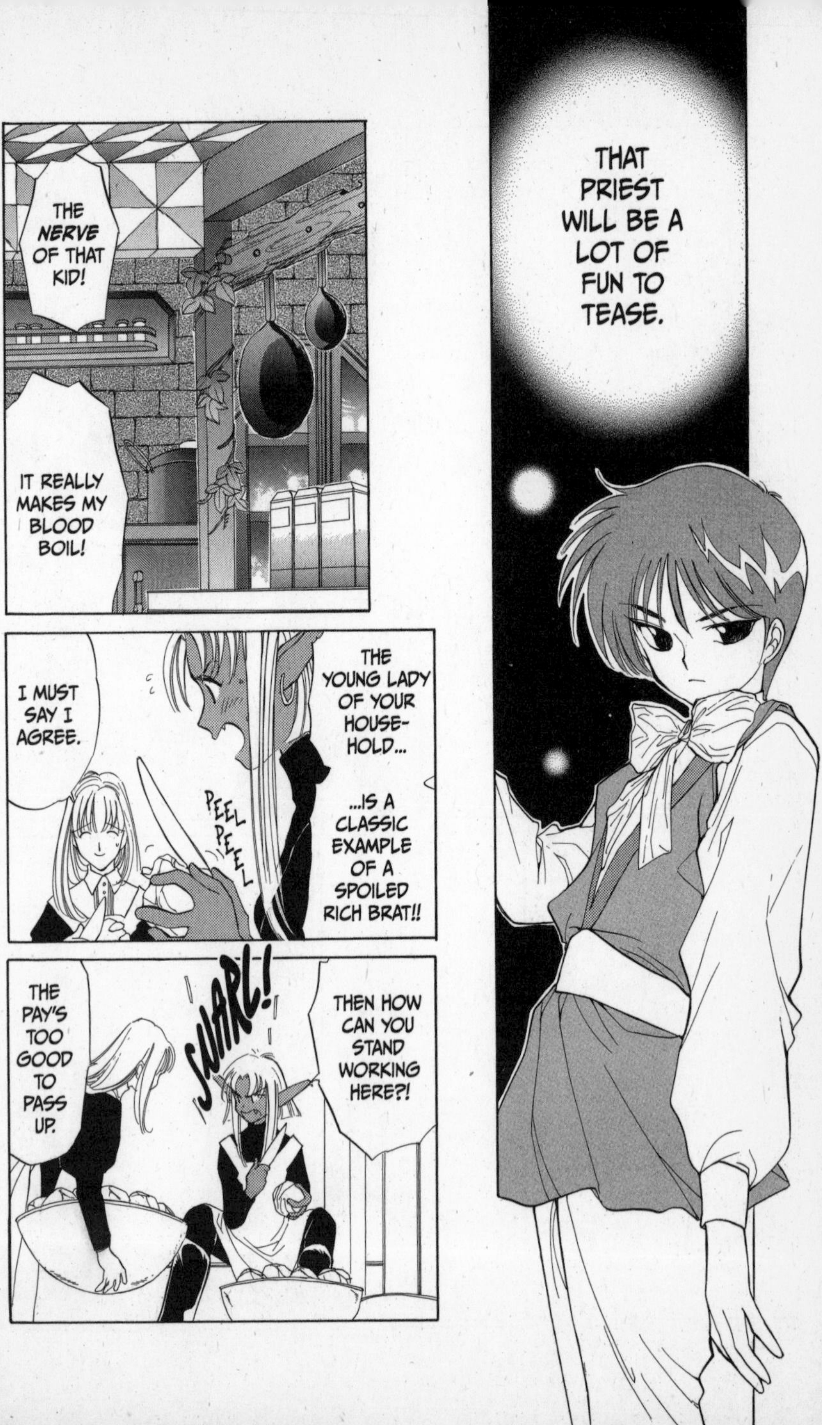
THAT PRIEST WILL BE A LOT OF FUN TO TEASE.
THE NERVE OF THAT KID!
IT REALLY MAKES MY BLOOD BOIL!
THE YOUNG LADY OF YOUR HOUSE-HOLD...
...IS A CLASSIC EXAMPLE OF A SPOILED RICH BRAT!!
PEEL PEEL
I MUST SAY I AGREE.
THEN HOW CAN YOU STAND WORKING HERE?!
SNARL!
THE PAY'S TOO GOOD TO PASS UP.

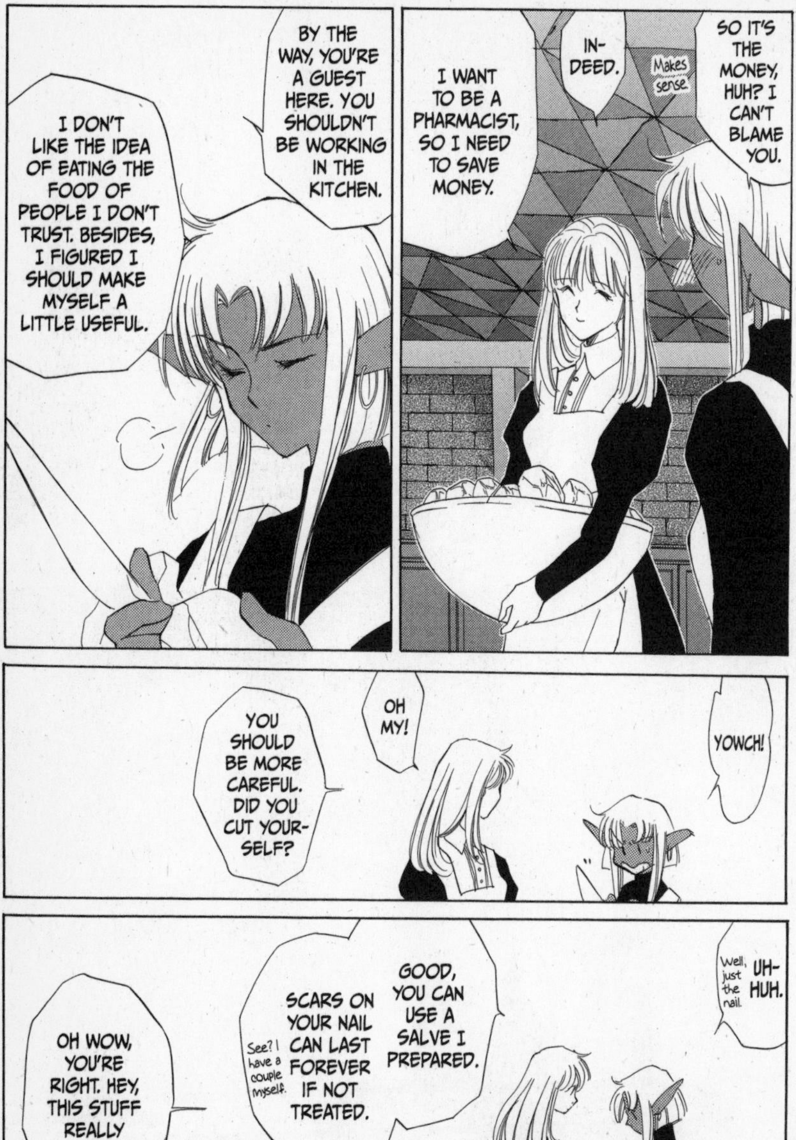

SO IT'S THE MONEY, HUH? I CAN'T BLAME YOU.
Makes sense.
IN-DEED.
I WANT TO BE A PHARMACIST, SO I NEED TO SAVE MONEY.
BY THE WAY, YOU'RE A GUEST HERE. YOU SHOULDN'T BE WORKING IN THE KITCHEN.
I DON'T LIKE THE IDEA OF EATING THE FOOD OF PEOPLE I DON'T TRUST. BESIDES, I FIGURED I SHOULD MAKE MYSELF A LITTLE USEFUL.
YOWCH!
OH MY!
YOU SHOULD BE MORE CAREFUL. DID YOU CUT YOUR-SELF?
UH-HUH.
Well, just the nail.
GOOD, YOU CAN USE A SALVE I PREPARED.
SCARS ON YOUR NAIL CAN LAST FOREVER IF NOT TREATED.
See? I have a couple myself.
OH WOW, YOU'RE RIGHT. HEY, THIS STUFF REALLY WORKS!

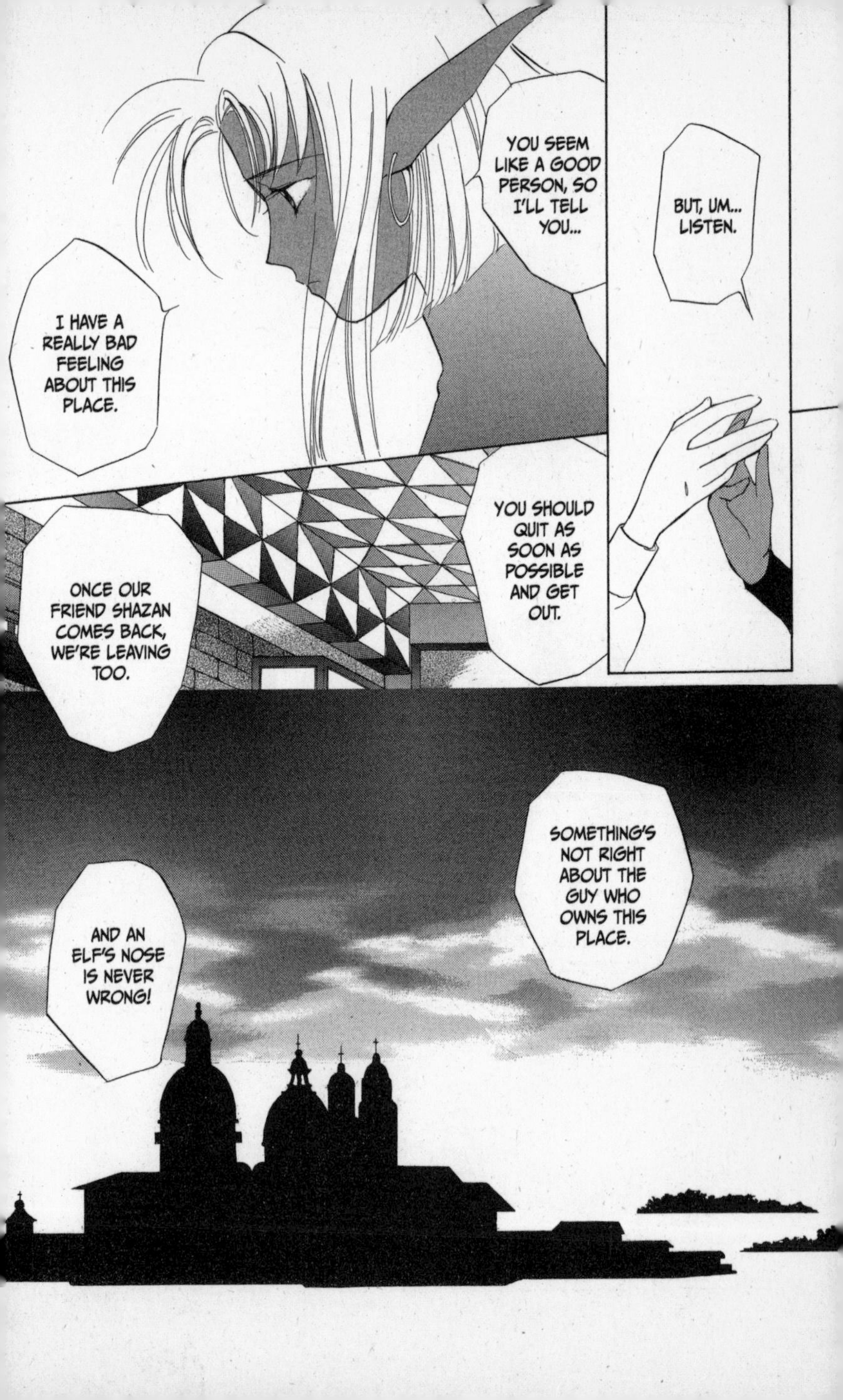
BUT, UM... LISTEN.
YOU SEEM LIKE A GOOD PERSON, SO I'LL TELL YOU...
I HAVE A REALLY BAD FEELING ABOUT THIS PLACE.
YOU SHOULD QUIT AS SOON AS POSSIBLE AND GET OUT.
ONCE OUR FRIEND SHAZAN COMES BACK, WE'RE LEAVING TOO.
SOMETHING'S NOT RIGHT ABOUT THE GUY WHO OWNS THIS PLACE.
AND AN ELF'S NOSE IS NEVER WRONG!

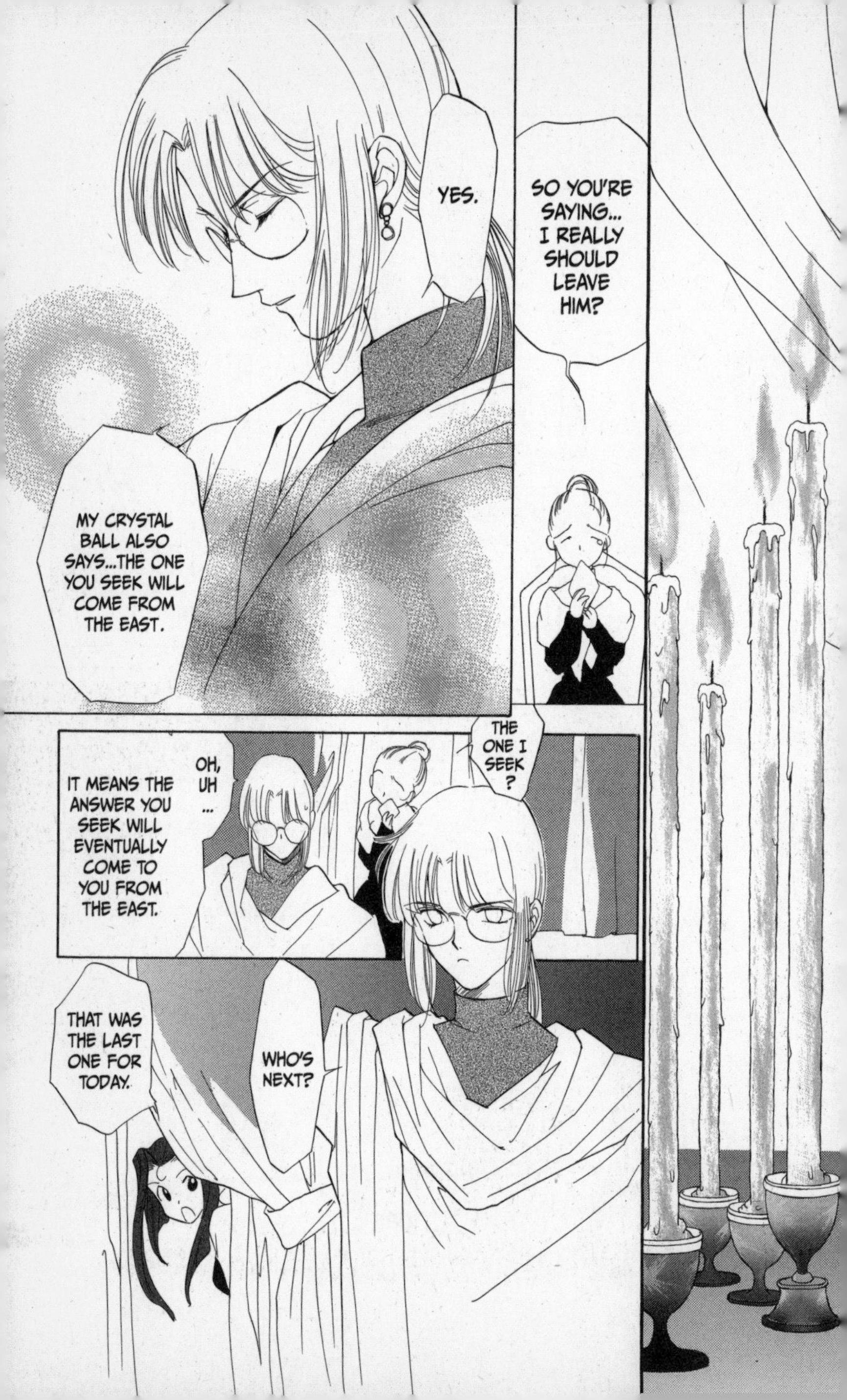

SO YOU'RE SAYING... I REALLY SHOULD LEAVE HIM?
YES.
MY CRYSTAL BALL ALSO SAYS...THE ONE YOU SEEK WILL COME FROM THE EAST.
THE ONE I SEEK?
OH, UH ...
IT MEANS THE ANSWER YOU SEEK WILL EVENTUALLY COME TO YOU FROM THE EAST.
WHO'S NEXT?
THAT WAS THE LAST ONE FOR TODAY.

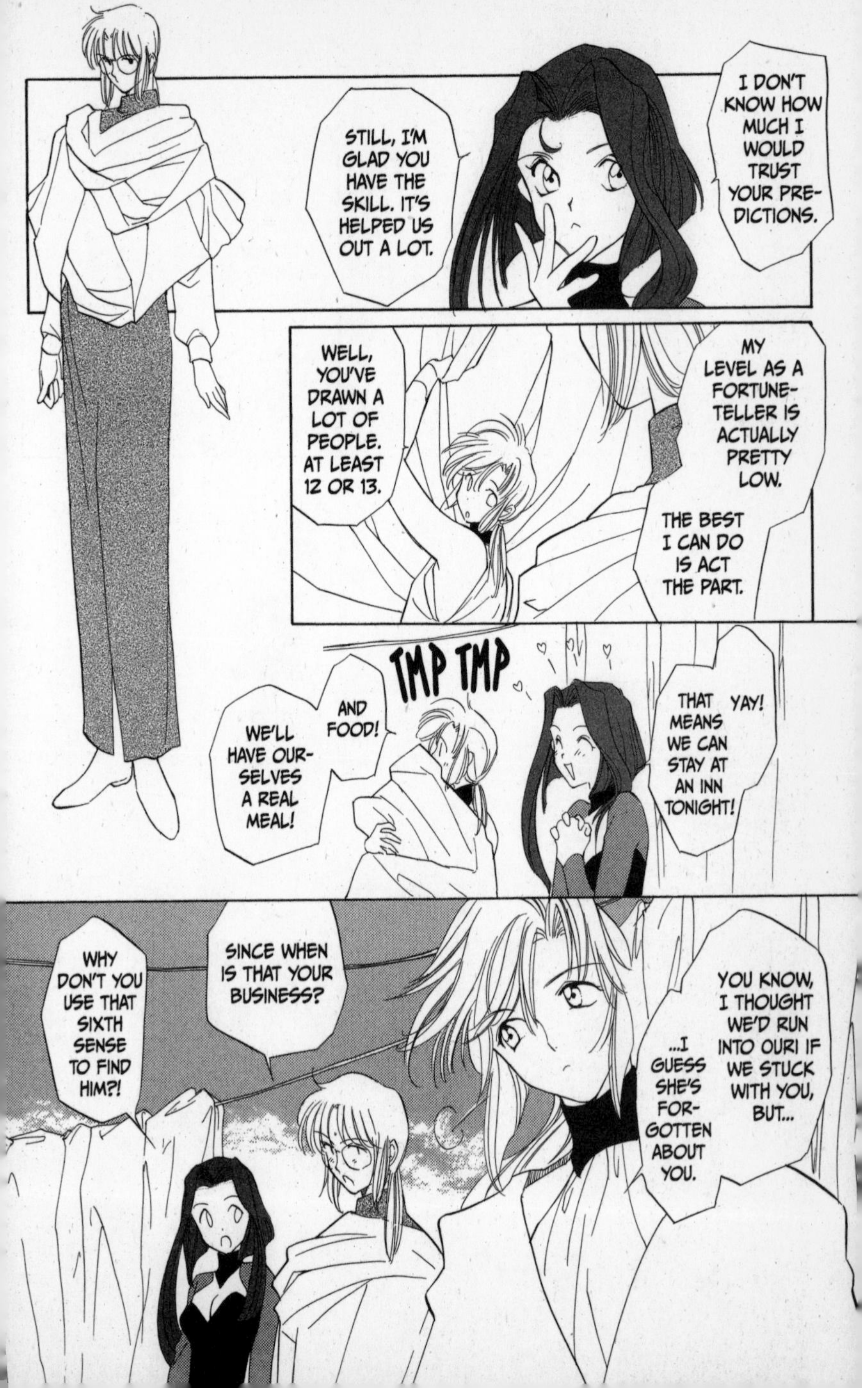
I DON'T KNOW HOW MUCH I WOULD TRUST YOUR PREDICTIONS.
STILL, I'M GLAD YOU HAVE THE SKILL. IT'S HELPED US OUT A LOT.
MY LEVEL AS A FORTUNE-TELLER IS ACTUALLY PRETTY LOW.
THE BEST I CAN DO IS ACT THE PART.
WELL, YOU'VE DRAWN A LOT OF PEOPLE. AT LEAST 12 OR 13.
YAY!
THAT MEANS WE CAN STAY AT AN INN TONIGHT!
TMP TMP
AND FOOD!
WE'LL HAVE OURSELVES A REAL MEAL!
YOU KNOW, I THOUGHT WE'D RUN INTO OURI IF WE STUCK WITH YOU, BUT...
...I GUESS SHE'S FORGOTTEN ABOUT YOU.
SINCE WHEN IS THAT YOUR BUSINESS?
WHY DON'T YOU USE THAT SIXTH SENSE TO FIND HIM?!

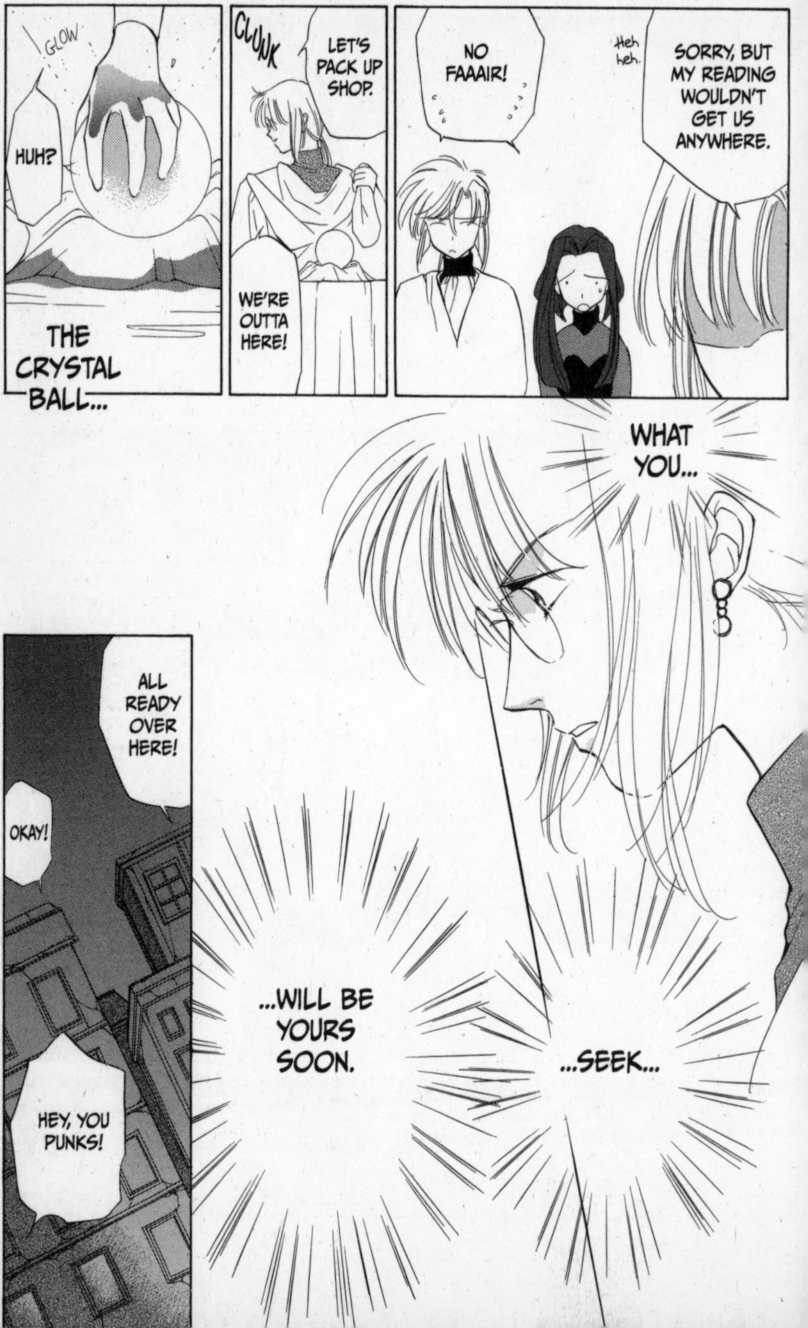
SORRY, BUT MY READING WOULDN'T GET US ANYWHERE.
Heh heh.
NO FAAAIR!
LET'S PACK UP SHOP.
CLUNK
WE'RE OUTTA HERE!
GLOW
HUH?
THE CRYSTAL BALL...
WHAT YOU...
...SEEK...
...WILL BE YOURS SOON.
ALL READY OVER HERE!
OKAY!
HEY, YOU PUNKS!

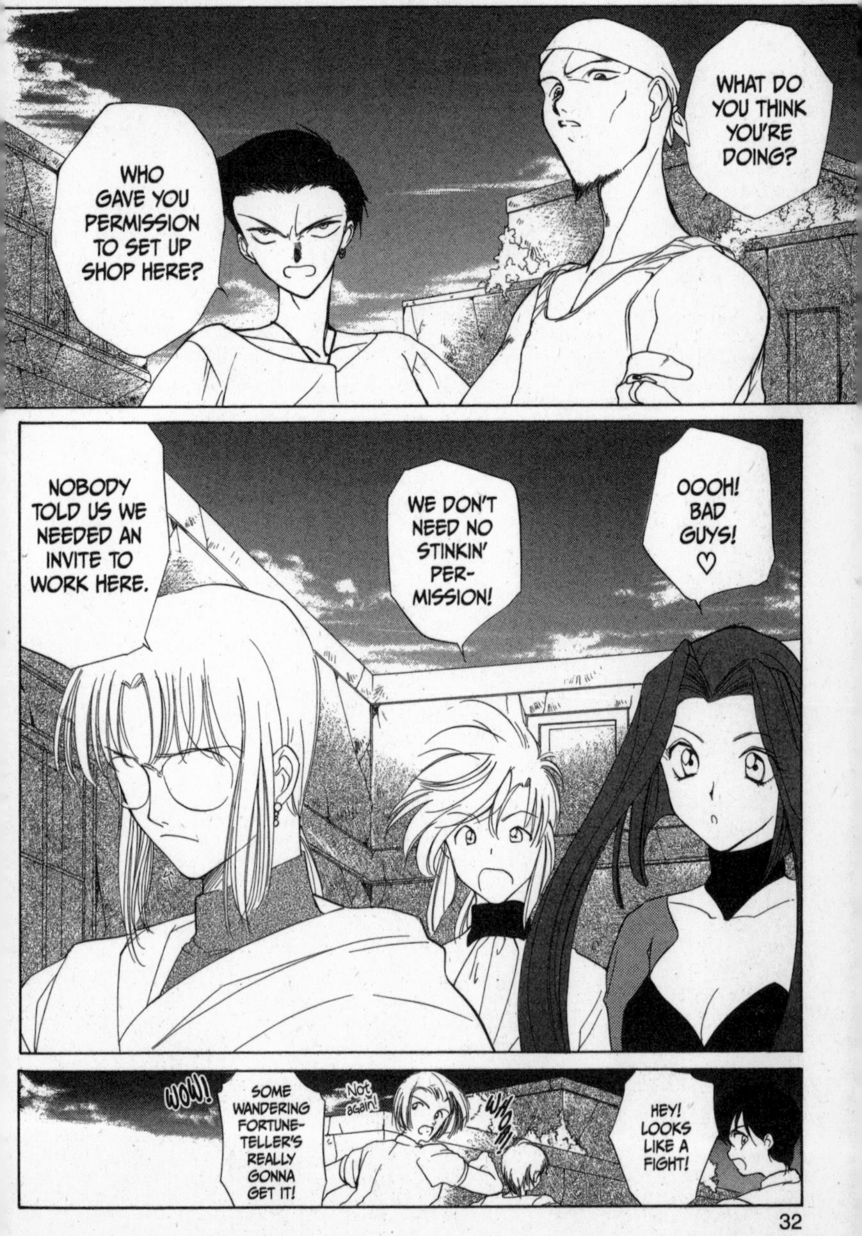
WHAT DO YOU THINK YOU'RE DOING?
WHO GAVE YOU PERMISSION TO SET UP SHOP HERE?
OOOH! BAD GUYS! ♡
WE DON'T NEED NO STINKIN' PER-MISSION!
NOBODY TOLD US WE NEEDED AN INVITE TO WORK HERE.
HEY! LOOKS LIKE A FIGHT!
WHOA!
Not again!
SOME WANDERING FORTUNE-TELLER'S REALLY GONNA GET IT!
WOW!

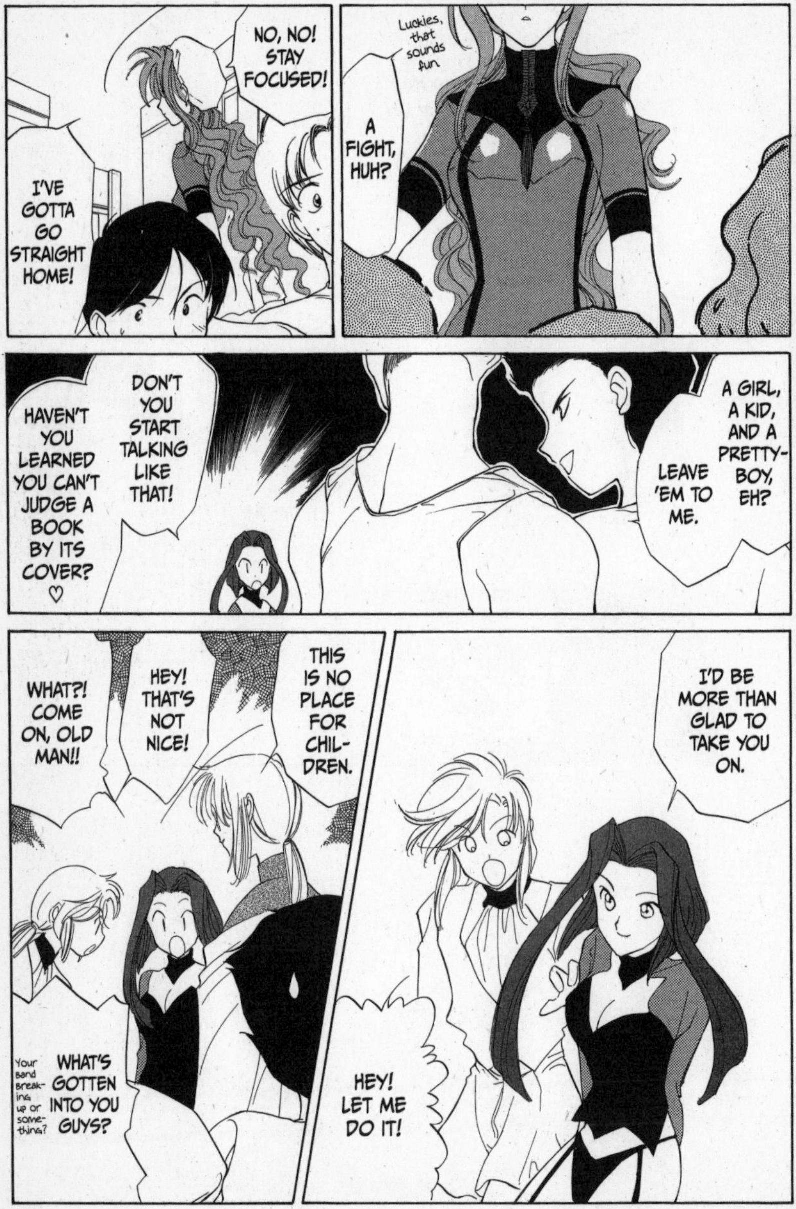
Luckies, that sounds fun.
A FIGHT, HUH?
NO, NO! STAY FOCUSED!
I'VE GOTTA GO STRAIGHT HOME!
A GIRL, A KID, AND A PRETTY-BOY, EH?
LEAVE 'EM TO ME.
DON'T YOU START TALKING LIKE THAT!
HAVEN'T YOU LEARNED YOU CAN'T JUDGE A BOOK BY ITS COVER? ♡
I'D BE MORE THAN GLAD TO TAKE YOU ON.
HEY! LET ME DO IT!
THIS IS NO PLACE FOR CHIL-DREN.
HEY! THAT'S NOT NICE!
WHAT?! COME ON, OLD MAN!!
WHAT'S GOTTEN INTO YOU GUYS?
Your band break-ing up or some-thing?

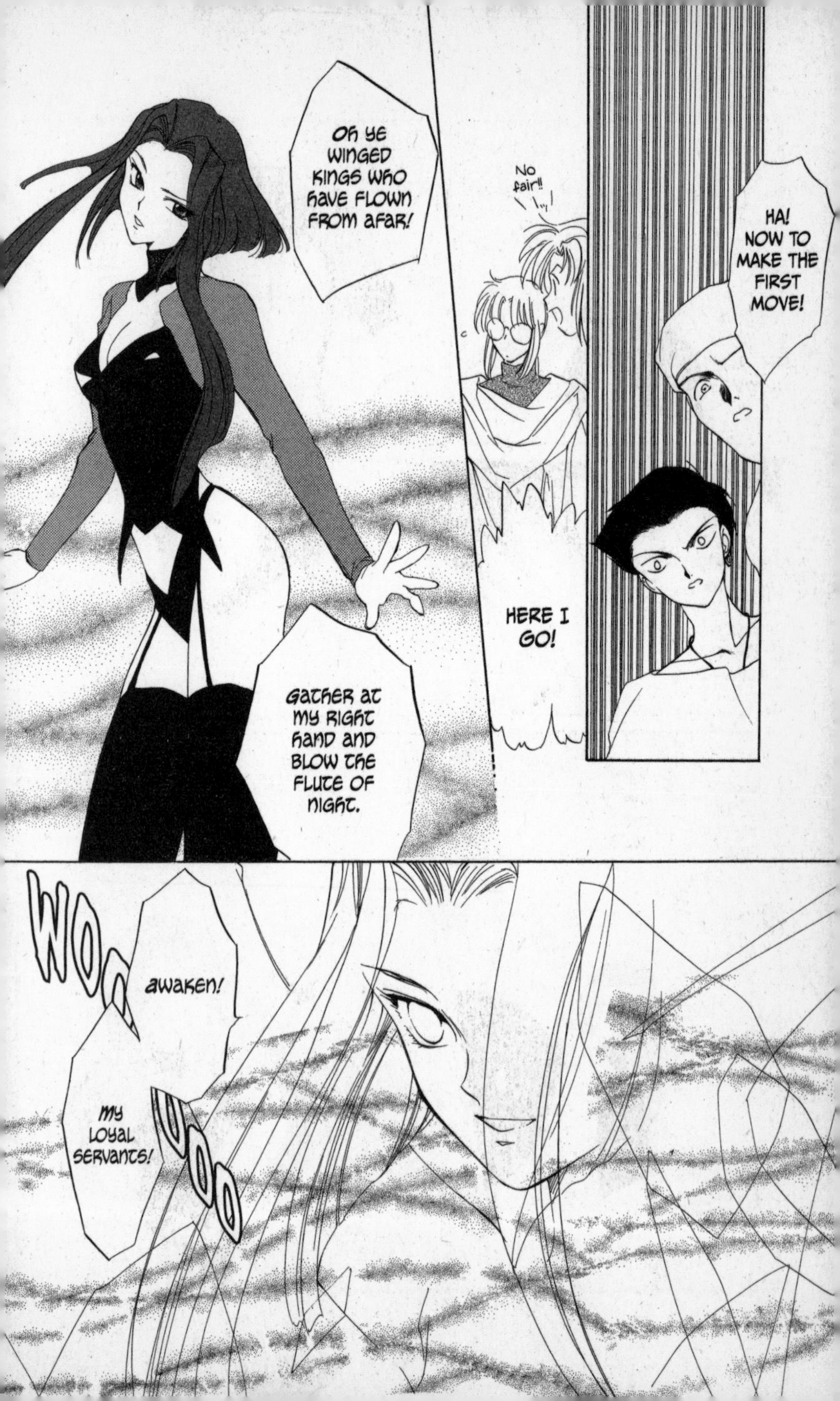
HA! NOW TO MAKE THE FIRST MOVE!
No fair!!
HERE I GO!
OH YE WINGED KINGS WHO HAVE FLOWN FROM AFAR!
GATHER AT MY RIGHT HAND AND BLOW THE FLUTE OF NIGHT.
AWAKEN!
MY LOYAL SERVANTS!
WOOOOOOO

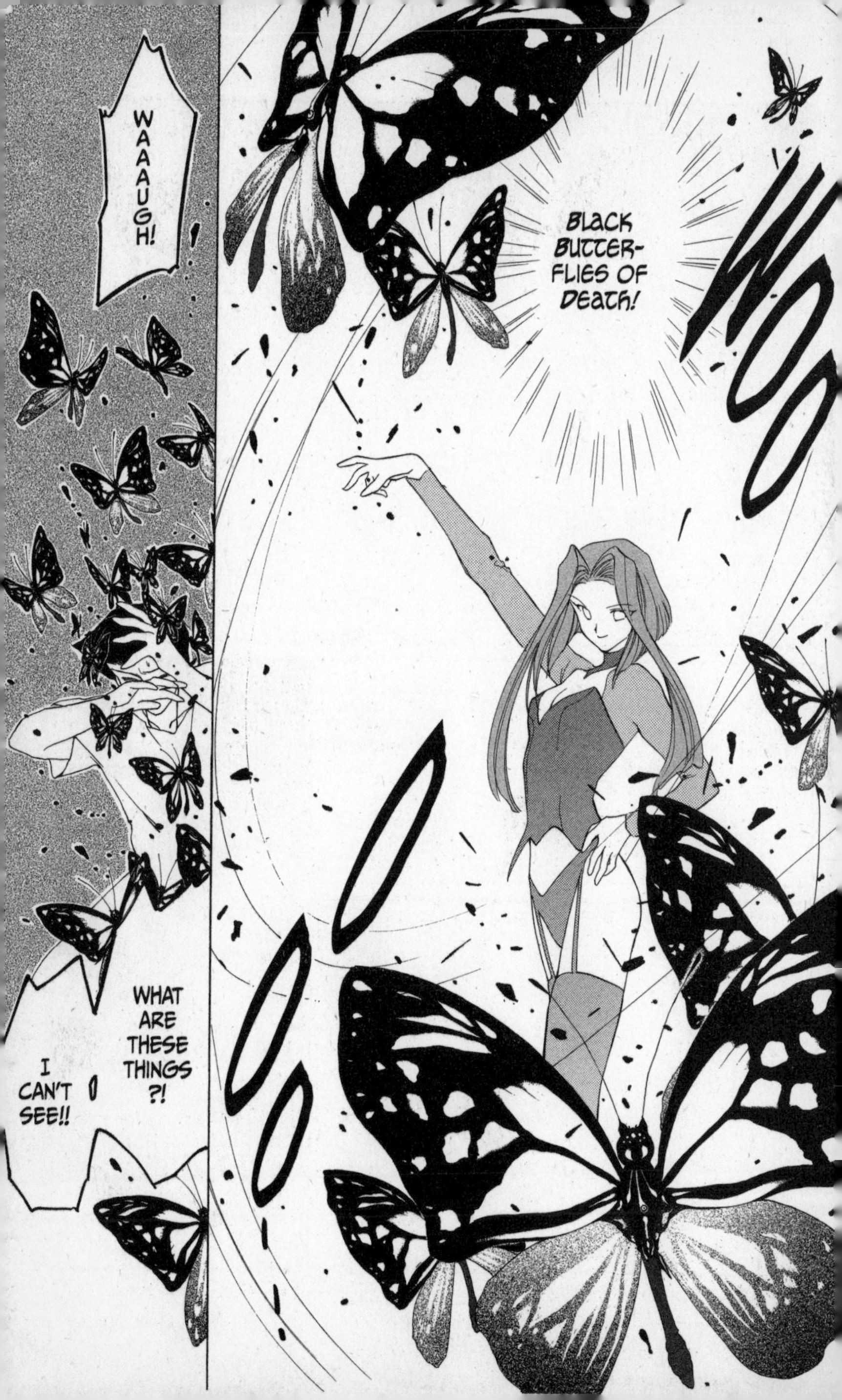
BLACK BUTTER-FLIES OF DEATH!
WAAAAUGH!
WHAT ARE THESE THINGS ?!
I CAN'T SEE!!

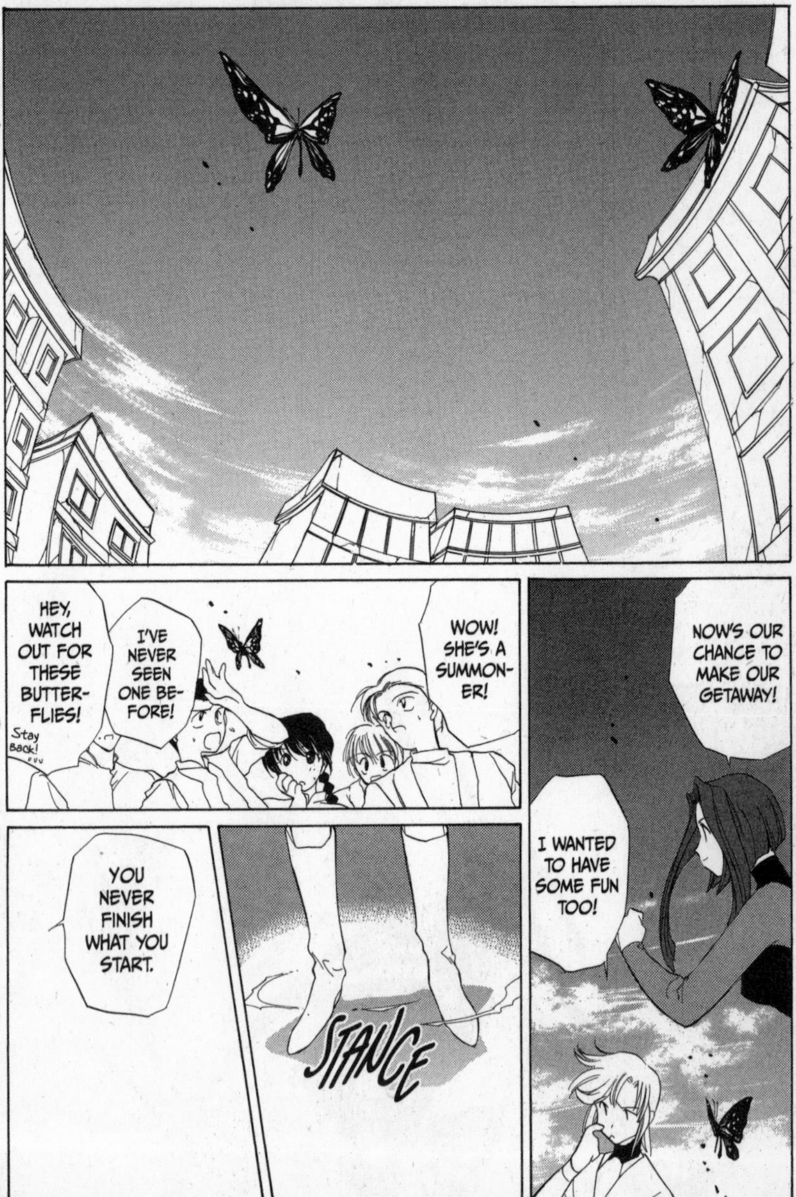
NOW'S OUR CHANCE TO MAKE OUR GETAWAY!
I WANTED TO HAVE SOME FUN TOO!
WOW! SHE'S A SUMMONER!
I'VE NEVER SEEN ONE BEFORE!
HEY, WATCH OUT FOR THESE BUTTERFLIES!
Stay Back!
STANCE
YOU NEVER FINISH WHAT YOU START.

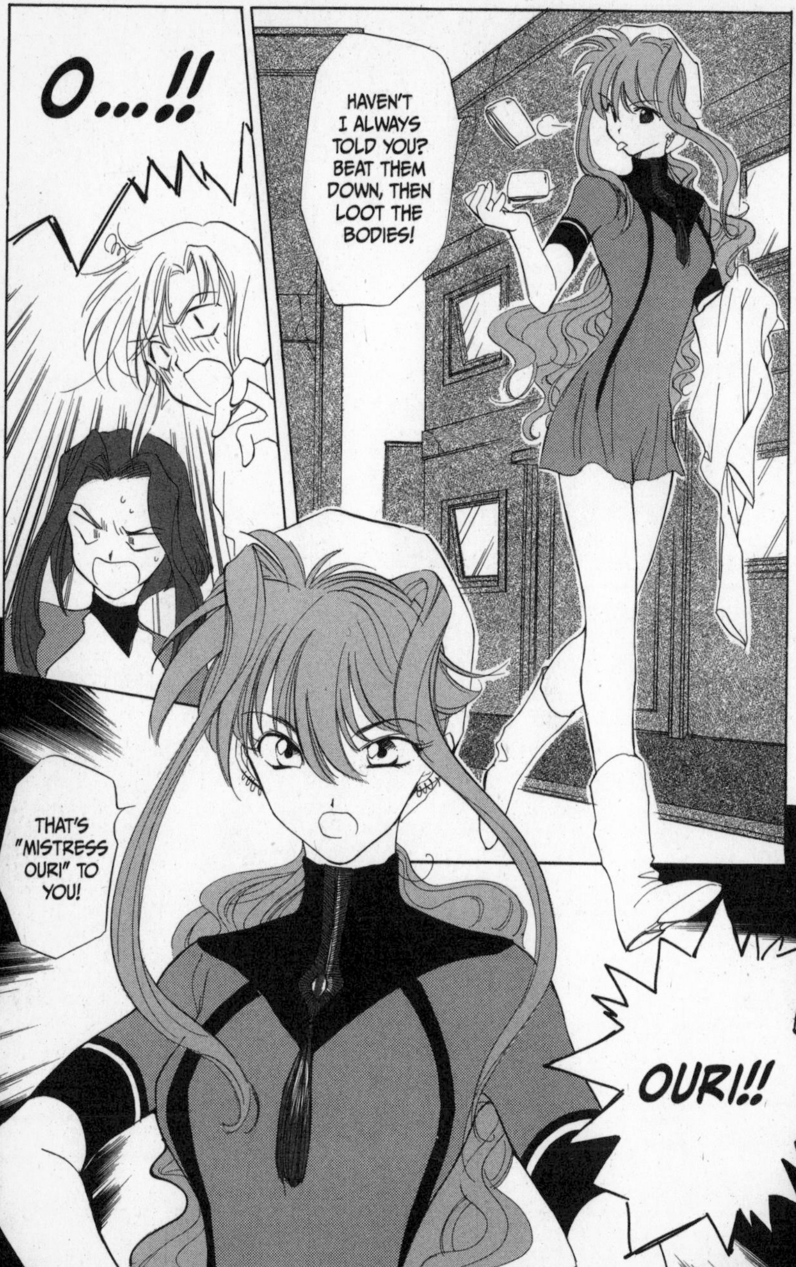
HAVEN'T I ALWAYS TOLD YOU? BEAT THEM DOWN, THEN LOOT THE BODIES!
O...!!
OURI!!
THAT'S "MISTRESS OURI" TO YOU!

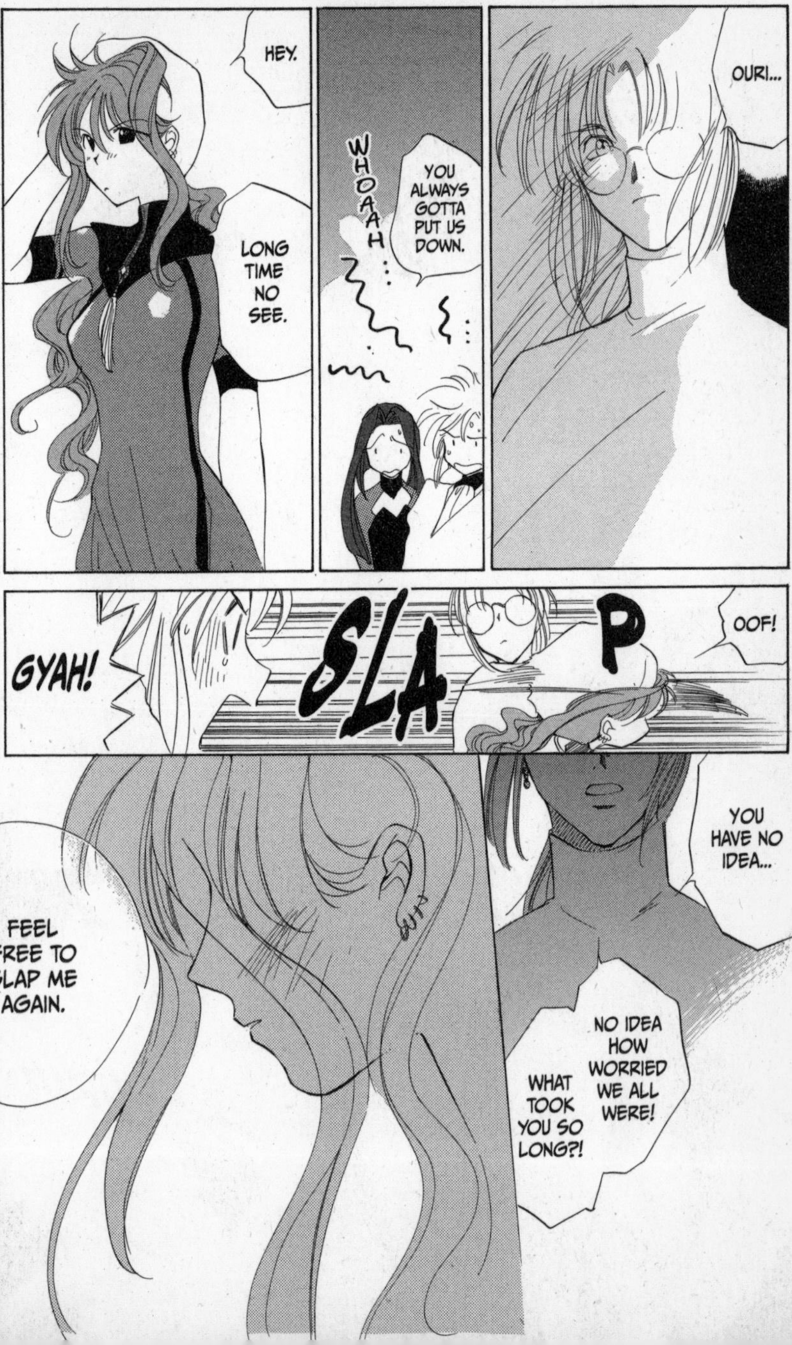
OURI...
YOU ALWAYS GOTTA PUT US DOWN.
WHOAAH...
HEY.
LONG TIME NO SEE.
OOF!
SLAP
GYAH!
YOU HAVE NO IDEA...
NO IDEA HOW WORRIED WE ALL WERE!
WHAT TOOK YOU SO LONG?!
FEEL FREE TO SLAP ME AGAIN.

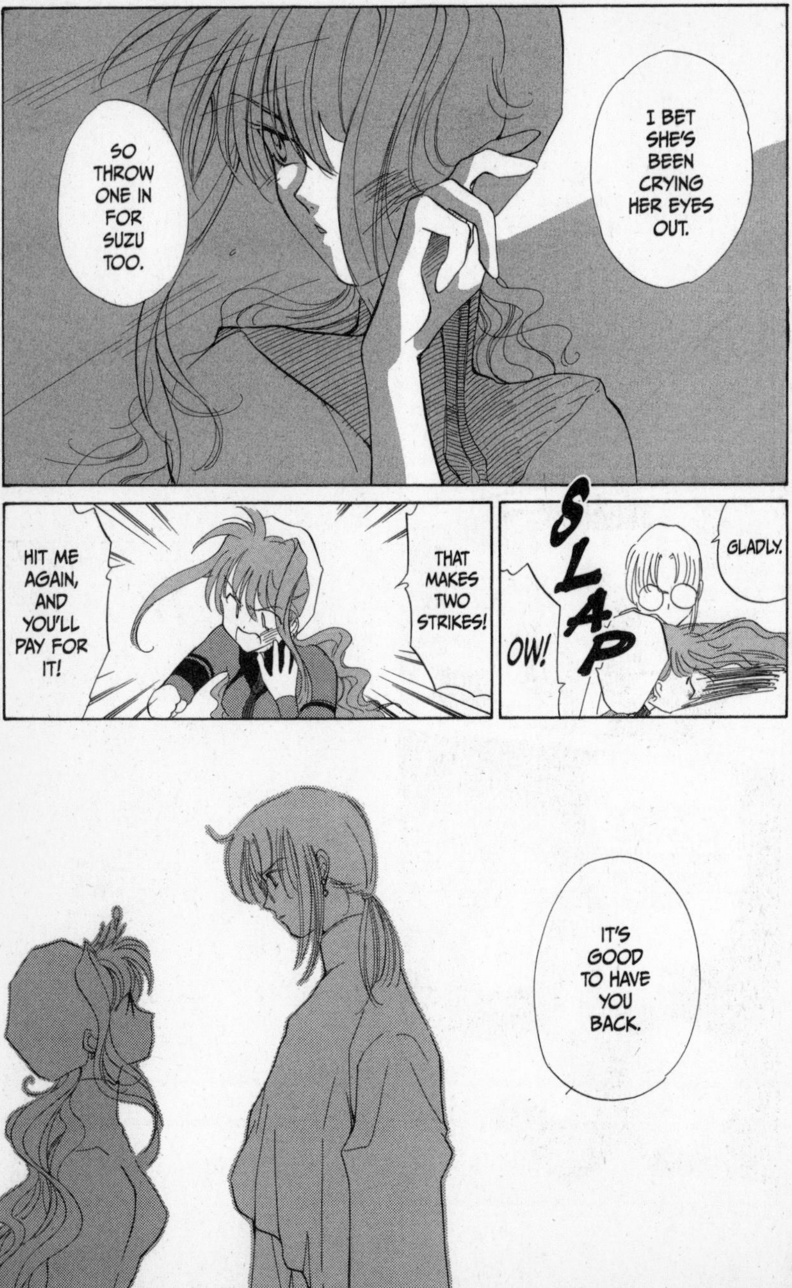
I BET SHE'S BEEN CRYING HER EYES OUT.
SO THROW ONE IN FOR SUZU TOO.
GLADLY.
SLAP
OW!
THAT MAKES TWO STRIKES!
HIT ME AGAIN, AND YOU'LL PAY FOR IT!
IT'S GOOD TO HAVE YOU BACK.

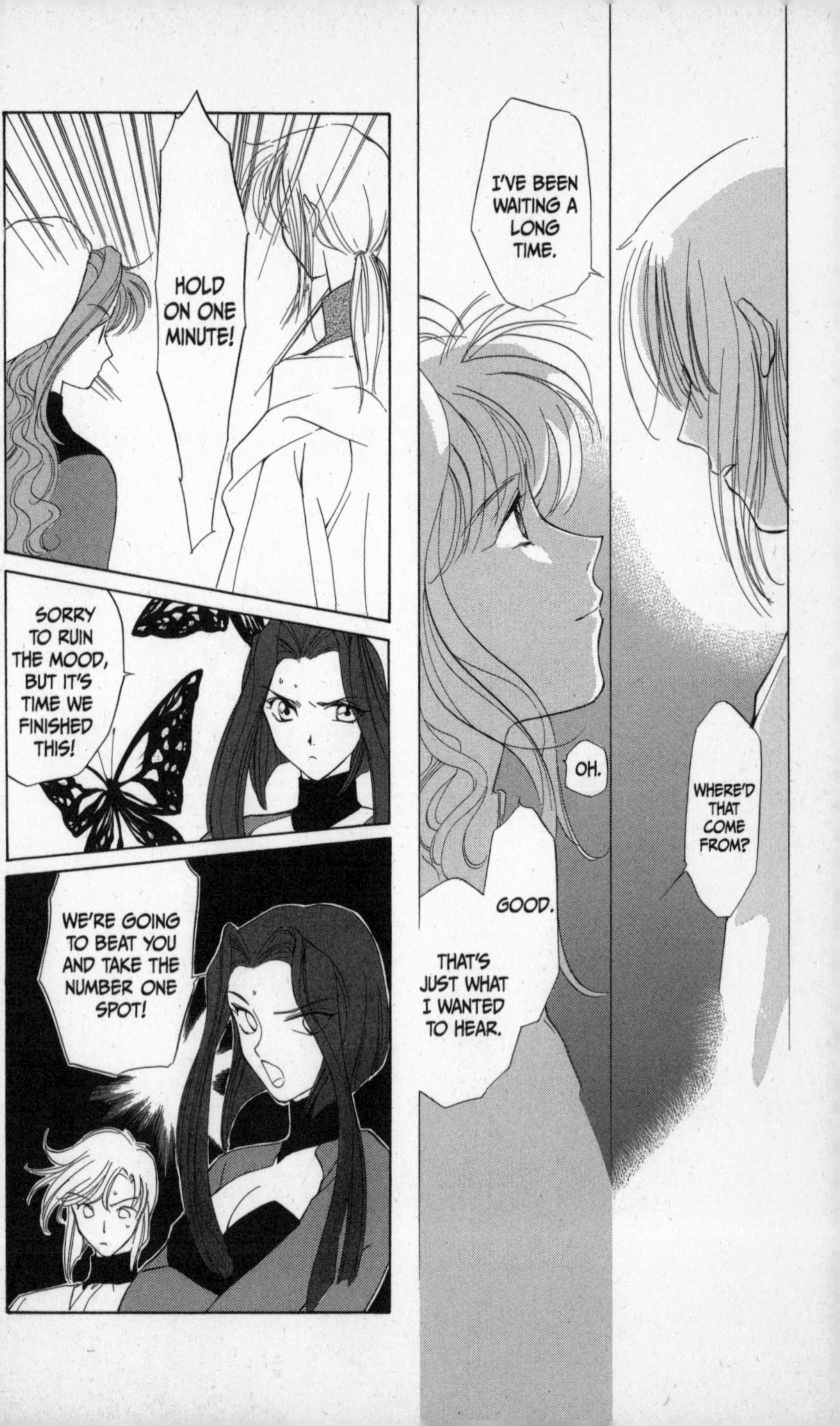
I'VE BEEN WAITING A LONG TIME.
WHERE'D THAT COME FROM?
OH.
GOOD.
THAT'S JUST WHAT I WANTED TO HEAR.
HOLD ON ONE MINUTE!
SORRY TO RUIN THE MOOD, BUT IT'S TIME WE FINISHED THIS!
WE'RE GOING TO BEAT YOU AND TAKE THE NUMBER ONE SPOT!

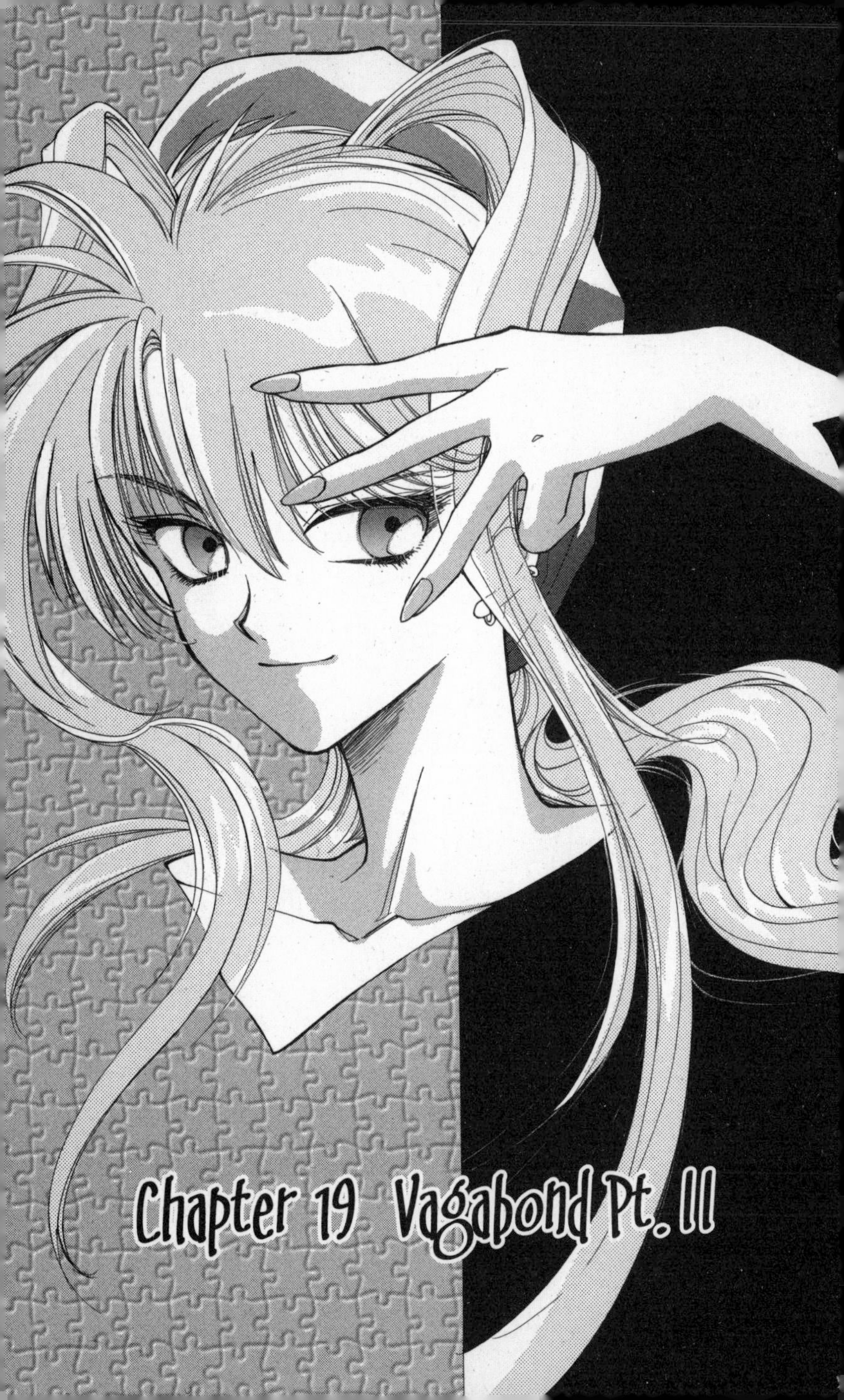
Chapter 19 Vagabond Pt. II

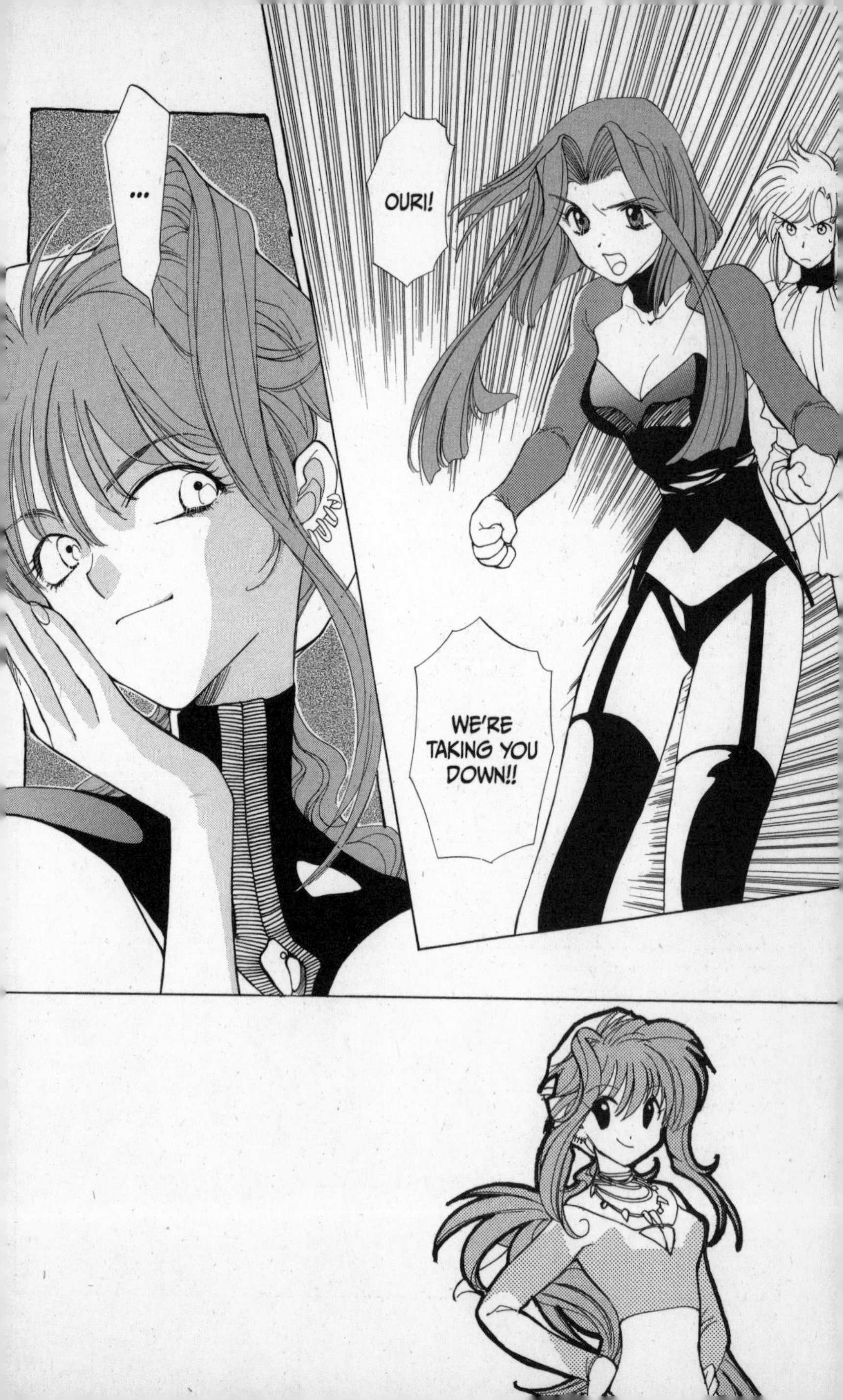
OURI!
WE'RE TAKING YOU DOWN!!
...

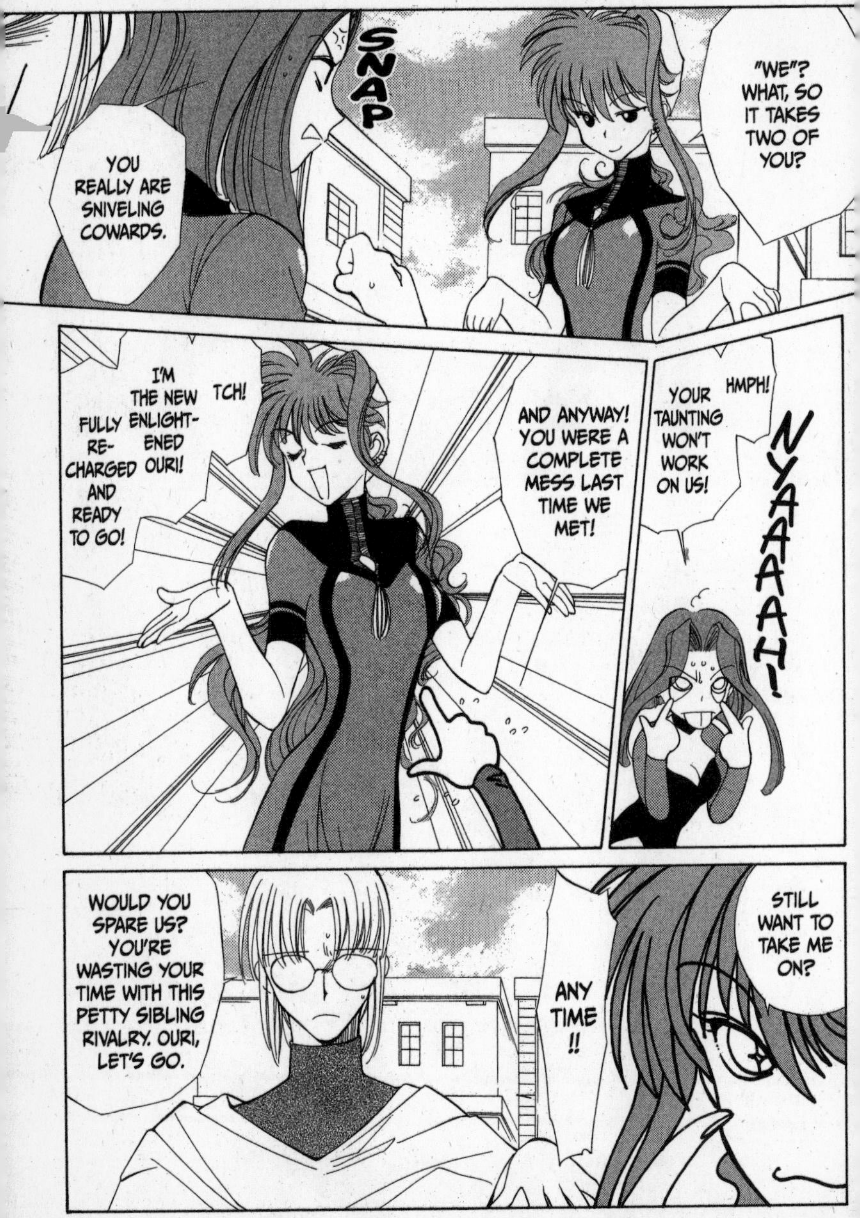
"WE"? WHAT, SO IT TAKES TWO OF YOU?
SNAP
YOU REALLY ARE SNIVELING COWARDS.
HMPH!
YOUR TAUNTING WON'T WORK ON US!
NYAAAAAH!
AND ANYWAY! YOU WERE A COMPLETE MESS LAST TIME WE MET!
TCH!
I'M THE NEW ENLIGHT-ENED OURI!
FULLY RE-CHARGED AND READY TO GO!
STILL WANT TO TAKE ME ON?
ANY TIME!!
WOULD YOU SPARE US? YOU'RE WASTING YOUR TIME WITH THIS PETTY SIBLING RIVALRY. OURI, LET'S GO.

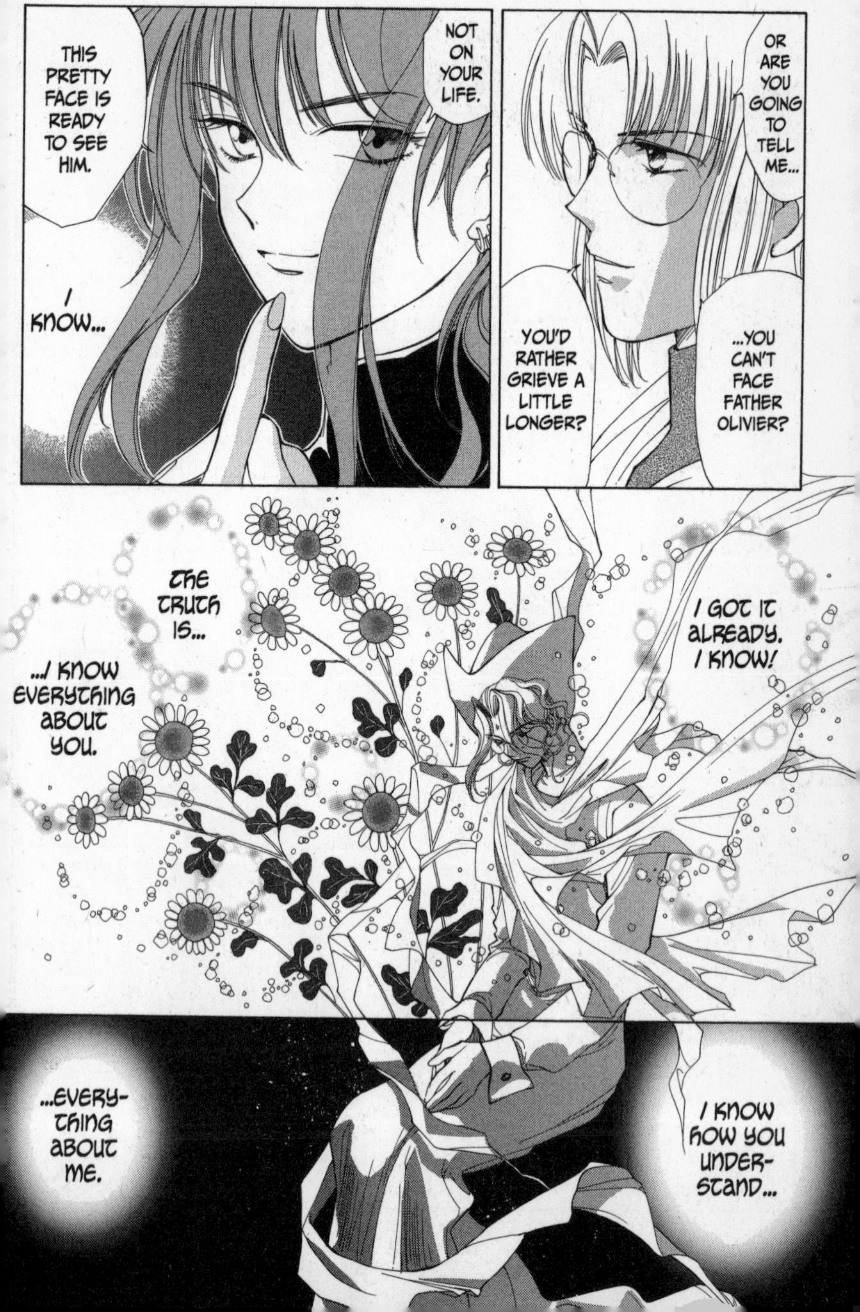
OR ARE YOU GOING TO TELL ME...
...YOU CAN'T FACE FATHER OLIVIER?
YOU'D RATHER GRIEVE A LITTLE LONGER?
NOT ON YOUR LIFE.
THIS PRETTY FACE IS READY TO SEE HIM.
I KNOW...
I GOT IT ALREADY. I KNOW!
THE TRUTH IS...
...I KNOW EVERYTHING ABOUT YOU.
I KNOW HOW YOU UNDER-STAND...
...EVERY-THING ABOUT ME.

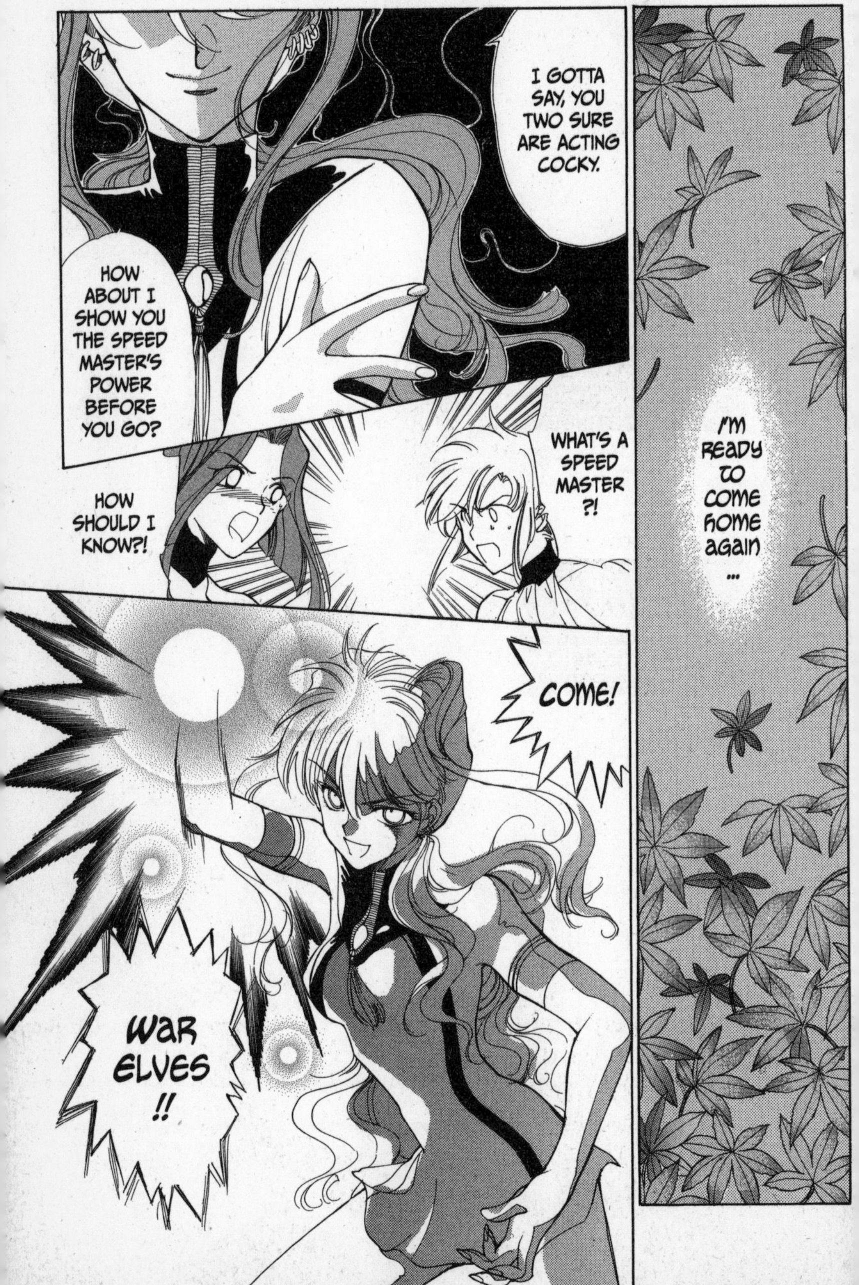
I'M READY TO COME HOME AGAIN...
I GOTTA SAY, YOU TWO SURE ARE ACTING COCKY.
HOW ABOUT I SHOW YOU THE SPEED MASTER'S POWER BEFORE YOU GO?
WHAT'S A SPEED MASTER?!
HOW SHOULD I KNOW?!
COME!
WAR ELVES!!

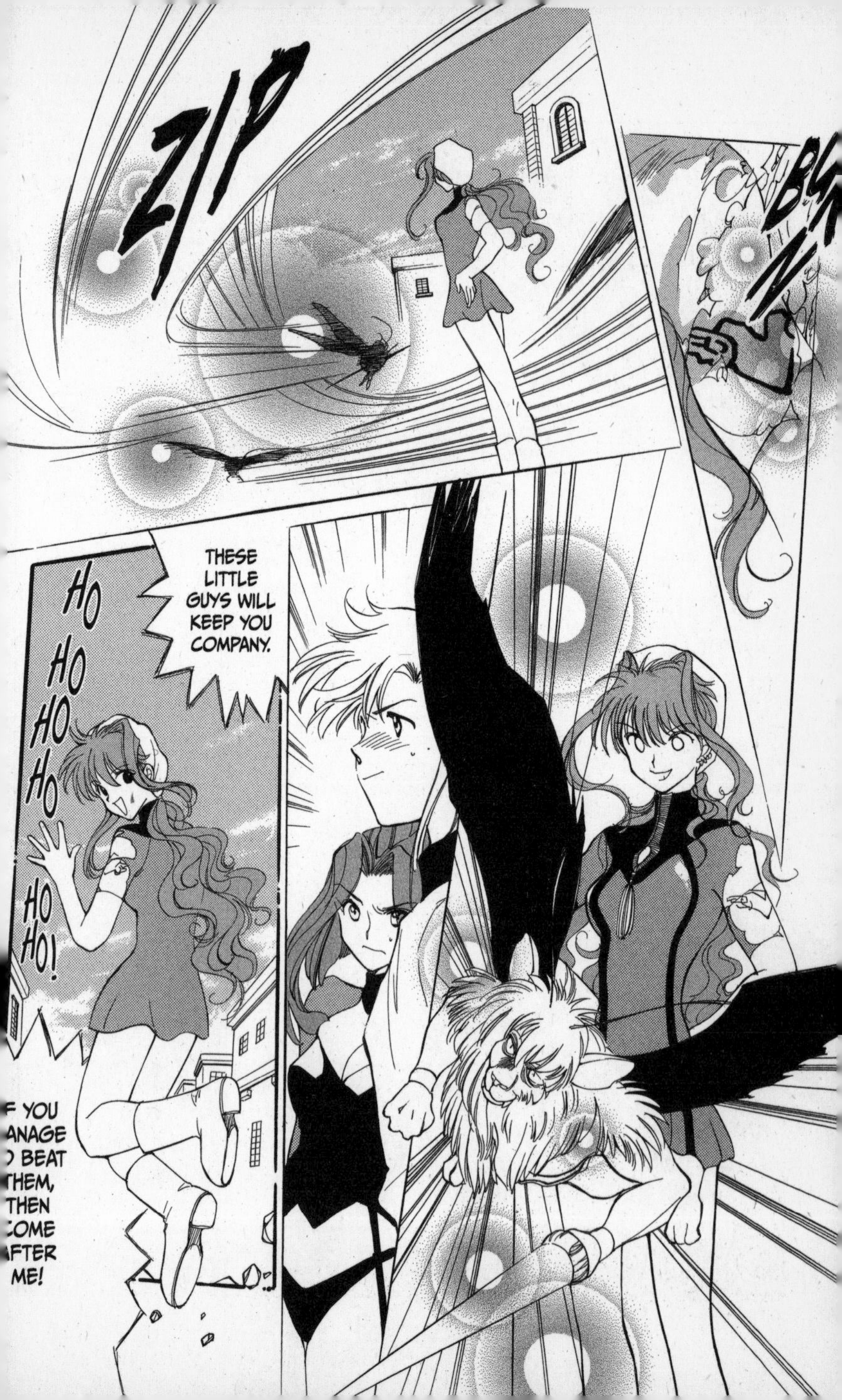
ZIP
THESE LITTLE GUYS WILL KEEP YOU COMPANY.
HO HO HO HO HO HO HO!
F YOU ANAGE D BEAT THEM, THEN COME FTER ME!

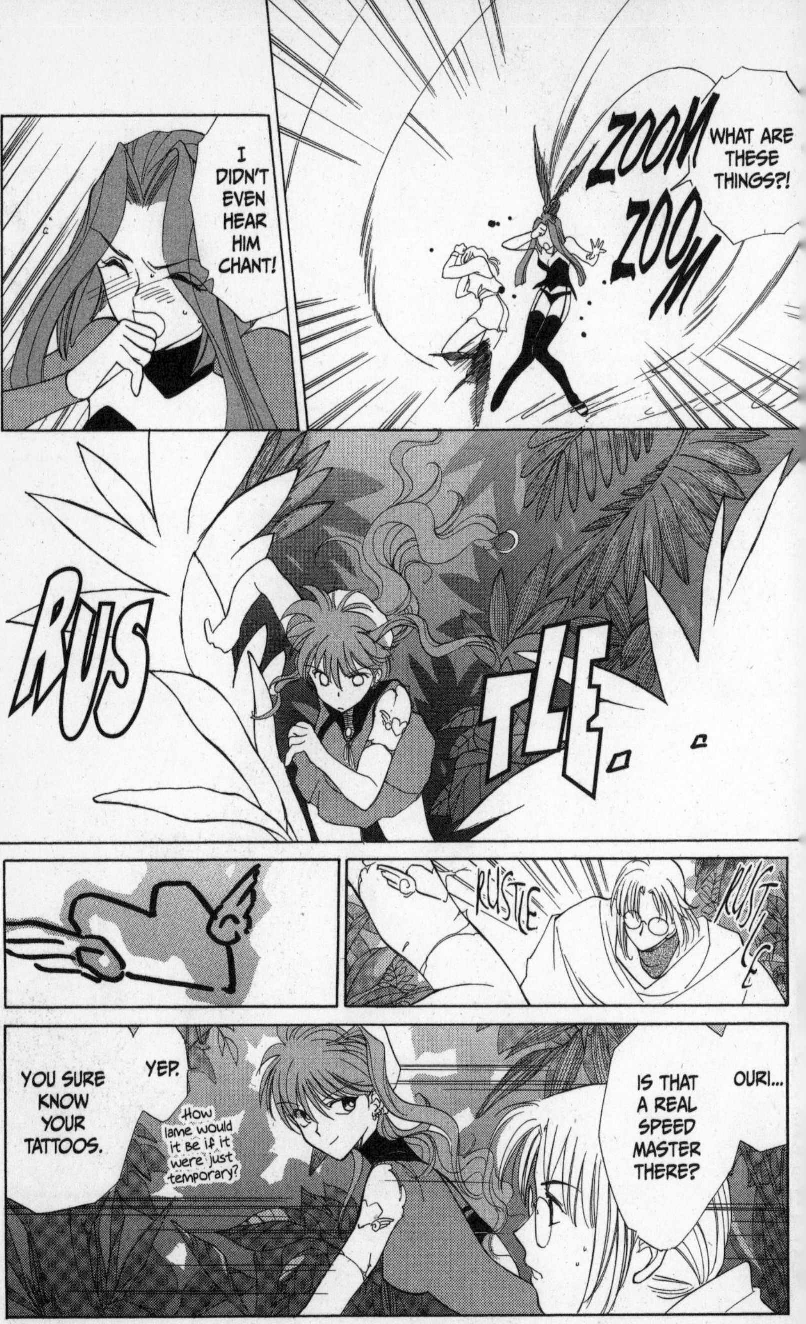
ZOOM
ZOOM
WHAT ARE THESE THINGS?!
I DIDN'T EVEN HEAR HIM CHANT!
RUS
TLE
RUSTLE
RUSTLE
OURI...
IS THAT A REAL SPEED MASTER THERE?
YEP.
How lame would it be if it were just temporary?
YOU SURE KNOW YOUR TATTOOS.

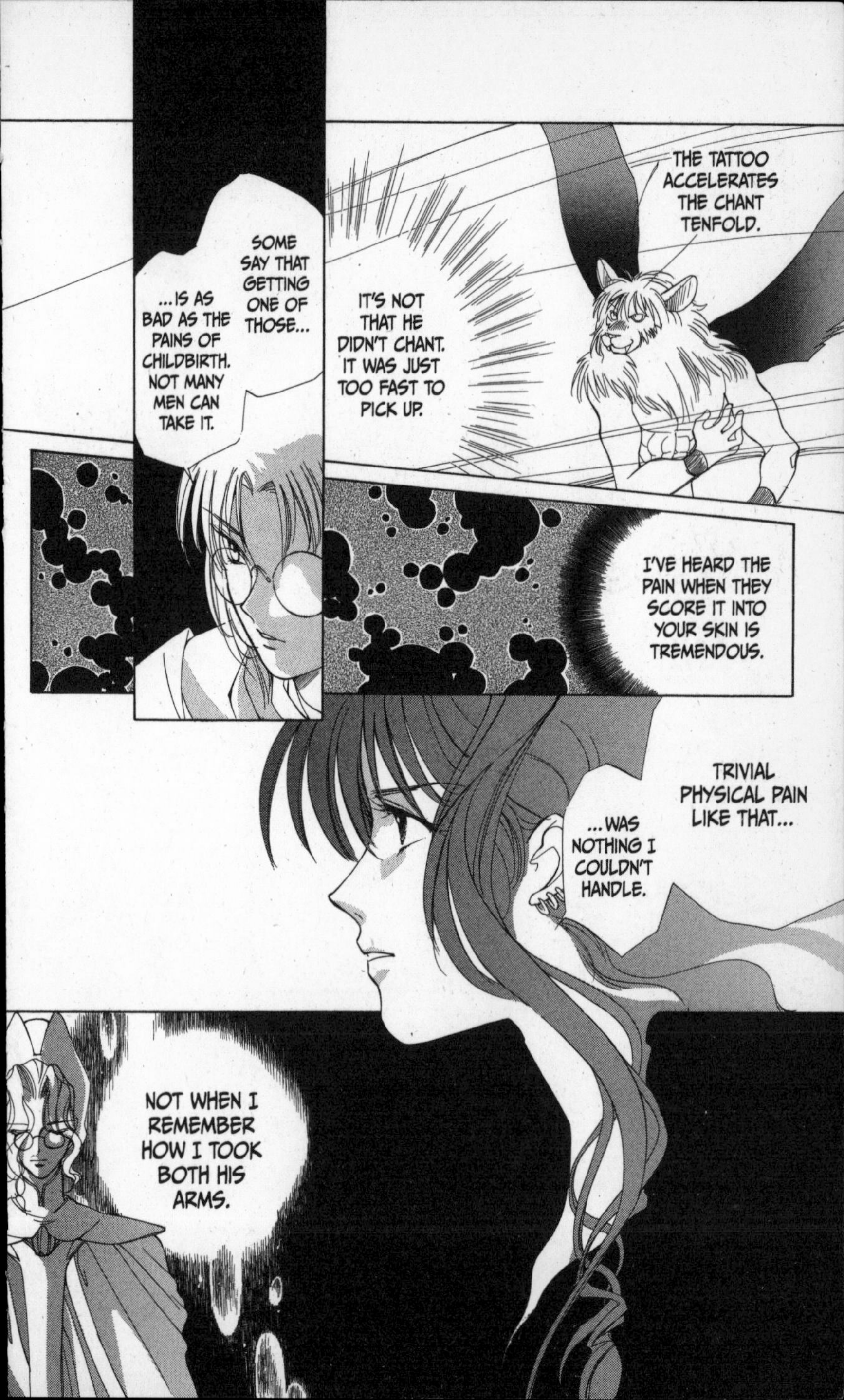
THE TATTOO ACCELERATES THE CHANT TENFOLD.
IT'S NOT THAT HE DIDN'T CHANT. IT WAS JUST TOO FAST TO PICK UP.
I'VE HEARD THE PAIN WHEN THEY SCORE IT INTO YOUR SKIN IS TREMENDOUS.
SOME SAY THAT GETTING ONE OF THOSE...
...IS AS BAD AS THE PAINS OF CHILDBIRTH. NOT MANY MEN CAN TAKE IT.
TRIVIAL PHYSICAL PAIN LIKE THAT...
...WAS NOTHING I COULDN'T HANDLE.
NOT WHEN I REMEMBER HOW I TOOK BOTH HIS ARMS.

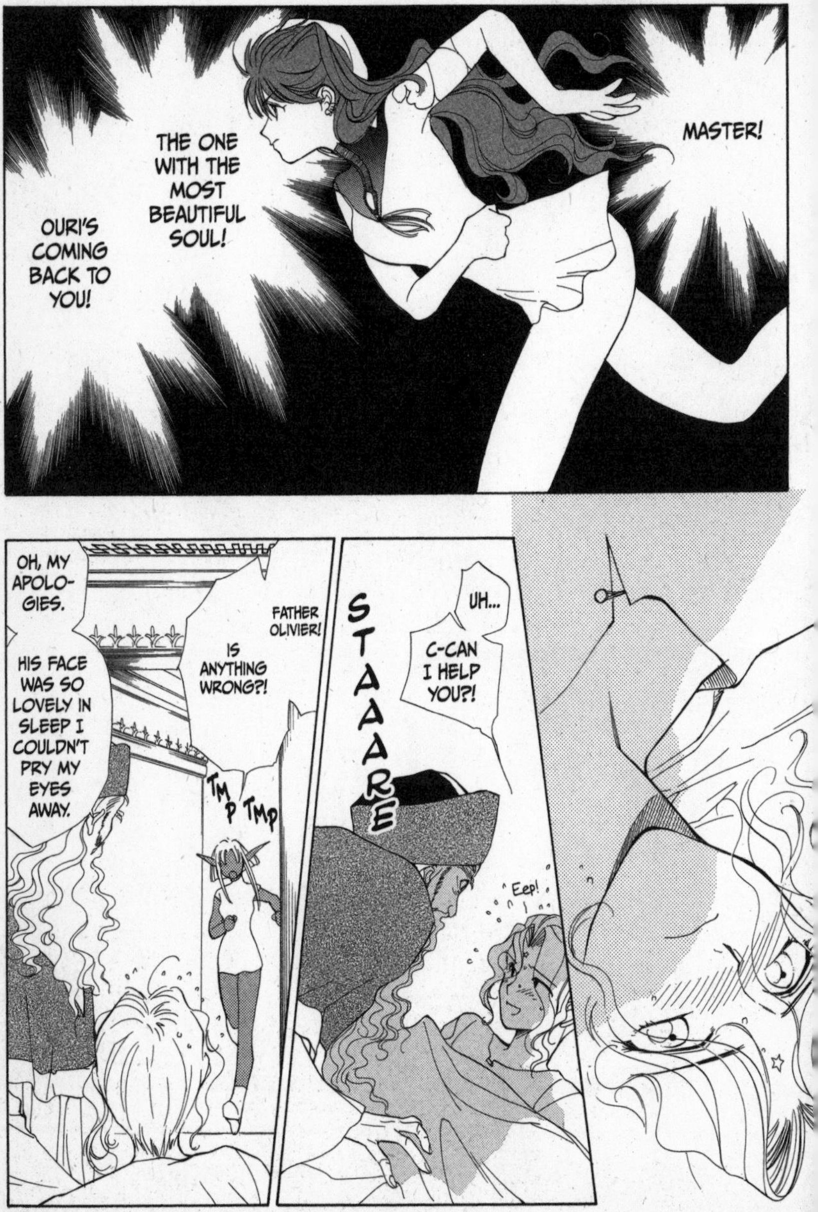
MASTER!
THE ONE WITH THE MOST BEAUTIFUL SOUL!
OURI'S COMING BACK TO YOU!
UH...
C-CAN I HELP YOU?!
STAAARE
Eep!
FATHER OLIVIER!
IS ANYTHING WRONG?!
OH, MY APOLOGIES.
HIS FACE WAS SO LOVELY IN SLEEP I COULDN'T PRY MY EYES AWAY.
TMP TMP

IT REALLY IS EXQUISITE...

SUZU...

LOOK! WE'VE ALREADY IMPOSED ON YOU FOR TOO LONG...

...I SEE.

THAT'S TOO BAD.

IN THAT CASE...

WHAT WAS THAT? CHILLS WENT DOWN MY SPINE.

TH-THAT'S WHY...

...WE'RE GOING TO SAY OUR GOODBYES SOON!

ONCE OUR FRIEND GETS BACK, WE'LL GO. SO THANKS FOR EVERYTHING YOU'VE DONE!

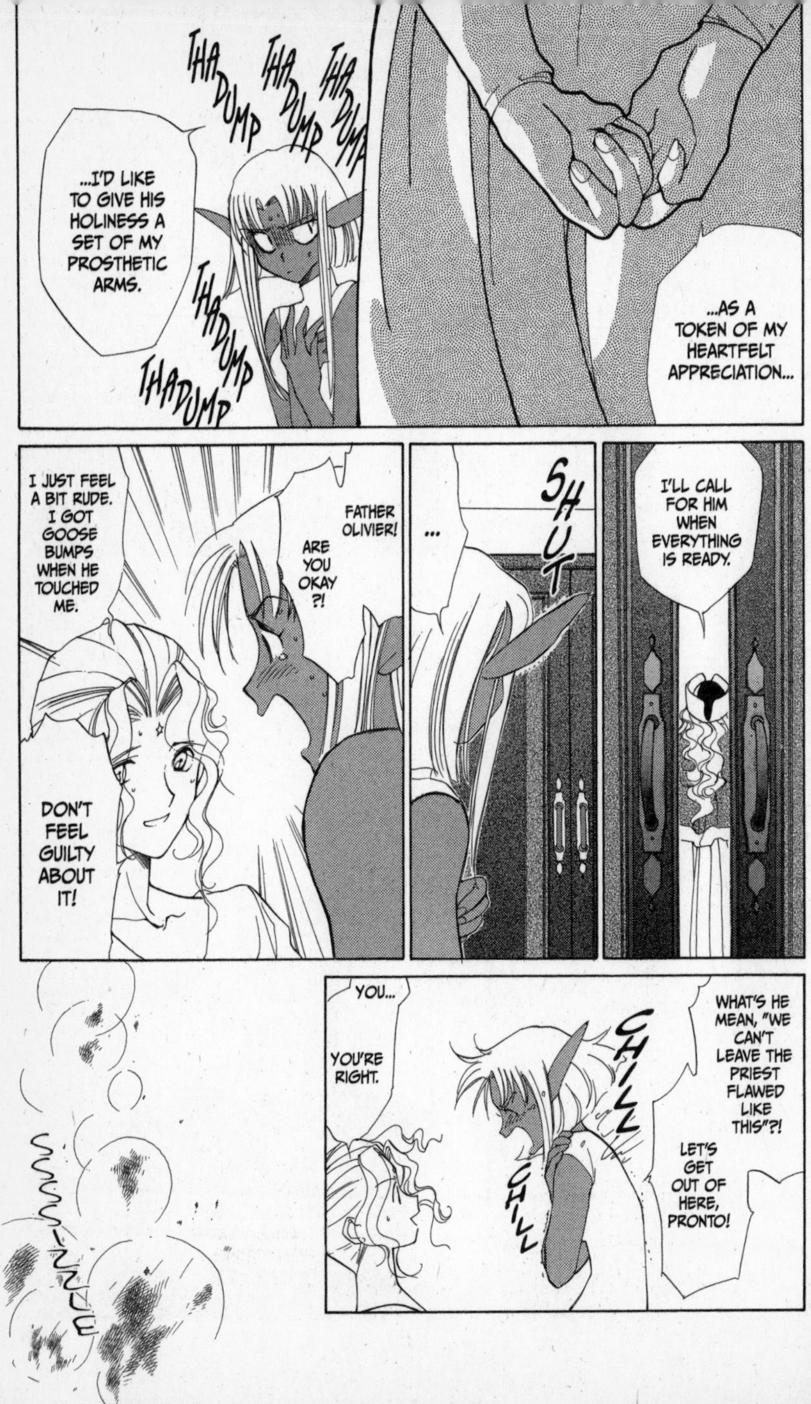
THADUMP THADUMP THADUMP
...I'D LIKE TO GIVE HIS HOLINESS A SET OF MY PROSTHETIC ARMS.
THADUMP THADUMP
...AS A TOKEN OF MY HEARTFELT APPRECIATION...
I'LL CALL FOR HIM WHEN EVERYTHING IS READY.
SHUT
...
FATHER OLIVIER!
ARE YOU OKAY?!
I JUST FEEL A BIT RUDE. I GOT GOOSE BUMPS WHEN HE TOUCHED ME.
DON'T FEEL GUILTY ABOUT IT!
WHAT'S HE MEAN, "WE CAN'T LEAVE THE PRIEST FLAWED LIKE THIS"?!
CHILL CHILL
LET'S GET OUT OF HERE, PRONTO!
YOU...
YOU'RE RIGHT.
SSSIZZLE

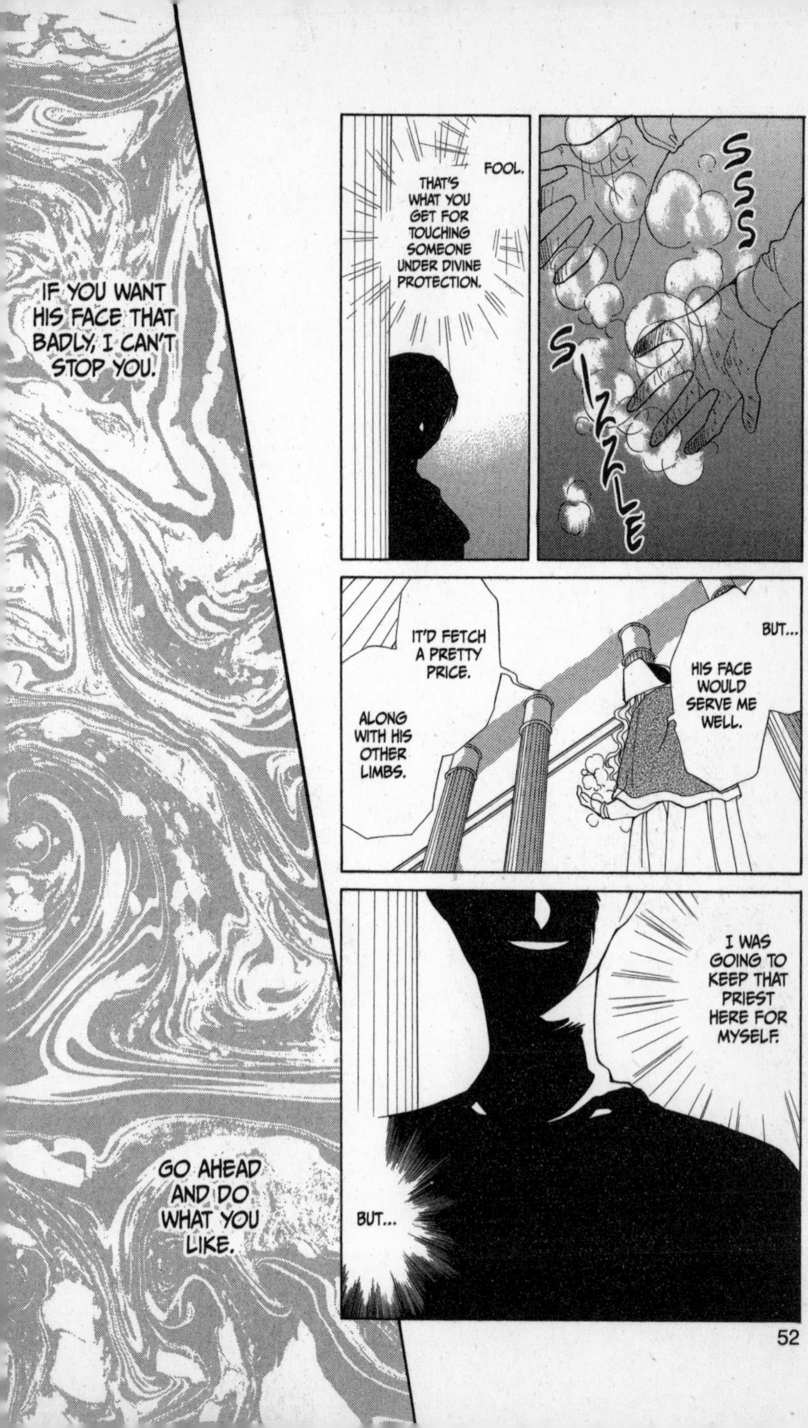
SSS
SIZZLE
FOOL.
THAT'S WHAT YOU GET FOR TOUCHING SOMEONE UNDER DIVINE PROTECTION.
BUT...
HIS FACE WOULD SERVE ME WELL.
IT'D FETCH A PRETTY PRICE.
ALONG WITH HIS OTHER LIMBS.
I WAS GOING TO KEEP THAT PRIEST HERE FOR MYSELF.
BUT...
IF YOU WANT HIS FACE THAT BADLY, I CAN'T STOP YOU.
GO AHEAD AND DO WHAT YOU LIKE.

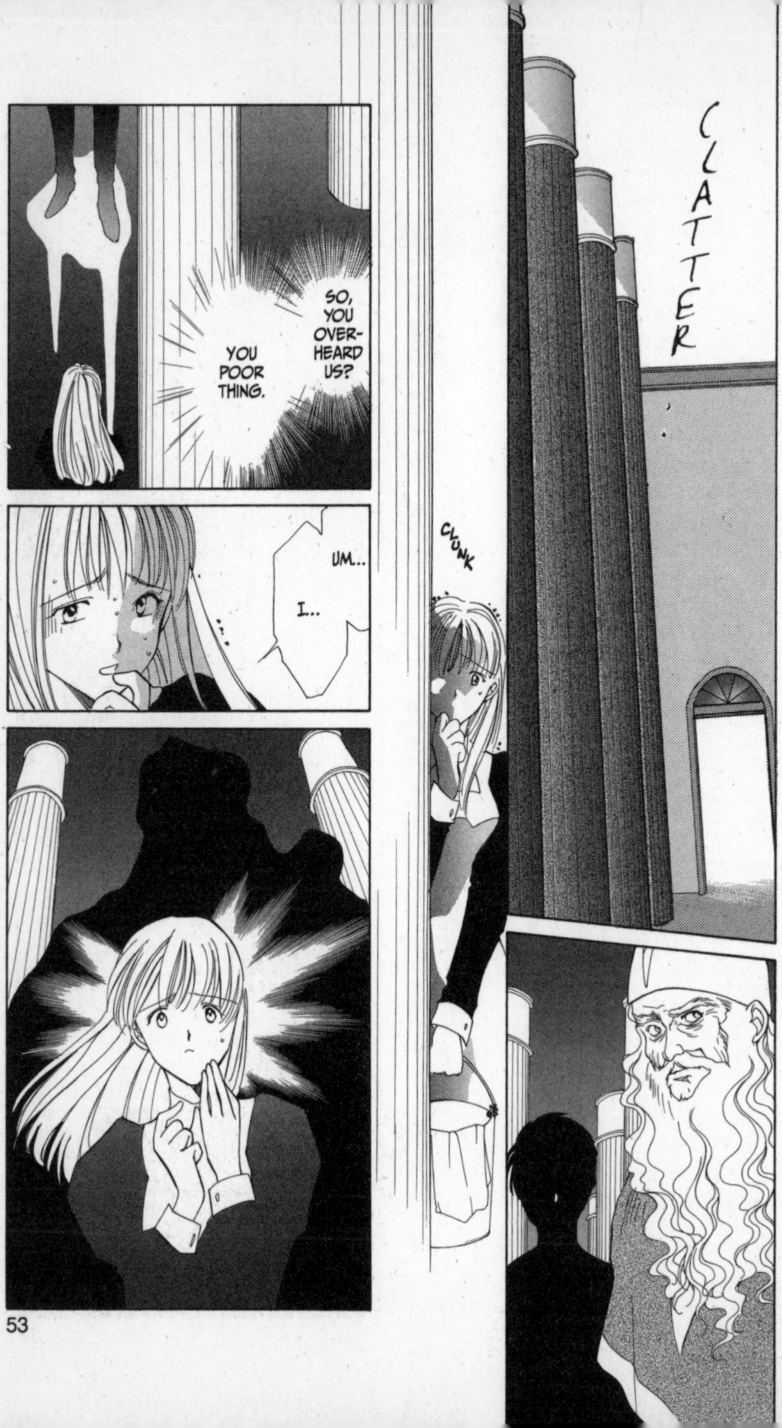
CLATTER
CLUNK
SO, YOU OVER-HEARD US?
YOU POOR THING.
UM...
I...

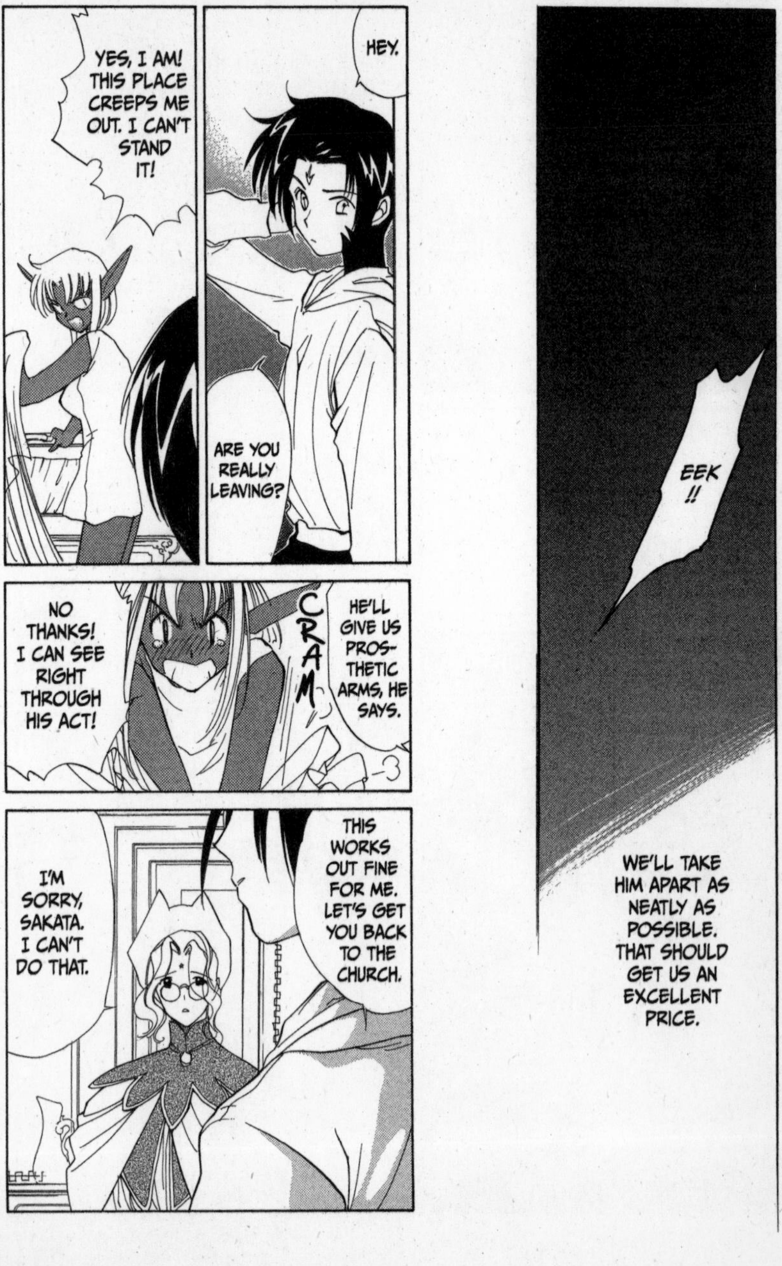
EEK!!
WE'LL TAKE HIM APART AS NEATLY AS POSSIBLE. THAT SHOULD GET US AN EXCELLENT PRICE.
HEY.
ARE YOU REALLY LEAVING?
YES, I AM! THIS PLACE CREEPS ME OUT. I CAN'T STAND IT!
HE'LL GIVE US PROS-THETIC ARMS, HE SAYS.
CRAM
NO THANKS! I CAN SEE RIGHT THROUGH HIS ACT!
THIS WORKS OUT FINE FOR ME. LET'S GET YOU BACK TO THE CHURCH.
I'M SORRY, SAKATA. I CAN'T DO THAT.

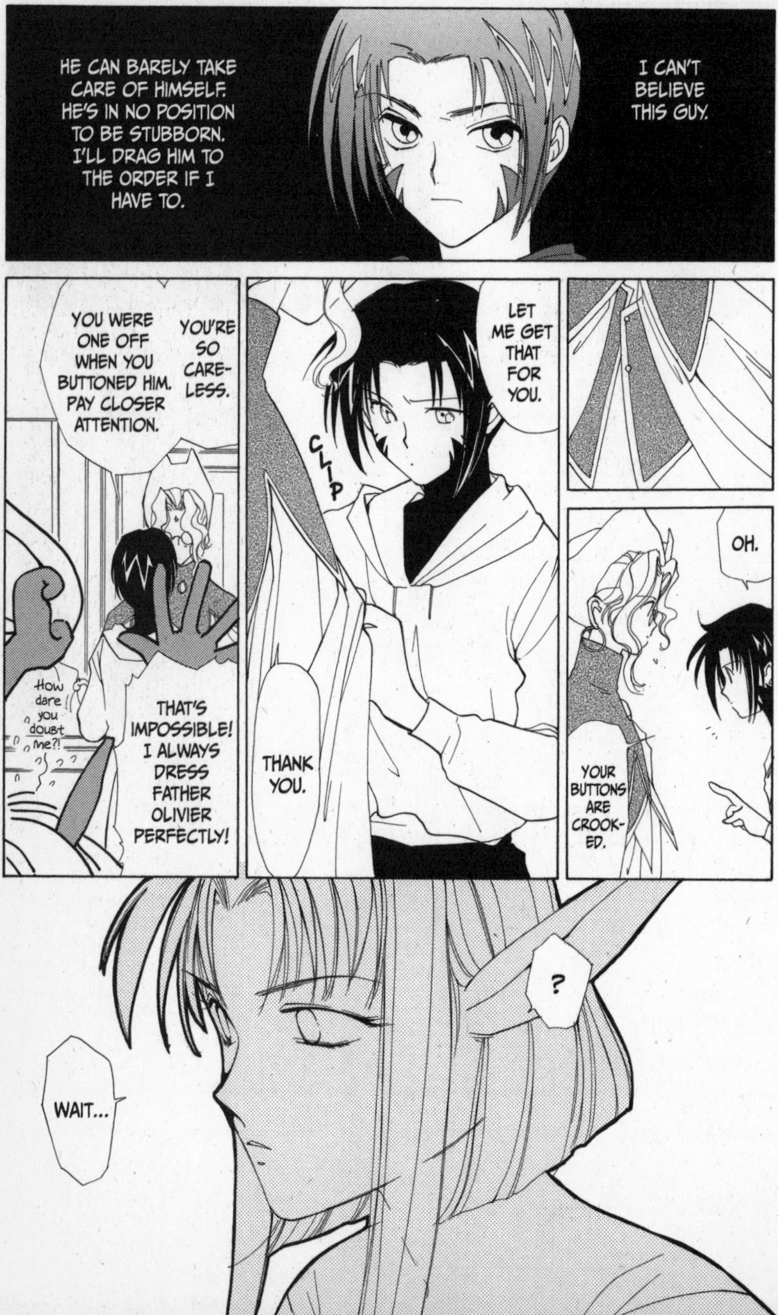
I CAN'T BELIEVE THIS GUY.
HE CAN BARELY TAKE CARE OF HIMSELF. HE'S IN NO POSITION TO BE STUBBORN. I'LL DRAG HIM TO THE ORDER IF I HAVE TO.
OH.
YOUR BUTTONS ARE CROOKED.
LET ME GET THAT FOR YOU.
CLIP
THANK YOU.
YOU'RE SO CARELESS.
YOU WERE ONE OFF WHEN YOU BUTTONED HIM. PAY CLOSER ATTENTION.
THAT'S IMPOSSIBLE! I ALWAYS DRESS FATHER OLIVIER PERFECTLY!
How dare you doubt me?!
?
WAIT...

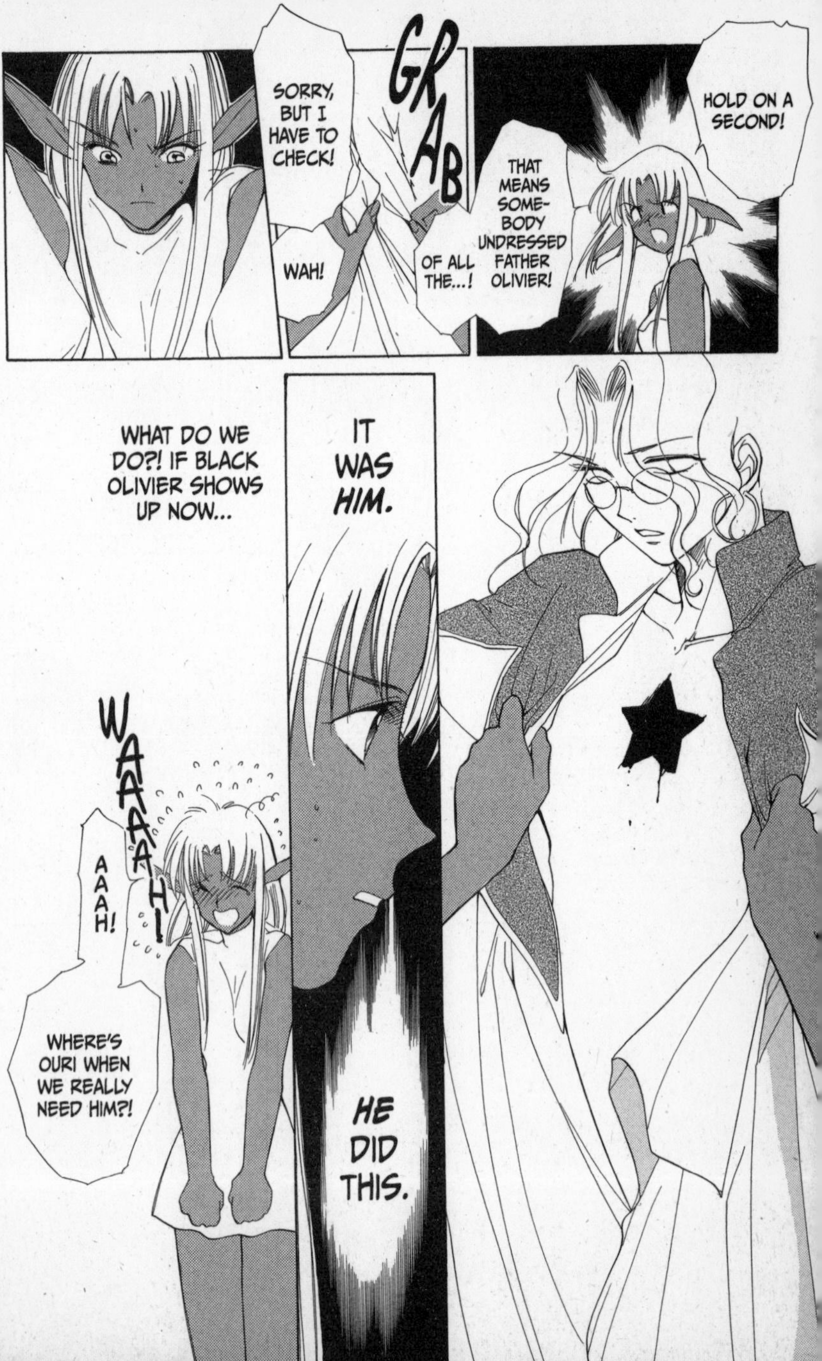
HOLD ON A SECOND!
THAT MEANS SOME-BODY UNDRESSED FATHER OLIVIER!
OF ALL THE...!
GRAB
SORRY, BUT I HAVE TO CHECK!
WAH!
IT WAS HIM.
HE DID THIS.
WHAT DO WE DO?! IF BLACK OLIVIER SHOWS UP NOW...
WAAAAAH!
AAAAH!
WHERE'S OURI WHEN WE REALLY NEED HIM?!

PSYCH.

GYAAAAH!!

BALD SPOT.

A-HA!

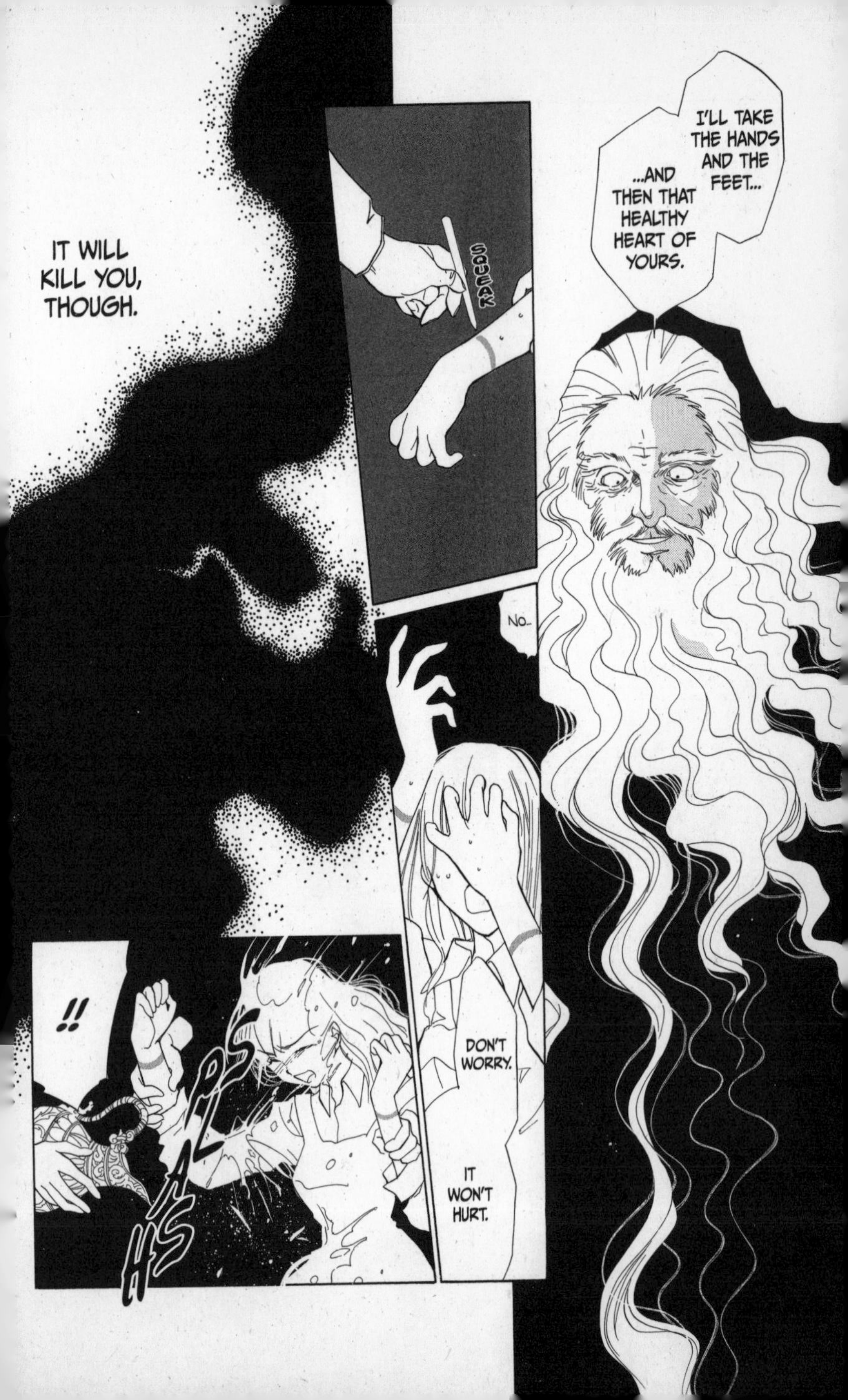
I'LL TAKE THE HANDS AND THE FEET...
...AND THEN THAT HEALTHY HEART OF YOURS.
SQUEAK
IT WILL KILL YOU, THOUGH.
No...
DON'T WORRY.
IT WON'T HURT.
!!
SPLASH

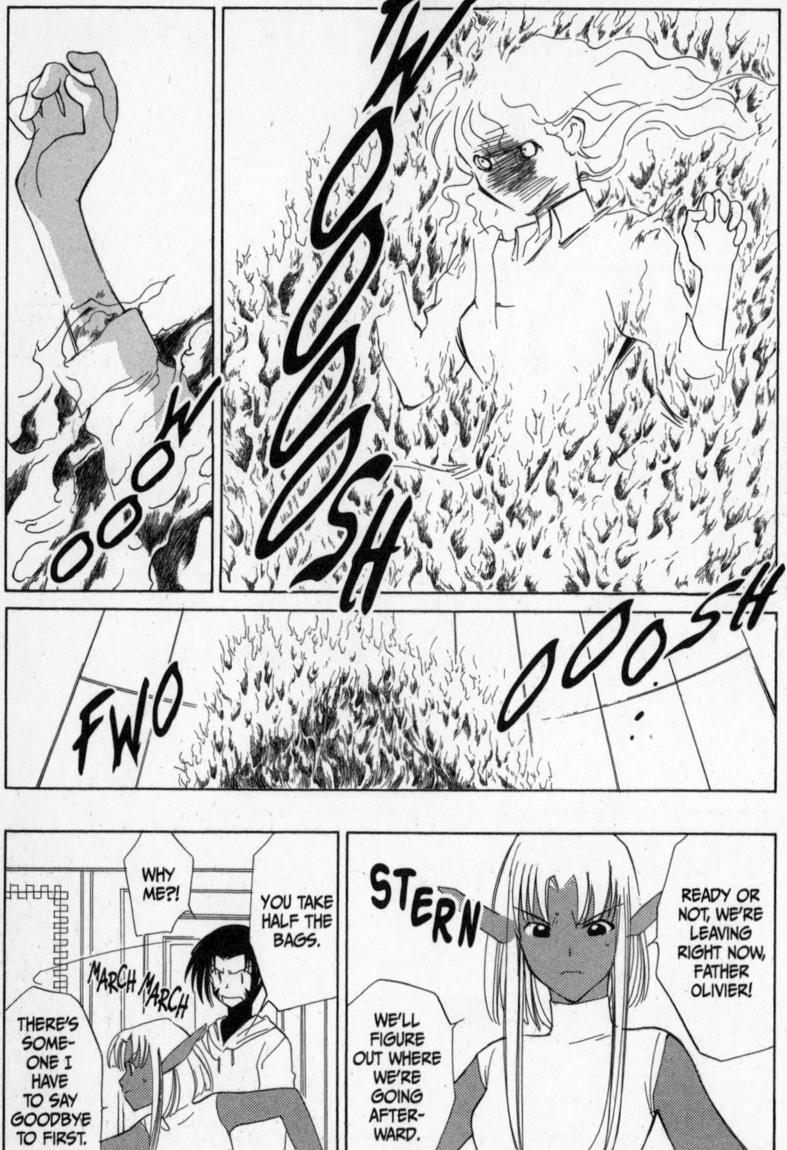
FWOOOOSH
OOOOW
FWO
OOOSH
READY OR NOT, WE'RE LEAVING RIGHT NOW, FATHER OLIVIER!
STERN
WE'LL FIGURE OUT WHERE WE'RE GOING AFTER-WARD.
YOU TAKE HALF THE BAGS.
WHY ME?!
MARCH MARCH
THERE'S SOME-ONE I HAVE TO SAY GOODBYE TO FIRST.
I'LL BE RIGHT BACK.

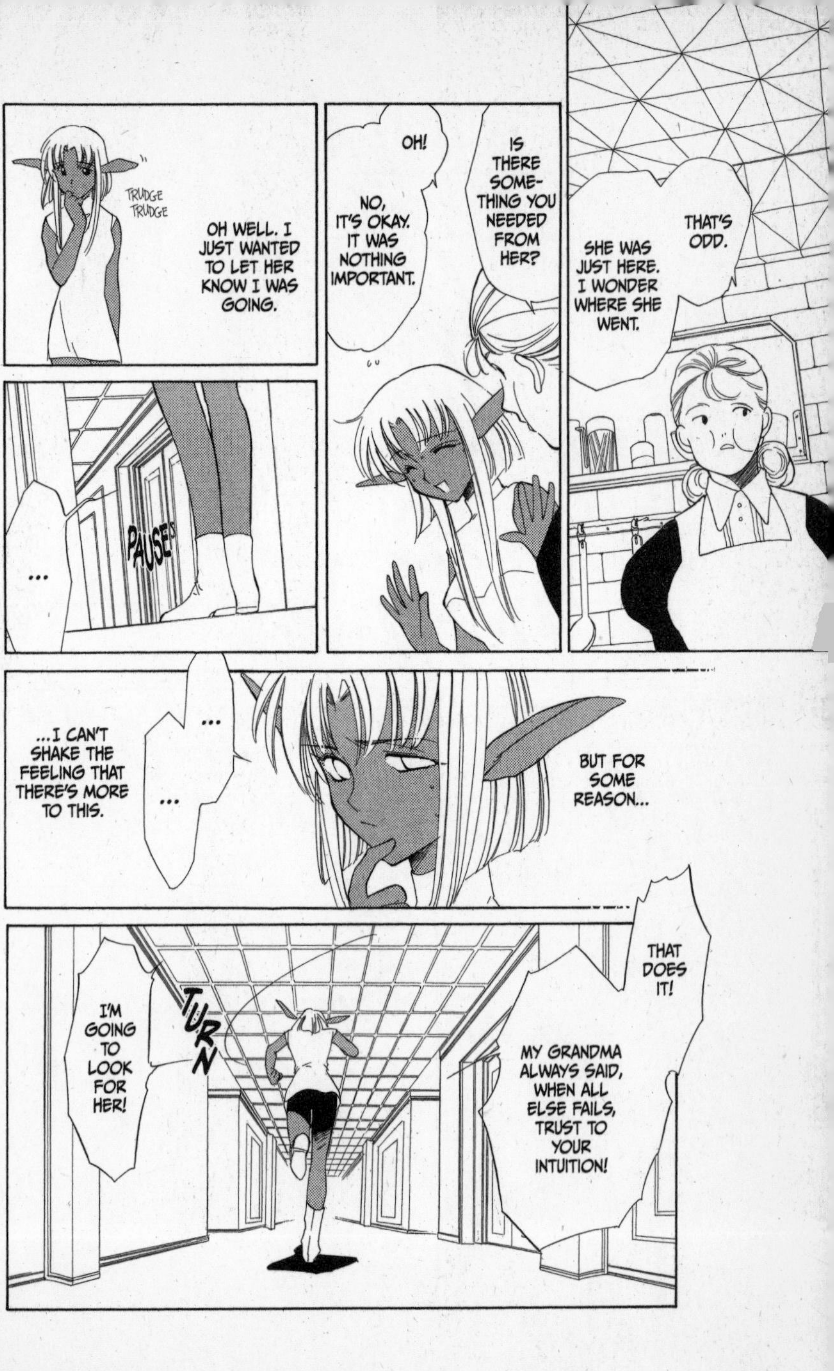
THAT'S ODD.
SHE WAS JUST HERE. I WONDER WHERE SHE WENT.
IS THERE SOME-THING YOU NEEDED FROM HER?
OH!
NO, IT'S OKAY. IT WAS NOTHING IMPORTANT.
TRUDGE TRUDGE
OH WELL. I JUST WANTED TO LET HER KNOW I WAS GOING.
PAUSE
...
BUT FOR SOME REASON...
...
...
...I CAN'T SHAKE THE FEELING THAT THERE'S MORE TO THIS.
THAT DOES IT!
MY GRANDMA ALWAYS SAID, WHEN ALL ELSE FAILS, TRUST TO YOUR INTUITION!
TURN
I'M GOING TO LOOK FOR HER!

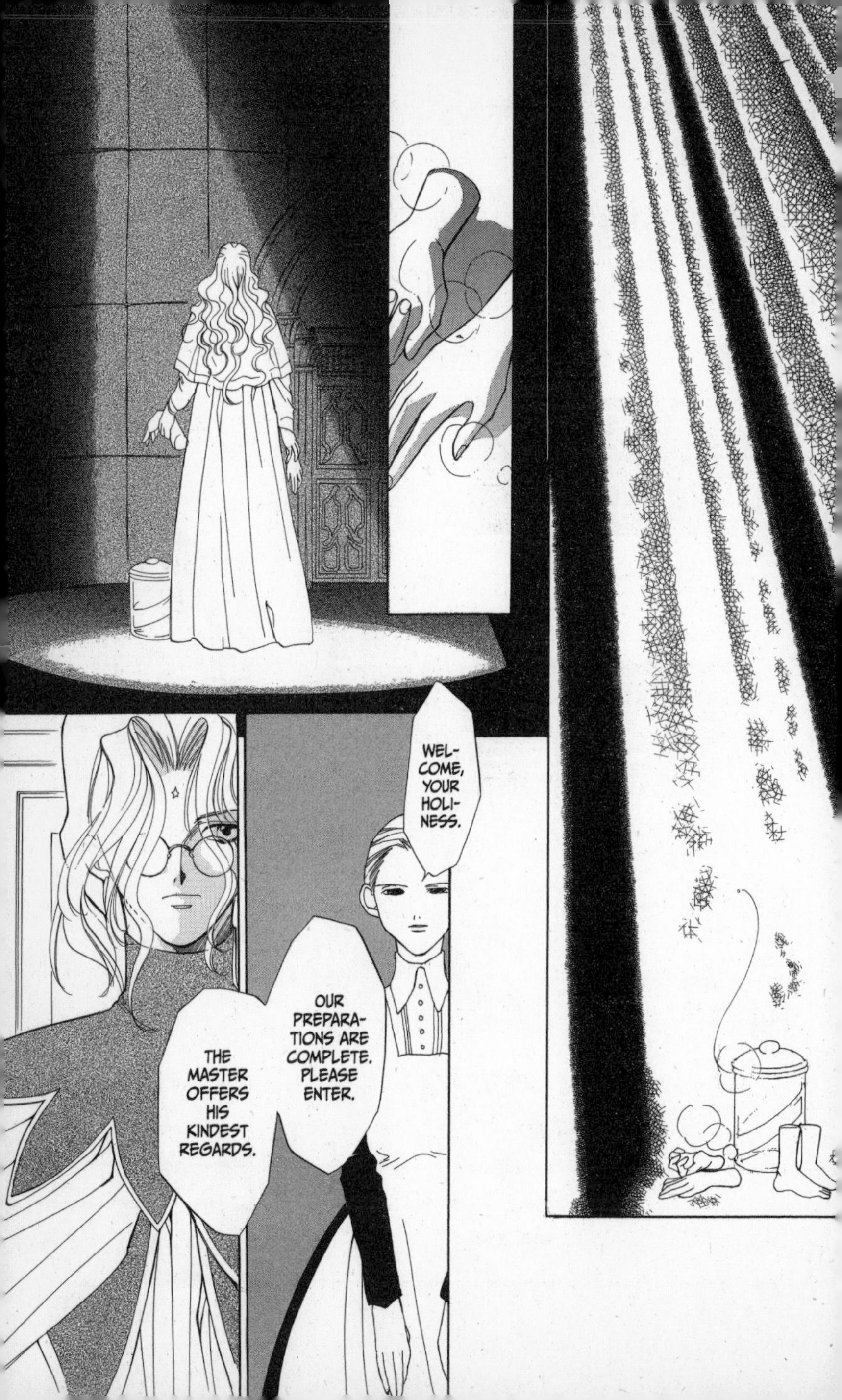
WEL-COME, YOUR HOLI-NESS.
OUR PREPARA-TIONS ARE COMPLETE. PLEASE ENTER.
THE MASTER OFFERS HIS KINDEST REGARDS.

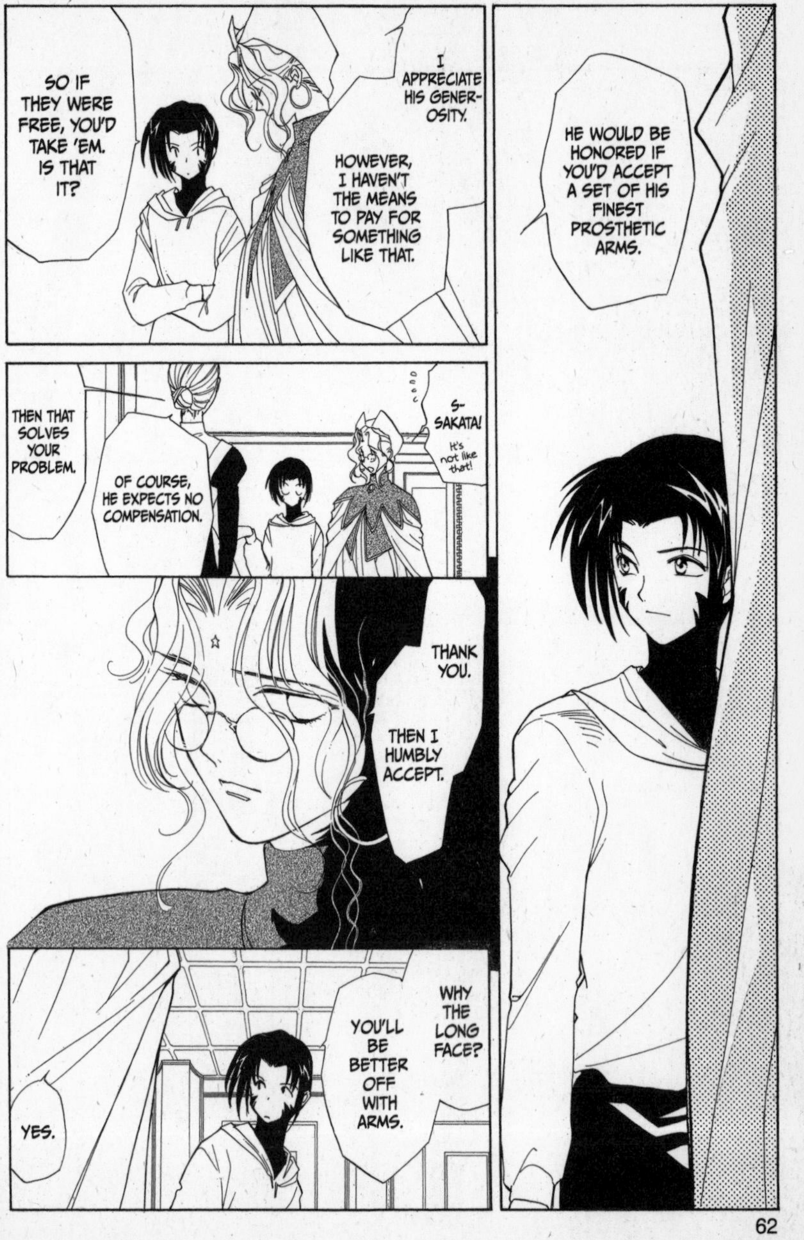
HE WOULD BE HONORED IF YOU'D ACCEPT A SET OF HIS FINEST PROSTHETIC ARMS.
I APPRECIATE HIS GENER-OSITY.
HOWEVER, I HAVEN'T THE MEANS TO PAY FOR SOMETHING LIKE THAT.
SO IF THEY WERE FREE, YOU'D TAKE 'EM. IS THAT IT?
S-SAKATA!
It's not like that!
OF COURSE, HE EXPECTS NO COMPENSATION.
THEN THAT SOLVES YOUR PROBLEM.
THANK YOU.
THEN I HUMBLY ACCEPT.
WHY THE LONG FACE?
YOU'LL BE BETTER OFF WITH ARMS.
YES.

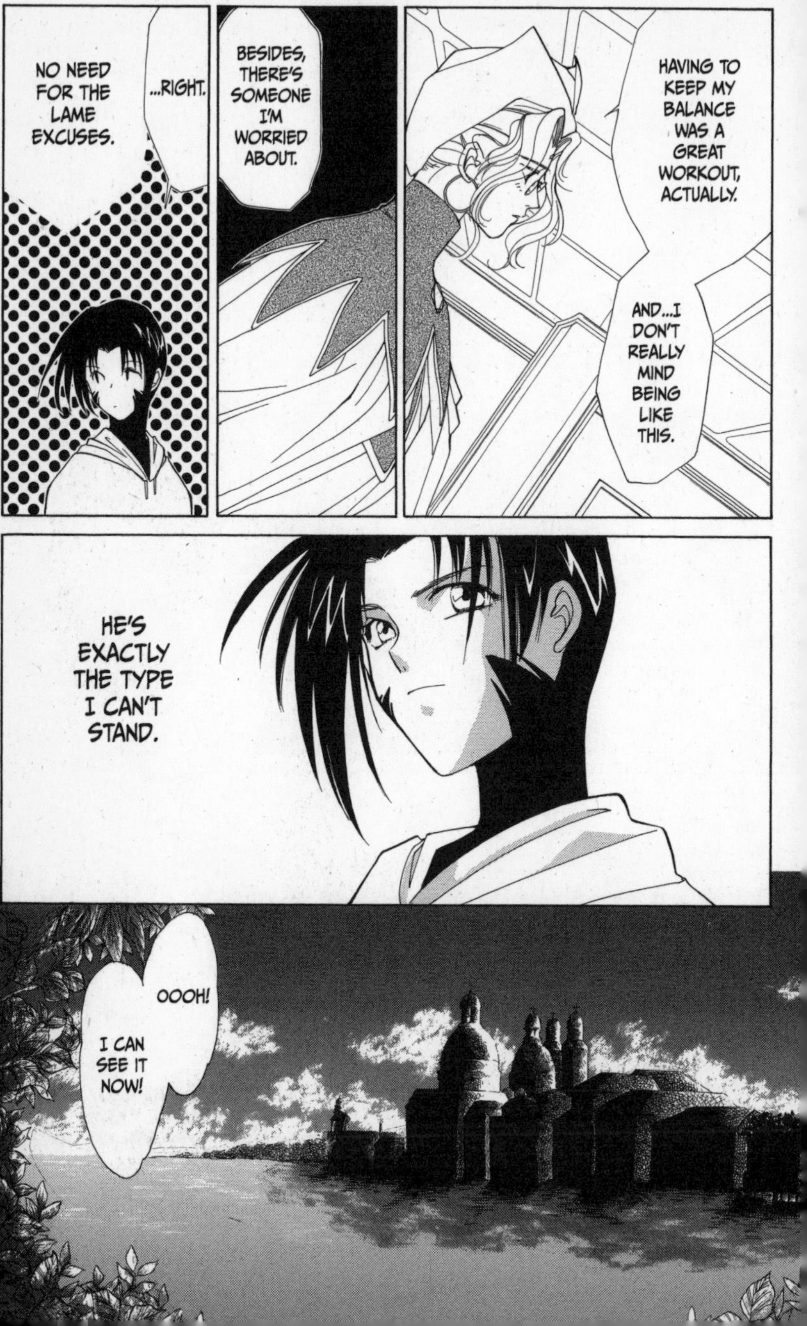
HAVING TO KEEP MY BALANCE WAS A GREAT WORKOUT, ACTUALLY.
AND...I DON'T REALLY MIND BEING LIKE THIS.
BESIDES, THERE'S SOMEONE I'M WORRIED ABOUT.
...RIGHT.
NO NEED FOR THE LAME EXCUSES.
HE'S EXACTLY THE TYPE I CAN'T STAND.
OOOH!
I CAN SEE IT NOW!

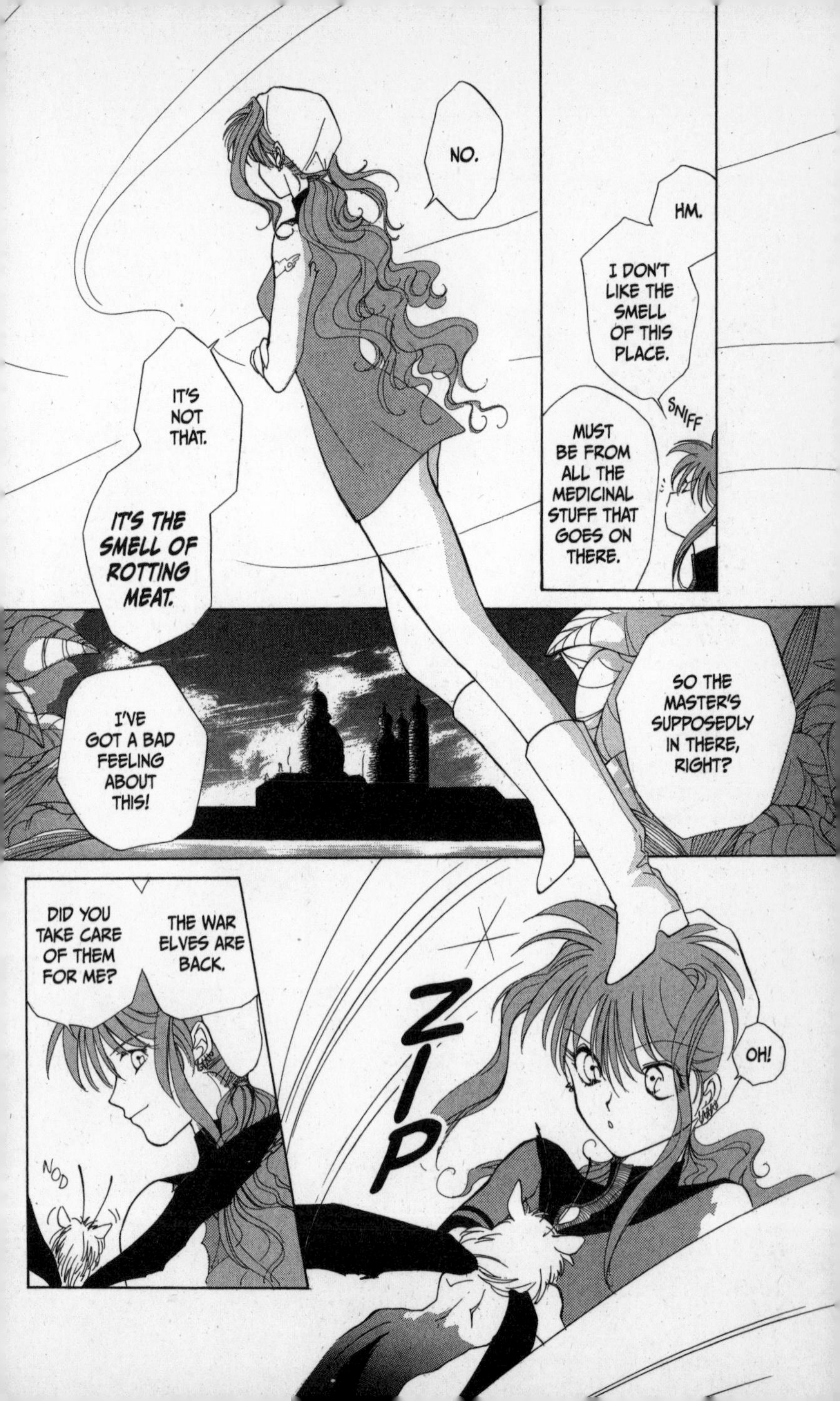
HM.
I DON'T LIKE THE SMELL OF THIS PLACE.
SNIFF
MUST BE FROM ALL THE MEDICINAL STUFF THAT GOES ON THERE.
NO.
IT'S NOT THAT.
IT'S THE SMELL OF ROTTING MEAT.
SO THE MASTER'S SUPPOSEDLY IN THERE, RIGHT?
I'VE GOT A BAD FEELING ABOUT THIS!
ZIP
OH!
THE WAR ELVES ARE BACK.
DID YOU TAKE CARE OF THEM FOR ME?
NOD

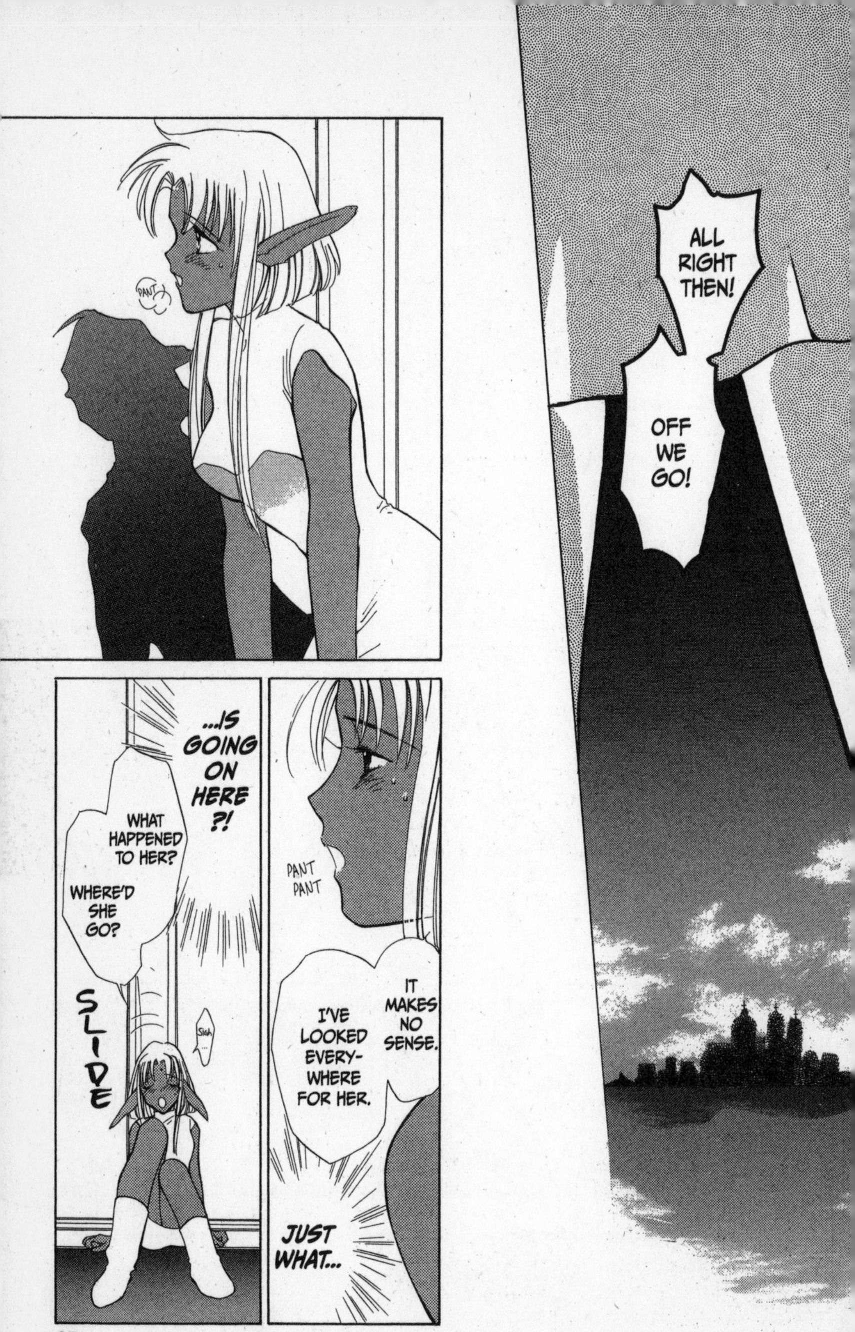
ALL RIGHT THEN!
OFF WE GO!
PANT
PANT PANT
IT MAKES NO SENSE.
I'VE LOOKED EVERYWHERE FOR HER.
JUST WHAT...
...IS GOING ON HERE?!
WHAT HAPPENED TO HER?
WHERE'D SHE GO?
SLIDE
Sigh...

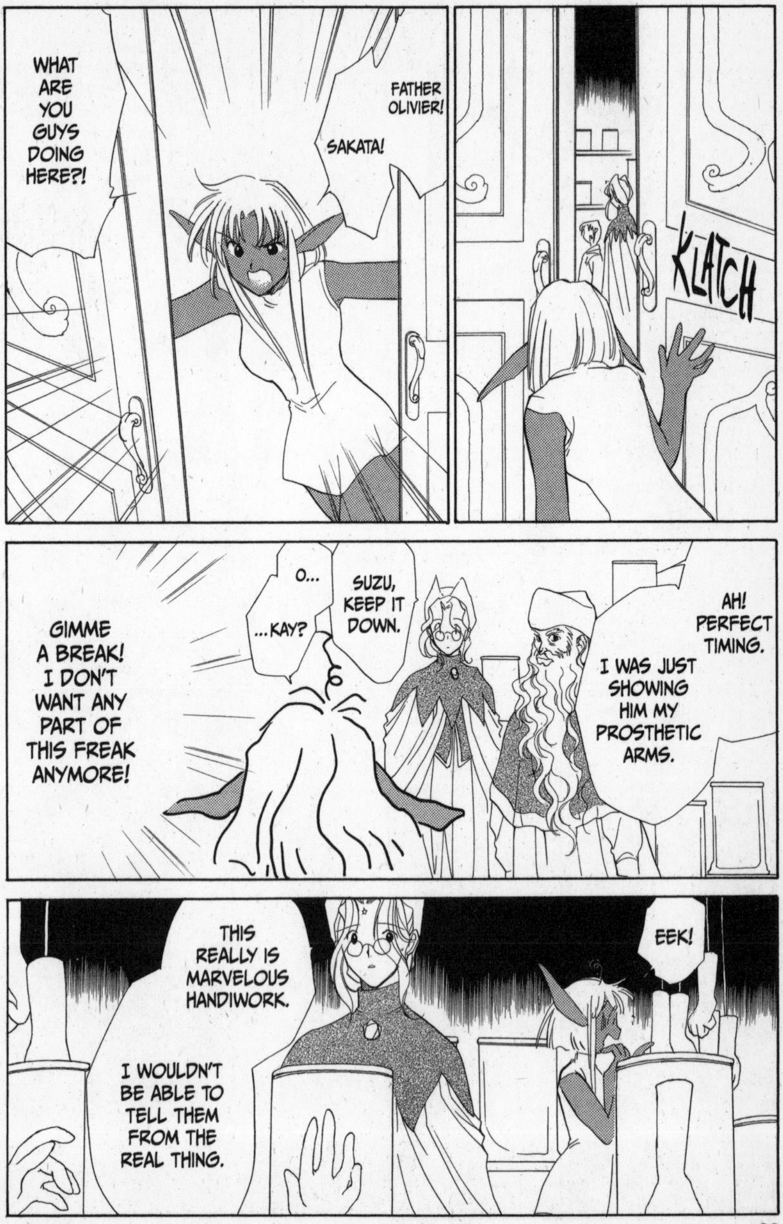
KLATCH
FATHER OLIVIER!
SAKATA!
WHAT ARE YOU GUYS DOING HERE?!
AH! PERFECT TIMING.
I WAS JUST SHOWING HIM MY PROSTHETIC ARMS.
SUZU, KEEP IT DOWN.
O...
...KAY?
GIMME A BREAK! I DON'T WANT ANY PART OF THIS FREAK ANYMORE!
EEK!
THIS REALLY IS MARVELOUS HANDIWORK.
I WOULDN'T BE ABLE TO TELL THEM FROM THE REAL THING.

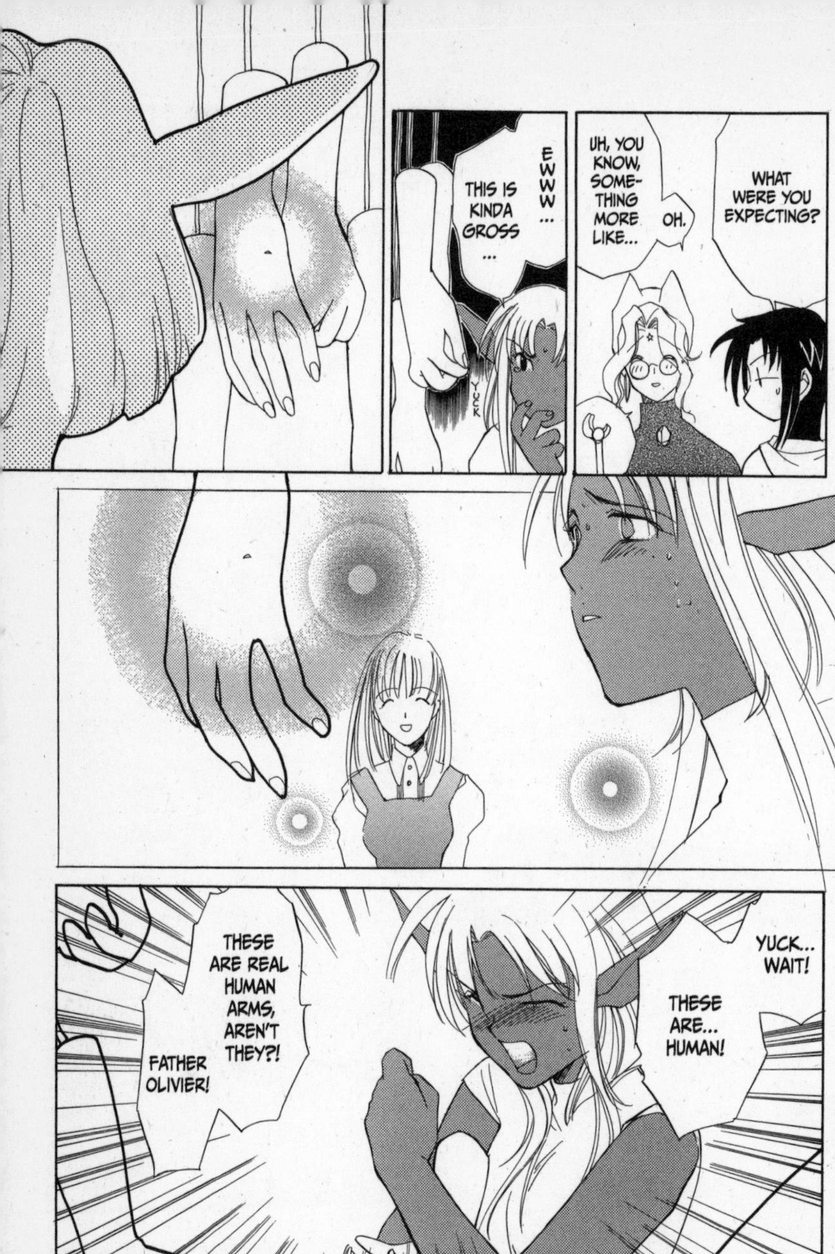
WHAT WERE YOU EXPECTING?
OH.
UH, YOU KNOW, SOME-THING MORE LIKE...
EWWW...
THIS IS KINDA GROSS...
YUCK
YUCK... WAIT!
THESE ARE... HUMAN!
THESE ARE REAL HUMAN ARMS, AREN'T THEY?!
FATHER OLIVIER!

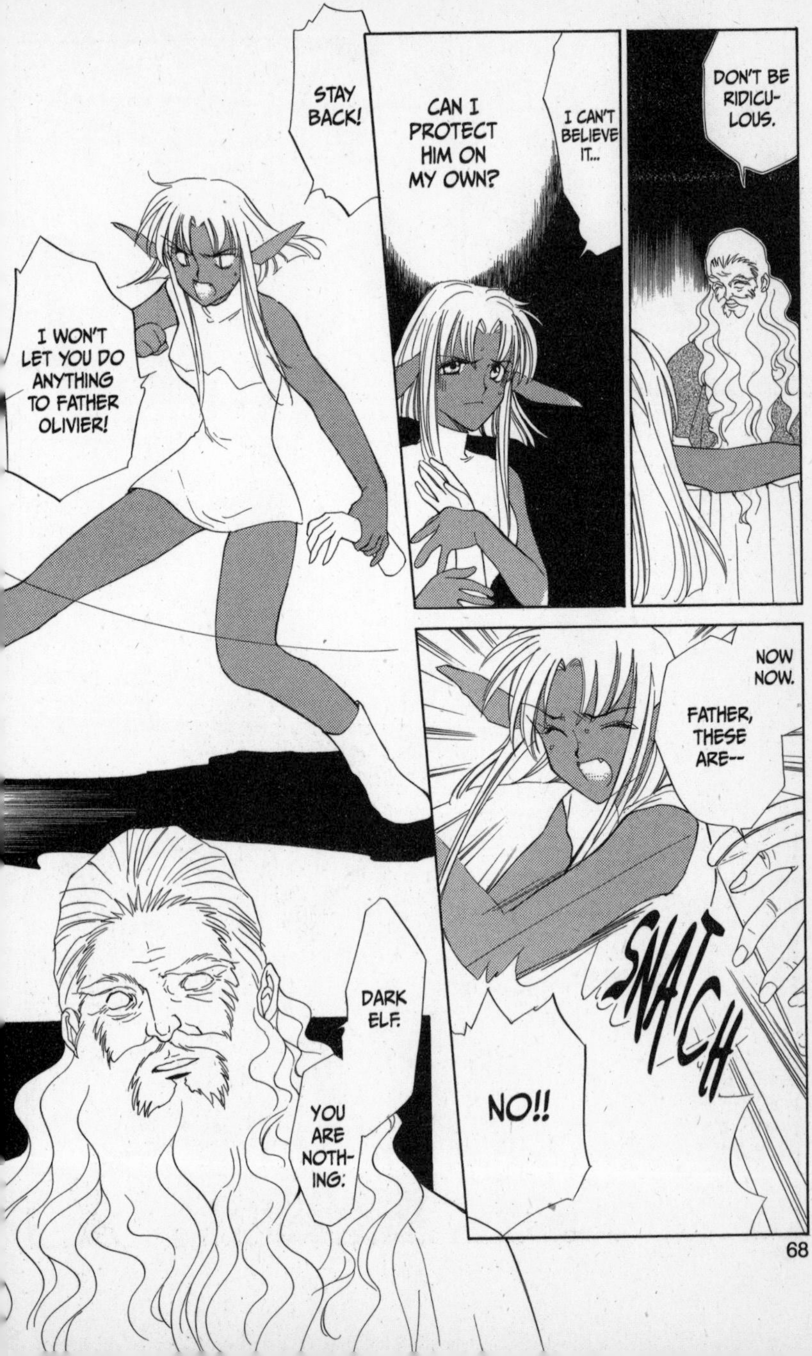
DON'T BE RIDICU-LOUS.
I CAN'T BELIEVE IT...
CAN I PROTECT HIM ON MY OWN?
STAY BACK!
I WON'T LET YOU DO ANYTHING TO FATHER OLIVIER!
NOW NOW.
FATHER, THESE ARE--
SNATCH
NO!!
DARK ELF.
YOU ARE NOTH-ING.

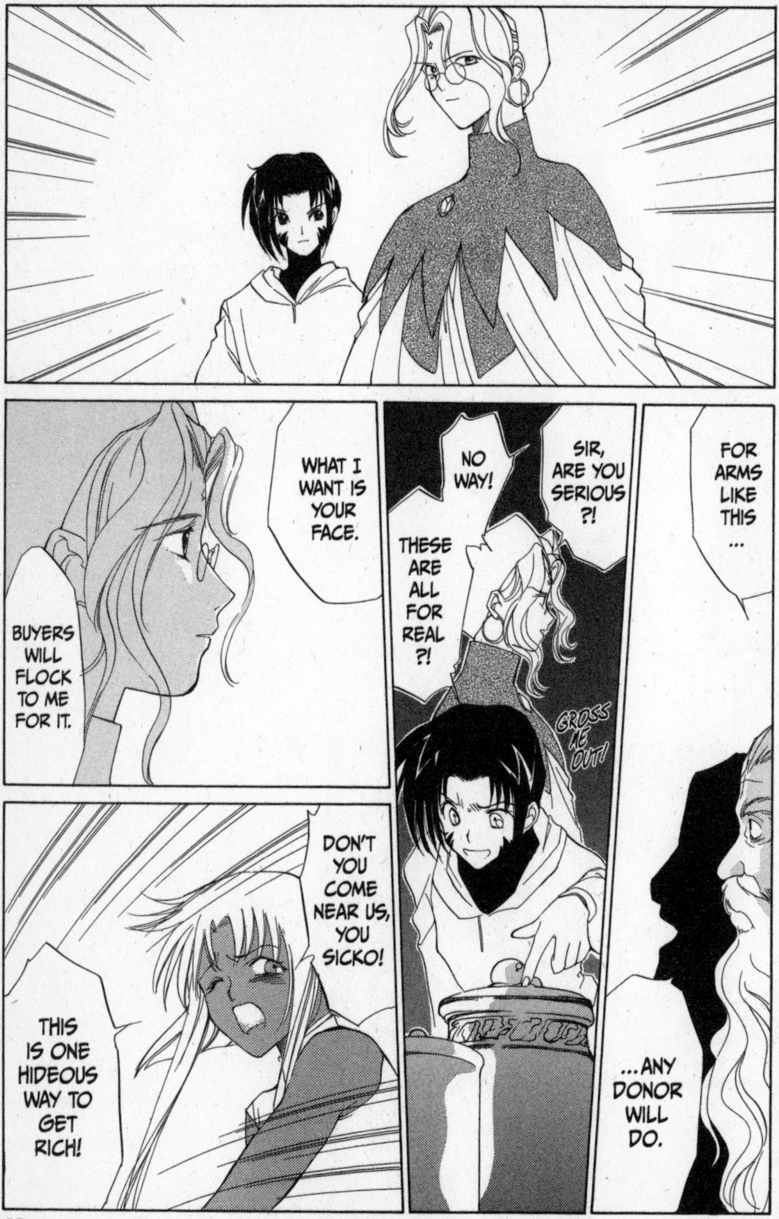
FOR ARMS LIKE THIS ...
...ANY DONOR WILL DO.
SIR, ARE YOU SERIOUS ?!
NO WAY!
THESE ARE ALL FOR REAL ?!
GROSS ME OUT!
WHAT I WANT IS YOUR FACE.
BUYERS WILL FLOCK TO ME FOR IT.
DON'T YOU COME NEAR US, YOU SICKO!
THIS IS ONE HIDEOUS WAY TO GET RICH!

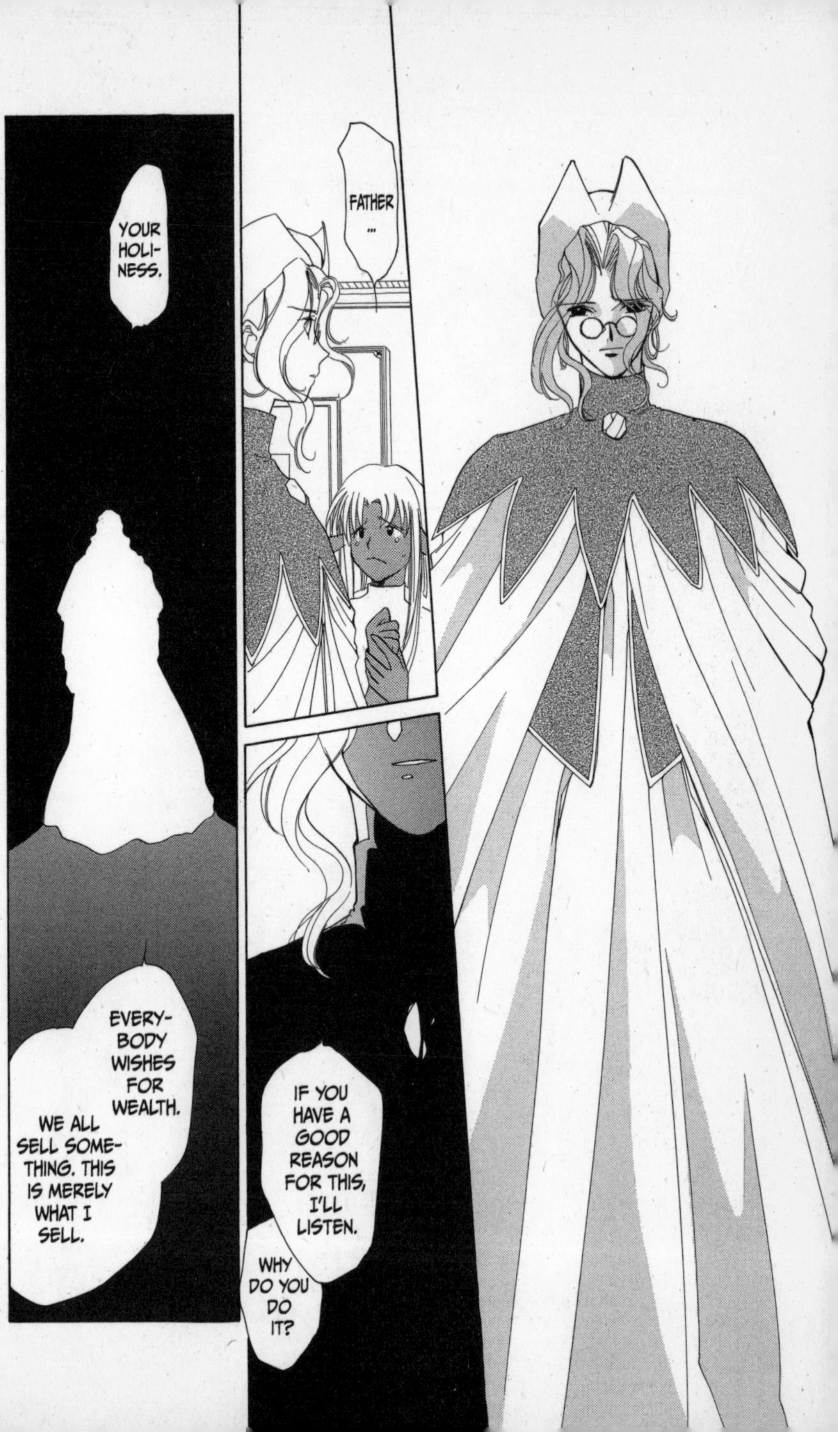
FATHER ...
IF YOU HAVE A GOOD REASON FOR THIS, I'LL LISTEN.
WHY DO YOU DO IT?
YOUR HOLI-NESS.
EVERY-BODY WISHES FOR WEALTH.
WE ALL SELL SOME-THING. THIS IS MERELY WHAT I SELL.

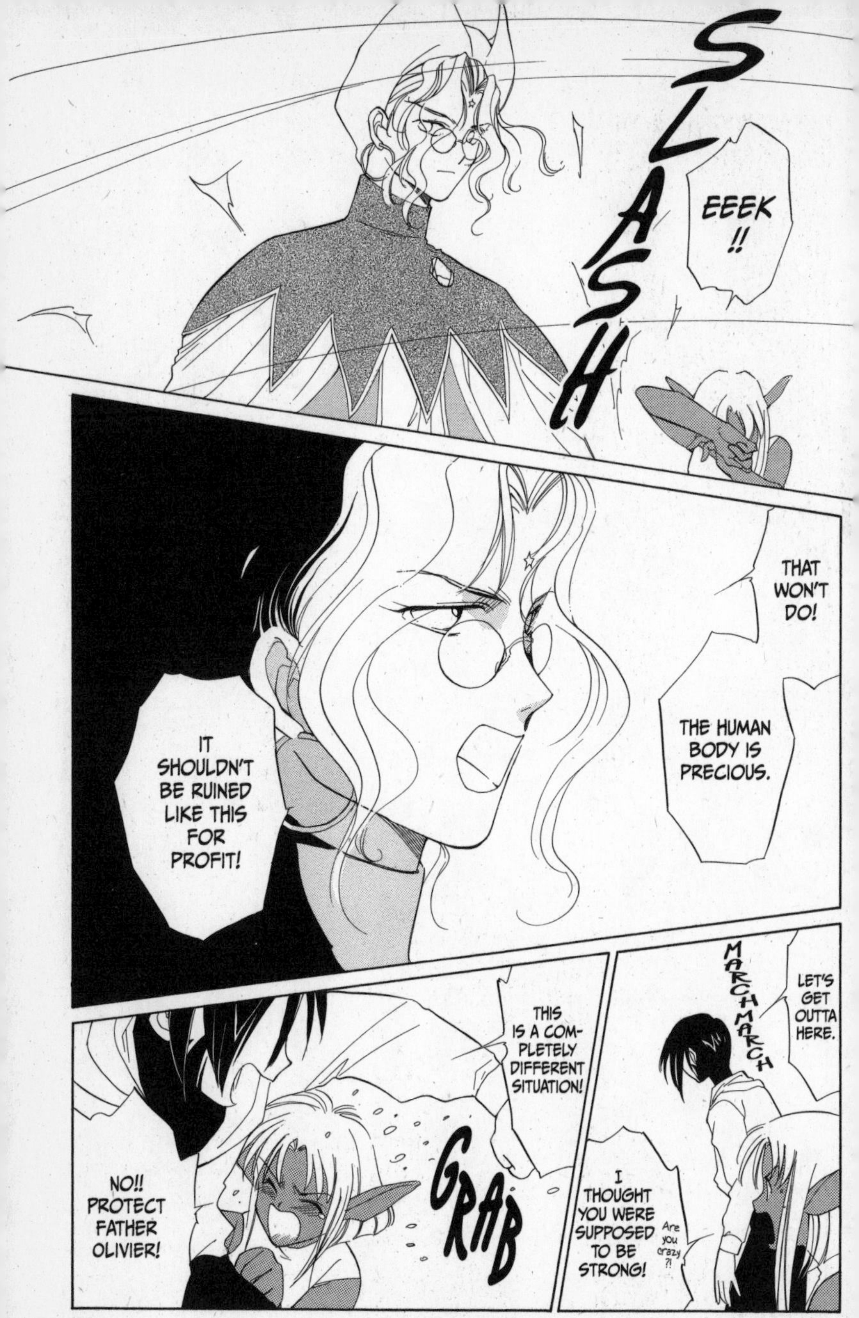
SLASH
EEEK!!
THAT WON'T DO!
THE HUMAN BODY IS PRECIOUS.
IT SHOULDN'T BE RUINED LIKE THIS FOR PROFIT!
MARCHMARCH
LET'S GET OUTTA HERE.
I THOUGHT YOU WERE SUPPOSED TO BE STRONG!
Are you crazy?!
THIS IS A COM-PLETELY DIFFERENT SITUATION!
GRAB
NO!! PROTECT FATHER OLIVIER!

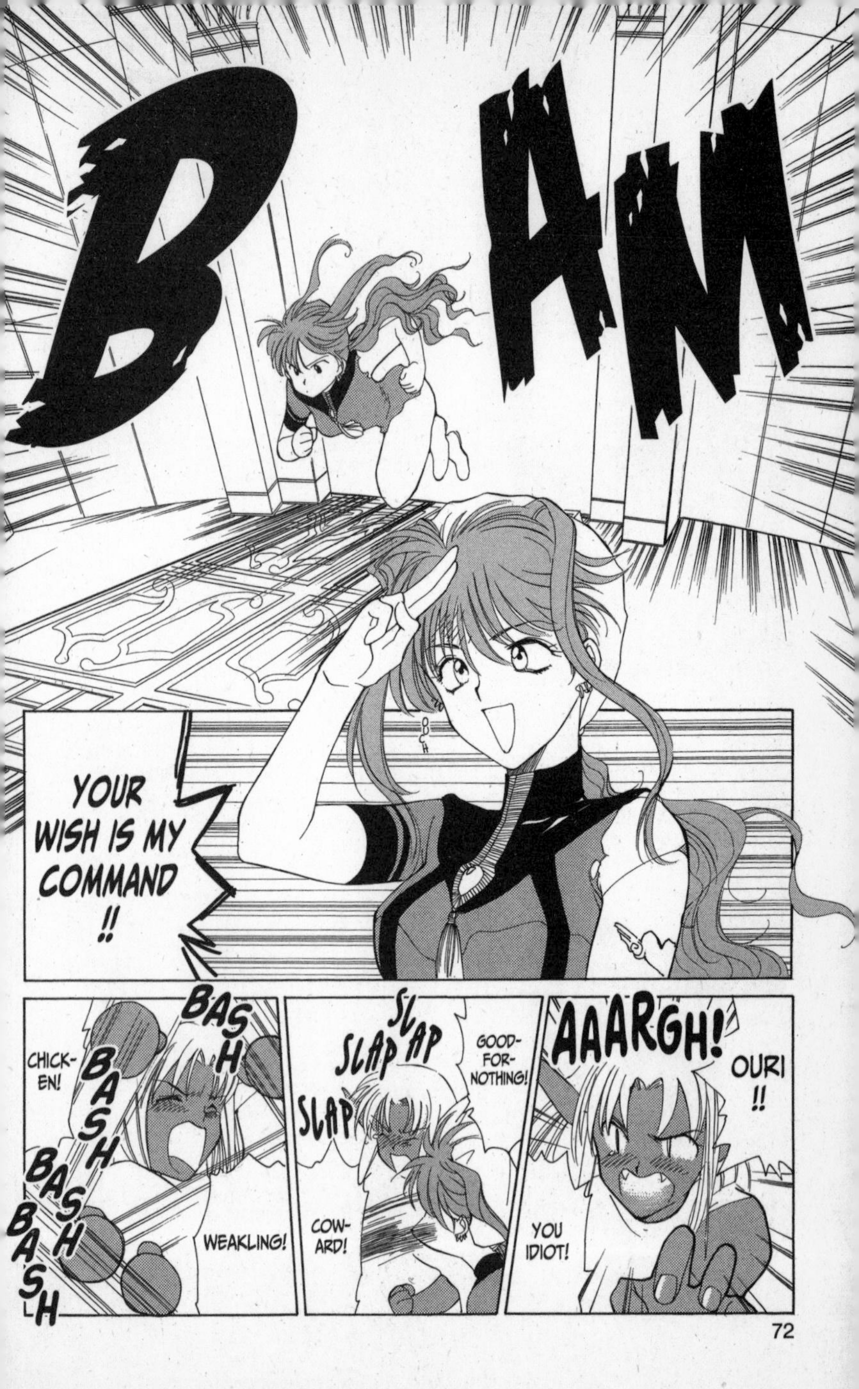
BAM
OUCH
YOUR WISH IS MY COMMAND!!
AAARGH!
OURI!!
YOU IDIOT!
SLAP SLAP
SLAP
SLAP
GOOD-FOR-NOTHING!
COW-ARD!
BASH
BASH
BASH
BASH
CHICK-EN!
WEAKLING!

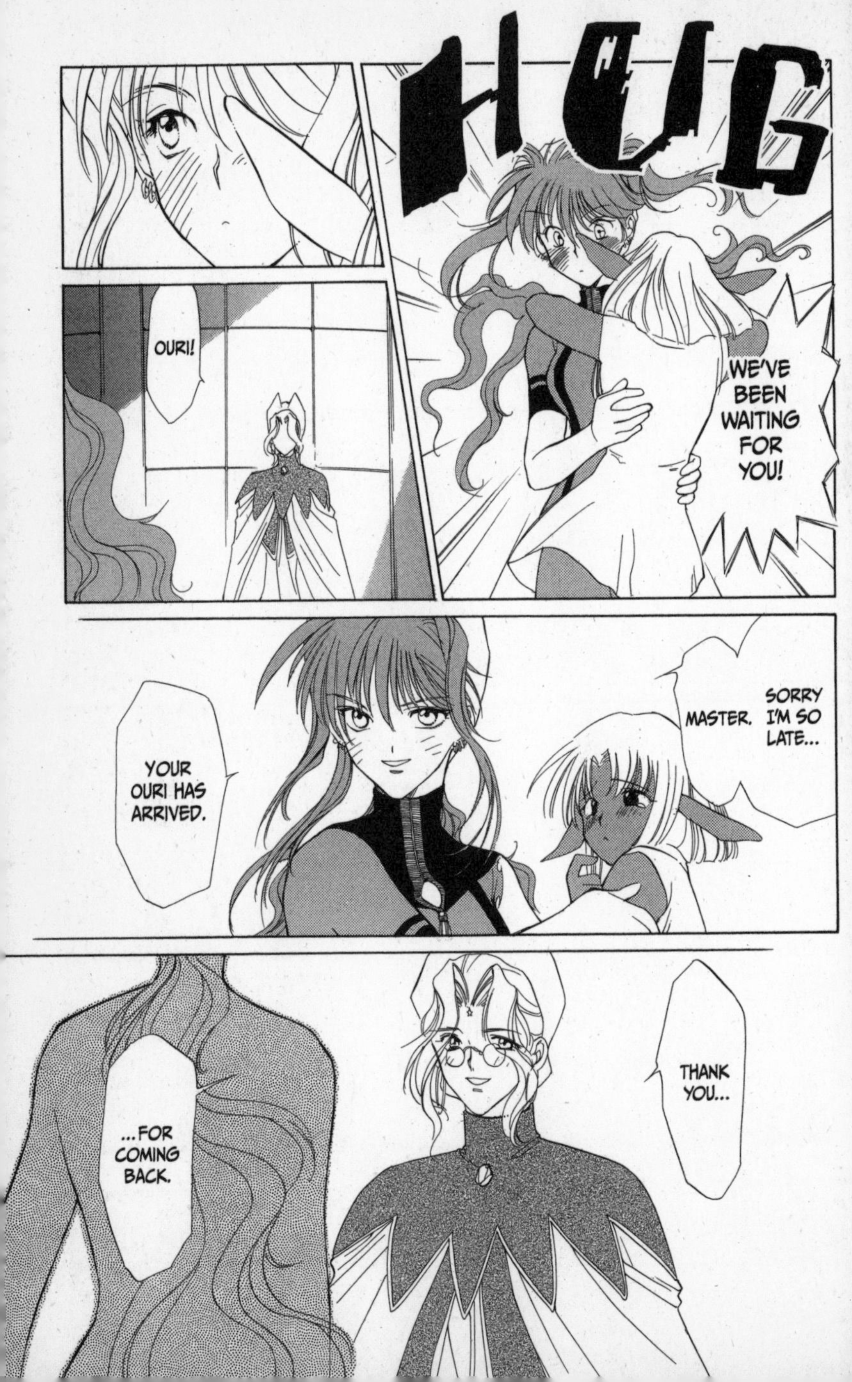
HUG
WE'VE BEEN WAITING FOR YOU!
OURI!
SORRY I'M SO LATE...
MASTER.
YOUR OURI HAS ARRIVED.
THANK YOU...
...FOR COMING BACK.

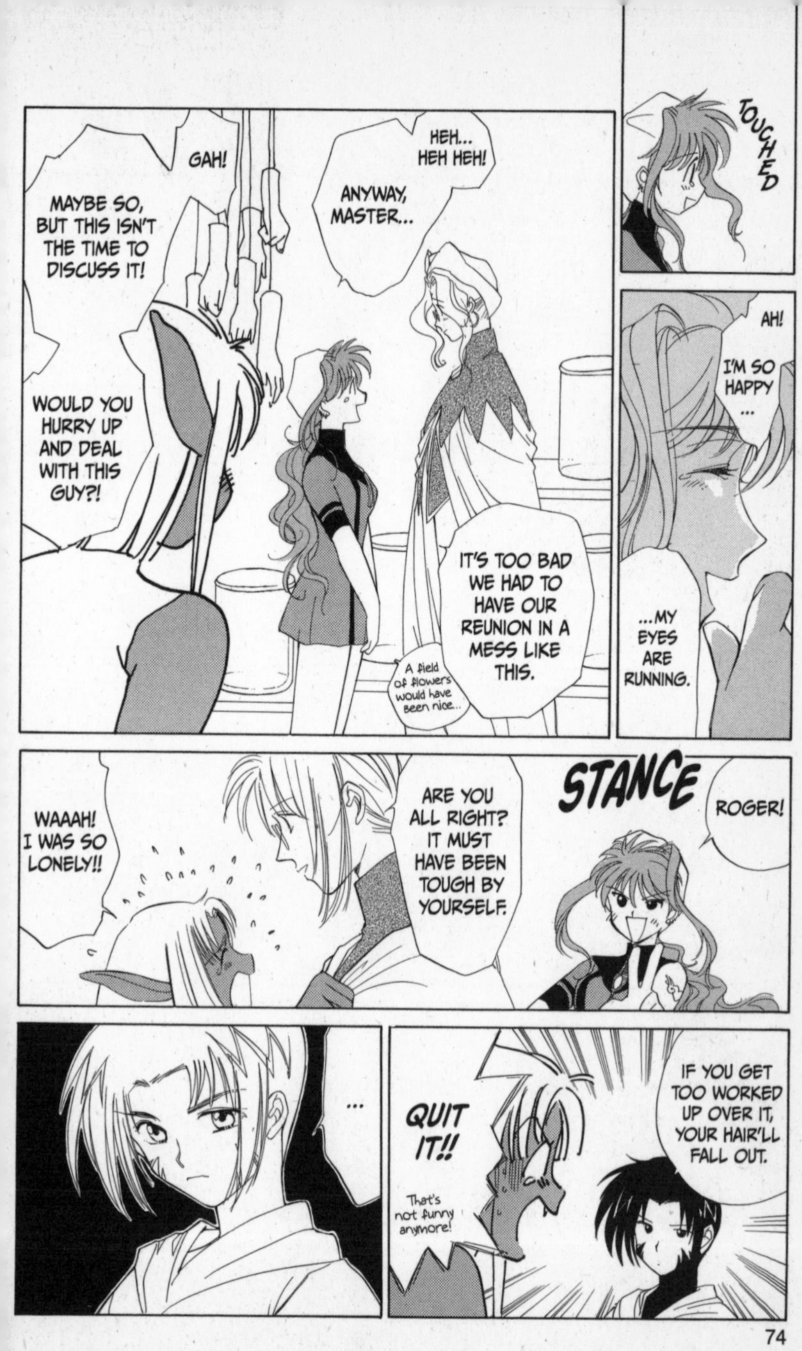
TOUCHED
AH!
I'M SO HAPPY ...
...MY EYES ARE RUNNING.
HEH... HEH HEH!
ANYWAY, MASTER...
GAH!
MAYBE SO, BUT THIS ISN'T THE TIME TO DISCUSS IT!
WOULD YOU HURRY UP AND DEAL WITH THIS GUY?!
IT'S TOO BAD WE HAD TO HAVE OUR REUNION IN A MESS LIKE THIS.
A field of flowers would have been nice...
ROGER!
STANCE
ARE YOU ALL RIGHT? IT MUST HAVE BEEN TOUGH BY YOURSELF.
WAAAH! I WAS SO LONELY!!
IF YOU GET TOO WORKED UP OVER IT, YOUR HAIR'LL FALL OUT.
QUIT IT!!
That's not funny anymore!
...

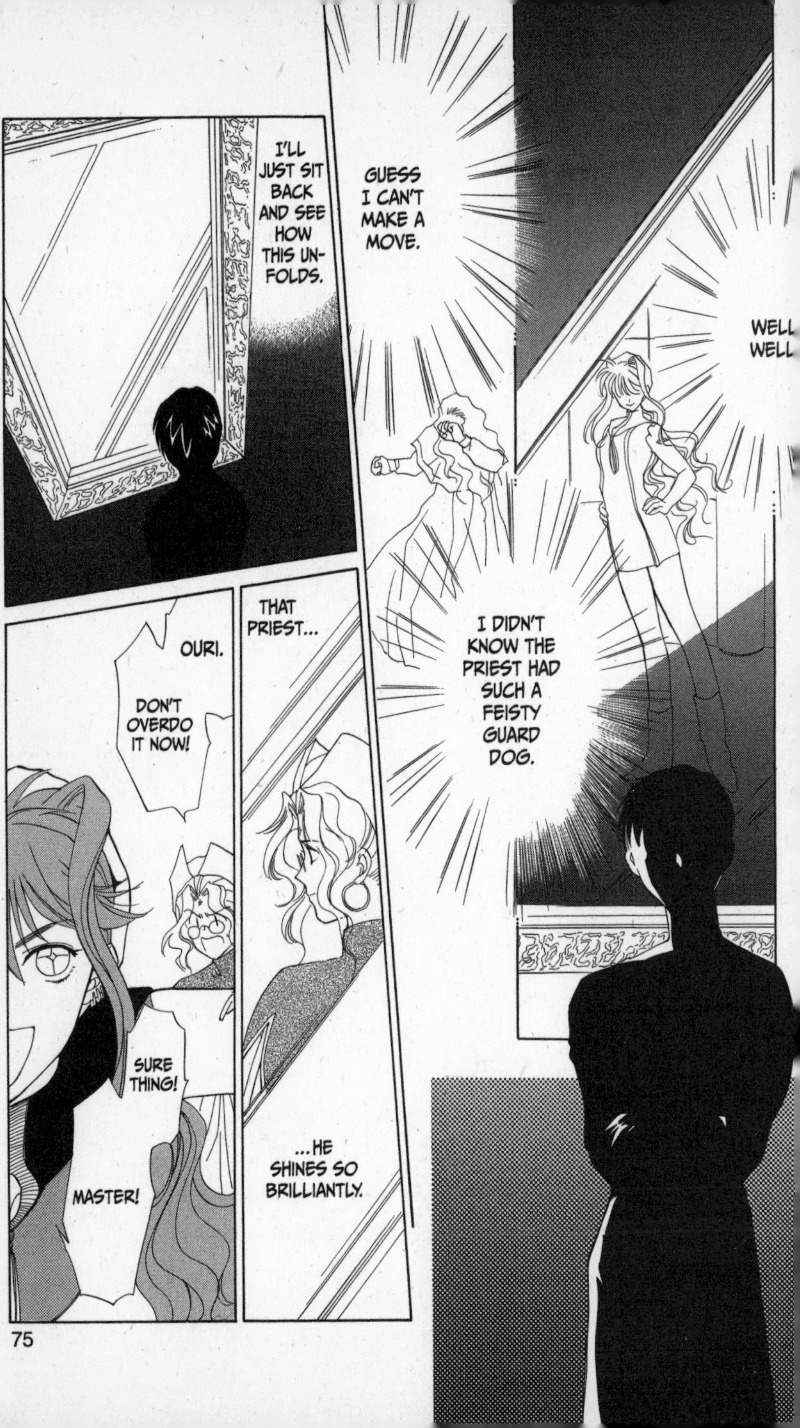
WELL WELL
I DIDN'T KNOW THE PRIEST HAD SUCH A FEISTY GUARD DOG.
GUESS I CAN'T MAKE A MOVE.
I'LL JUST SIT BACK AND SEE HOW THIS UN-FOLDS.
THAT PRIEST...
...HE SHINES SO BRILLIANTLY.
OURI.
DON'T OVERDO IT NOW!
SURE THING!
MASTER!

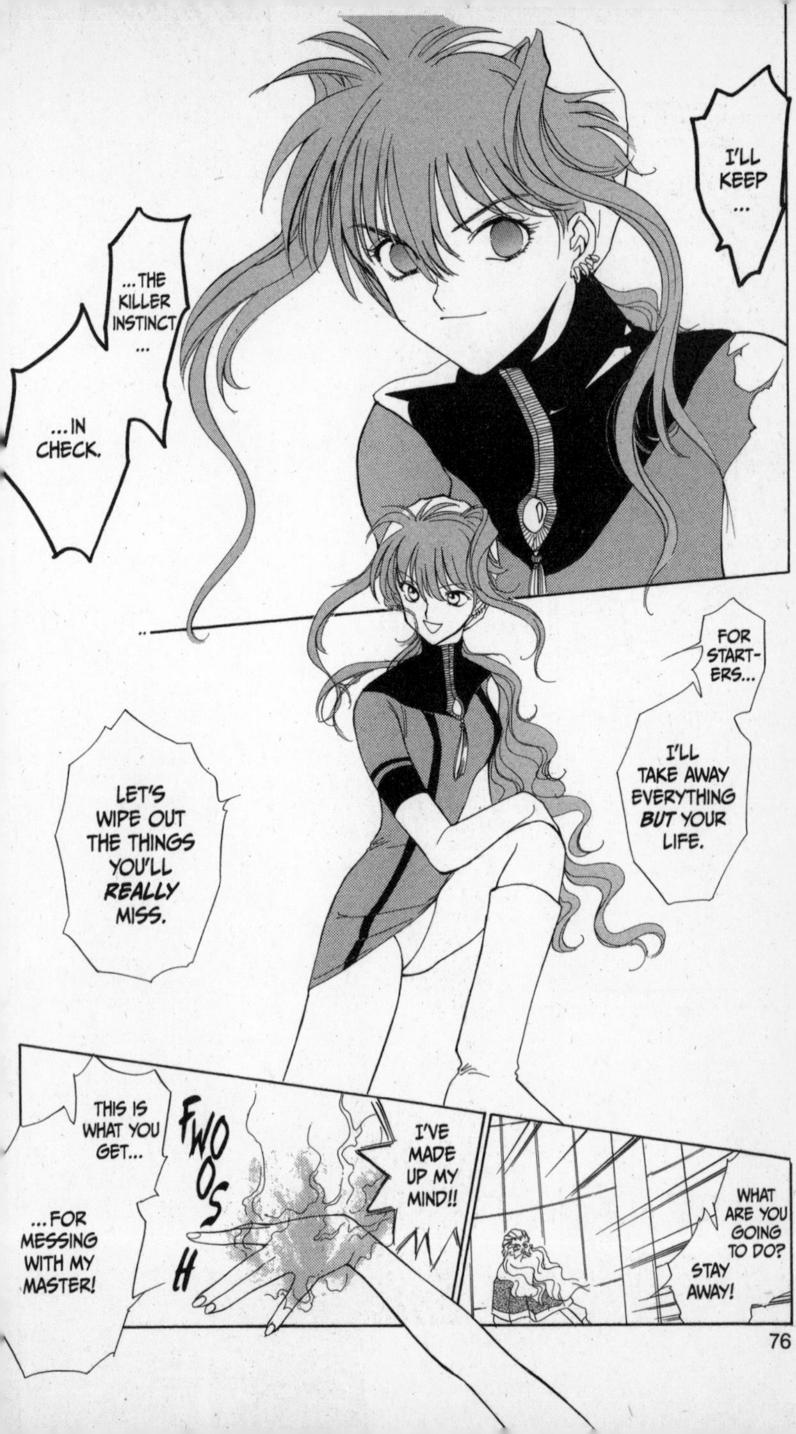
I'LL KEEP ...
...THE KILLER INSTINCT ...
...IN CHECK.
...
FOR STARTERS...
I'LL TAKE AWAY EVERYTHING *BUT* YOUR LIFE.
LET'S WIPE OUT THE THINGS YOU'LL *REALLY* MISS.
WHAT ARE YOU GOING TO DO?
STAY AWAY!
I'VE MADE UP MY MIND!!
FWOOSH
THIS IS WHAT YOU GET...
...FOR MESSING WITH MY MASTER!

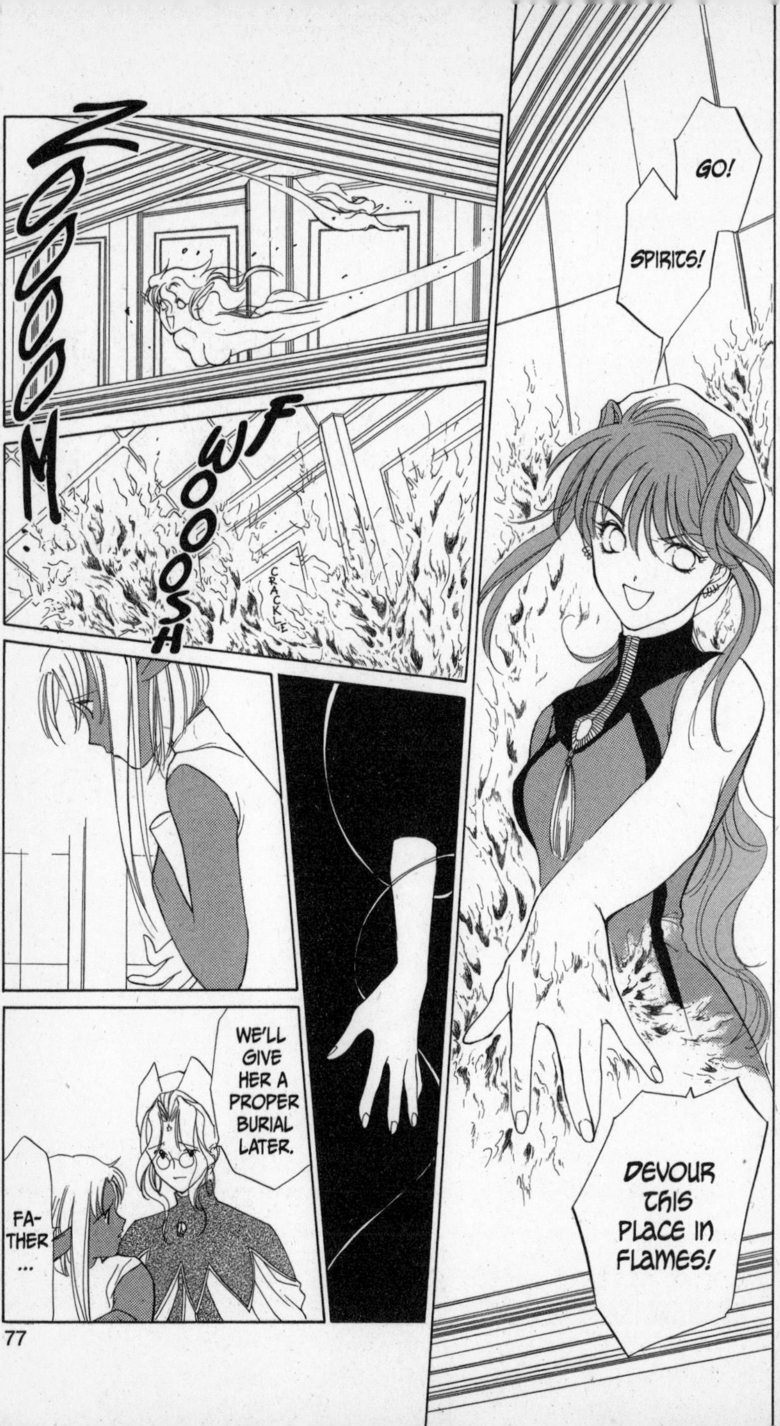
GO!
SPIRITS!
DEVOUR THIS PLACE IN FLAMES!
ZOOOOOM
WOOOOOSH
WF
CRACKLE
WE'LL GIVE HER A PROPER BURIAL LATER.
FA-THER ...

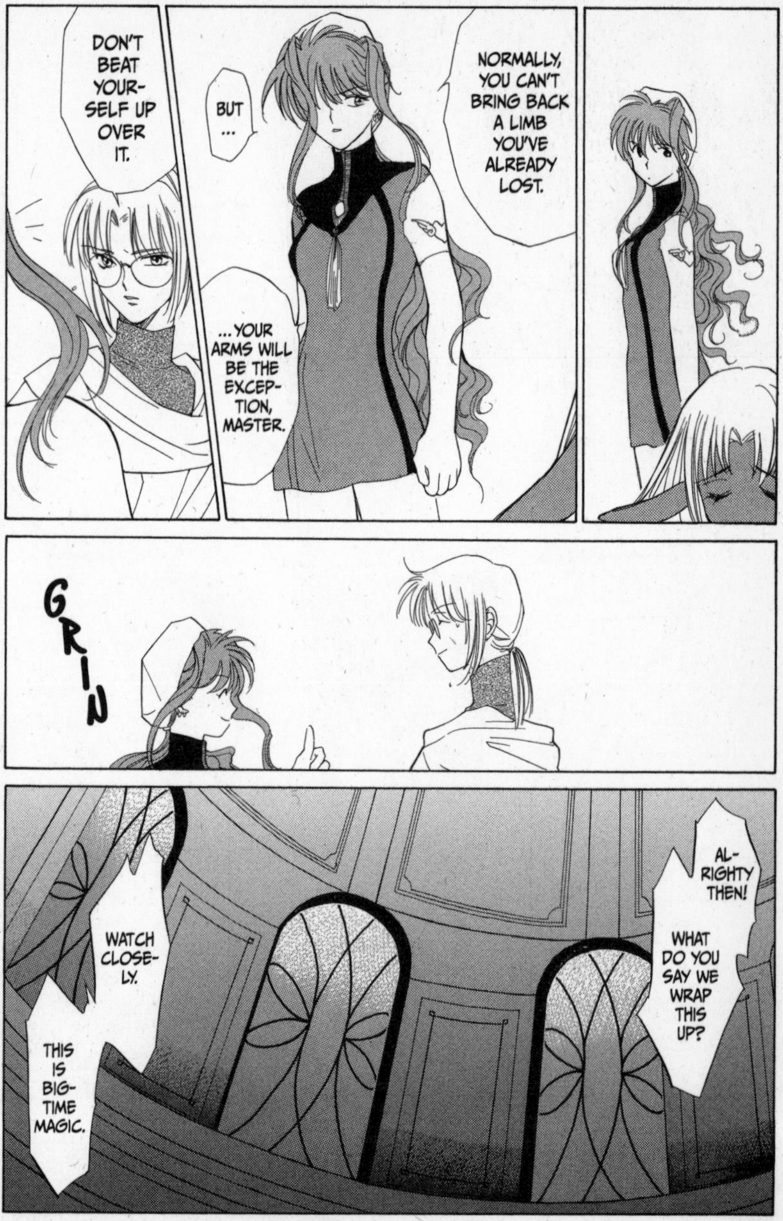
NORMALLY, YOU CAN'T BRING BACK A LIMB YOU'VE ALREADY LOST.
BUT ...
...YOUR ARMS WILL BE THE EXCEP-TION, MASTER.
DON'T BEAT YOUR-SELF UP OVER IT.
GRIN
AL-RIGHTY THEN!
WHAT DO YOU SAY WE WRAP THIS UP?
WATCH CLOSE-LY.
THIS IS BIG-TIME MAGIC.

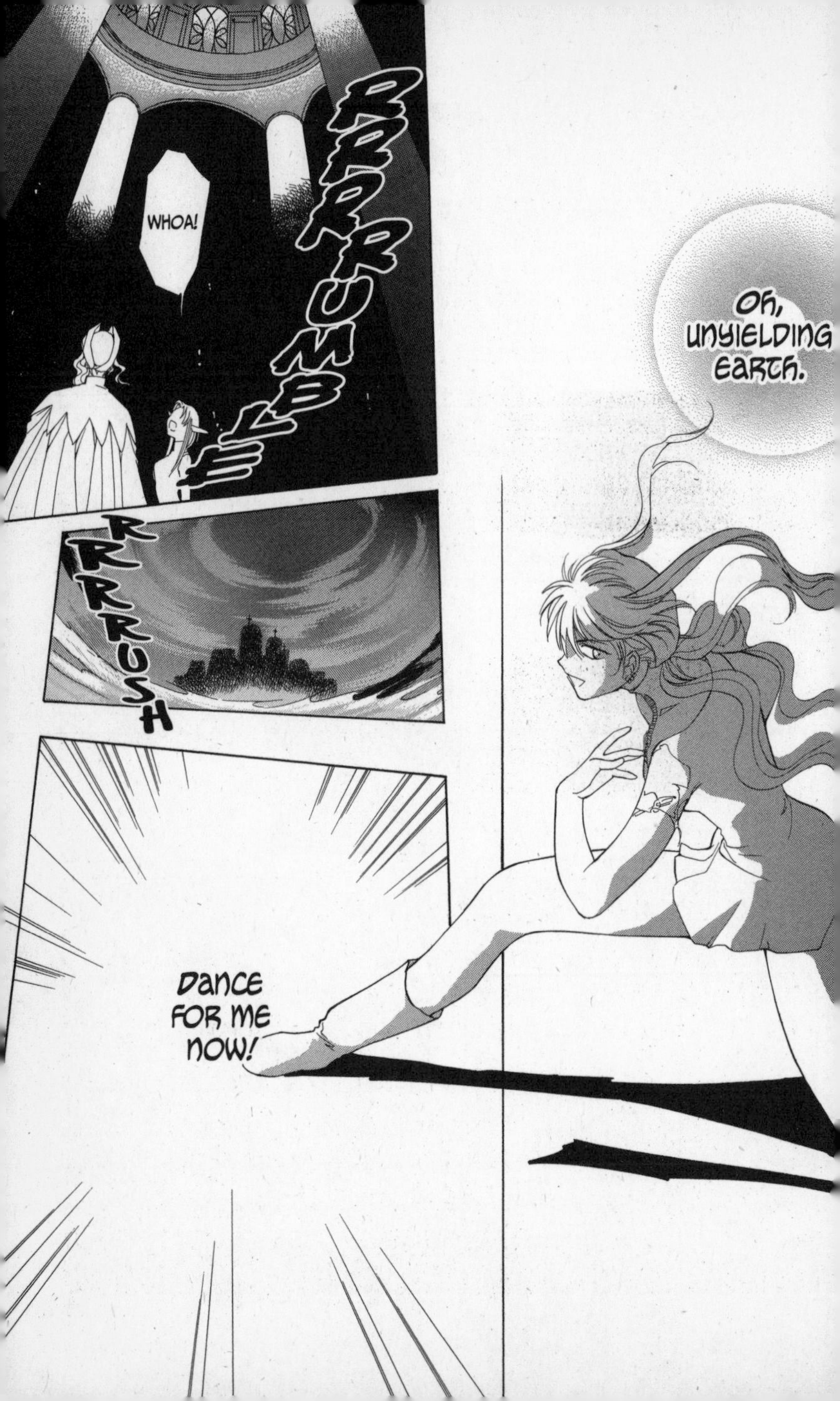
OH, UNYIELDING EARTH.
RRRRUMBLE
WHOA!
RRRRUSH
DANCE FOR ME NOW!

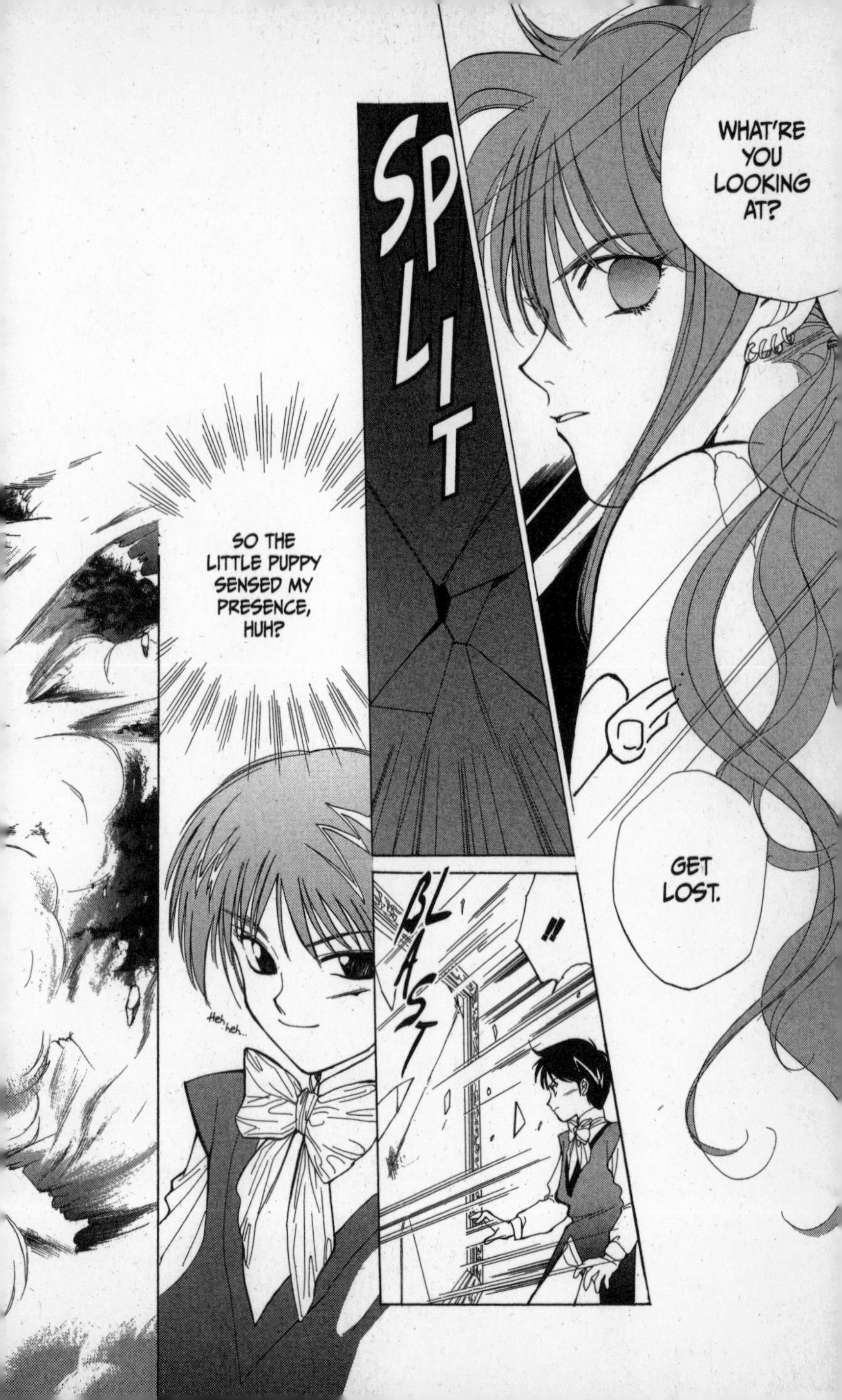
WHAT'RE YOU LOOKING AT?
GET LOST.
SPLIT
BLAST
!!
SO THE LITTLE PUPPY SENSED MY PRESENCE, HUH?
Heh heh...

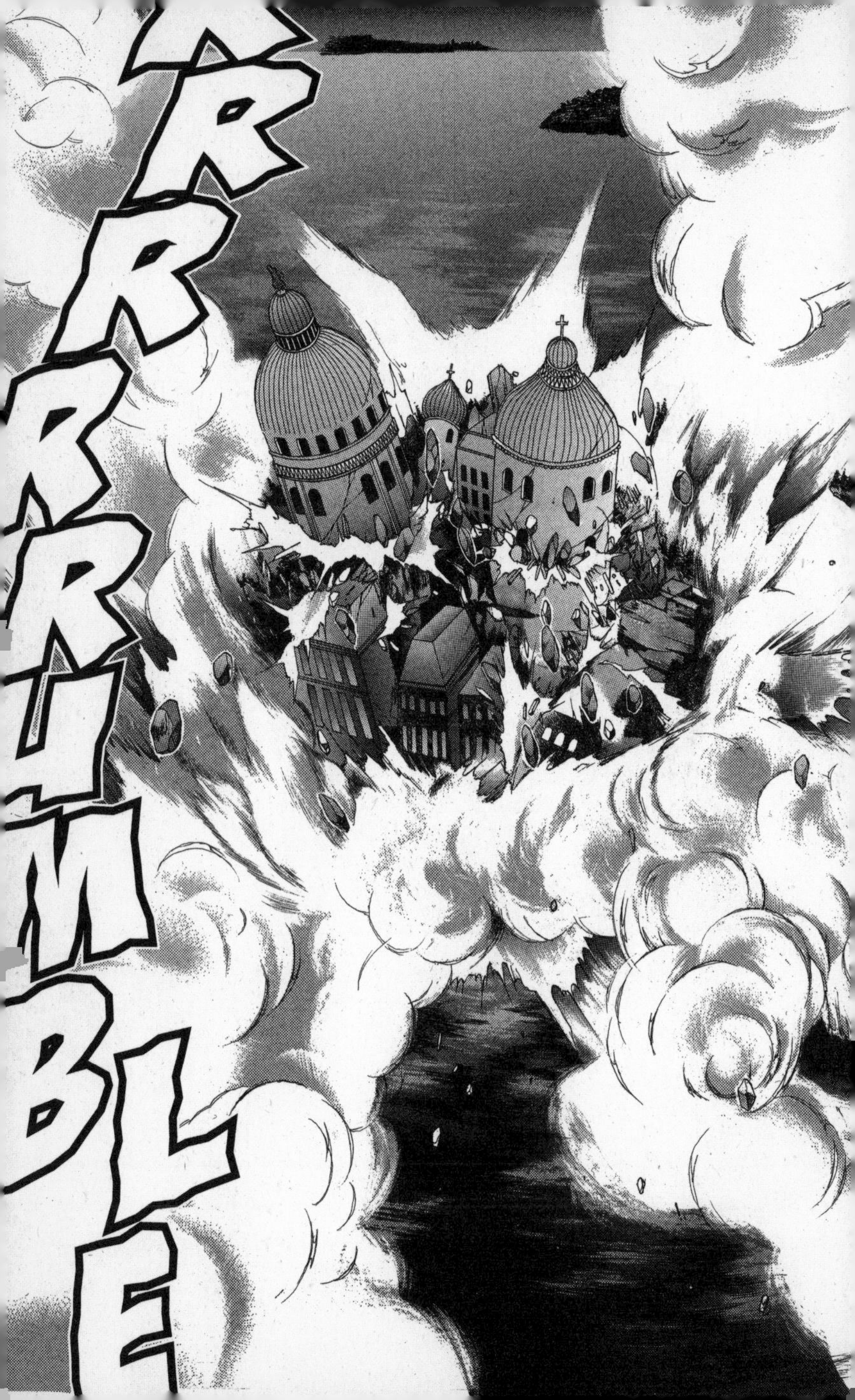
RRRRUMBLE

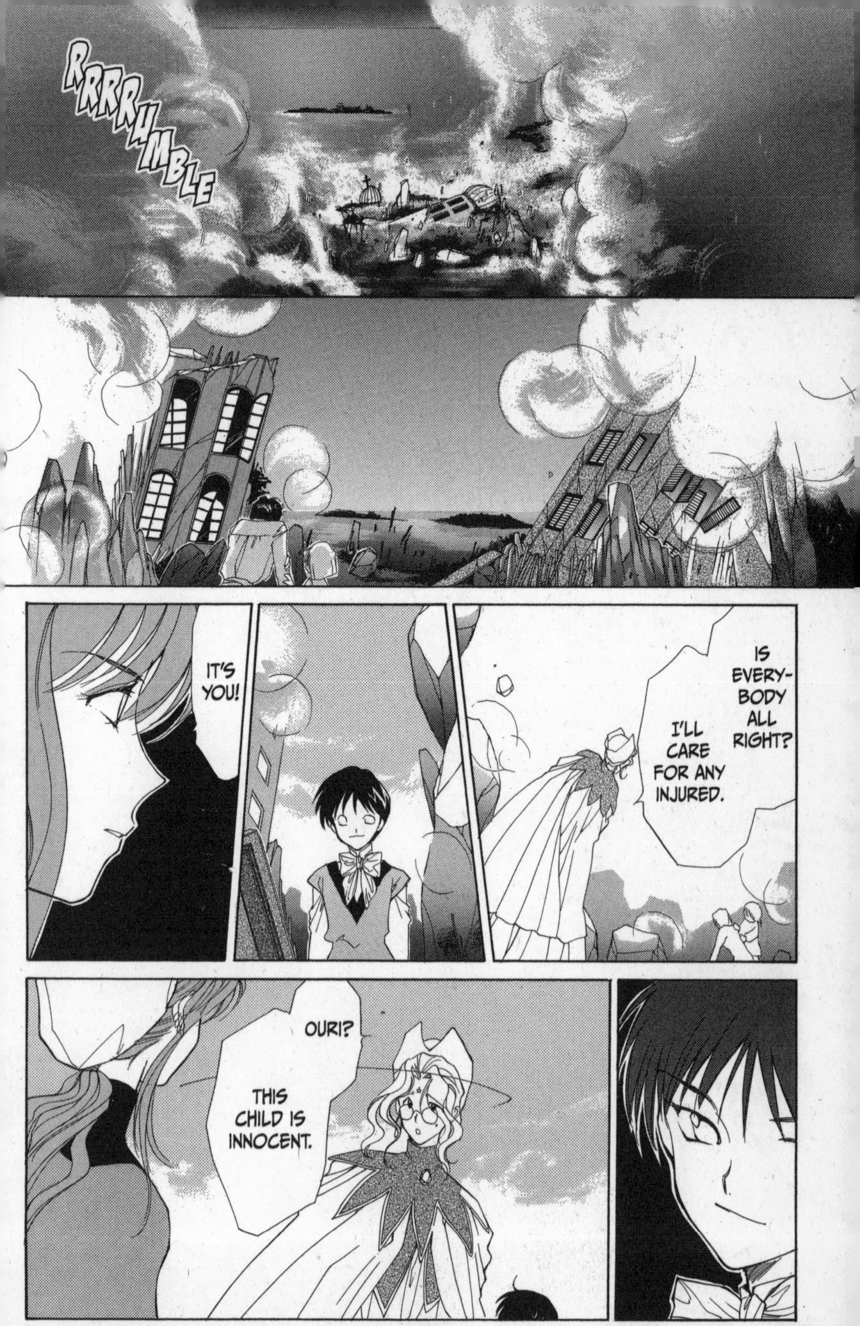
RRRRUMBLE
IS EVERYBODY ALL RIGHT?
I'LL CARE FOR ANY INJURED.
IT'S YOU!
OURI?
THIS CHILD IS INNOCENT.

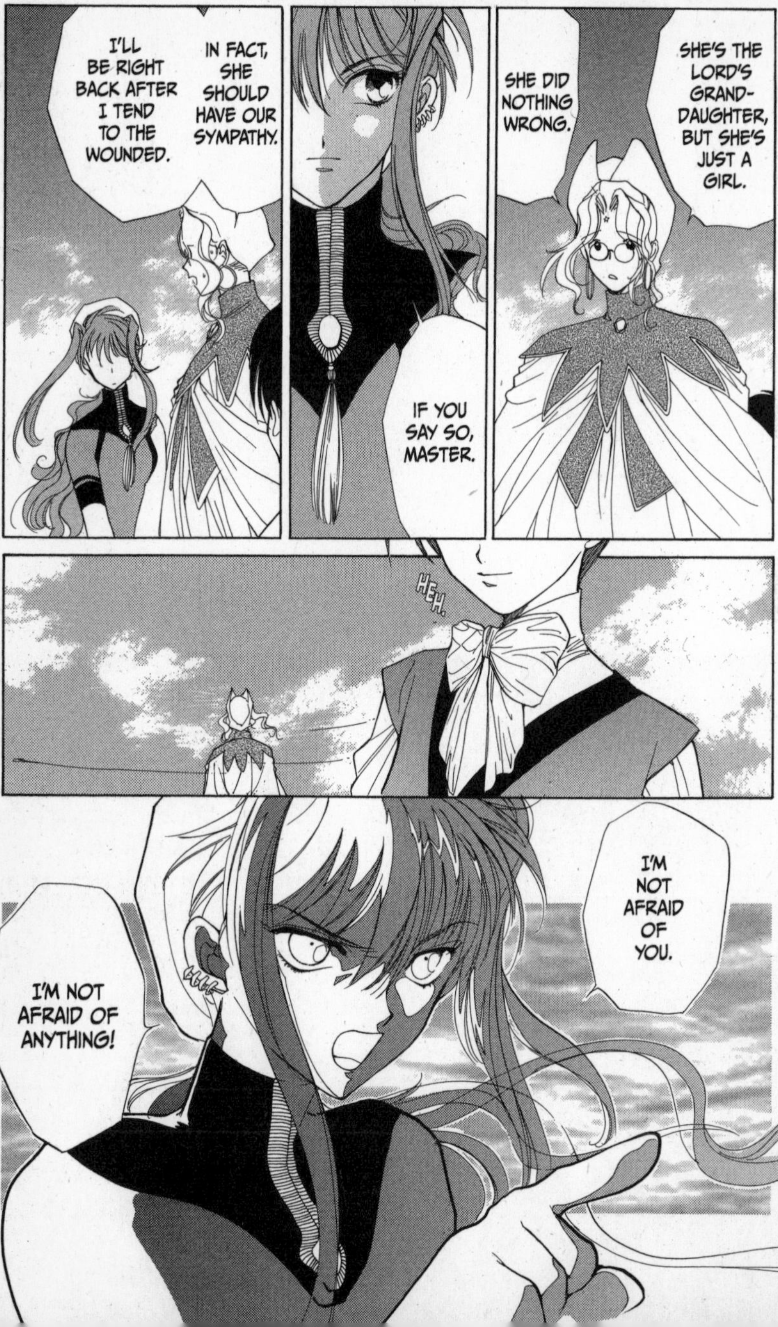
SHE'S THE LORD'S GRAND-DAUGHTER, BUT SHE'S JUST A GIRL.
SHE DID NOTHING WRONG.
IF YOU SAY SO, MASTER.
IN FACT, SHE SHOULD HAVE OUR SYMPATHY.
I'LL BE RIGHT BACK AFTER I TEND TO THE WOUNDED.
HEH.
I'M NOT AFRAID OF YOU.
I'M NOT AFRAID OF ANYTHING!

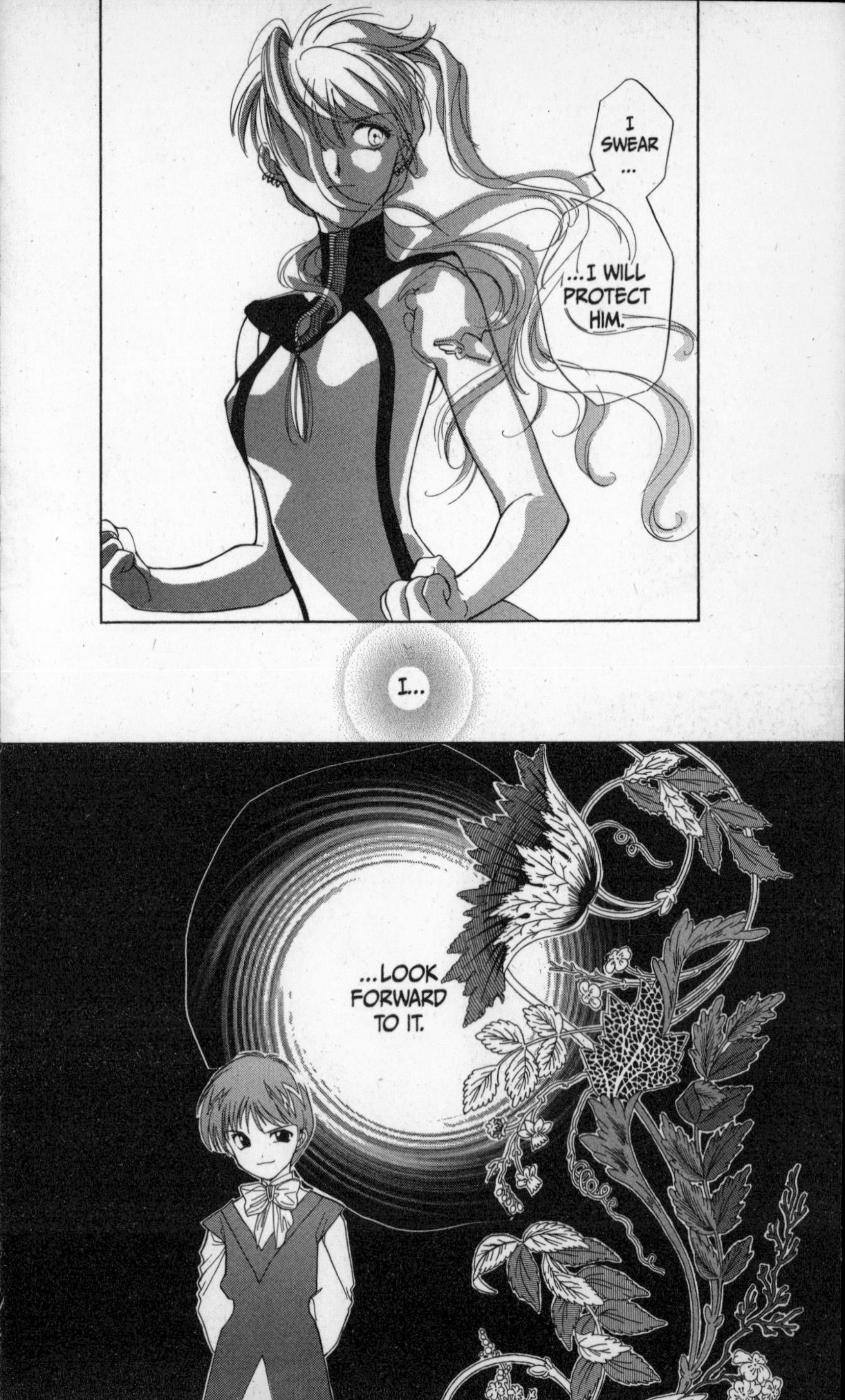
I SWEAR ...
...I WILL PROTECT HIM.
I...
...LOOK FORWARD TO IT.

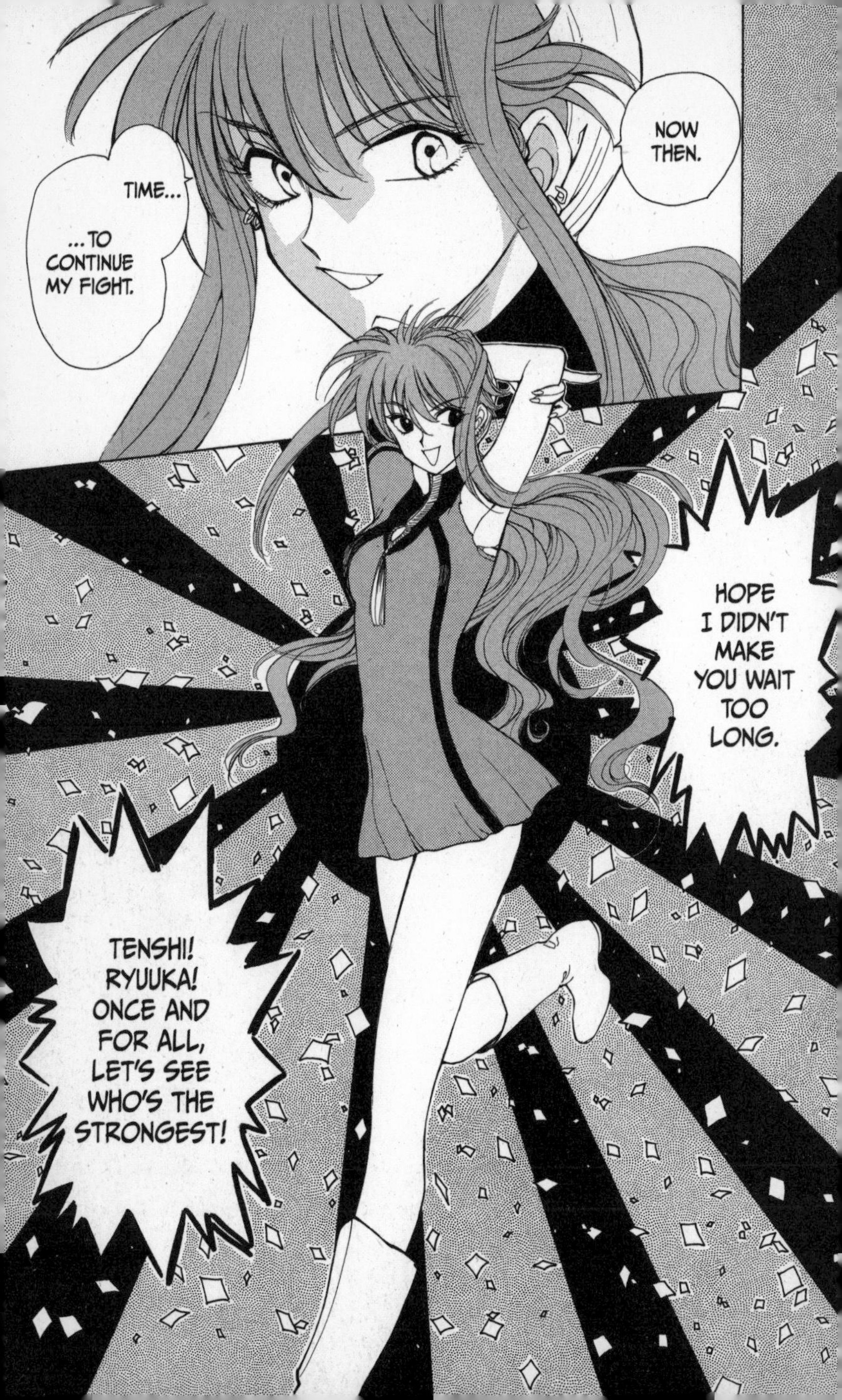
NOW THEN.
TIME...
...TO CONTINUE MY FIGHT.
HOPE I DIDN'T MAKE YOU WAIT TOO LONG.
TENSHI! RYUUKA! ONCE AND FOR ALL, LET'S SEE WHO'S THE STRONGEST!

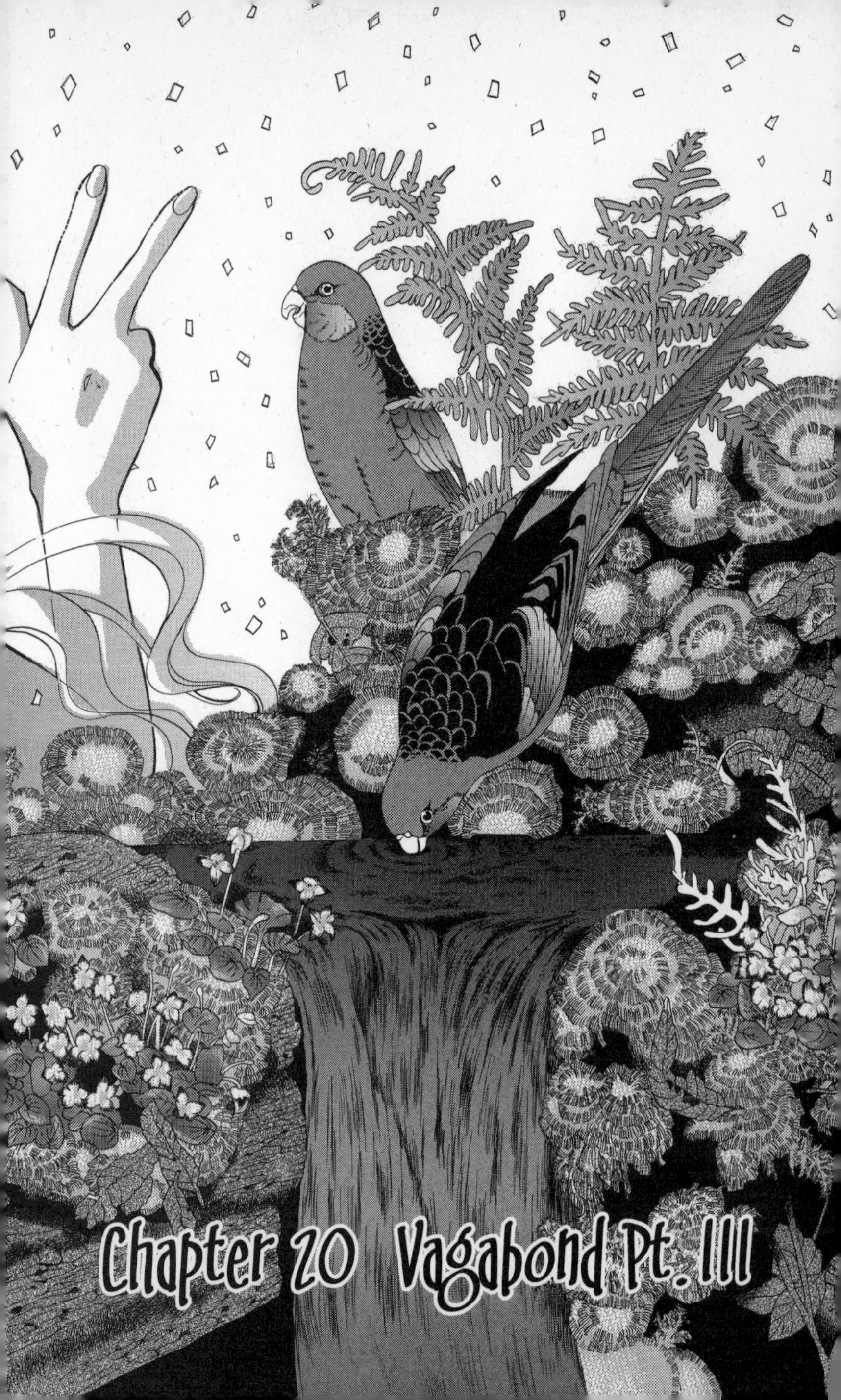
Chapter 20 Vagabond Pt. III

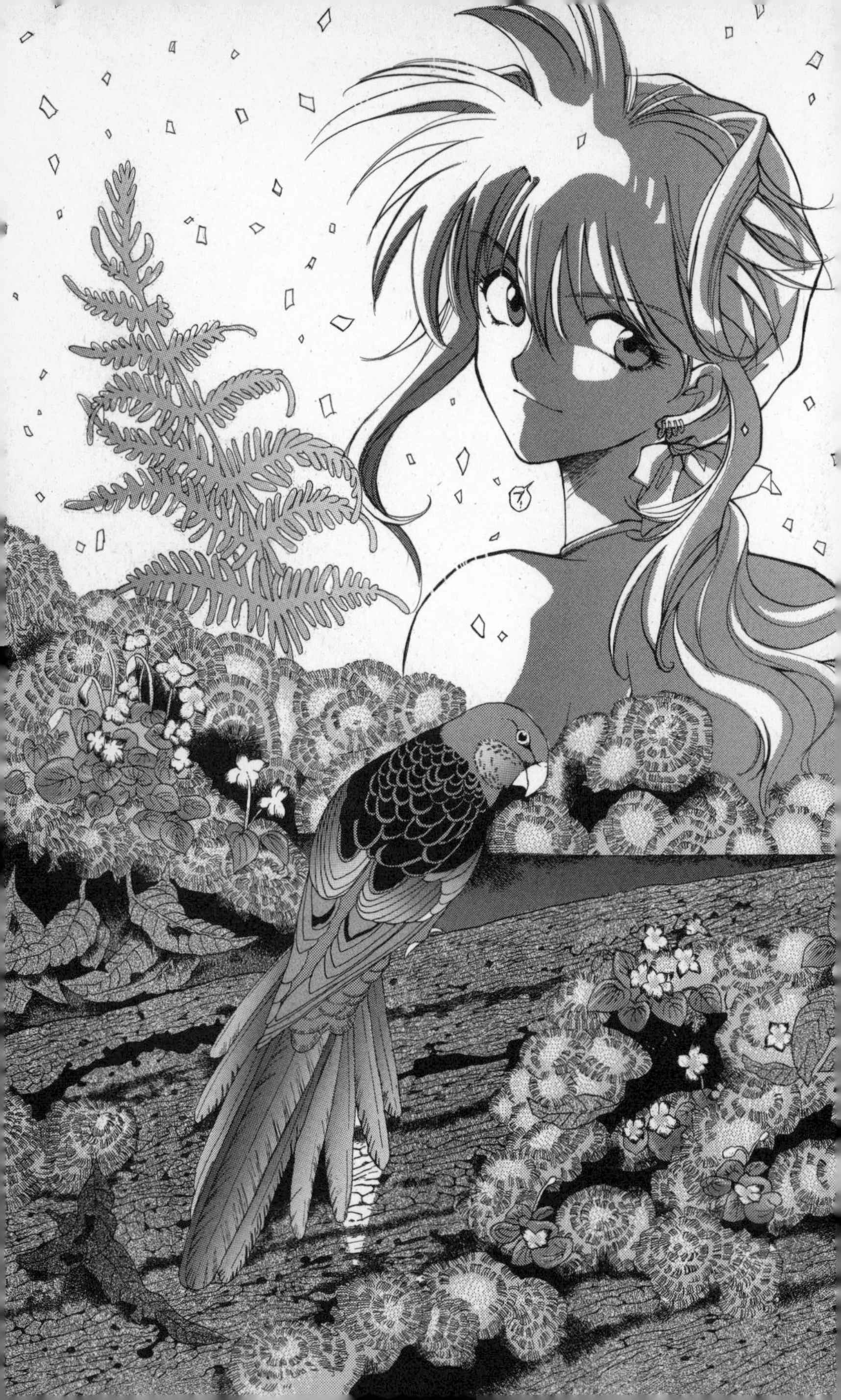

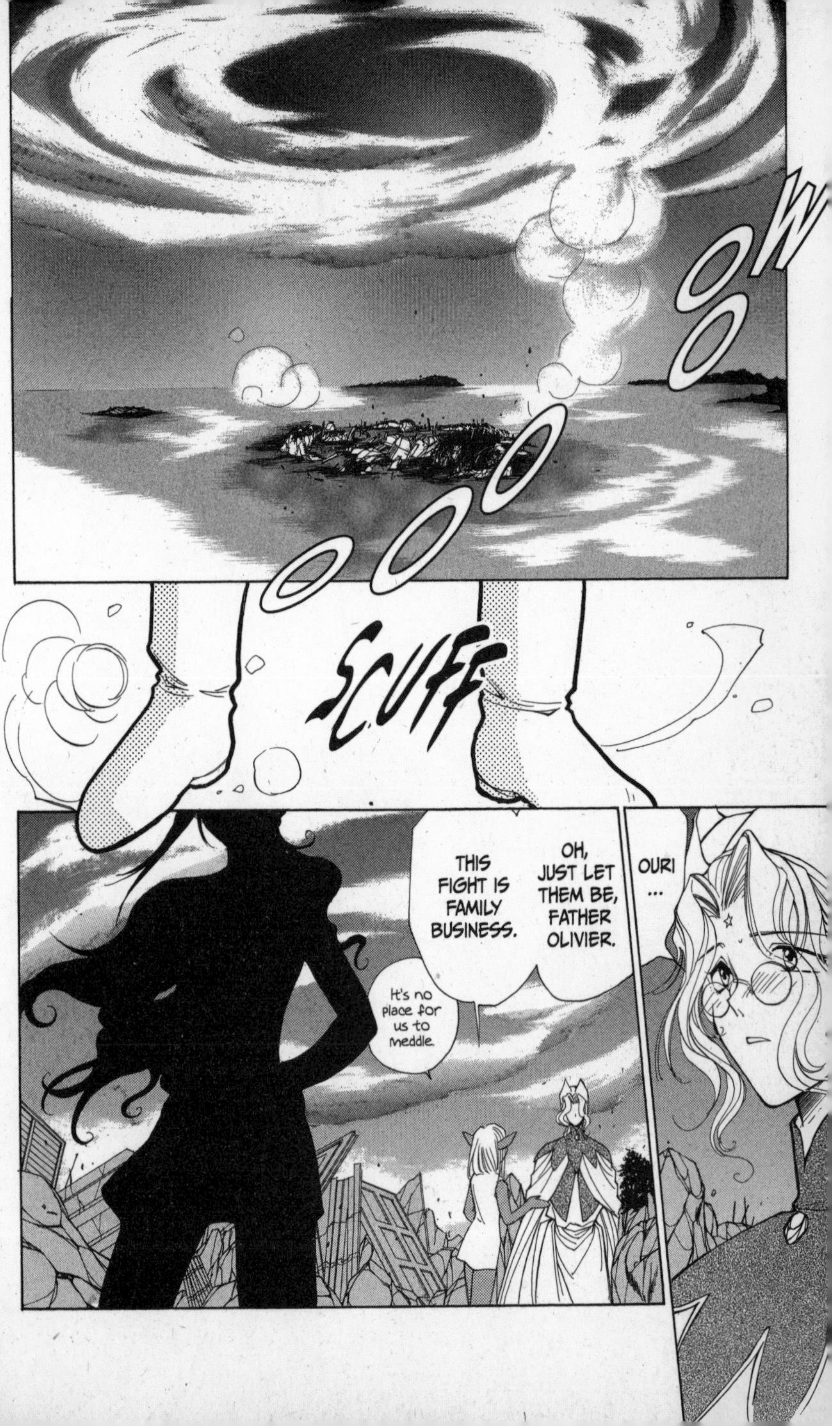
OOOOOOW
SCUFF
OURI ...
OH, JUST LET THEM BE, FATHER OLIVIER.
THIS FIGHT IS FAMILY BUSINESS.
It's no place for us to meddle.

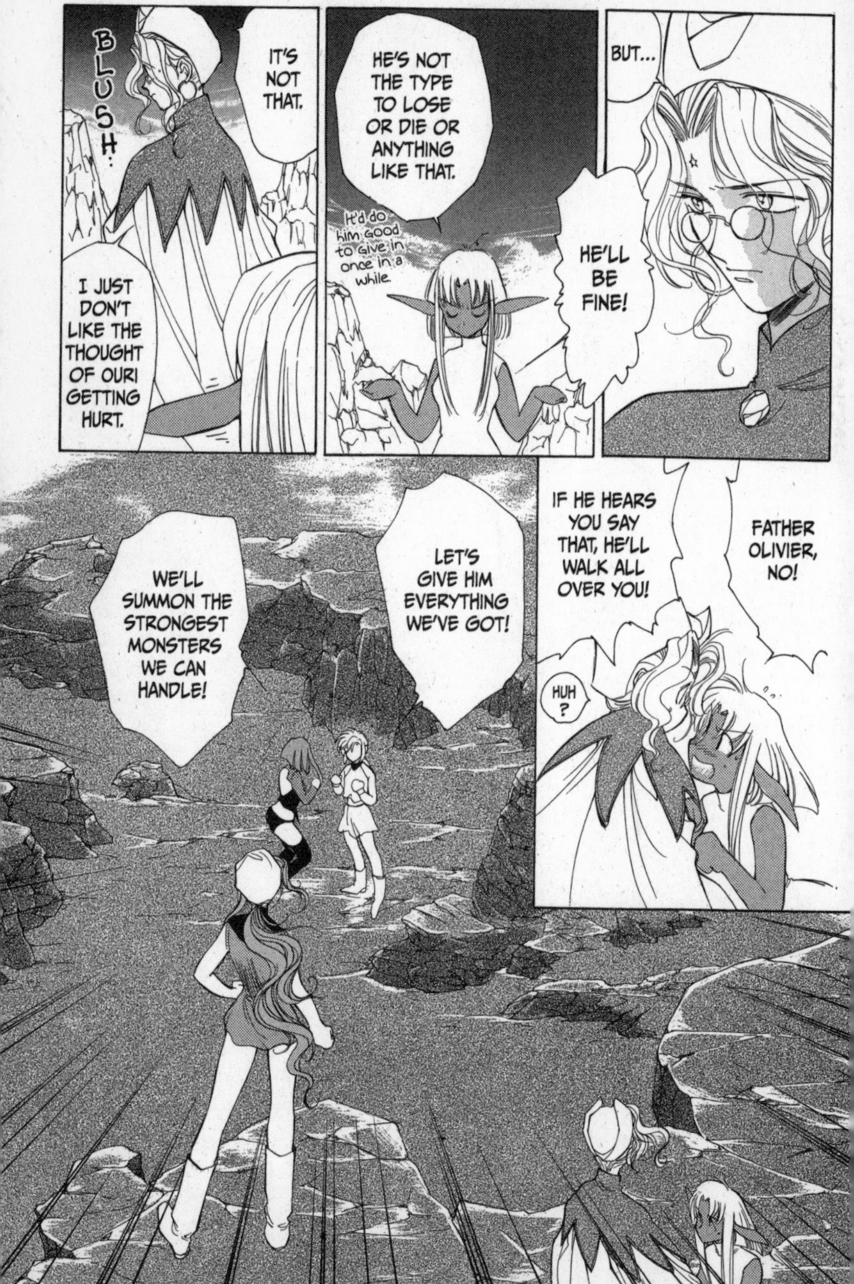
BUT...
HE'LL BE FINE!
HE'S NOT THE TYPE TO LOSE OR DIE OR ANYTHING LIKE THAT.
It'd do him good to give in once in a while.
IT'S NOT THAT.
BLUSH...
I JUST DON'T LIKE THE THOUGHT OF OURI GETTING HURT.
FATHER OLIVIER, NO!
IF HE HEARS YOU SAY THAT, HE'LL WALK ALL OVER YOU!
HUH?
LET'S GIVE HIM EVERYTHING WE'VE GOT!
WE'LL SUMMON THE STRONGEST MONSTERS WE CAN HANDLE!

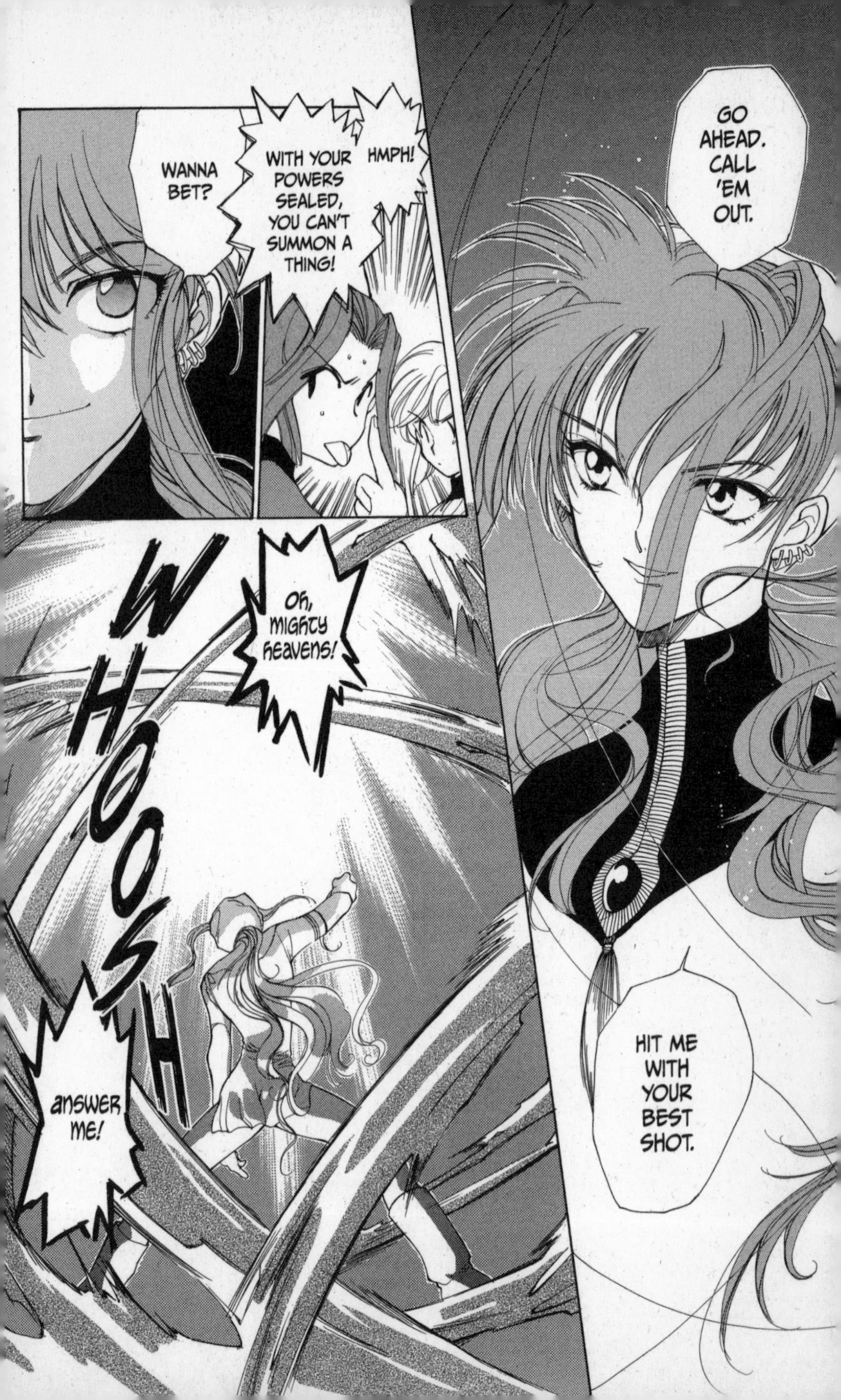
GO AHEAD. CALL 'EM OUT.
HIT ME WITH YOUR BEST SHOT.
HMPH!
WITH YOUR POWERS SEALED, YOU CAN'T SUMMON A THING!
WANNA BET?
Oh, mighty heavens!
WHOOSH
answer me!

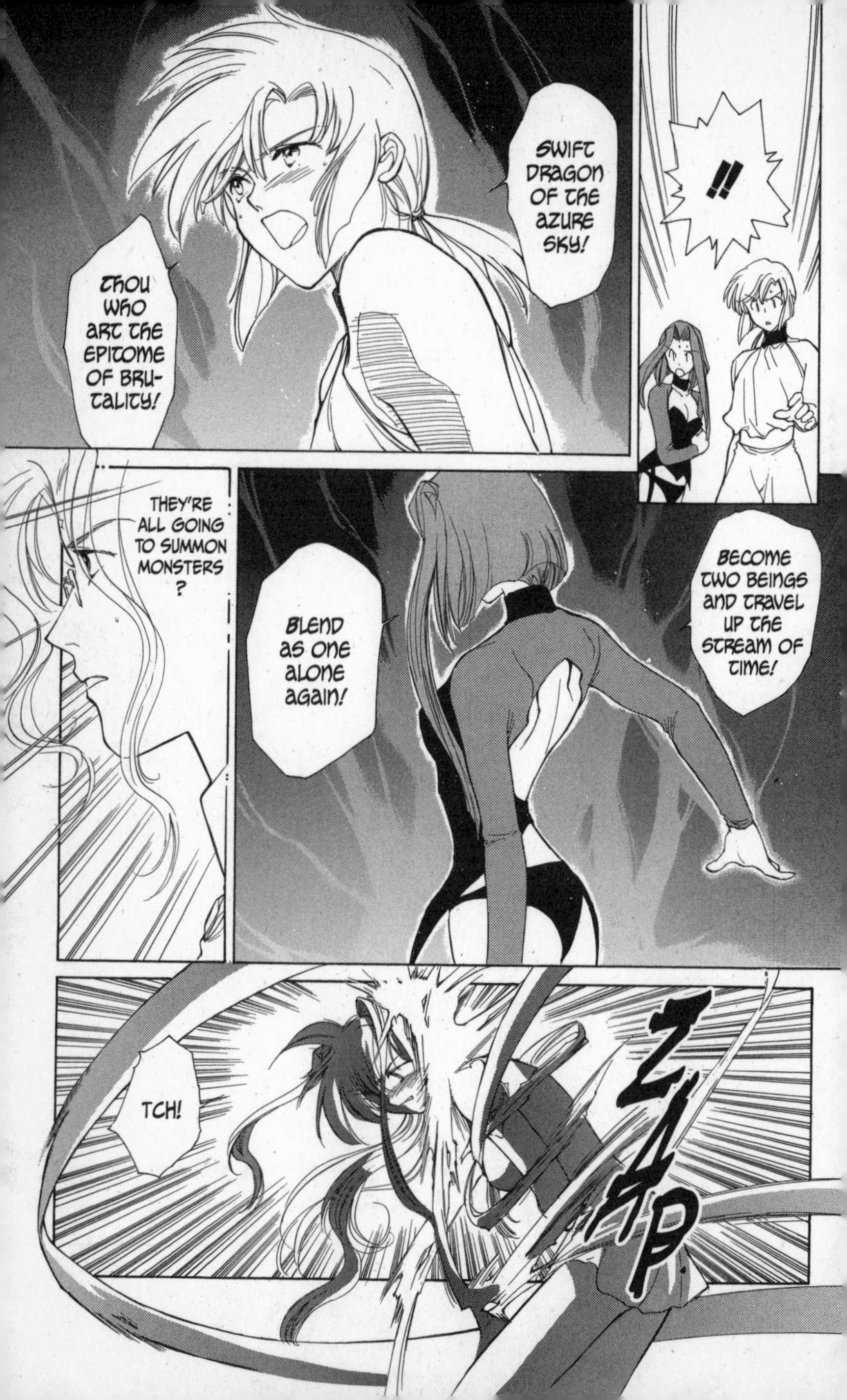
!!
SWIFT DRAGON OF THE AZURE SKY!
THOU WHO ART THE EPITOME OF BRU-TALITY!
BECOME TWO BEINGS AND TRAVEL UP THE STREAM OF TIME!
BLEND AS ONE ALONE AGAIN!
THEY'RE ALL GOING TO SUMMON MONSTERS?
ZAP
TCH!

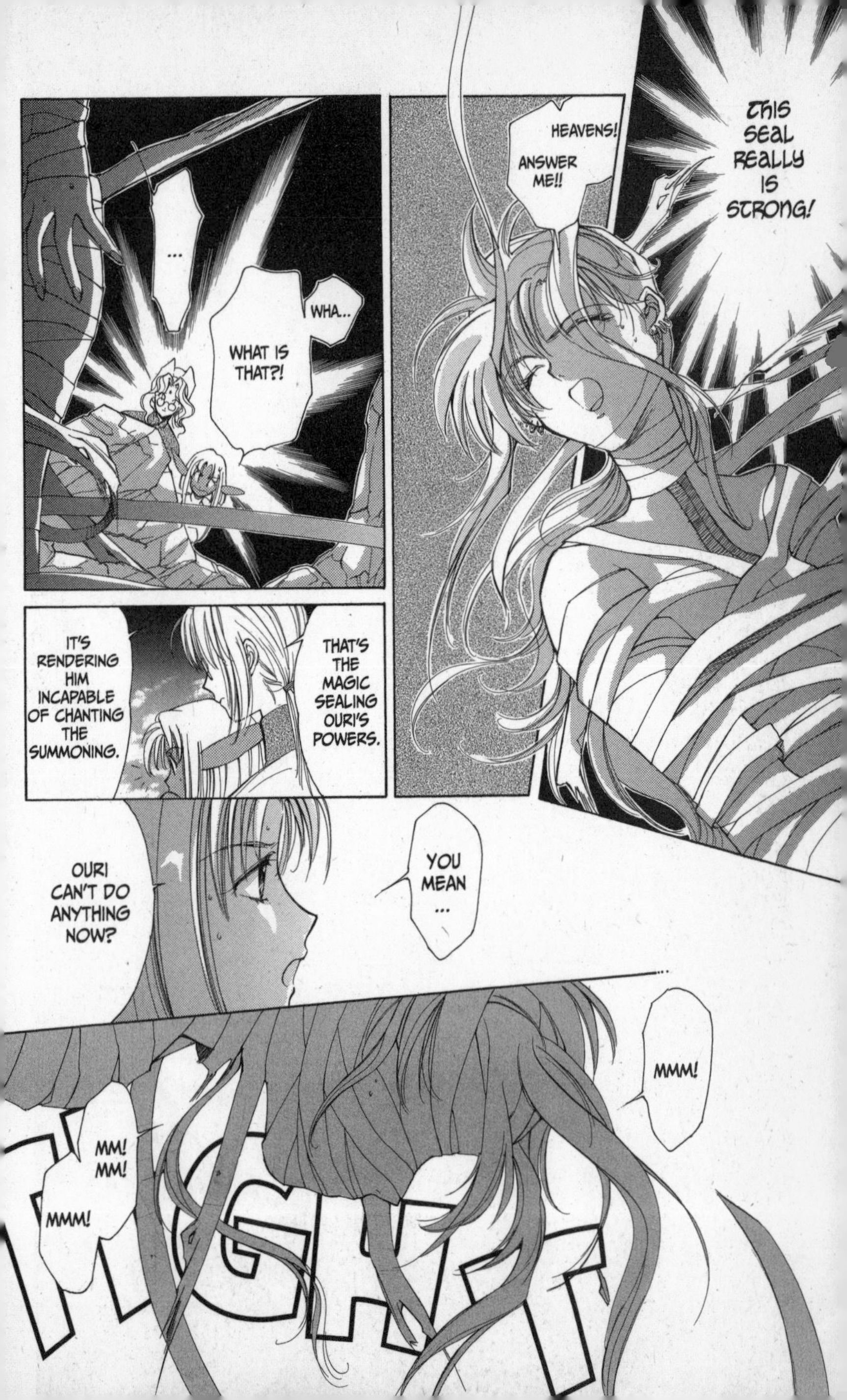
THIS SEAL REALLY IS STRONG!
HEAVENS!
ANSWER ME!!
WHA...
WHAT IS THAT?!
...
THAT'S THE MAGIC SEALING OURI'S POWERS.
IT'S RENDERING HIM INCAPABLE OF CHANTING THE SUMMONING.
YOU MEAN ...
OURI CAN'T DO ANYTHING NOW?
MMM!
MM! MM!
MMM!
TIGHT

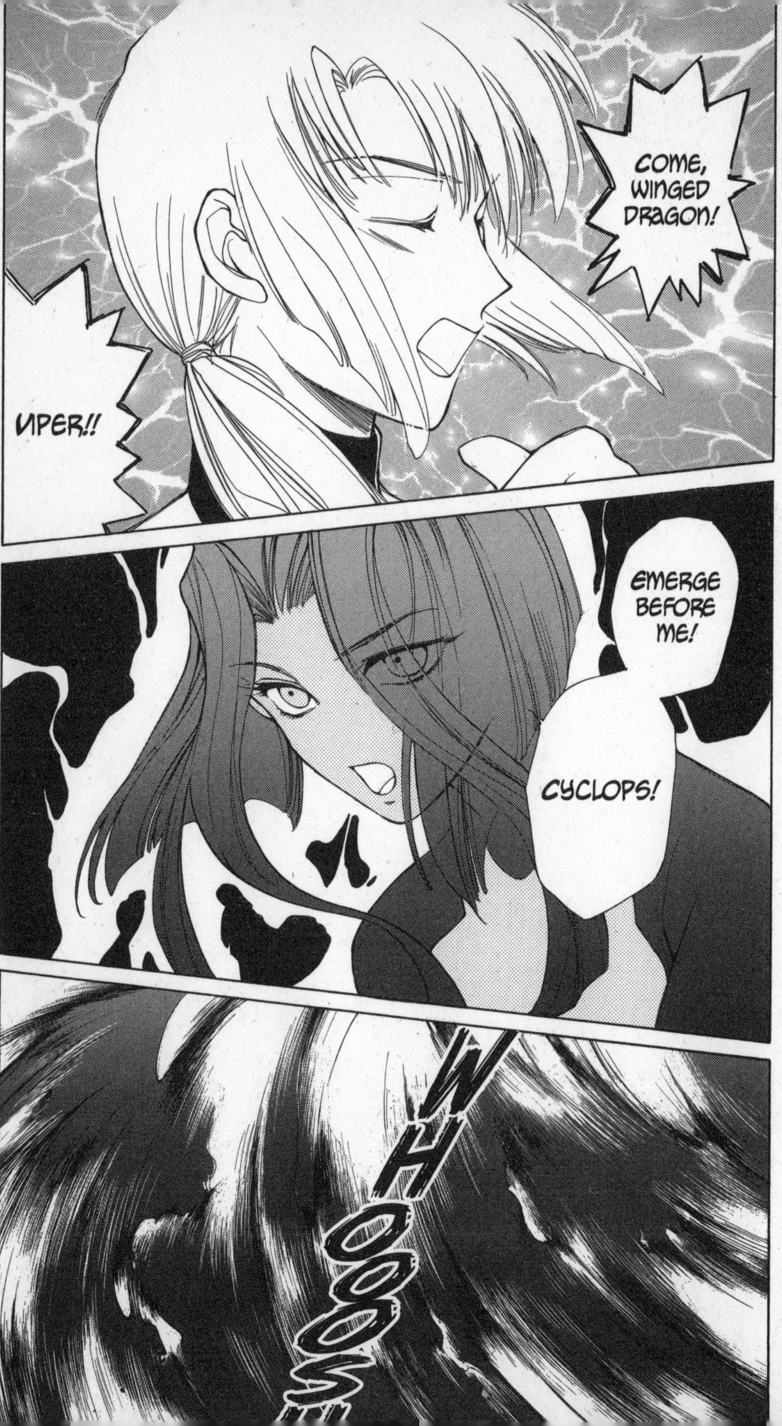
COME, WINGED DRAGON!
VIPER!!
EMERGE BEFORE ME!
CYCLOPS!
WHOOOSH

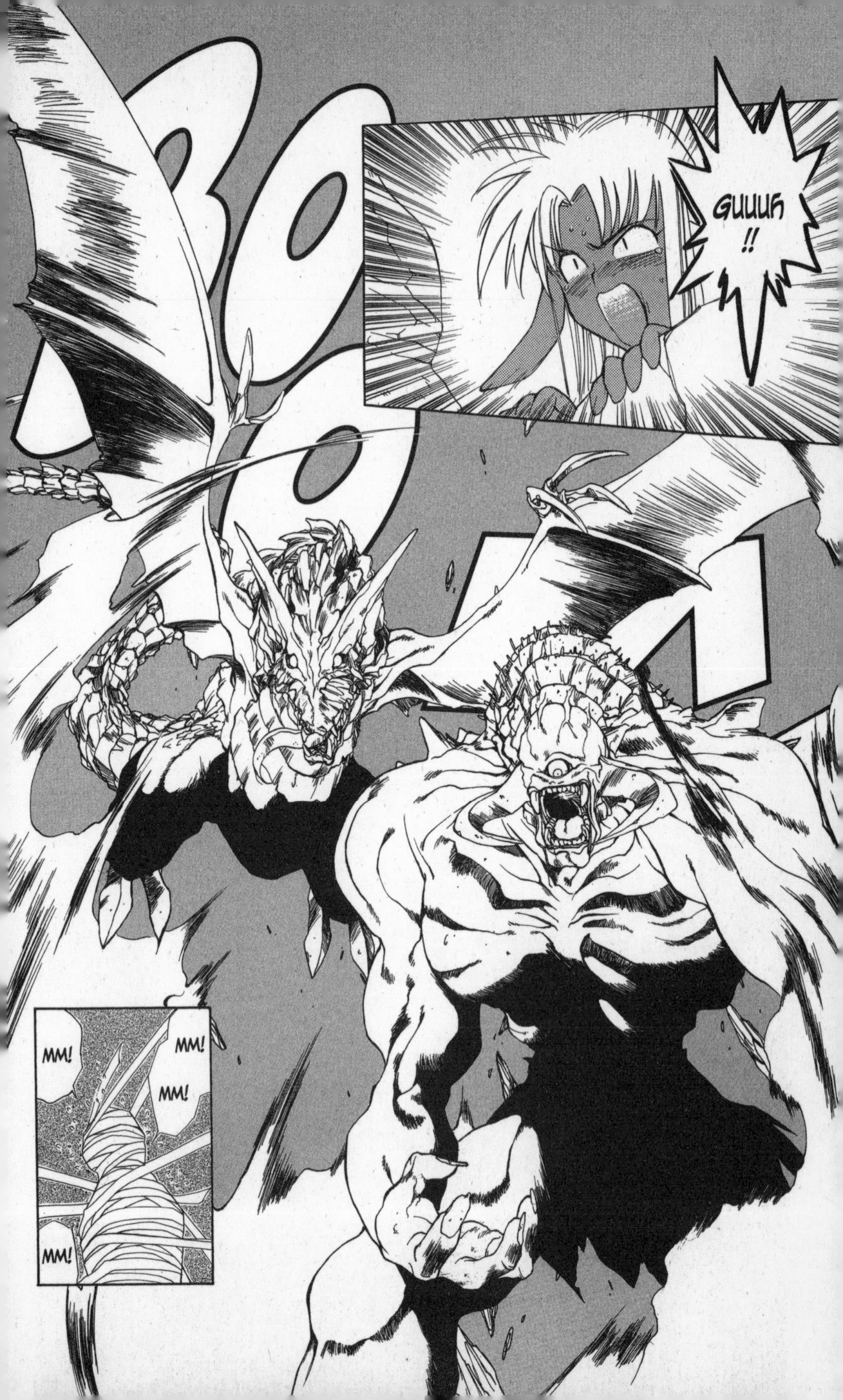
GUUUH !!
MM!
MM!
MM!
MM!

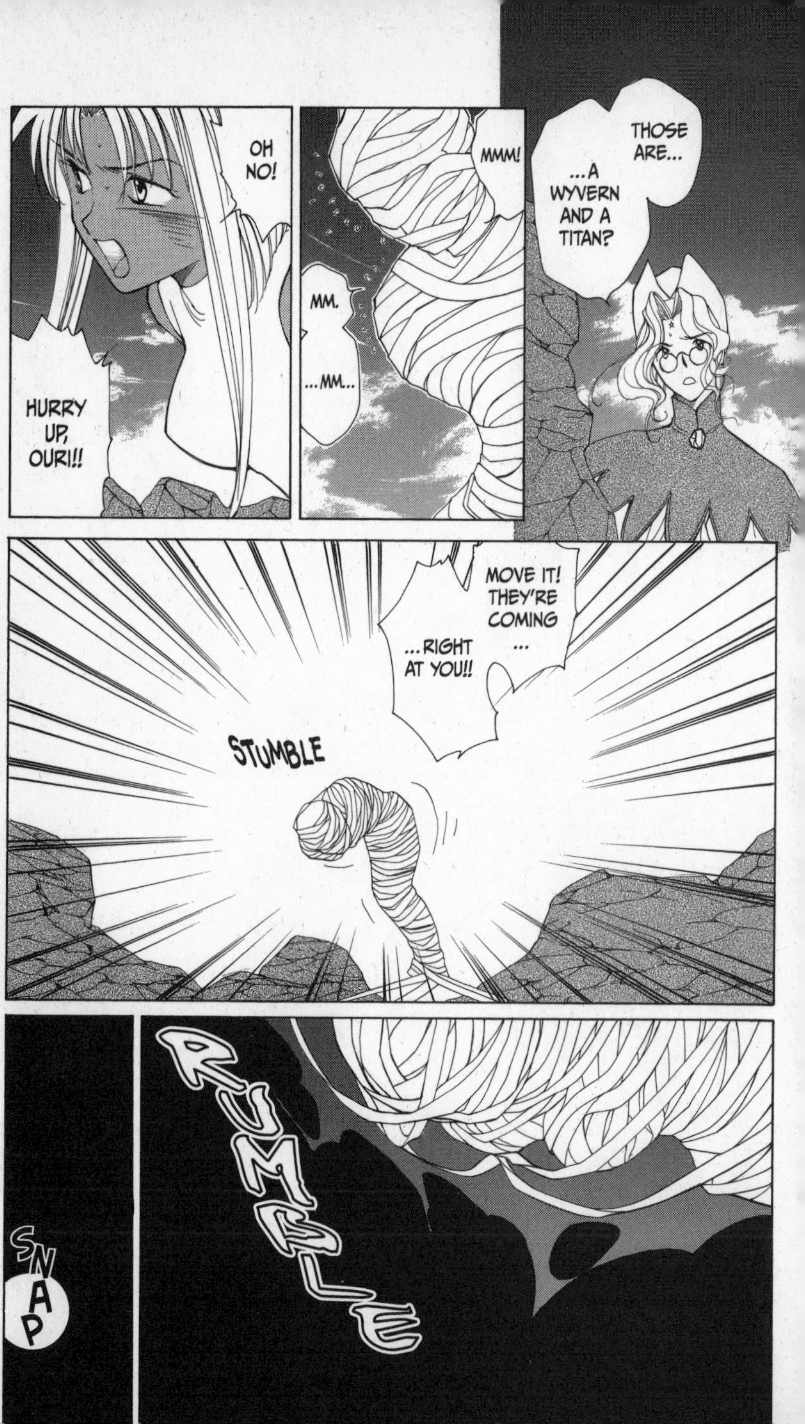
THOSE ARE...
...A WYVERN AND A TITAN?
MMM!
MM.
...MM...
OH NO!
HURRY UP, OURI!!
MOVE IT! THEY'RE COMING ...
...RIGHT AT YOU!!
STUMBLE
RUMBLE
SNAP

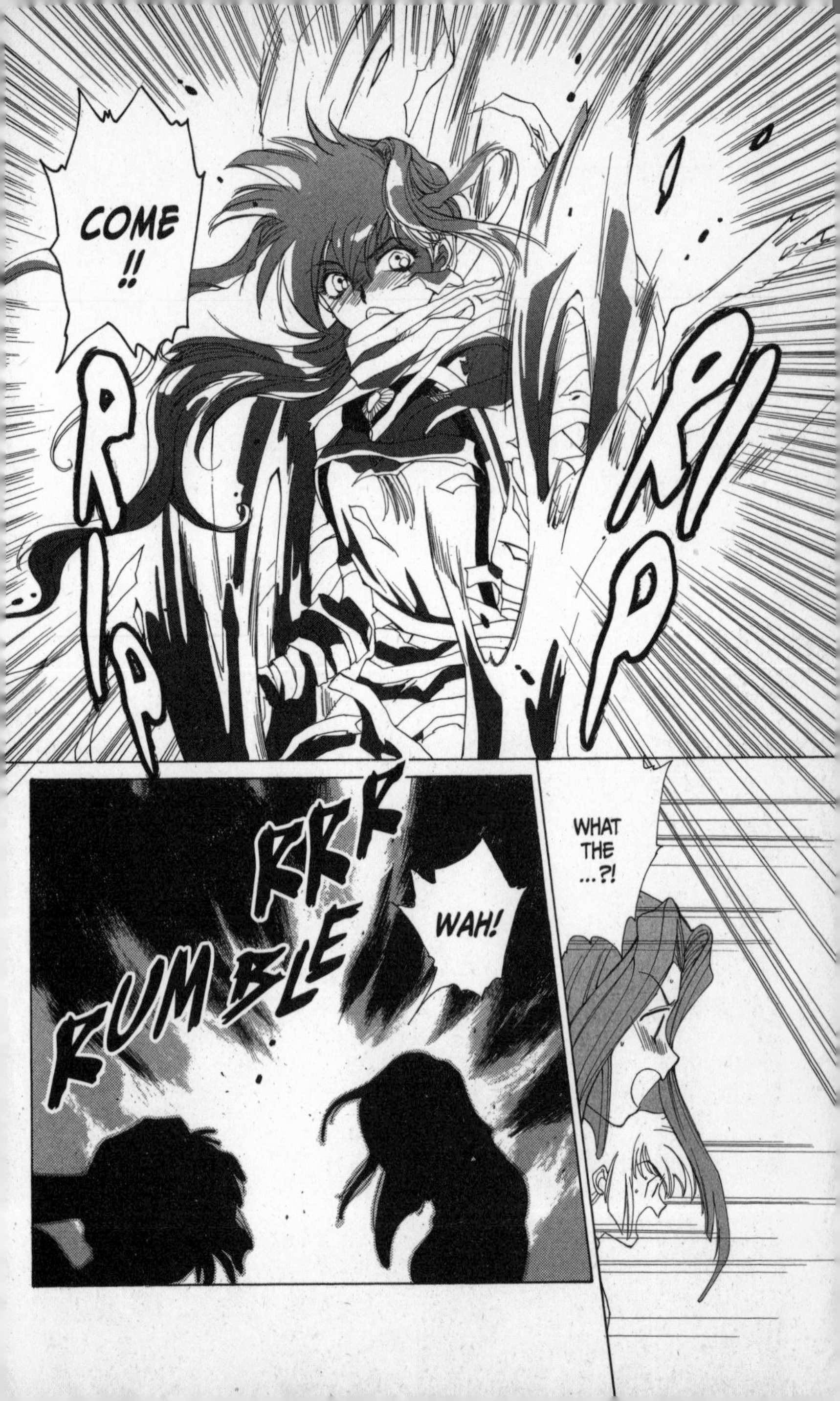
COME !!
RIP
RIP
WHAT THE ...?!
RRR RUMBLE
WAH!

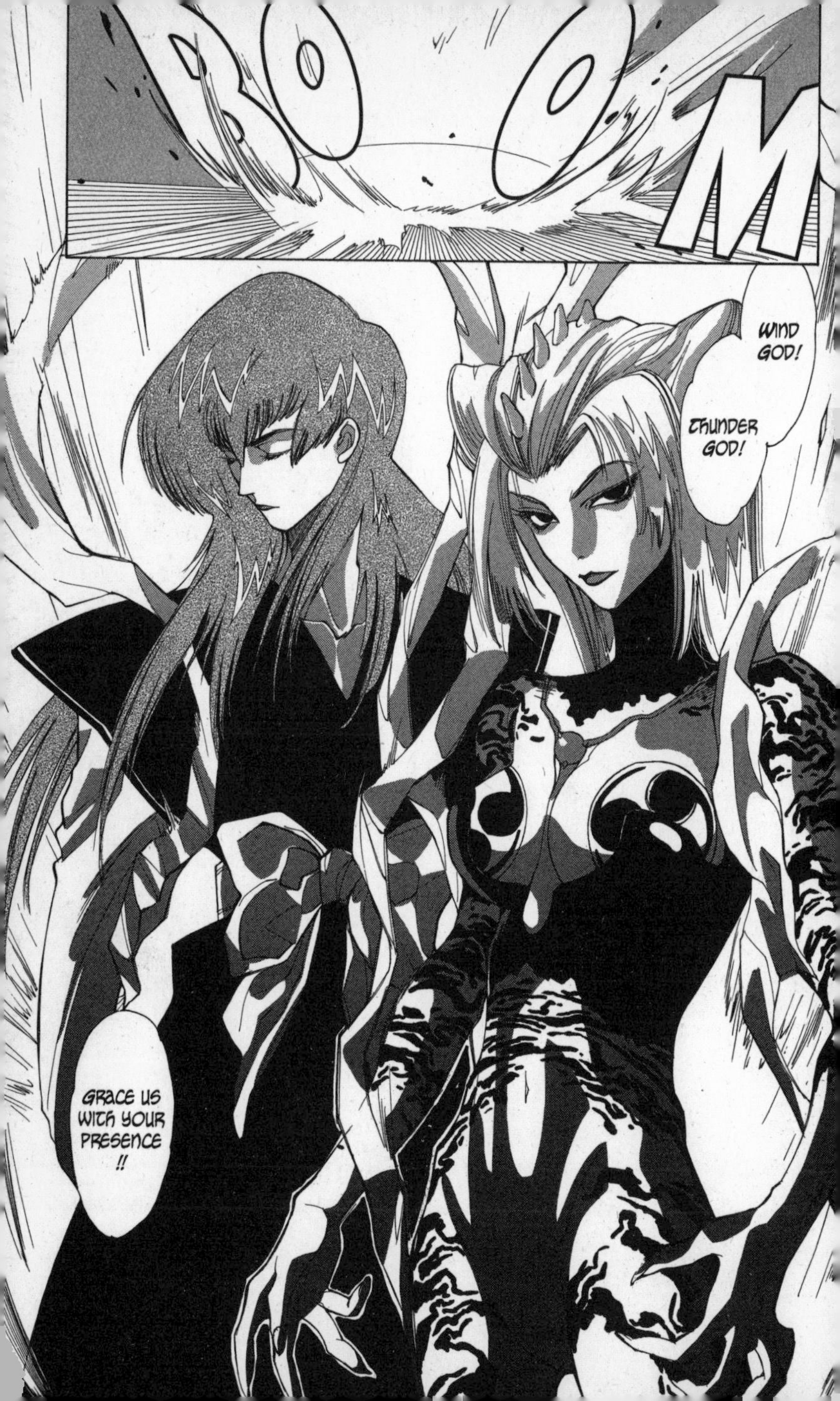
BOOOM
WIND GOD!
THUNDER GOD!
GRACE US WITH YOUR PRESENCE !!

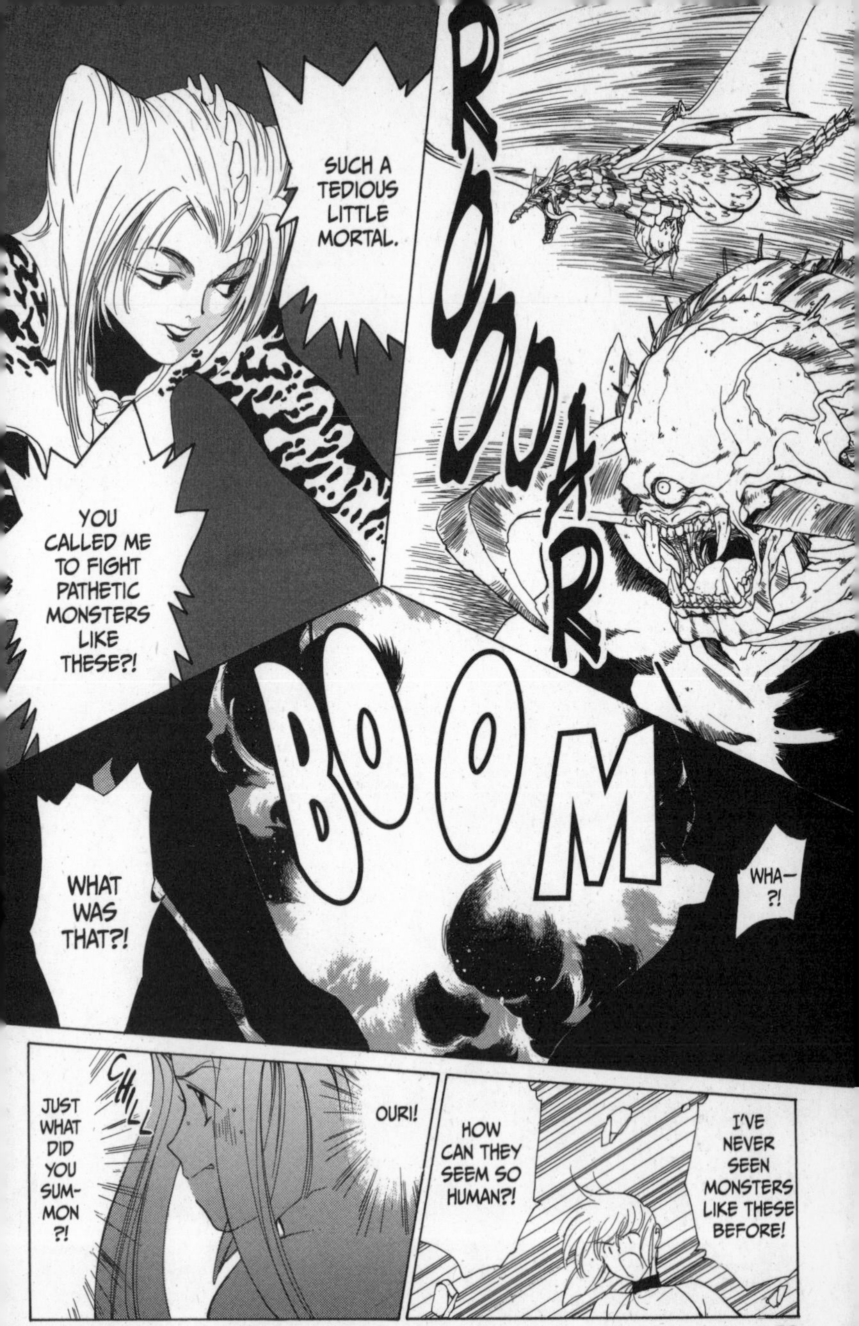
ROOOOAR
SUCH A TEDIOUS LITTLE MORTAL.
YOU CALLED ME TO FIGHT PATHETIC MONSTERS LIKE THESE?!
BOOM
WHA- ?!
WHAT WAS THAT?!
I'VE NEVER SEEN MONSTERS LIKE THESE BEFORE!
HOW CAN THEY SEEM SO HUMAN?!
OURI!
CHILL
JUST WHAT DID YOU SUM-MON ?!

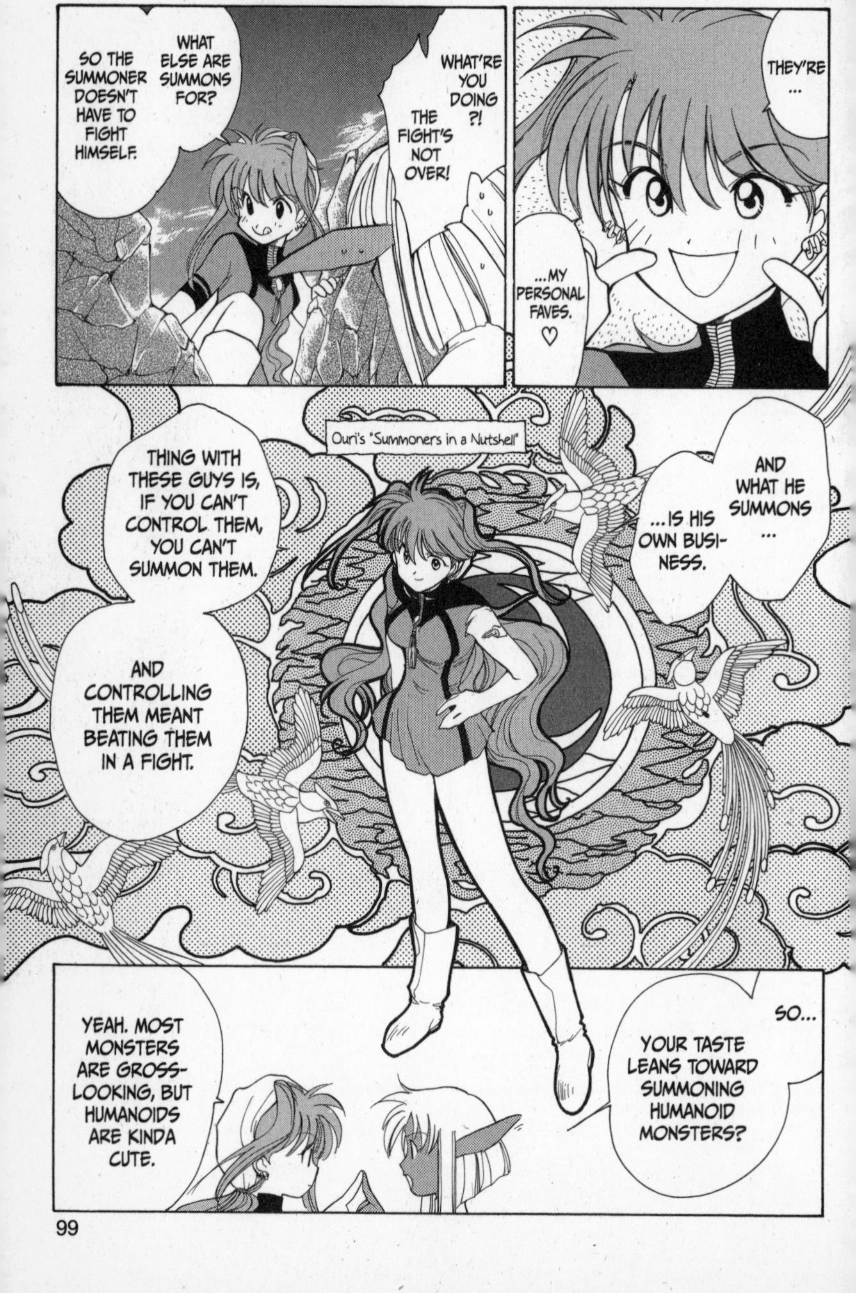
THEY'RE ...
...MY PERSONAL FAVES. ♡
WHAT'RE YOU DOING ?!
THE FIGHT'S NOT OVER!
WHAT ELSE ARE SUMMONS FOR?
SO THE SUMMONER DOESN'T HAVE TO FIGHT HIMSELF.
Ouri's "Summoners in a Nutshell"
AND WHAT HE SUMMONS ...
...IS HIS OWN BUSINESS.
THING WITH THESE GUYS IS, IF YOU CAN'T CONTROL THEM, YOU CAN'T SUMMON THEM.
AND CONTROLLING THEM MEANT BEATING THEM IN A FIGHT.
SO...
YOUR TASTE LEANS TOWARD SUMMONING HUMANOID MONSTERS?
YEAH. MOST MONSTERS ARE GROSS-LOOKING, BUT HUMANOIDS ARE KINDA CUTE.

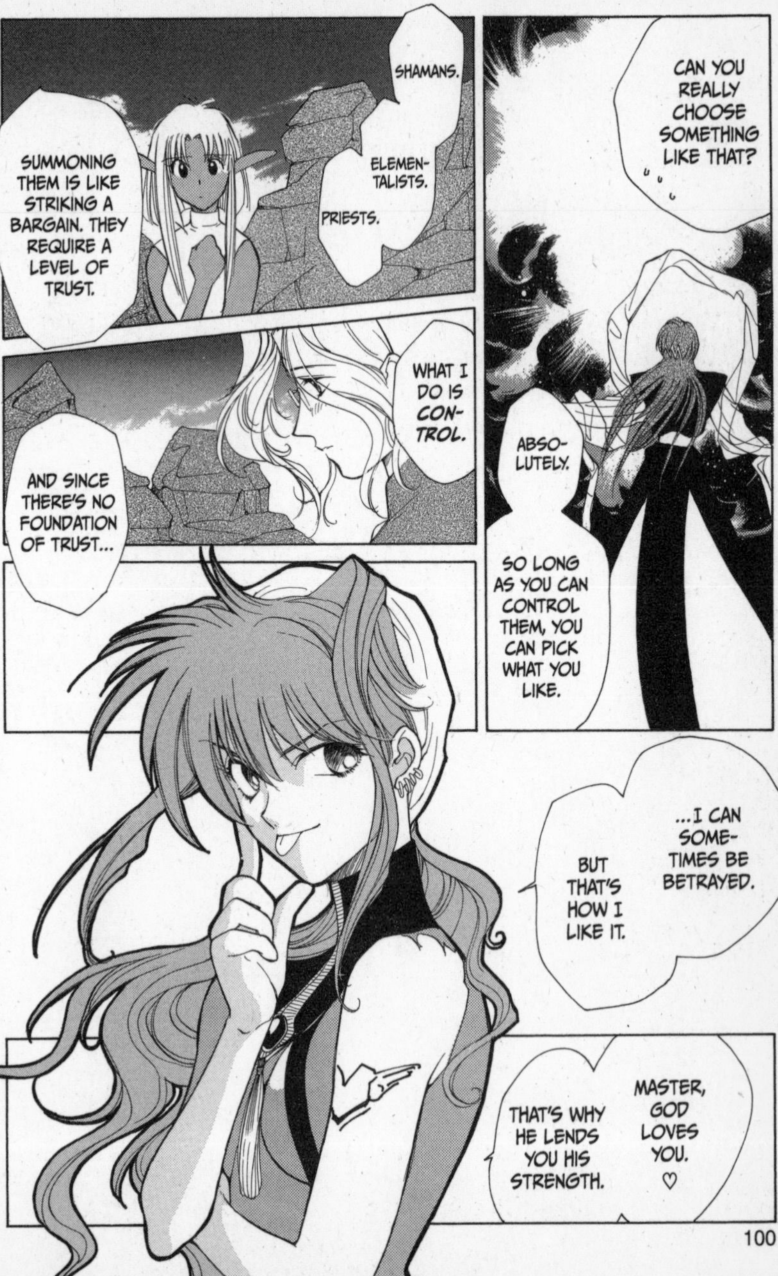
CAN YOU REALLY CHOOSE SOMETHING LIKE THAT?
ABSOLUTELY.
SO LONG AS YOU CAN CONTROL THEM, YOU CAN PICK WHAT YOU LIKE.
SHAMANS.
ELEMENTALISTS.
PRIESTS.
SUMMONING THEM IS LIKE STRIKING A BARGAIN. THEY REQUIRE A LEVEL OF TRUST.
WHAT I DO IS *CONTROL.*
AND SINCE THERE'S NO FOUNDATION OF TRUST...
...I CAN SOMETIMES BE BETRAYED.
BUT THAT'S HOW I LIKE IT.
MASTER, GOD LOVES YOU. ♡
THAT'S WHY HE LENDS YOU HIS STRENGTH.

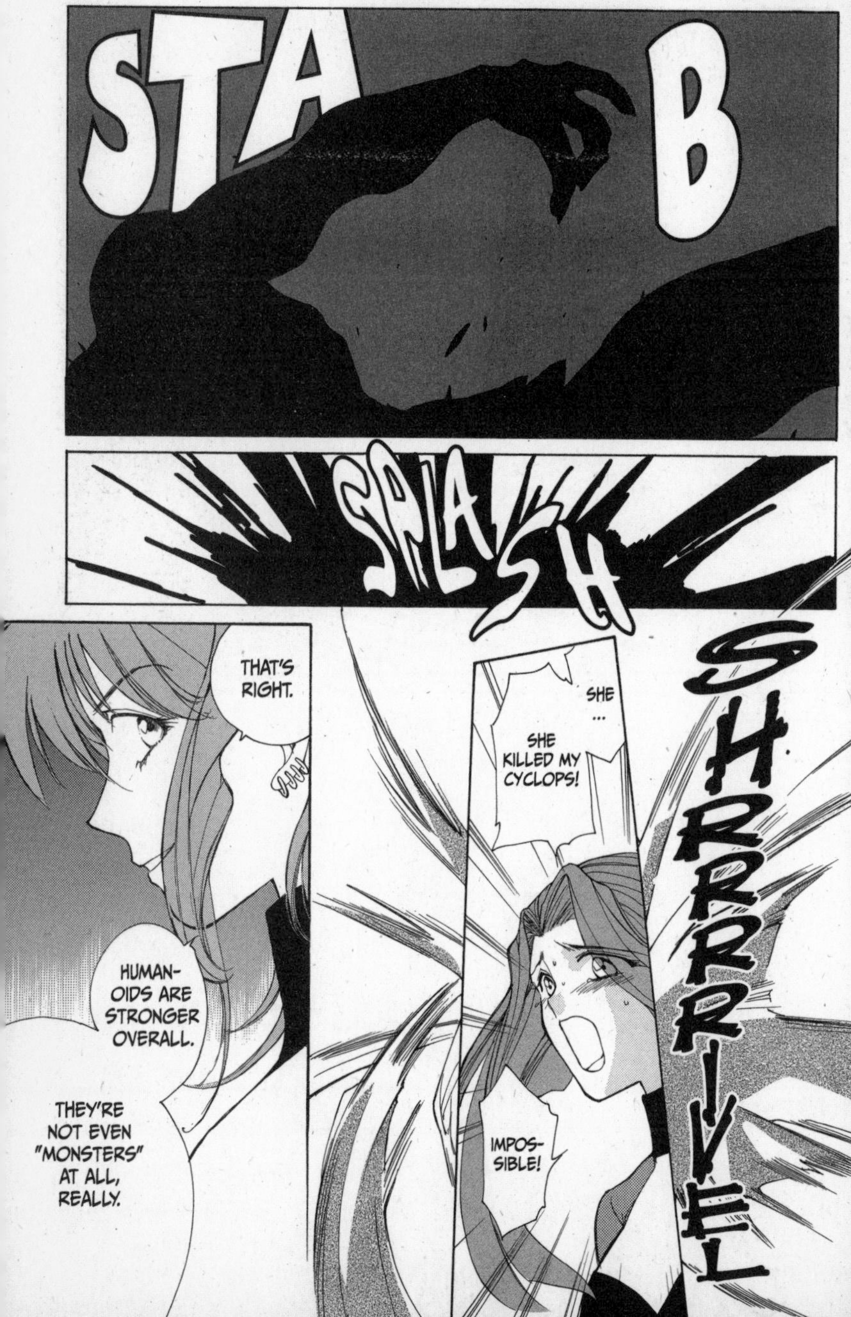
STAB
SPLASH
SHRRRIVEL
SHE ...
SHE KILLED MY CYCLOPS!
IMPOSSIBLE!
THAT'S RIGHT.
HUMANOIDS ARE STRONGER OVERALL.
THEY'RE NOT EVEN "MONSTERS" AT ALL, REALLY.

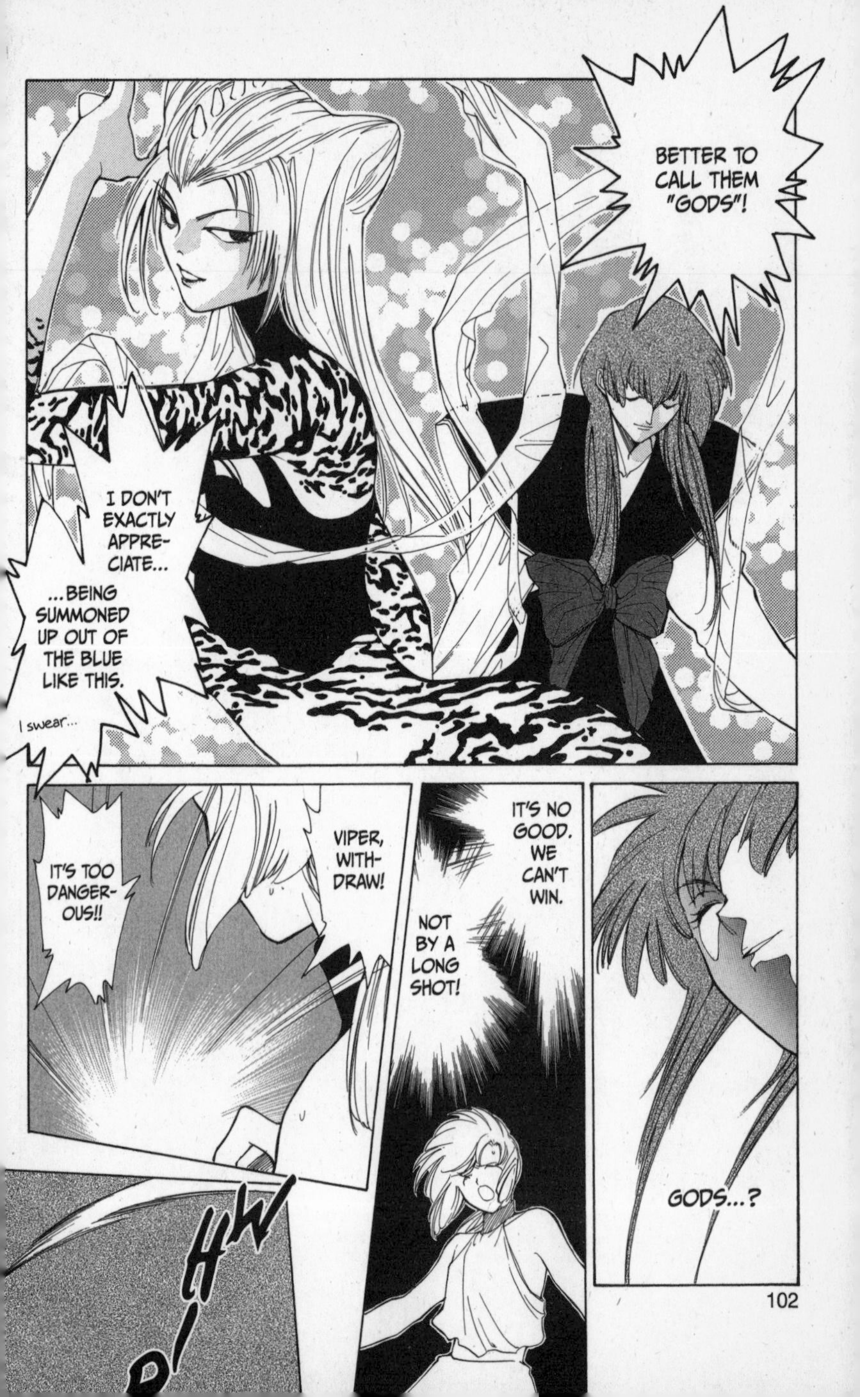
BETTER TO CALL THEM "GODS"!
I DON'T EXACTLY APPRECIATE...
...BEING SUMMONED UP OUT OF THE BLUE LIKE THIS.
I swear...
GODS...?
IT'S NO GOOD. WE CAN'T WIN.
NOT BY A LONG SHOT!
VIPER, WITH-DRAW!
IT'S TOO DANGER-OUS!!

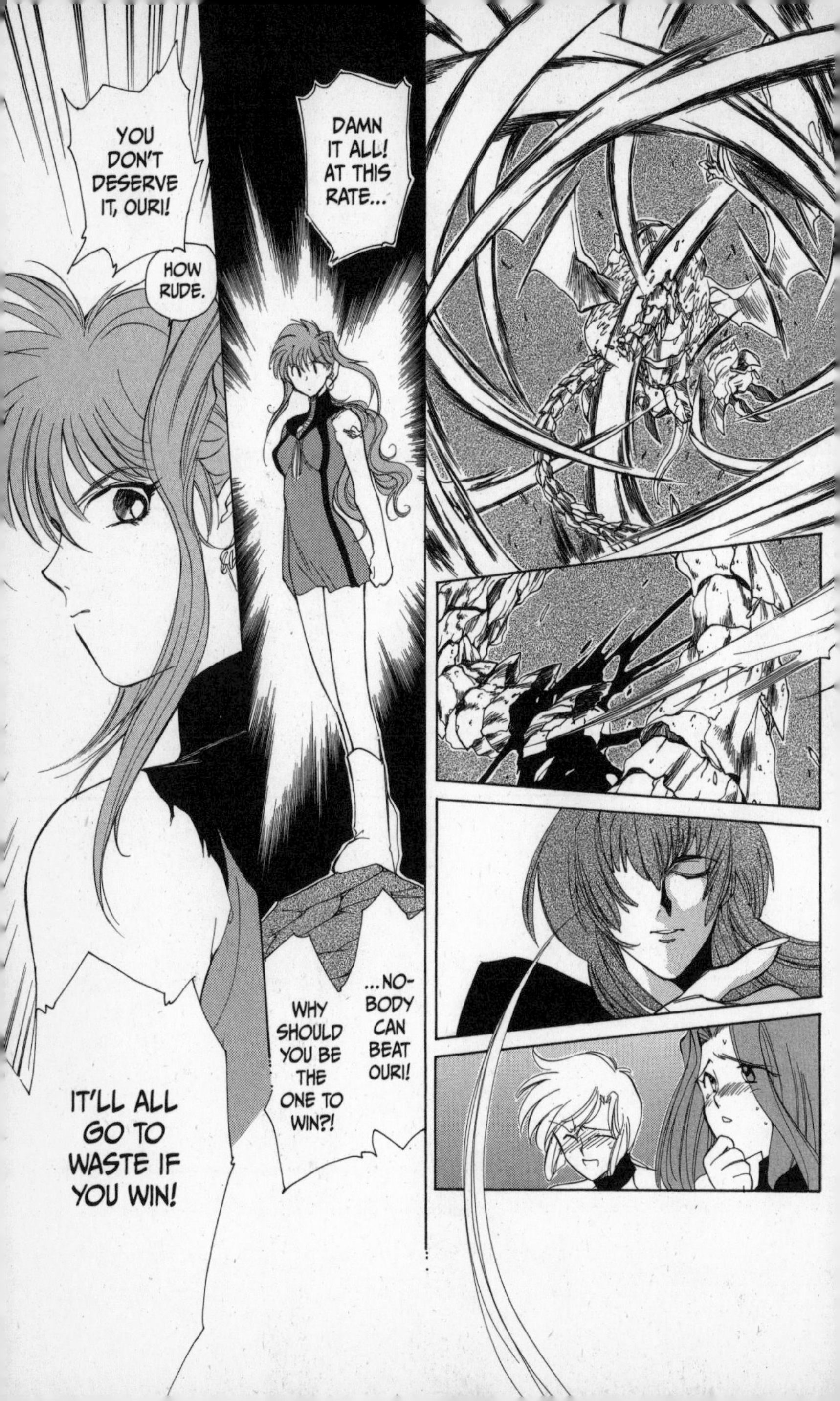
DAMN IT ALL! AT THIS RATE...
...NO-BODY CAN BEAT OURI!
WHY SHOULD YOU BE THE ONE TO WIN?!
YOU DON'T DESERVE IT, OURI!
HOW RUDE.
IT'LL ALL GO TO WASTE IF YOU WIN!

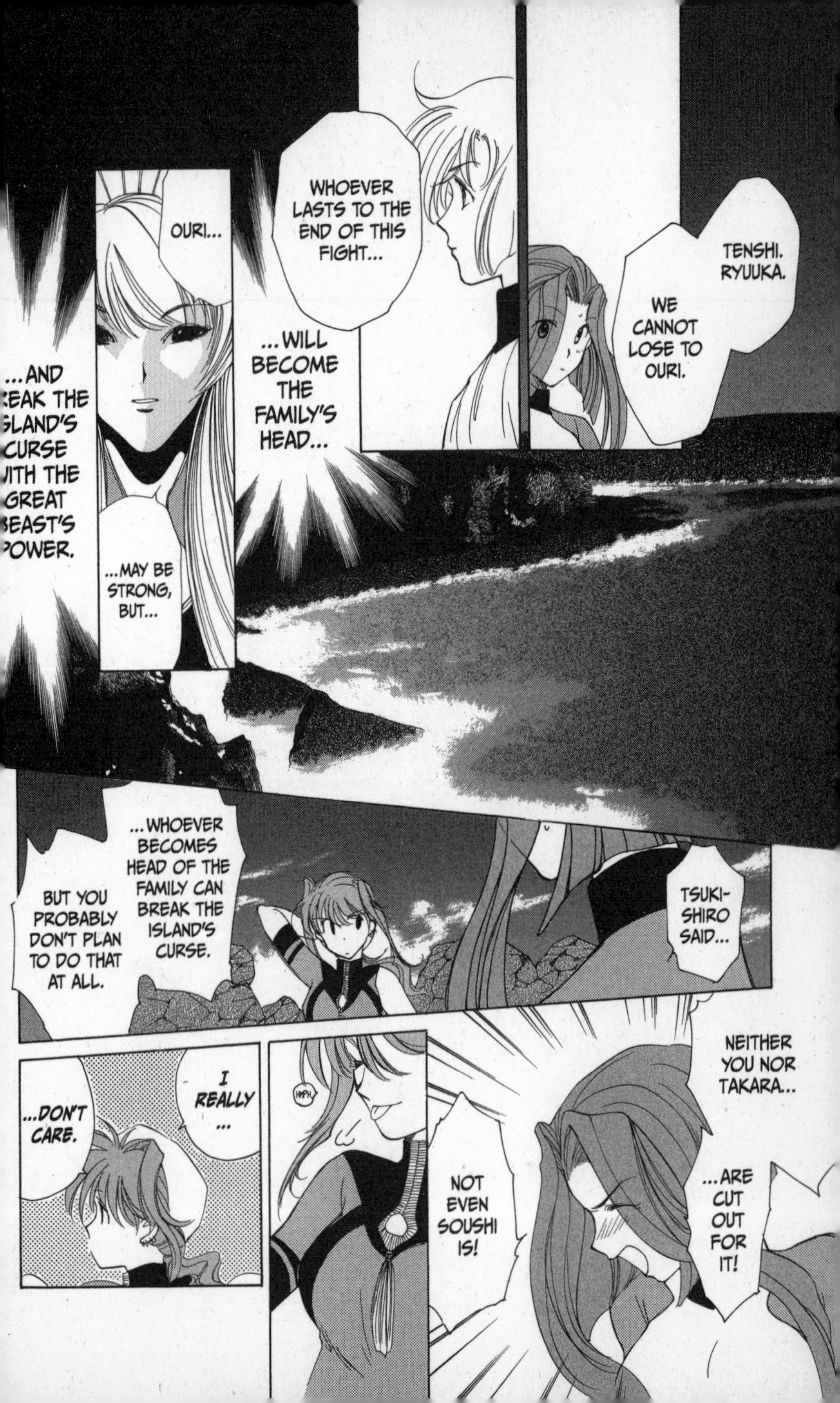
TENSHI. RYUUKA.
WE CANNOT LOSE TO OURI.
WHOEVER LASTS TO THE END OF THIS FIGHT...
...WILL BECOME THE FAMILY'S HEAD...
...AND EAK THE LAND'S CURSE ITH THE GREAT EAST'S OWER.
OURI...
...MAY BE STRONG, BUT...
TSUKI-SHIRO SAID...
...WHOEVER BECOMES HEAD OF THE FAMILY CAN BREAK THE ISLAND'S CURSE.
BUT YOU PROBABLY DON'T PLAN TO DO THAT AT ALL.
NEITHER YOU NOR TAKARA...
...ARE CUT OUT FOR IT!
NOT EVEN SOUSHI IS!
HMPH
I REALLY...
...DON'T CARE.

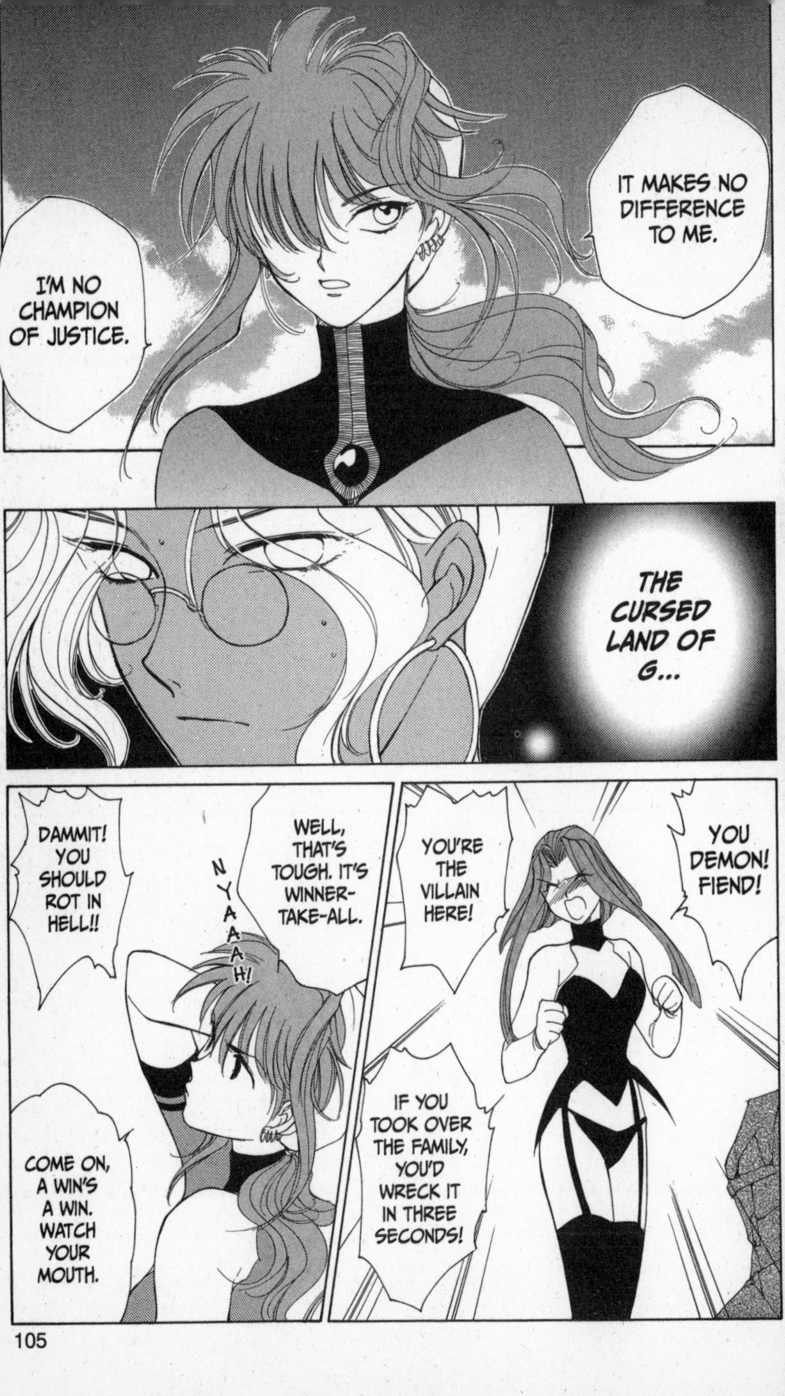
IT MAKES NO DIFFERENCE TO ME.
I'M NO CHAMPION OF JUSTICE.
THE CURSED LAND OF G...
YOU DEMON! FIEND!
YOU'RE THE VILLAIN HERE!
IF YOU TOOK OVER THE FAMILY, YOU'D WRECK IT IN THREE SECONDS!
WELL, THAT'S TOUGH. IT'S WINNER-TAKE-ALL.
NYAAAH!
DAMMIT! YOU SHOULD ROT IN HELL!!
COME ON, A WIN'S A WIN. WATCH YOUR MOUTH.

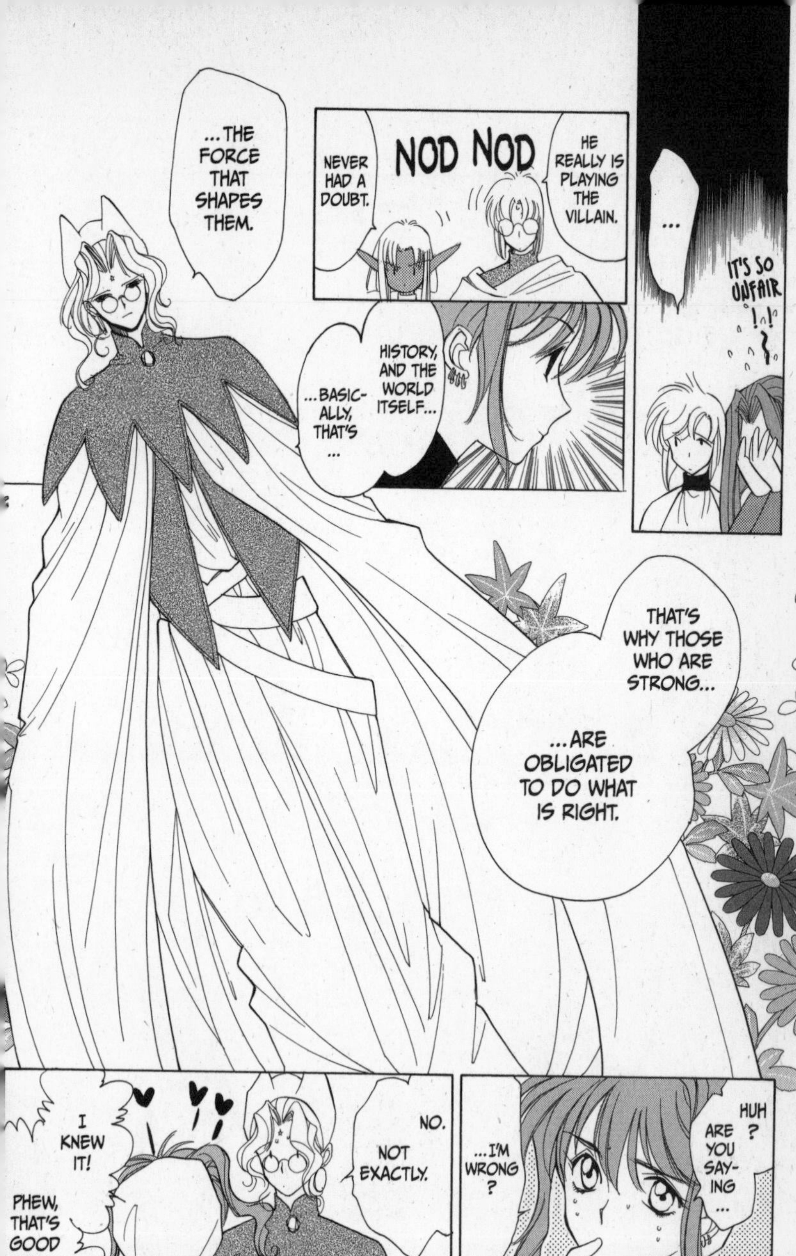
...
IT'S SO UNFAIR !?!
HE REALLY IS PLAYING THE VILLAIN.
NOD NOD
NEVER HAD A DOUBT.
HISTORY, AND THE WORLD ITSELF...
...BASIC-ALLY, THAT'S ...
...THE FORCE THAT SHAPES THEM.
THAT'S WHY THOSE WHO ARE STRONG...
...ARE OBLIGATED TO DO WHAT IS RIGHT.
HUH ? ARE YOU SAY-ING ...
...I'M WRONG ?
NO.
NOT EXACTLY.
I KNEW IT!
PHEW, THAT'S GOOD TO HEAR!

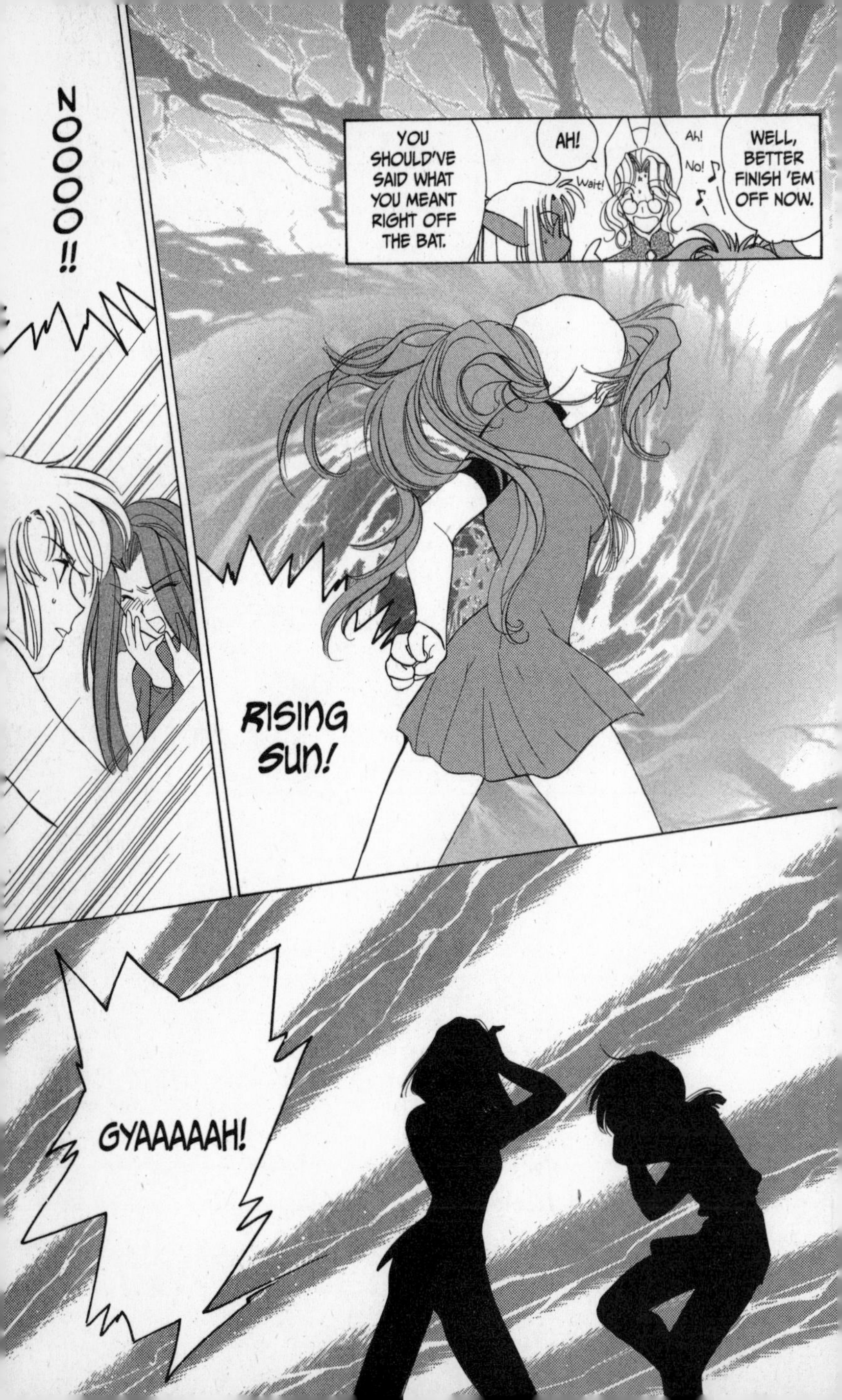
WELL, BETTER FINISH 'EM OFF NOW.
Ah! No!
AH!
Wait!
YOU SHOULD'VE SAID WHAT YOU MEANT RIGHT OFF THE BAT.
RISING SUN!
NOOOO!!
GYAAAAAH!

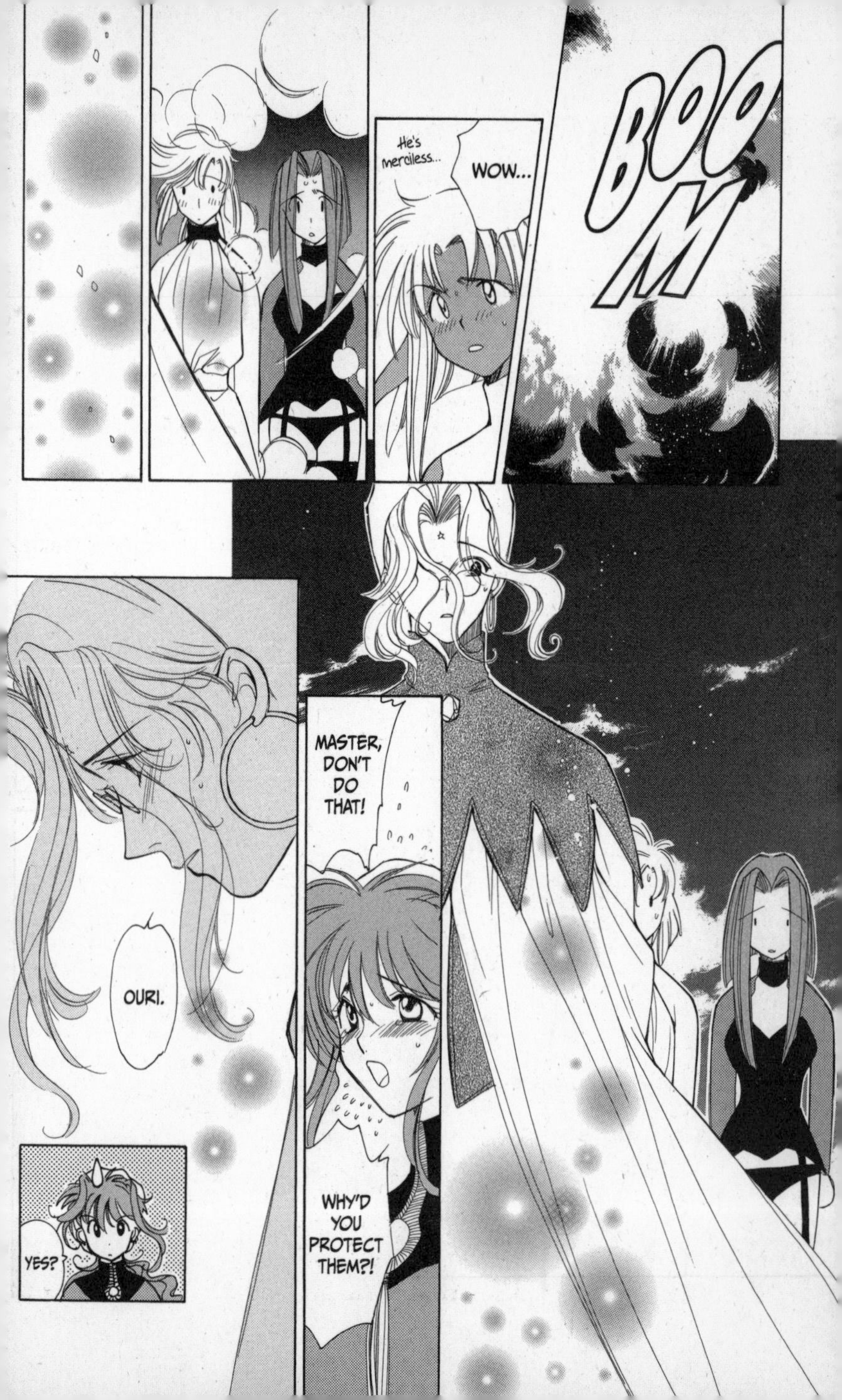
BOOM
WOW...
He's merciless...
MASTER, DON'T DO THAT!
WHY'D YOU PROTECT THEM?!
OURI.
YES?

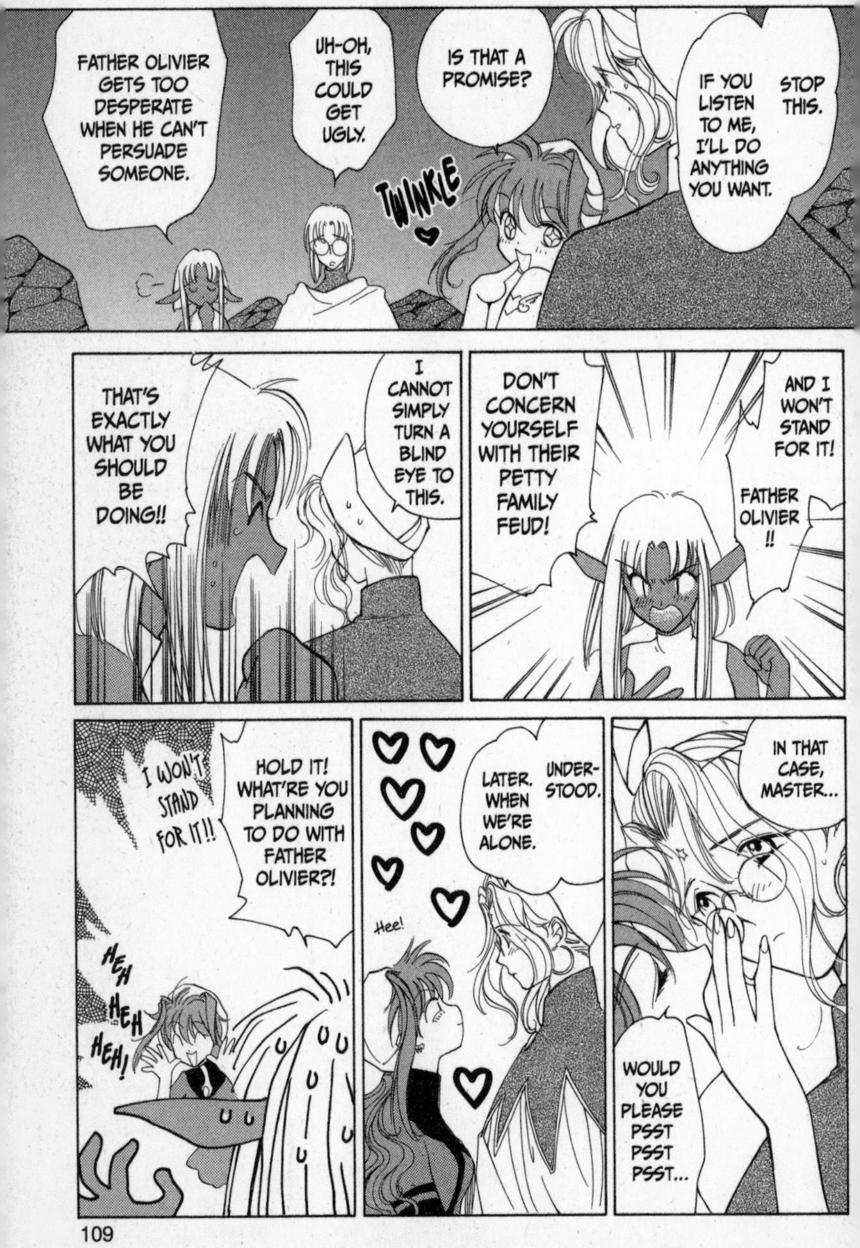
STOP THIS.
IF YOU LISTEN TO ME, I'LL DO ANYTHING YOU WANT.
IS THAT A PROMISE?
TWINKLE
UH-OH, THIS COULD GET UGLY.
FATHER OLIVIER GETS TOO DESPERATE WHEN HE CAN'T PERSUADE SOMEONE.
AND I WON'T STAND FOR IT!
FATHER OLIVIER!!
DON'T CONCERN YOURSELF WITH THEIR PETTY FAMILY FEUD!
I CANNOT SIMPLY TURN A BLIND EYE TO THIS.
THAT'S EXACTLY WHAT YOU SHOULD BE DOING!!
IN THAT CASE, MASTER...
WOULD YOU PLEASE PSST PSST PSST...
UNDER-STOOD.
LATER. WHEN WE'RE ALONE.
Hee!
HOLD IT! WHAT'RE YOU PLANNING TO DO WITH FATHER OLIVIER?!
I WON'T STAND FOR IT!!
HEH HEH HEH!

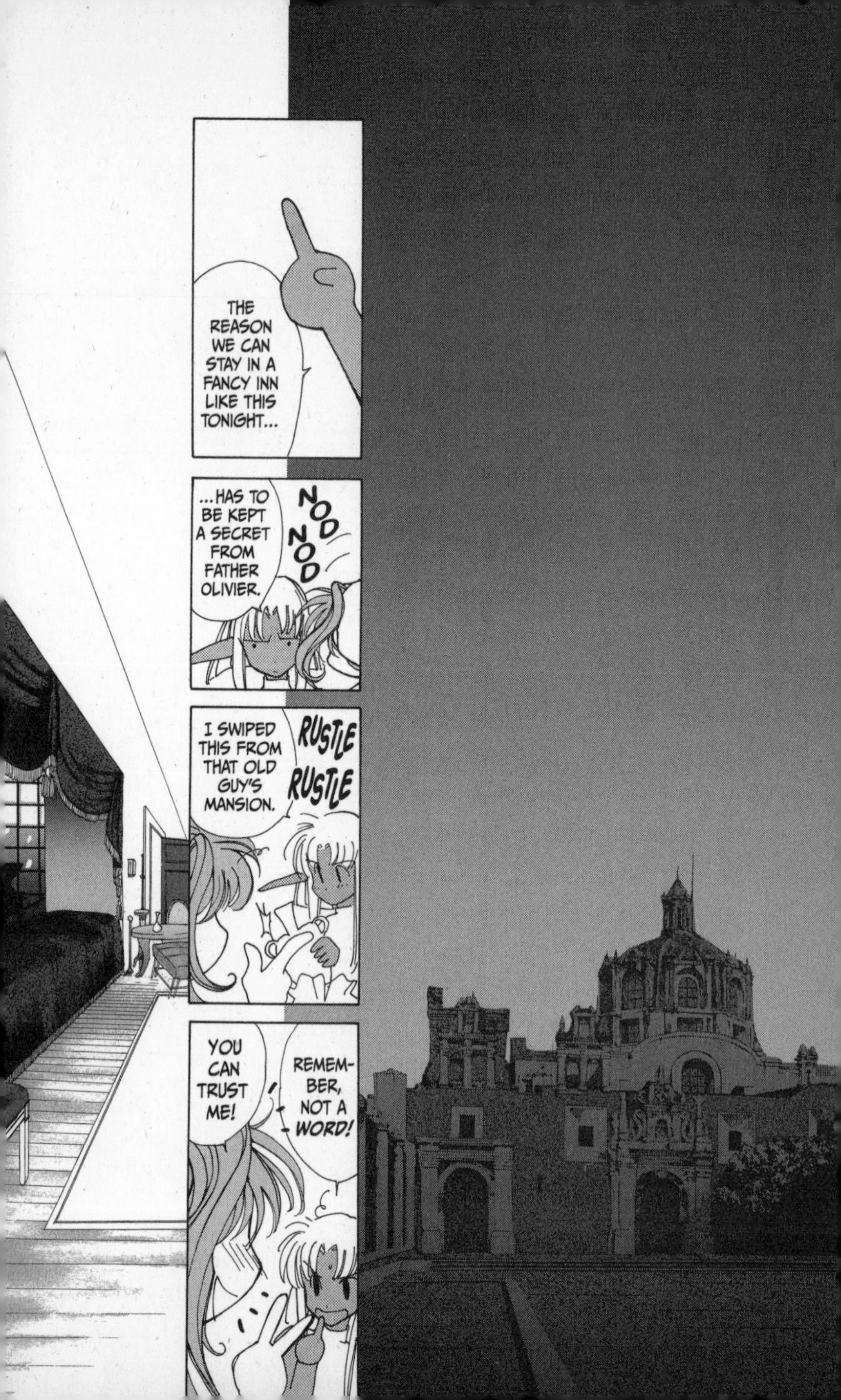
THE REASON WE CAN STAY IN A FANCY INN LIKE THIS TONIGHT...
...HAS TO BE KEPT A SECRET FROM FATHER OLIVIER.
NOD NOD
RUSTLE RUSTLE
I SWIPED THIS FROM THAT OLD GUY'S MANSION.
REMEMBER, NOT A WORD!
YOU CAN TRUST ME!

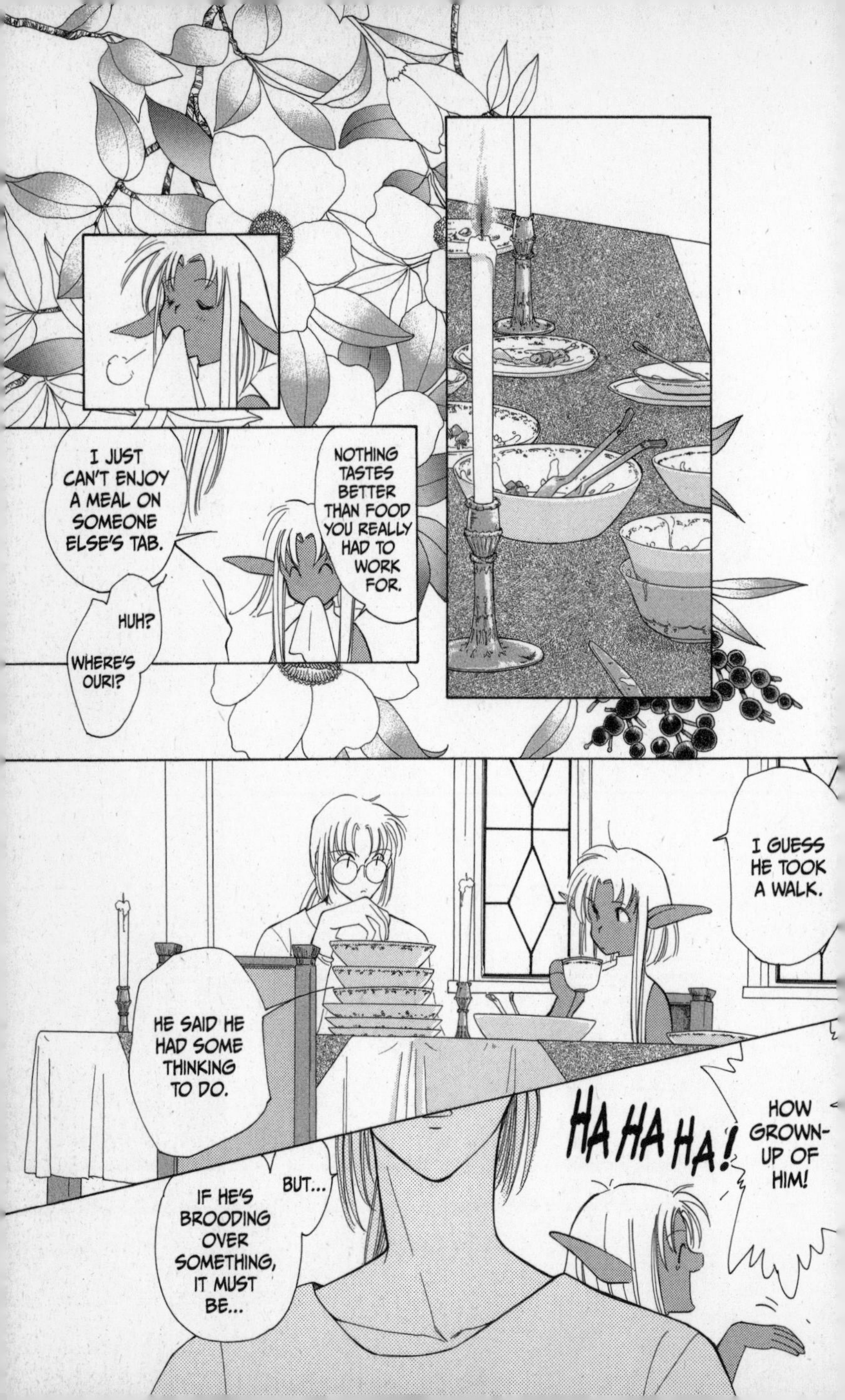
NOTHING TASTES BETTER THAN FOOD YOU REALLY HAD TO WORK FOR.
I JUST CAN'T ENJOY A MEAL ON SOMEONE ELSE'S TAB.
HUH? WHERE'S OURI?
I GUESS HE TOOK A WALK.
HE SAID HE HAD SOME THINKING TO DO.
HA HA HA!
HOW GROWN-UP OF HIM!
BUT...
IF HE'S BROODING OVER SOMETHING, IT MUST BE...

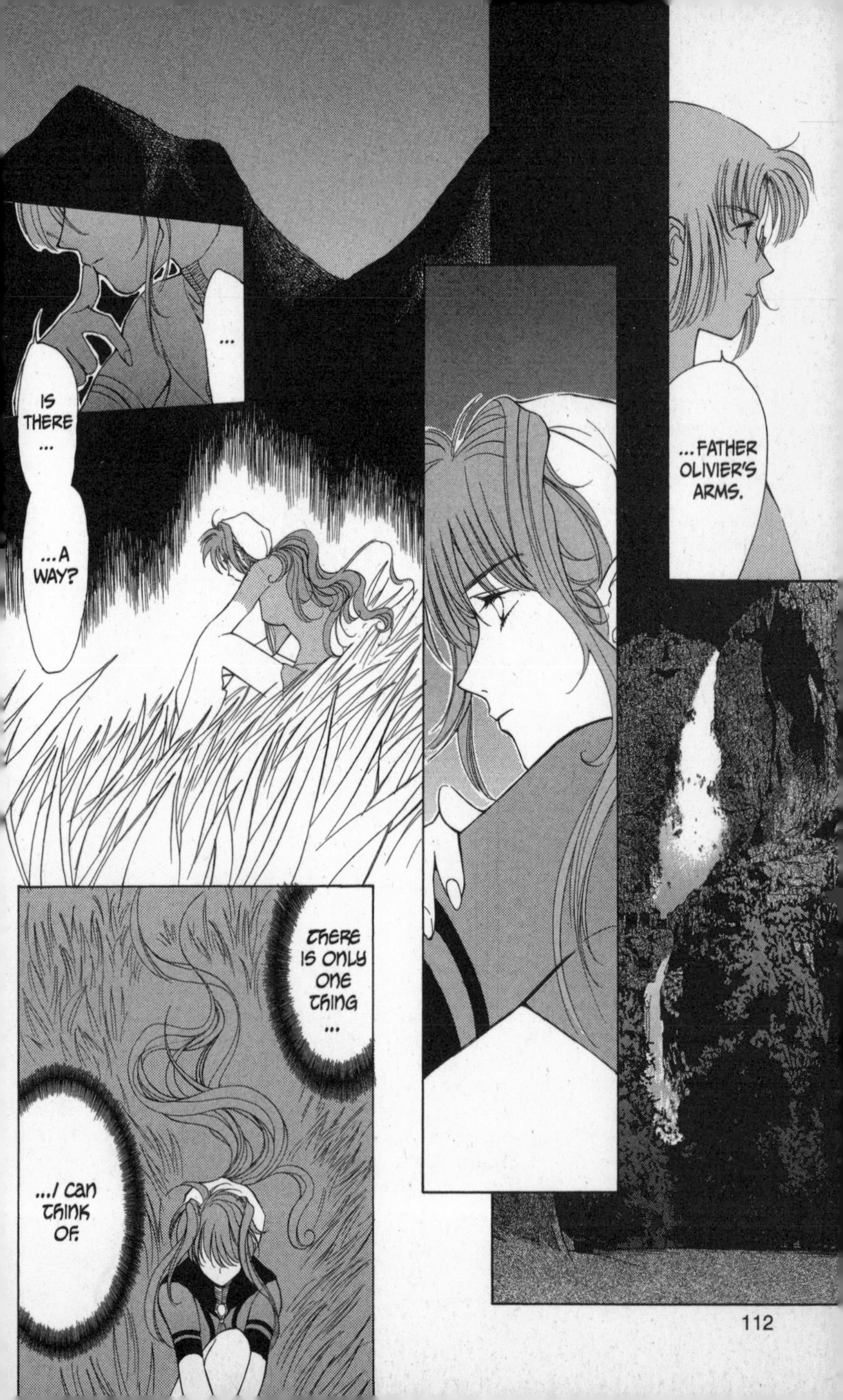
...FATHER OLIVIER'S ARMS.
...
IS THERE ...
...A WAY?
THERE IS ONLY ONE THING ...
...I CAN THINK OF.

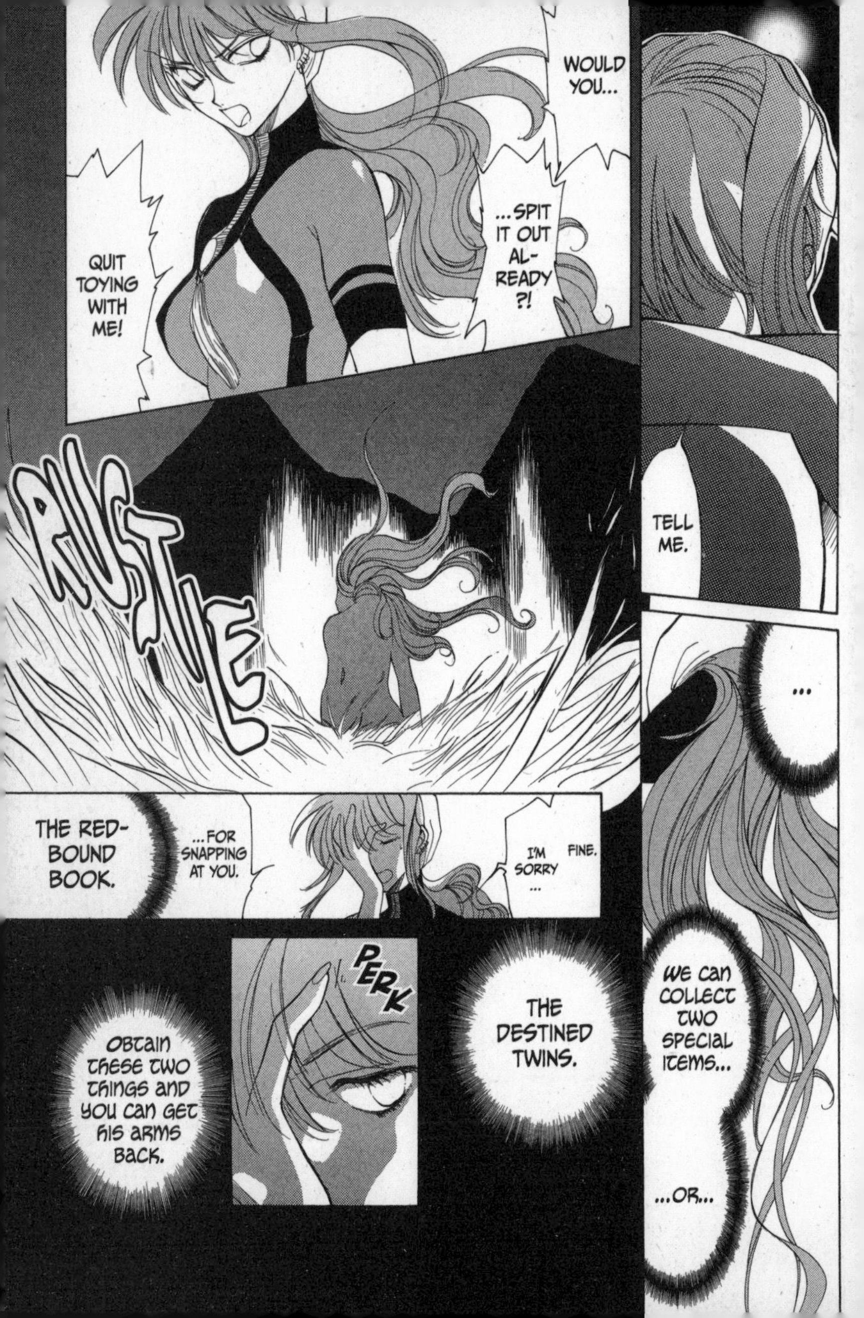
TELL ME.
...
WE CAN COLLECT TWO SPECIAL ITEMS...
...OR...
WOULD YOU...
...SPIT IT OUT AL-READY?!
QUIT TOYING WITH ME!
RUSTLE
FINE.
I'M SORRY...
...FOR SNAPPING AT YOU.
THE RED-BOUND BOOK.
THE DESTINED TWINS.
PERK
OBTAIN THESE TWO THINGS AND YOU CAN GET HIS ARMS BACK.

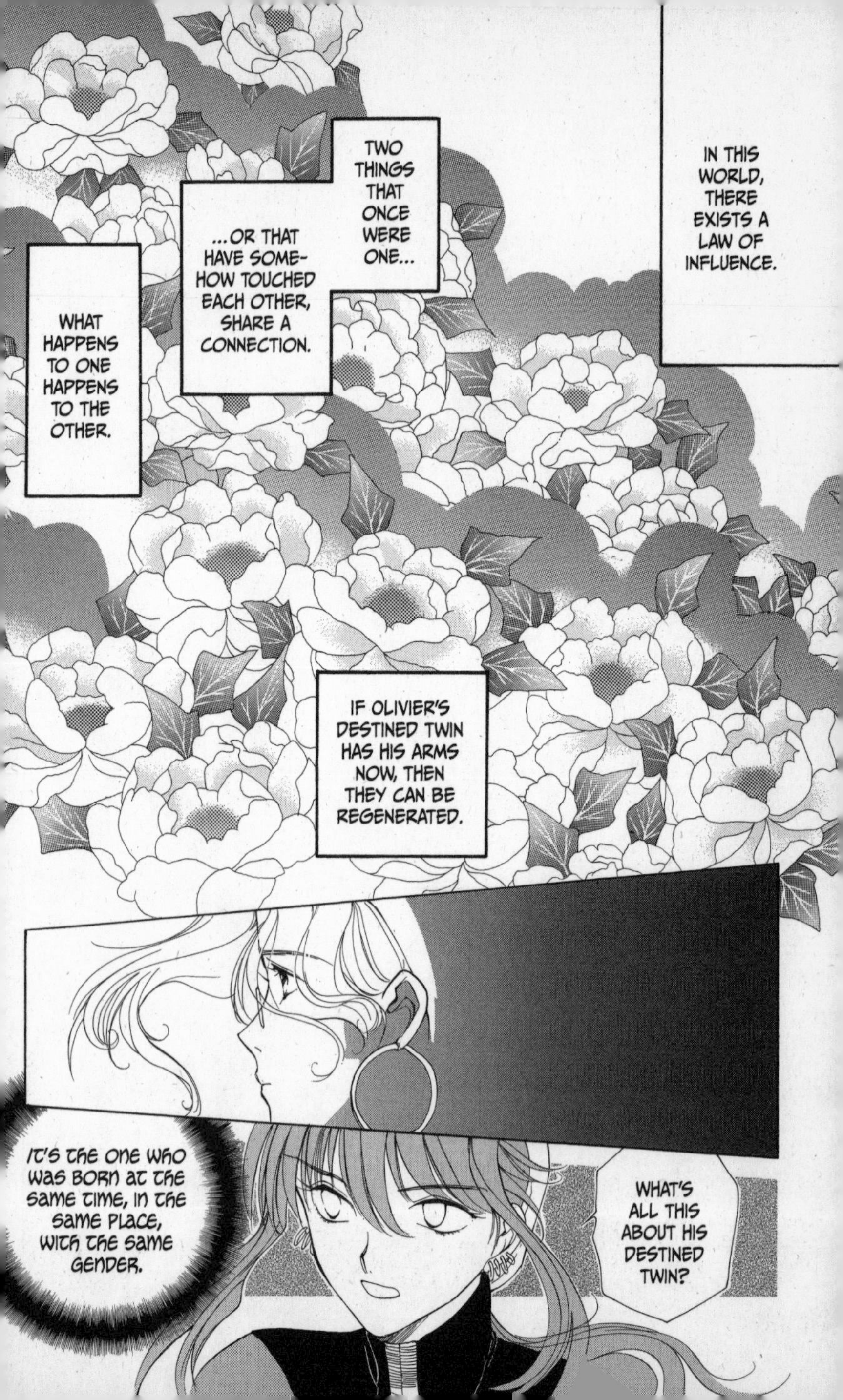
IN THIS WORLD, THERE EXISTS A LAW OF INFLUENCE.
TWO THINGS THAT ONCE WERE ONE...
...OR THAT HAVE SOME-HOW TOUCHED EACH OTHER, SHARE A CONNECTION.
WHAT HAPPENS TO ONE HAPPENS TO THE OTHER.
IF OLIVIER'S DESTINED TWIN HAS HIS ARMS NOW, THEN THEY CAN BE REGENERATED.
WHAT'S ALL THIS ABOUT HIS DESTINED TWIN?
IT'S THE ONE WHO WAS BORN AT THE SAME TIME, IN THE SAME PLACE, WITH THE SAME GENDER.

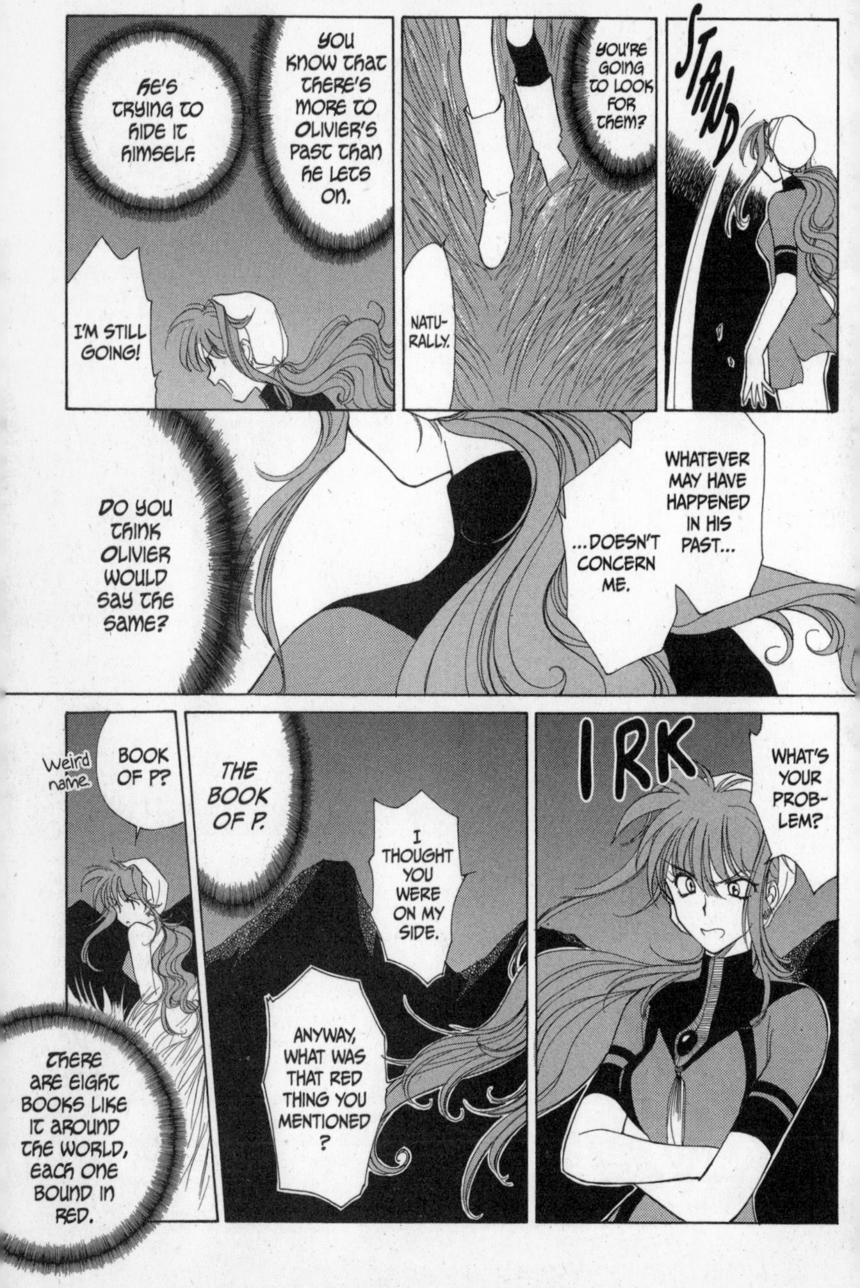
STAND
YOU'RE GOING TO LOOK FOR THEM?
NATU-RALLY.
YOU KNOW THAT THERE'S MORE TO OLIVIER'S PAST THAN HE LETS ON.
HE'S TRYING TO HIDE IT HIMSELF.
I'M STILL GOING!
WHATEVER MAY HAVE HAPPENED IN HIS PAST...
...DOESN'T CONCERN ME.
DO YOU THINK OLIVIER WOULD SAY THE SAME?
IRK
WHAT'S YOUR PROB-LEM?
I THOUGHT YOU WERE ON MY SIDE.
ANYWAY, WHAT WAS THAT RED THING YOU MENTIONED?
THE BOOK OF P.
BOOK OF P?
Weird name.
THERE ARE EIGHT BOOKS LIKE IT AROUND THE WORLD, EACH ONE BOUND IN RED.

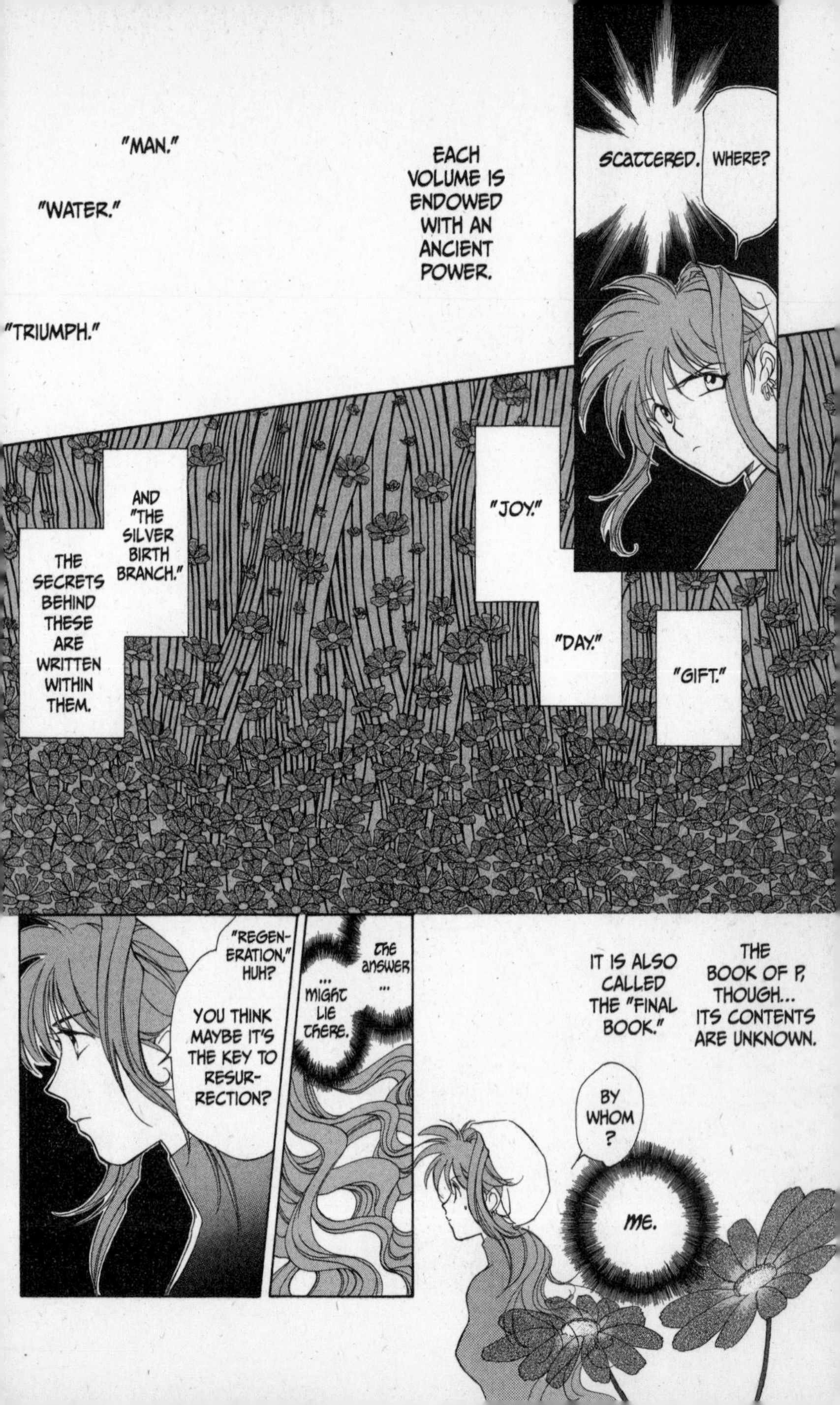

SCATTERED.
WHERE?
EACH VOLUME IS ENDOWED WITH AN ANCIENT POWER.
"MAN."
"WATER."
"TRIUMPH."
"JOY."
"DAY."
"GIFT."
AND "THE SILVER BIRTH BRANCH."
THE SECRETS BEHIND THESE ARE WRITTEN WITHIN THEM.
THE BOOK OF P, THOUGH... ITS CONTENTS ARE UNKNOWN.
IT IS ALSO CALLED THE "FINAL BOOK."
BY WHOM?
ME.
THE ANSWER...
...MIGHT LIE THERE.
"REGENERATION," HUH?
YOU THINK MAYBE IT'S THE KEY TO RESURRECTION?

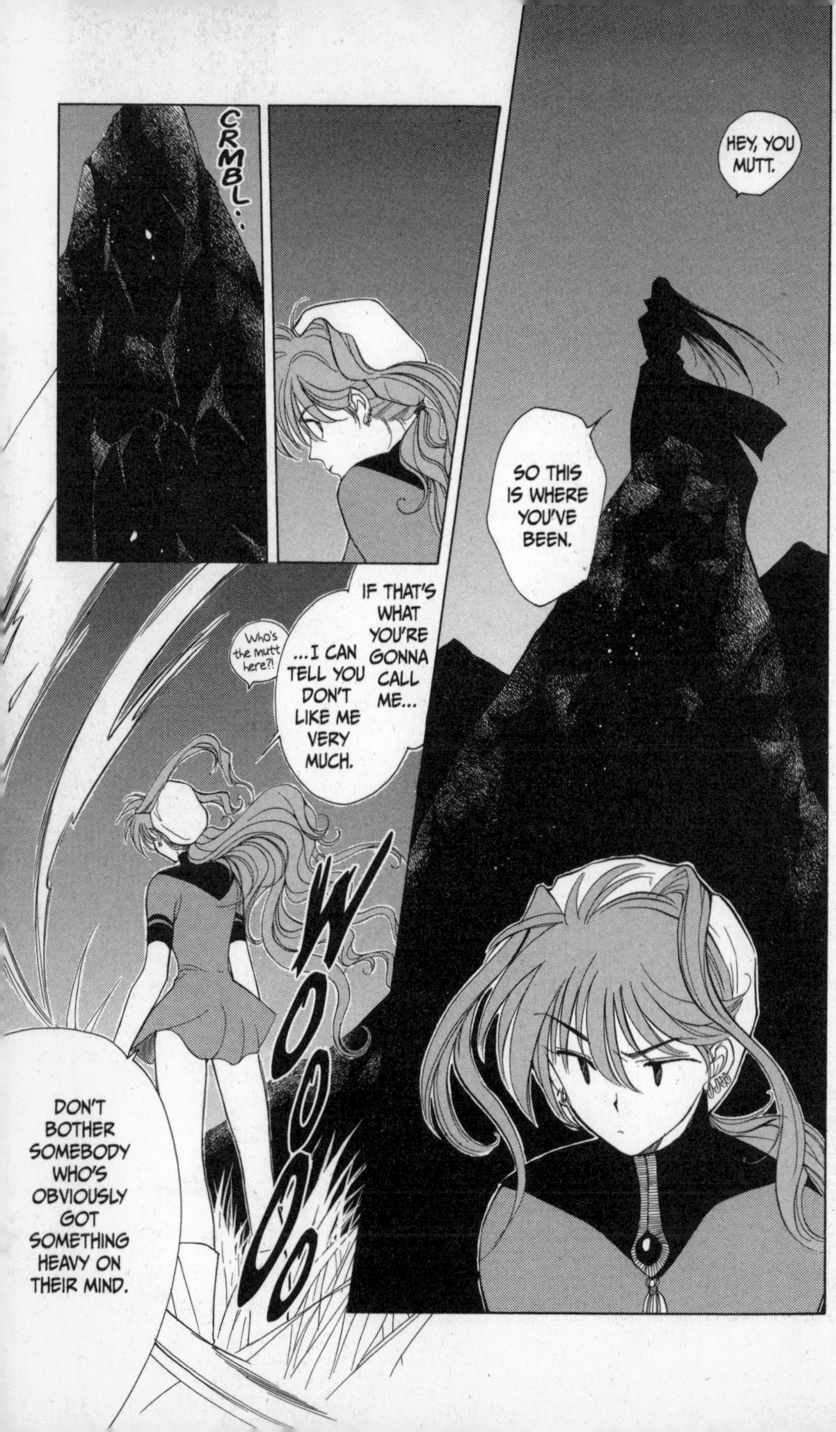
HEY, YOU MUTT.
SO THIS IS WHERE YOU'VE BEEN.
CRMBL..
IF THAT'S WHAT YOU'RE GONNA CALL ME...
...I CAN TELL YOU DON'T LIKE ME VERY MUCH.
Who's the mutt here?!
WOOOOO
DON'T BOTHER SOMEBODY WHO'S OBVIOUSLY GOT SOMETHING HEAVY ON THEIR MIND.

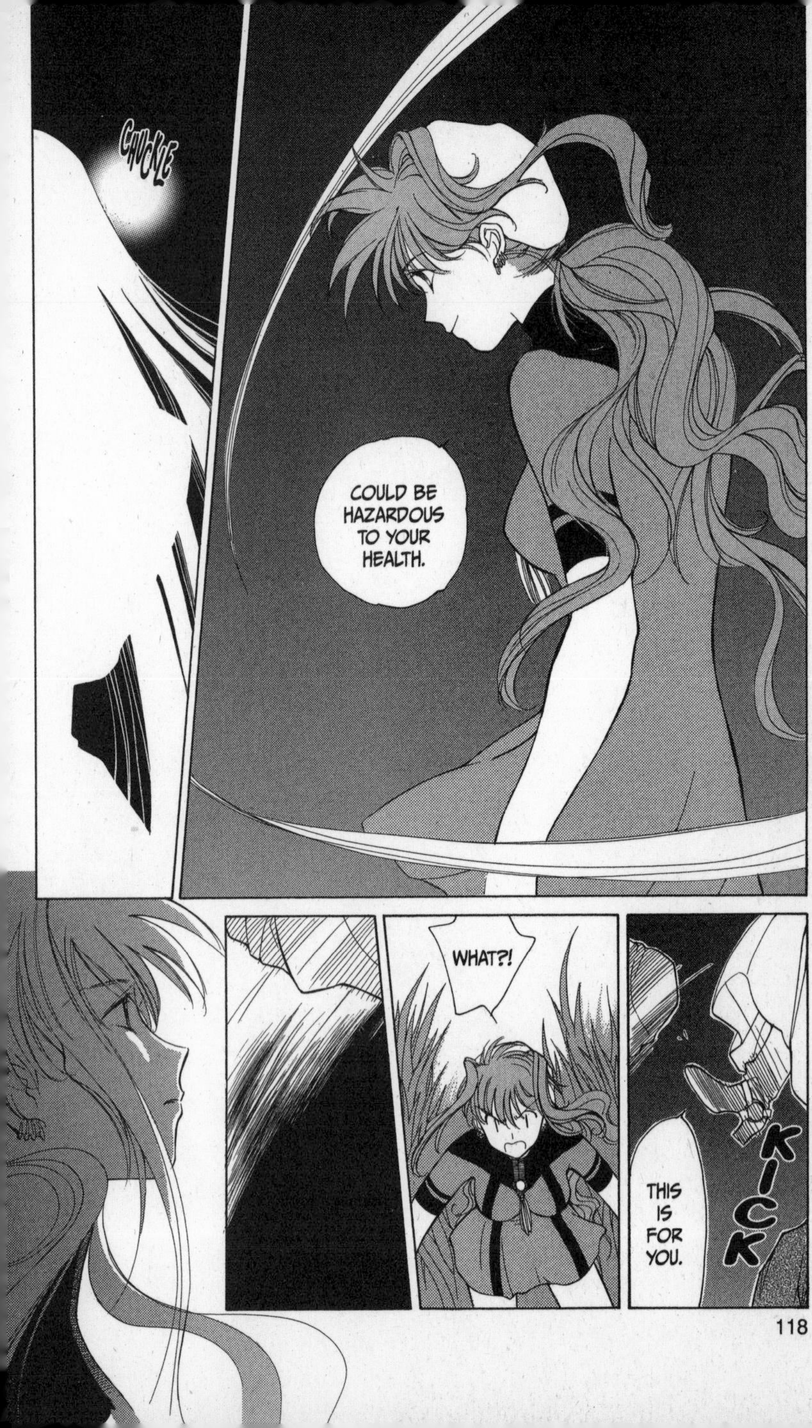
COULD BE HAZARDOUS TO YOUR HEALTH.
CHUCKLE
KICK
THIS IS FOR YOU.
WHAT?!

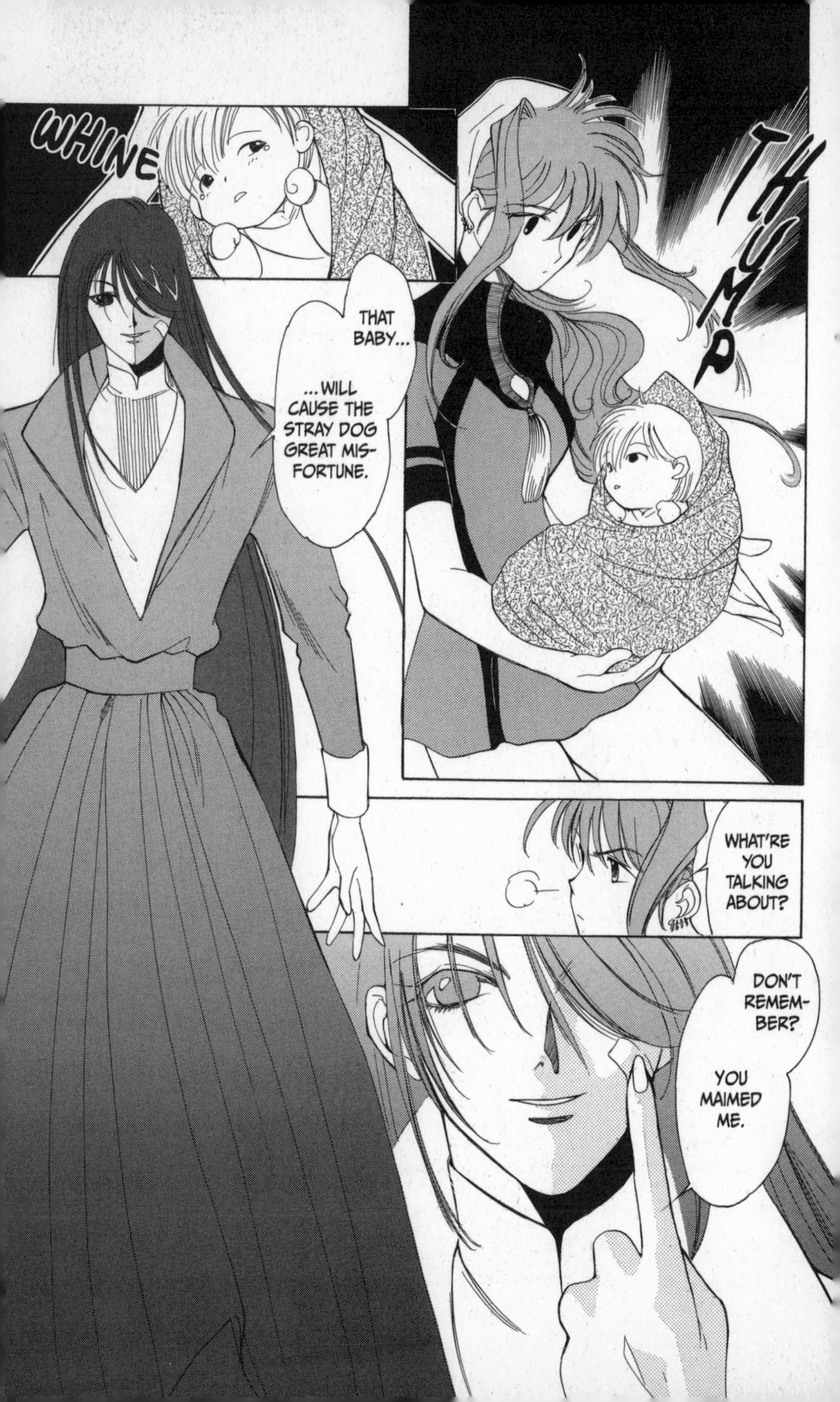
THUMP
WHINE
THAT BABY...
...WILL CAUSE THE STRAY DOG GREAT MIS-FORTUNE.
WHAT'RE YOU TALKING ABOUT?
DON'T REMEM-BER?
YOU MAIMED ME.

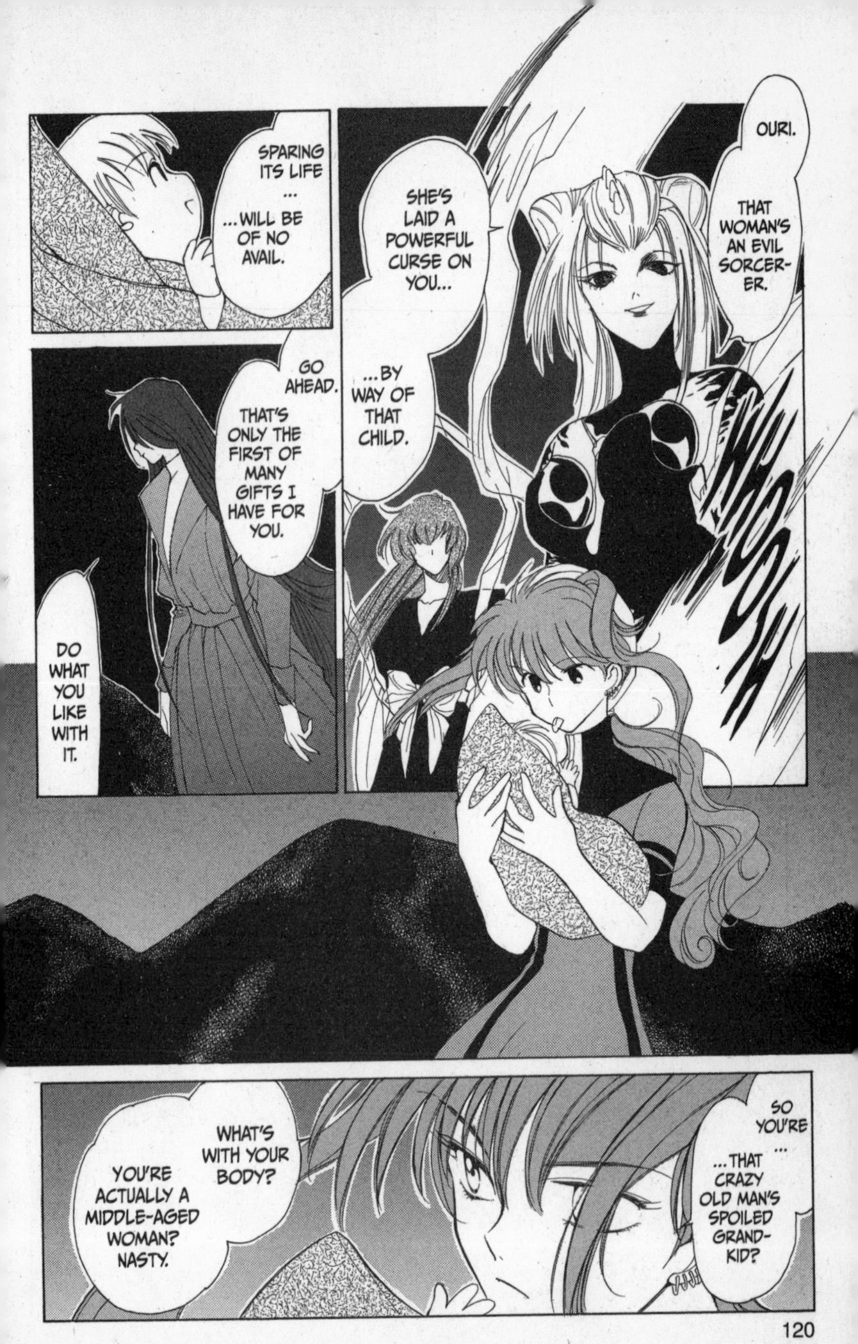
OURI.
THAT WOMAN'S AN EVIL SORCERER.
SHE'S LAID A POWERFUL CURSE ON YOU...
...BY WAY OF THAT CHILD.
SPARING ITS LIFE ... ...WILL BE OF NO AVAIL.
GO AHEAD.
THAT'S ONLY THE FIRST OF MANY GIFTS I HAVE FOR YOU.
DO WHAT YOU LIKE WITH IT.
SO YOU'RE ... ...THAT CRAZY OLD MAN'S SPOILED GRANDKID?
WHAT'S WITH YOUR BODY?
YOU'RE ACTUALLY A MIDDLE-AGED WOMAN? NASTY.

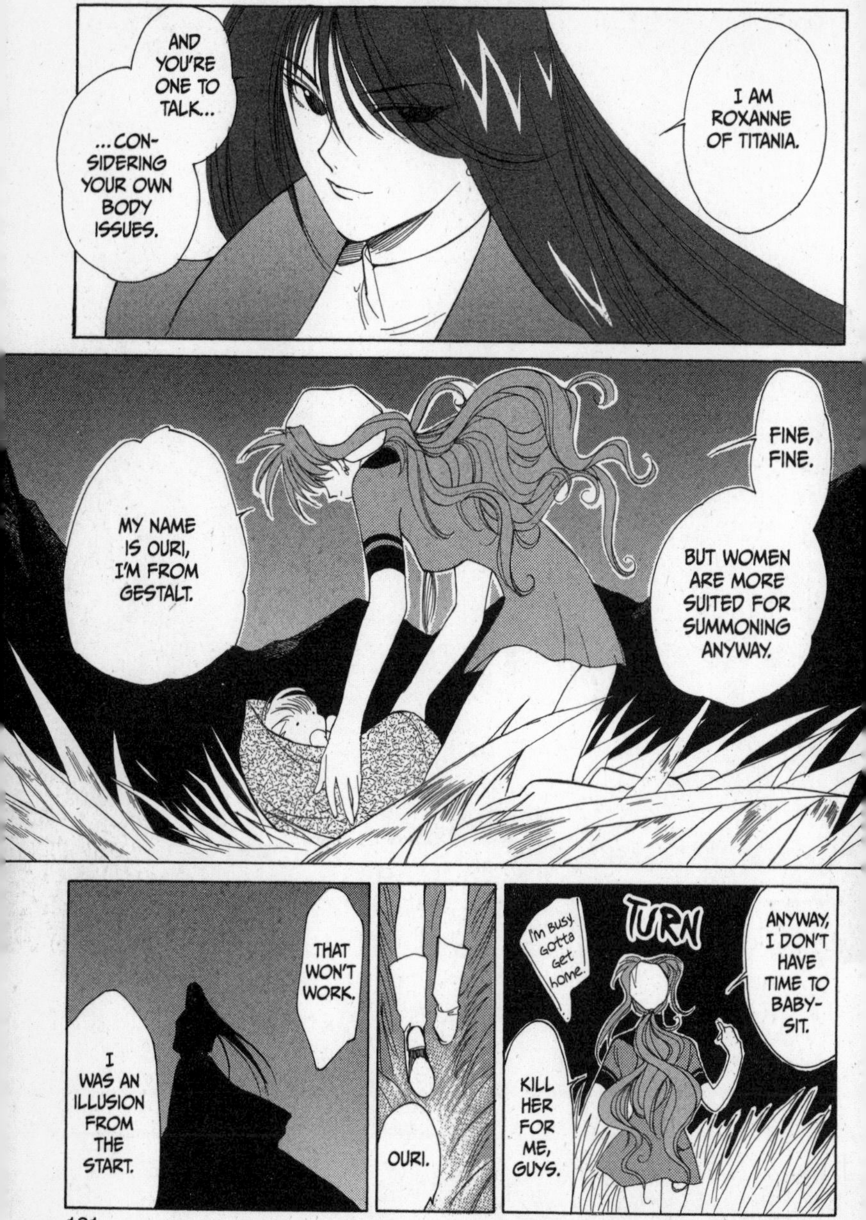
I AM ROXANNE OF TITANIA.
AND YOU'RE ONE TO TALK...
...CON-SIDERING YOUR OWN BODY ISSUES.
FINE, FINE.
BUT WOMEN ARE MORE SUITED FOR SUMMONING ANYWAY.
MY NAME IS OURI, I'M FROM GESTALT.
TURN
ANYWAY, I DON'T HAVE TIME TO BABY-SIT.
I'm busy. Gotta get home.
KILL HER FOR ME, GUYS.
THAT WON'T WORK.
OURI.
I WAS AN ILLUSION FROM THE START.

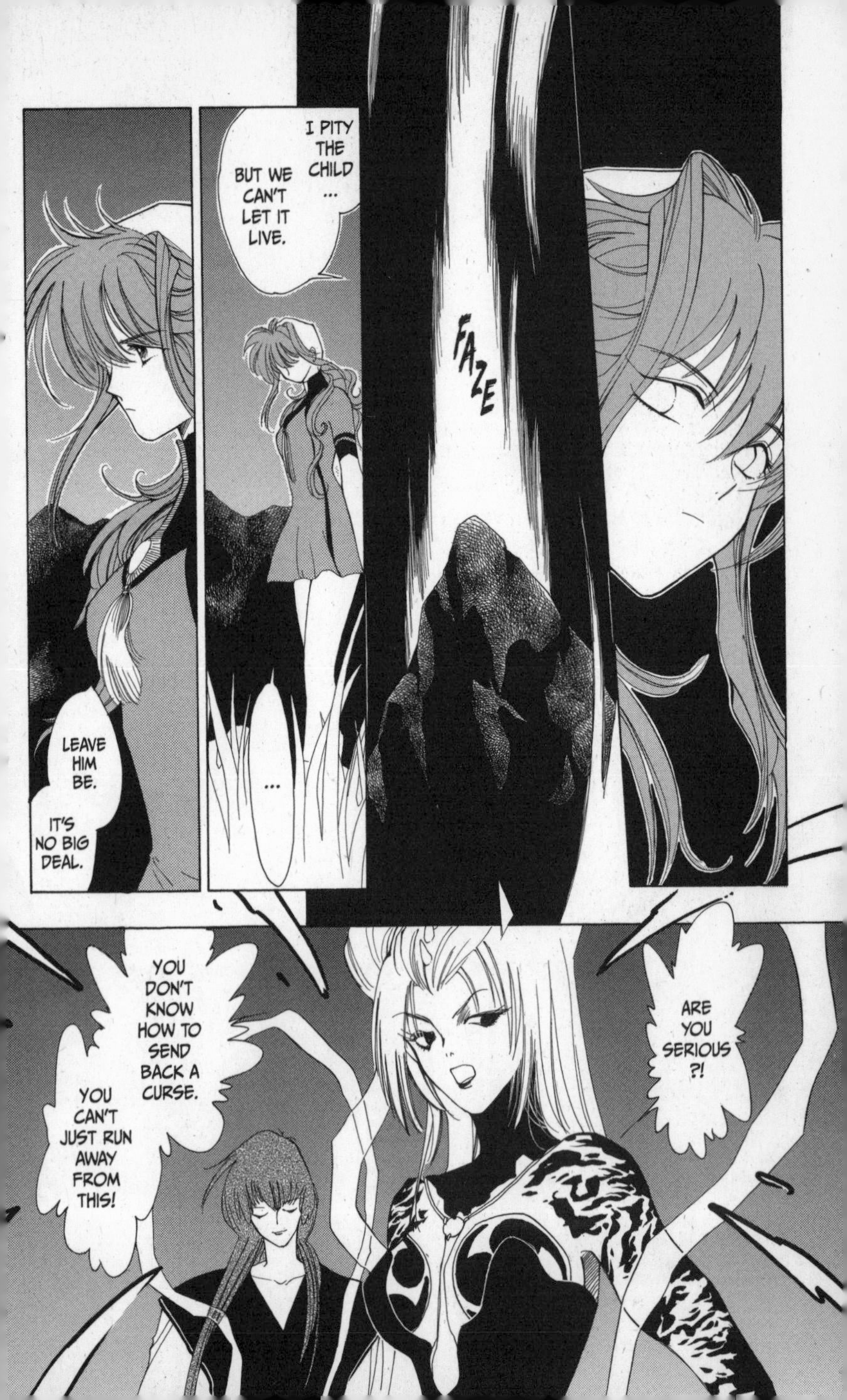
FAZE
I PITY THE CHILD ...
BUT WE CAN'T LET IT LIVE.
...
LEAVE HIM BE.
IT'S NO BIG DEAL.
ARE YOU SERIOUS ?!
YOU DON'T KNOW HOW TO SEND BACK A CURSE.
YOU CAN'T JUST RUN AWAY FROM THIS!

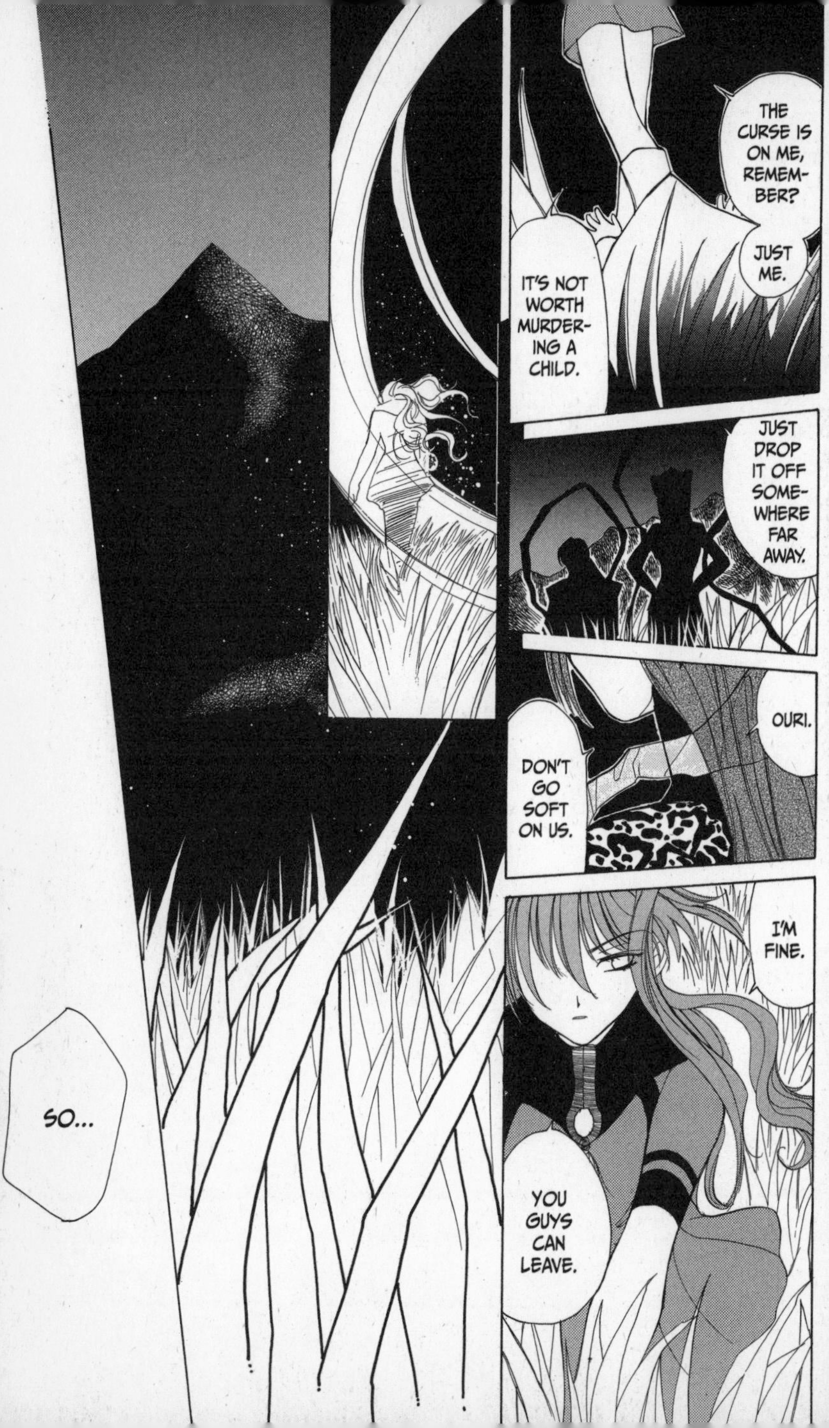
THE CURSE IS ON ME, REMEMBER?
JUST ME.
IT'S NOT WORTH MURDERING A CHILD.
JUST DROP IT OFF SOMEWHERE FAR AWAY.
OURI.
DON'T GO SOFT ON US.
I'M FINE.
YOU GUYS CAN LEAVE.
SO...

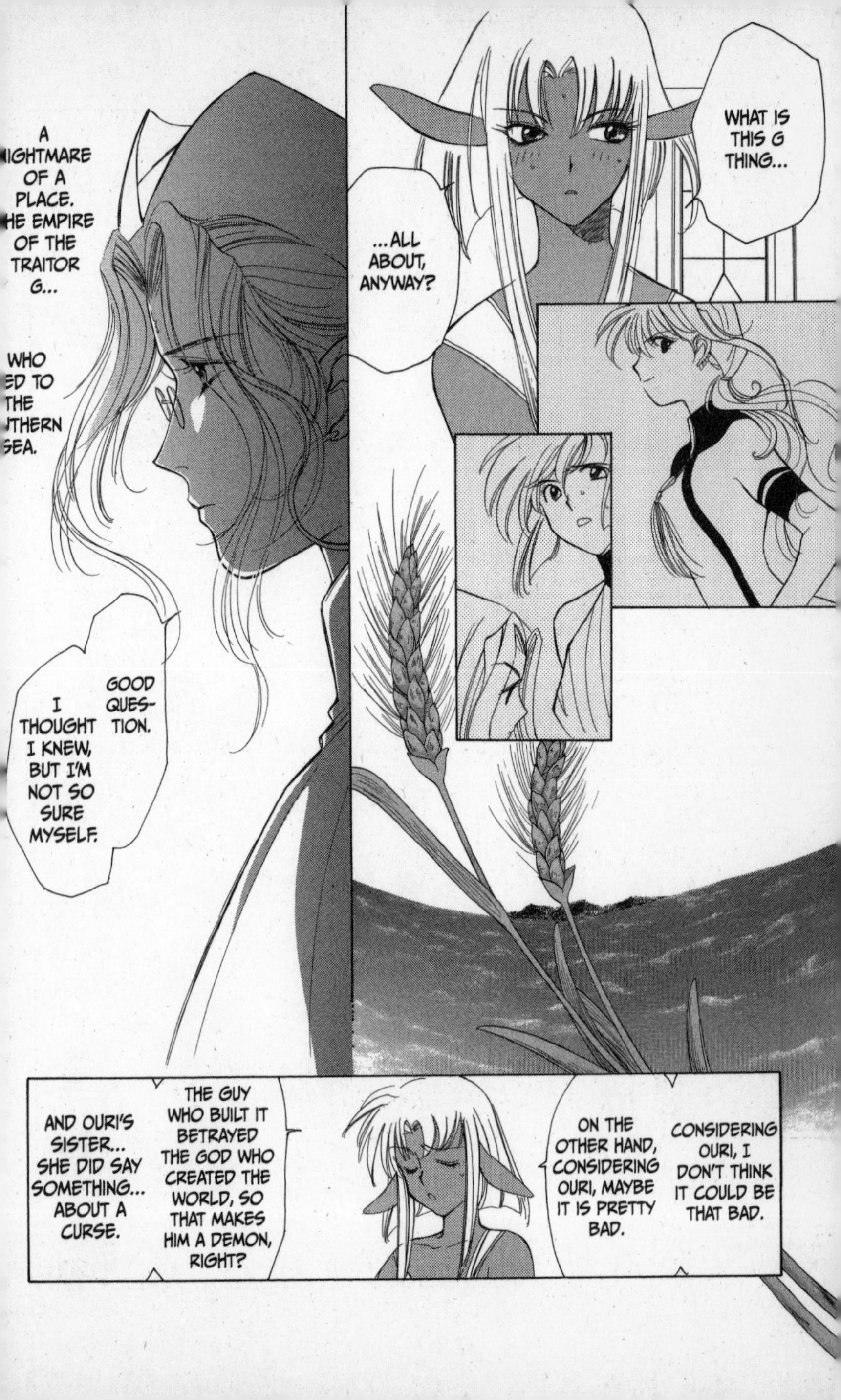
WHAT IS THIS G THING...
...ALL ABOUT, ANYWAY?
A IGHTMARE OF A PLACE. HE EMPIRE OF THE TRAITOR G...
WHO ED TO THE UTHERN SEA.
GOOD QUES- TION.
I THOUGHT I KNEW, BUT I'M NOT SO SURE MYSELF.
CONSIDERING OURI, I DON'T THINK IT COULD BE THAT BAD.
ON THE OTHER HAND, CONSIDERING OURI, MAYBE IT IS PRETTY BAD.
THE GUY WHO BUILT IT BETRAYED THE GOD WHO CREATED THE WORLD, SO THAT MAKES HIM A DEMON, RIGHT?
AND OURI'S SISTER... SHE DID SAY SOMETHING... ABOUT A CURSE.

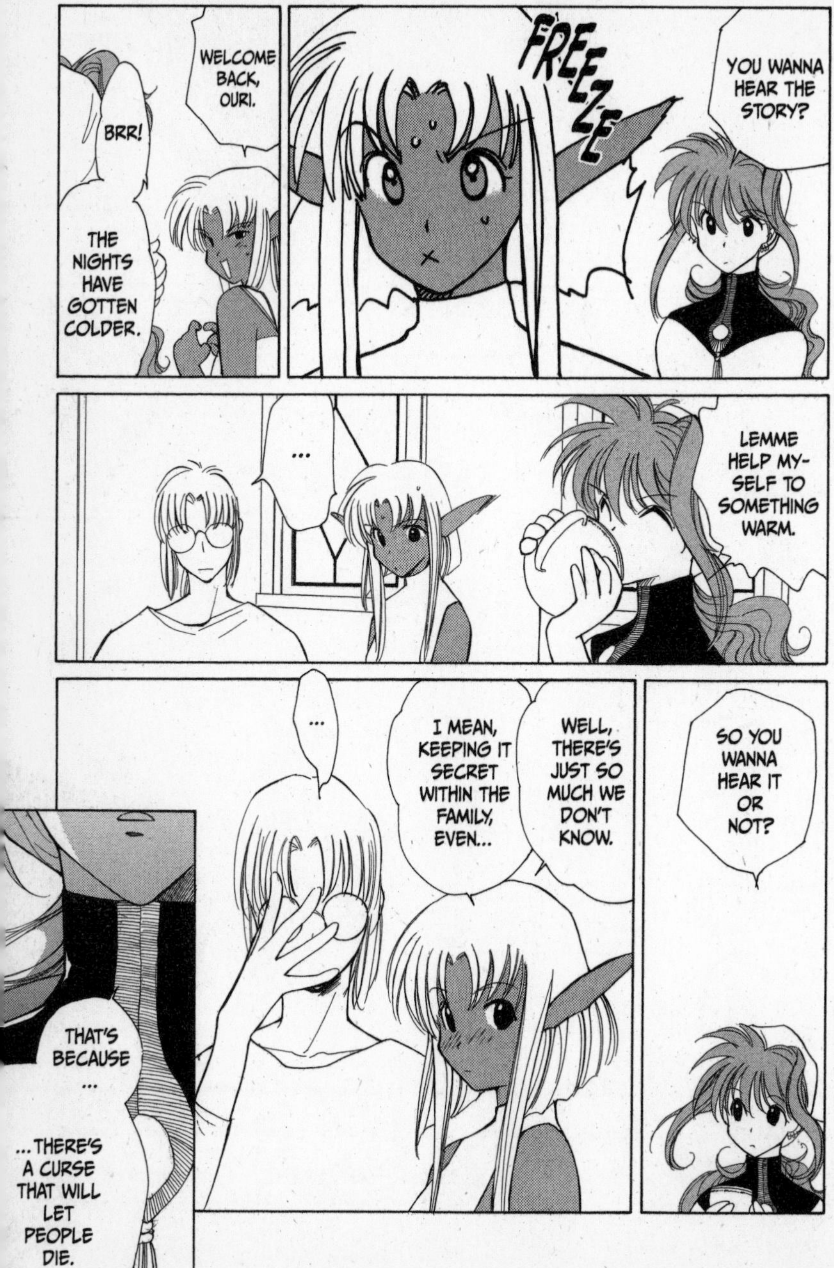
YOU WANNA HEAR THE STORY?
FREEZE
WELCOME BACK, OURI.
BRR!
THE NIGHTS HAVE GOTTEN COLDER.
LEMME HELP MY-SELF TO SOMETHING WARM.
...
SO YOU WANNA HEAR IT OR NOT?
WELL, THERE'S JUST SO MUCH WE DON'T KNOW.
I MEAN, KEEPING IT SECRET WITHIN THE FAMILY, EVEN...
...
THAT'S BECAUSE ...
...THERE'S A CURSE THAT WILL LET PEOPLE DIE.

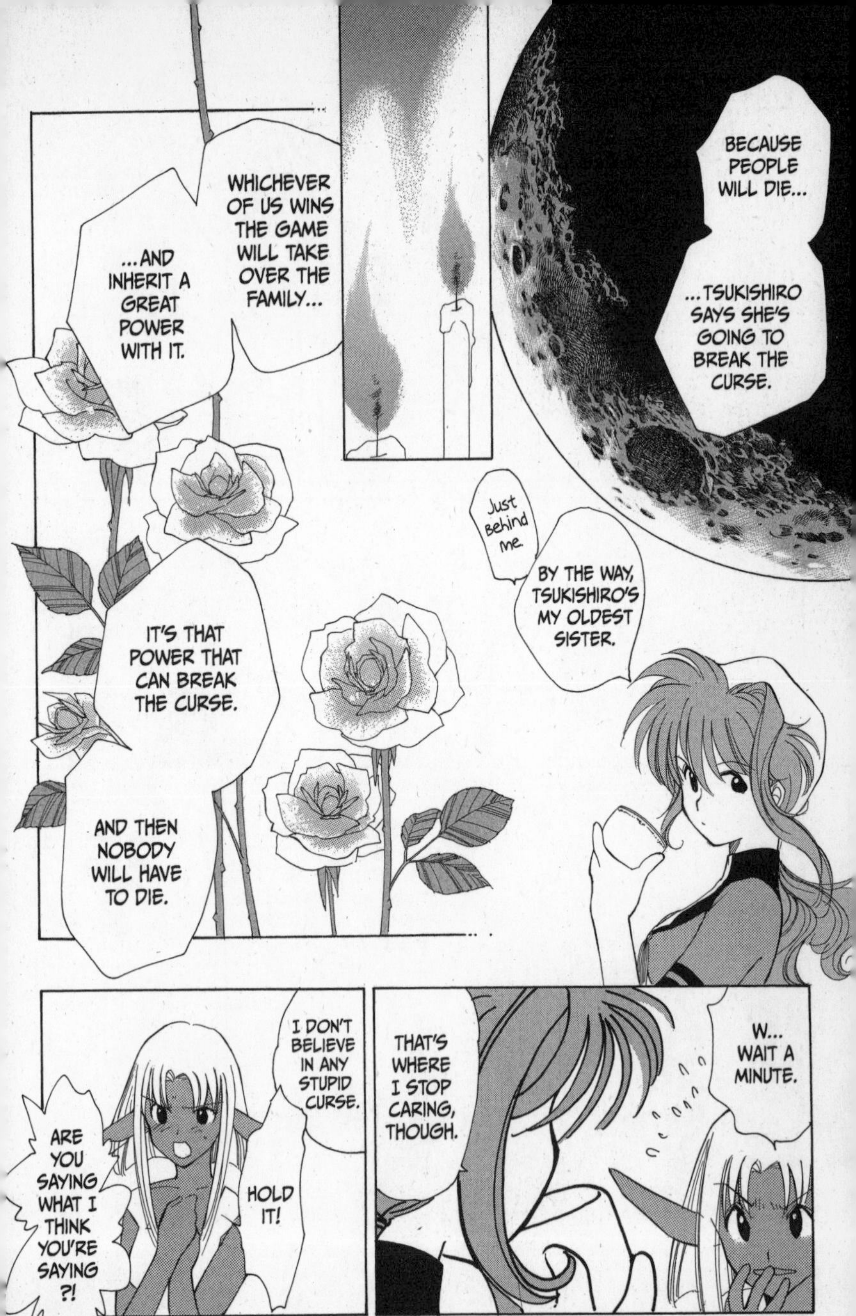

BECAUSE PEOPLE WILL DIE...
...TSUKISHIRO SAYS SHE'S GOING TO BREAK THE CURSE.
WHICHEVER OF US WINS THE GAME WILL TAKE OVER THE FAMILY...
...AND INHERIT A GREAT POWER WITH IT.
IT'S THAT POWER THAT CAN BREAK THE CURSE.
AND THEN NOBODY WILL HAVE TO DIE.
Just behind me.
BY THE WAY, TSUKISHIRO'S MY OLDEST SISTER.
W... WAIT A MINUTE.
THAT'S WHERE I STOP CARING, THOUGH.
I DON'T BELIEVE IN ANY STUPID CURSE.
HOLD IT!
ARE YOU SAYING WHAT I THINK YOU'RE SAYING?!

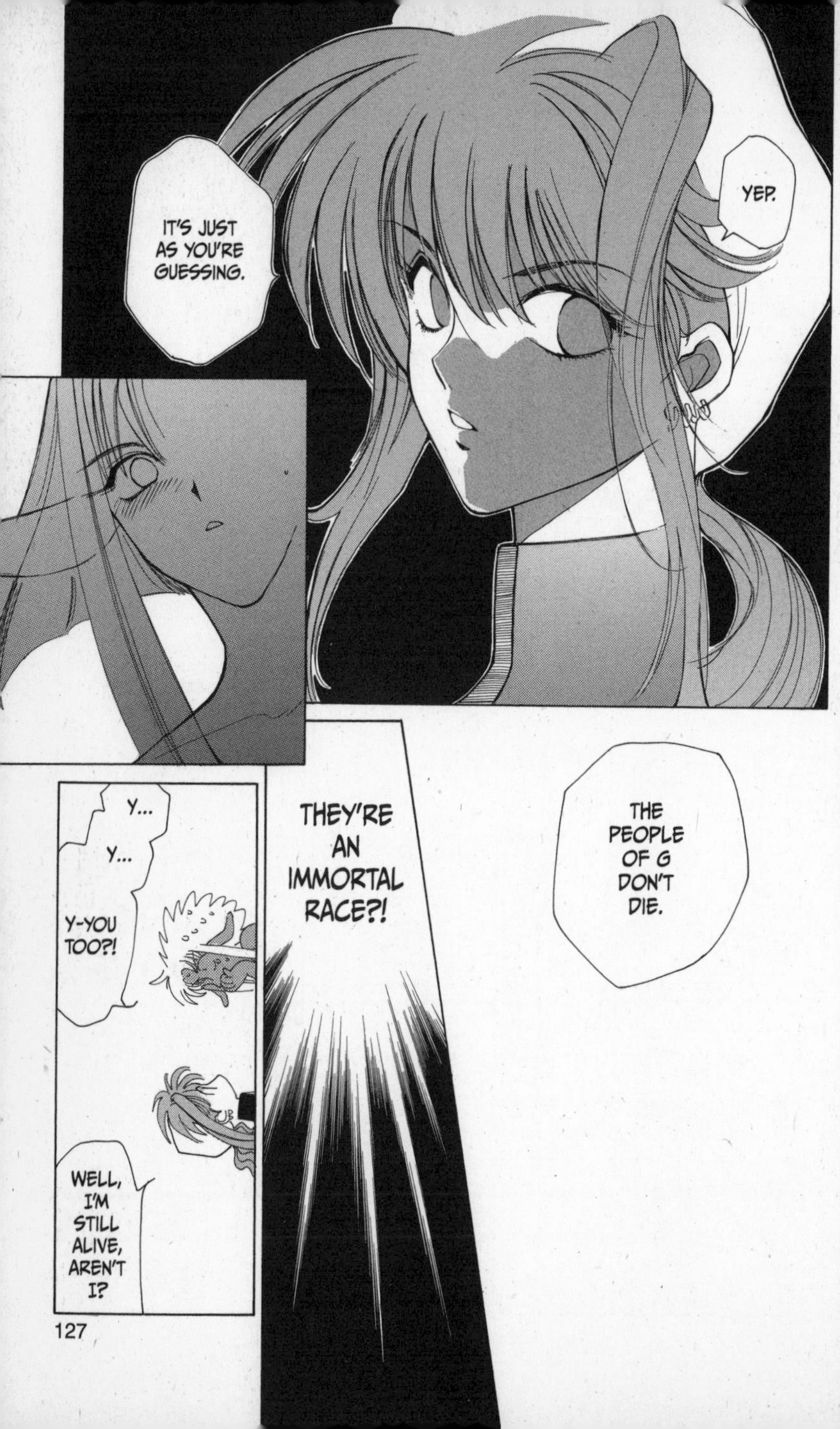
YEP.
IT'S JUST AS YOU'RE GUESSING.
THE PEOPLE OF G DON'T DIE.
THEY'RE AN IMMORTAL RACE?!
Y...
Y...
Y-YOU TOO?!
WELL, I'M STILL ALIVE, AREN'T I?

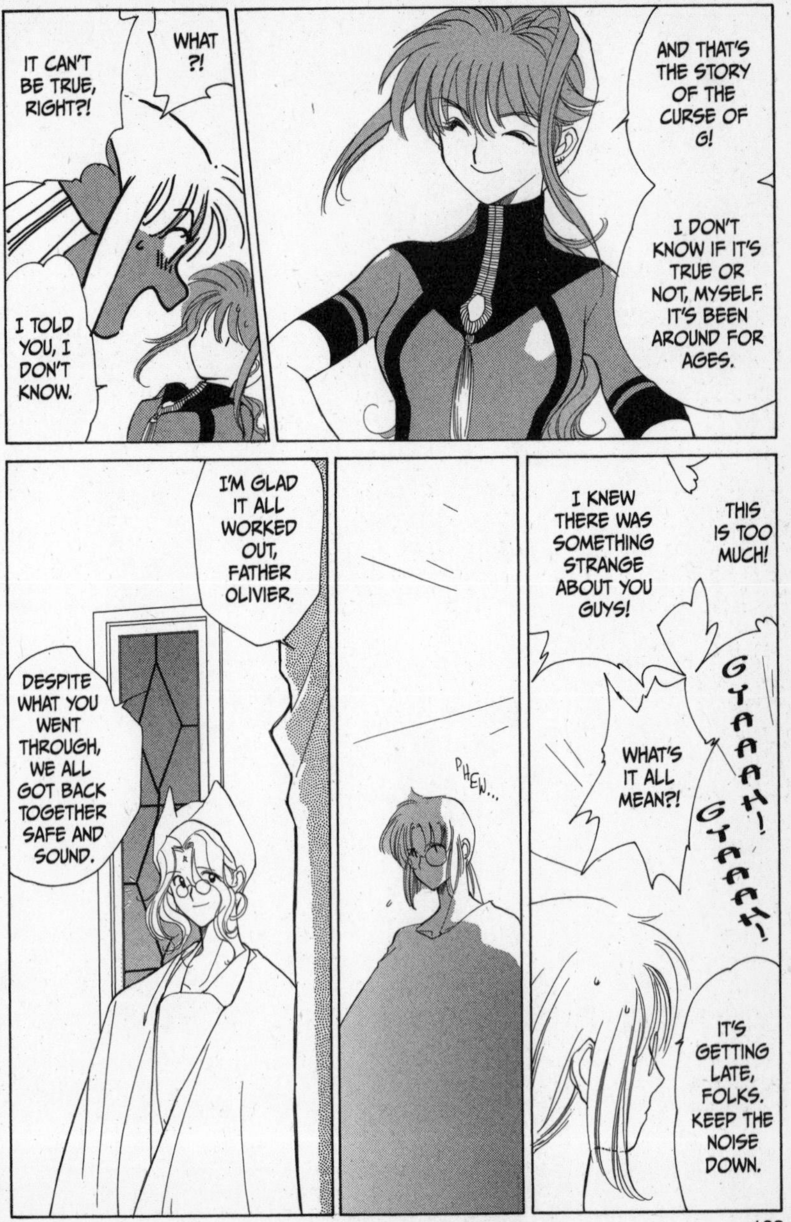
AND THAT'S THE STORY OF THE CURSE OF G!
I DON'T KNOW IF IT'S TRUE OR NOT, MYSELF. IT'S BEEN AROUND FOR AGES.
WHAT ?!
IT CAN'T BE TRUE, RIGHT?!
I TOLD YOU, I DON'T KNOW.
THIS IS TOO MUCH!
I KNEW THERE WAS SOMETHING STRANGE ABOUT YOU GUYS!
GYAAAAH!
GYAAAAH!
WHAT'S IT ALL MEAN?!
IT'S GETTING LATE, FOLKS. KEEP THE NOISE DOWN.
PHEW...
I'M GLAD IT ALL WORKED OUT, FATHER OLIVIER.
DESPITE WHAT YOU WENT THROUGH, WE ALL GOT BACK TOGETHER SAFE AND SOUND.

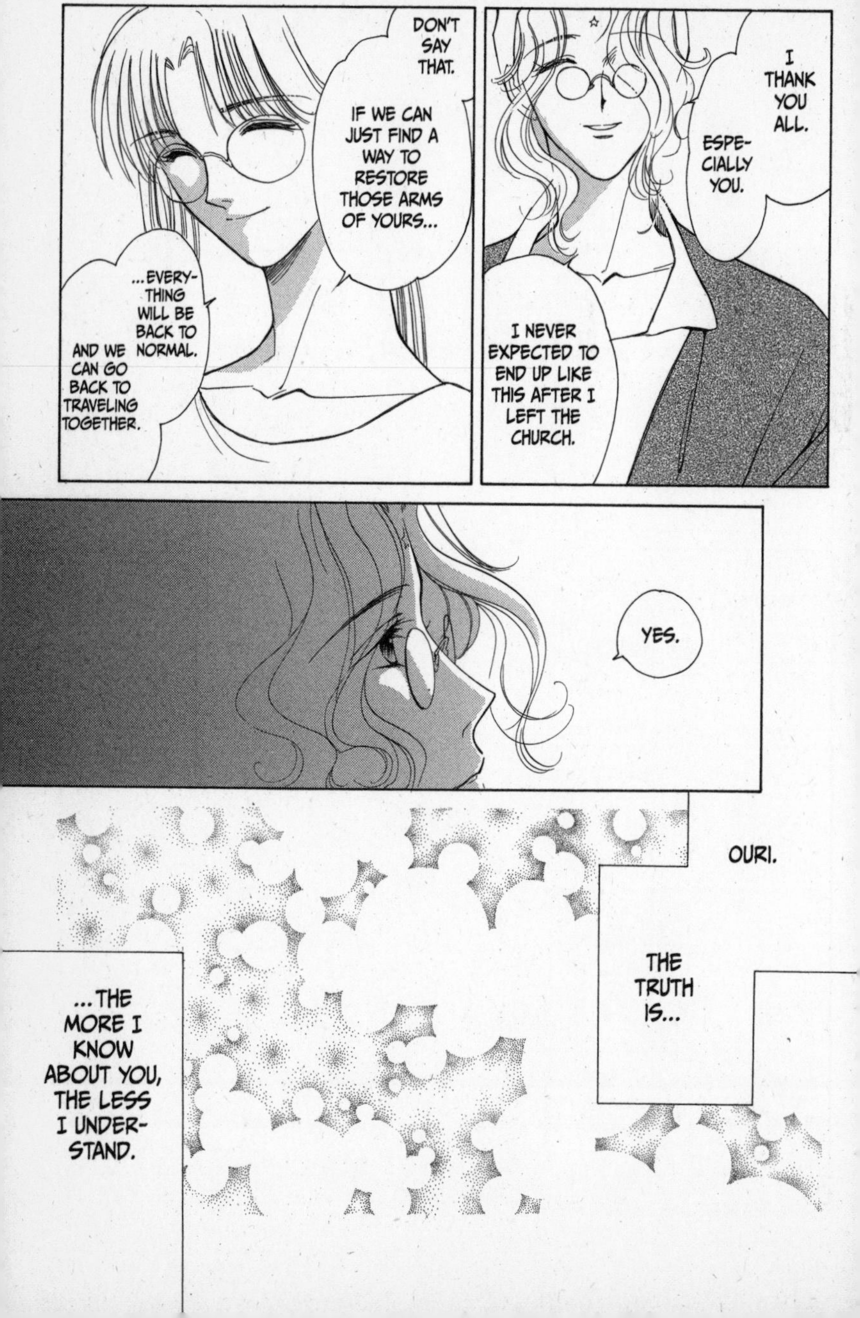
I THANK YOU ALL.
ESPE-CIALLY YOU.
I NEVER EXPECTED TO END UP LIKE THIS AFTER I LEFT THE CHURCH.
DON'T SAY THAT.
IF WE CAN JUST FIND A WAY TO RESTORE THOSE ARMS OF YOURS...
...EVERY-THING WILL BE BACK TO NORMAL.
AND WE CAN GO BACK TO TRAVELING TOGETHER.
YES.
OURI.
THE TRUTH IS...
...THE MORE I KNOW ABOUT YOU, THE LESS I UNDER-STAND.

WHICH
...

There.

EITHER WAY, IT SEEMS LIKE YOU'VE MADE UP YOUR MIND.

...IS THE REAL YOU?

WHAT IS IT?

WHAT'RE YOU STARING AT ME FOR?

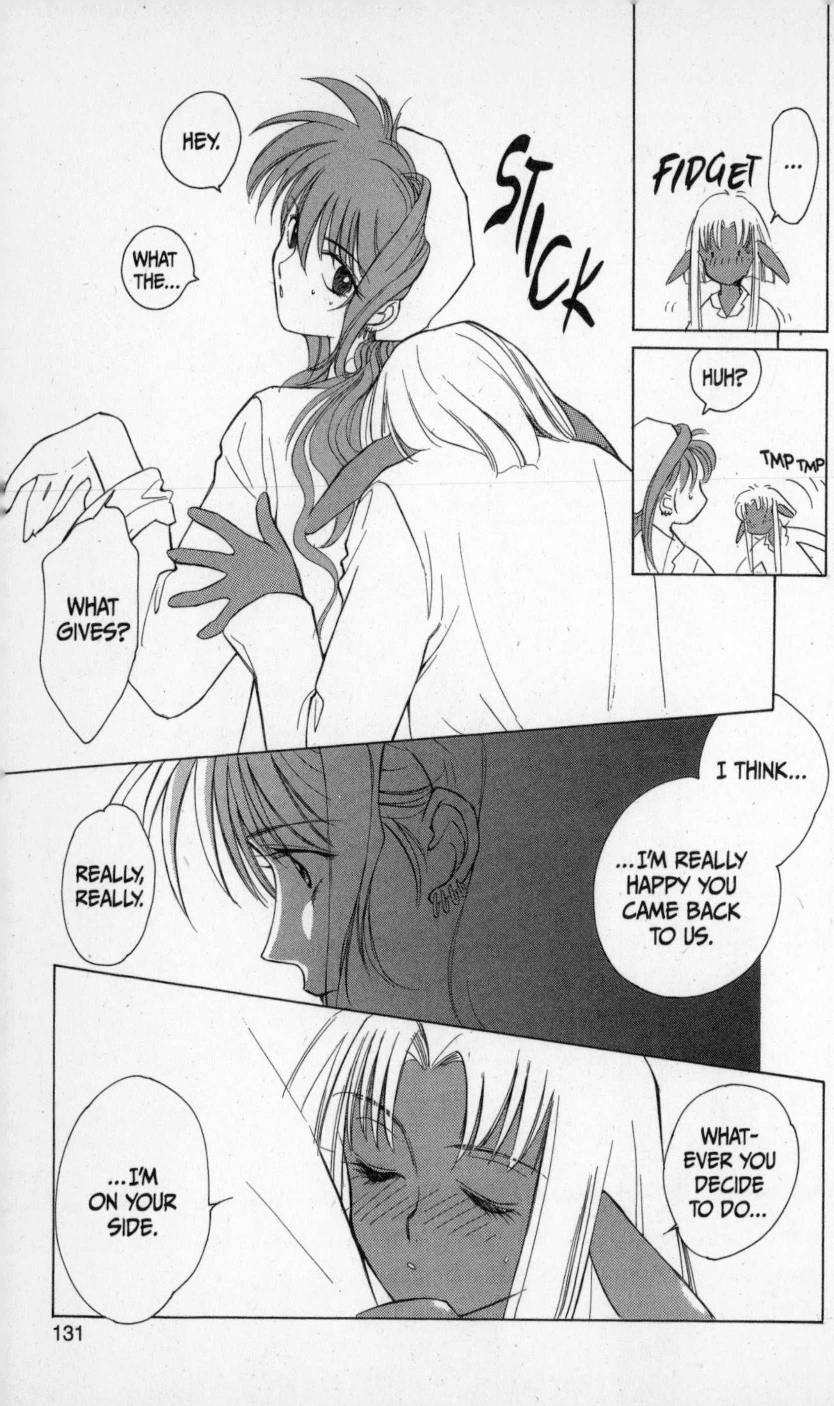
FIDGET
...
HUH?
TMP TMP
STICK
HEY.
WHAT THE...
WHAT GIVES?
I THINK...
...I'M REALLY HAPPY YOU CAME BACK TO US.
REALLY, REALLY.
WHAT-EVER YOU DECIDE TO DO...
...I'M ON YOUR SIDE.

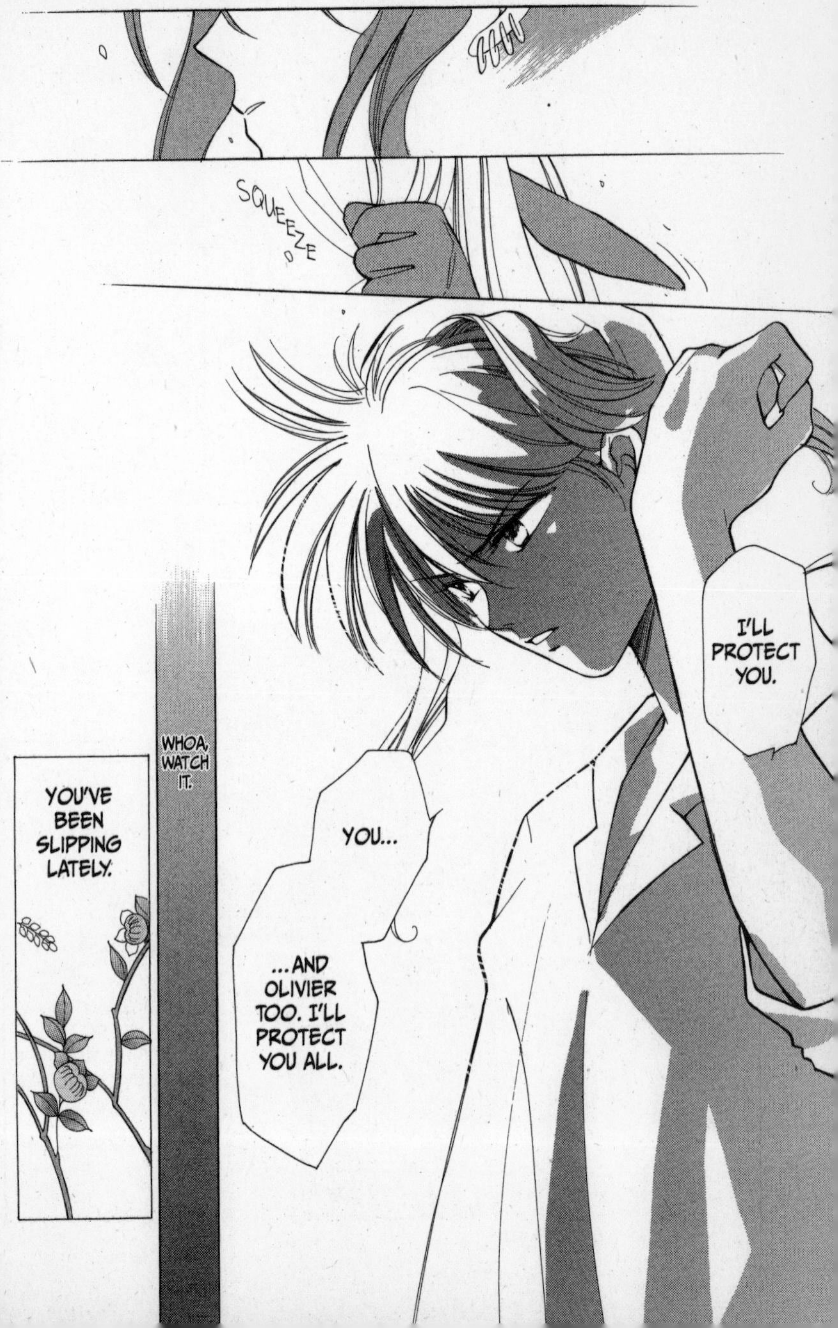
SQUEEEZE
I'LL PROTECT YOU.
YOU...
...AND OLIVIER TOO. I'LL PROTECT YOU ALL.
WHOA, WATCH IT.
YOU'VE BEEN SLIPPING LATELY.

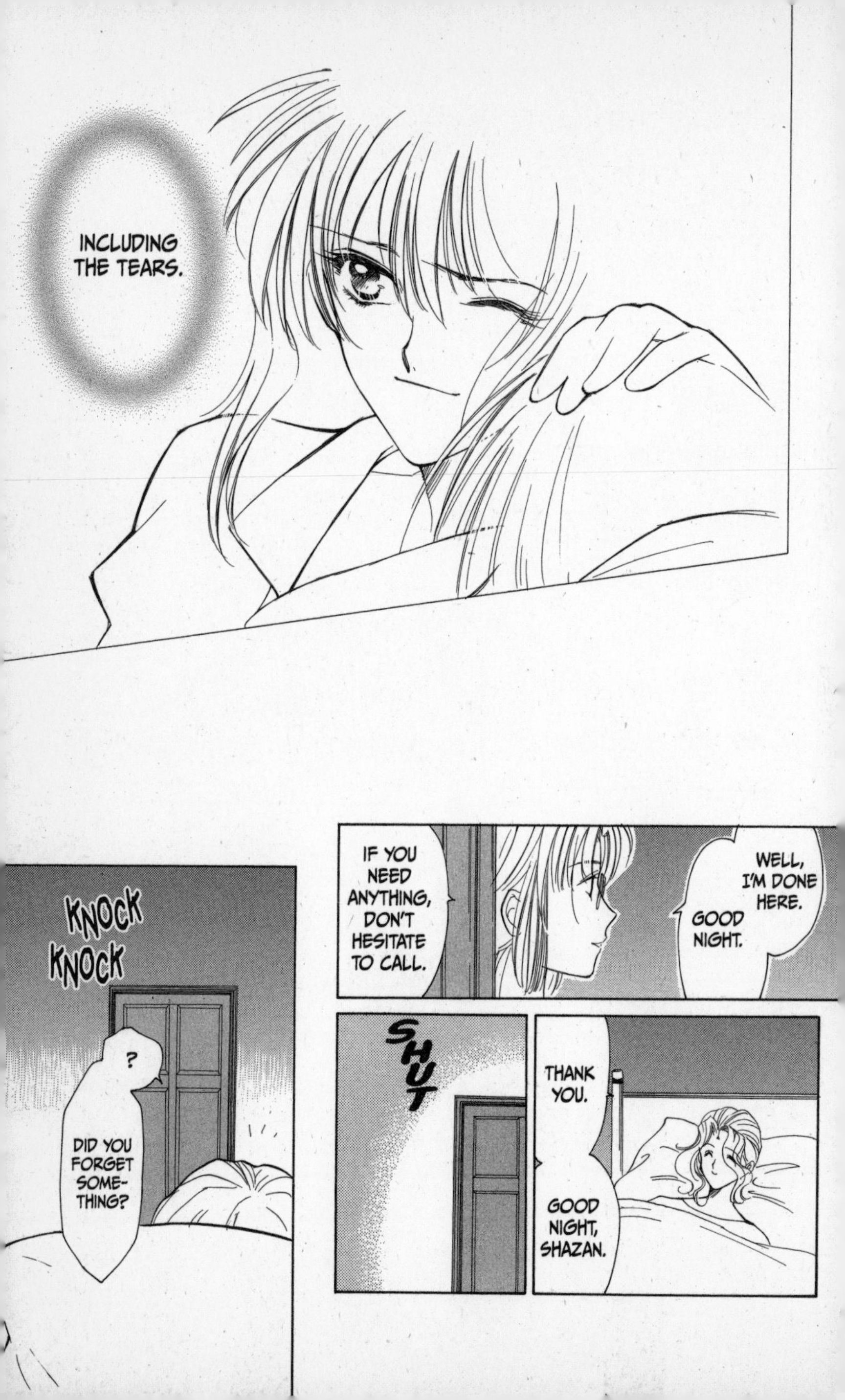
INCLUDING THE TEARS.
WELL, I'M DONE HERE.
GOOD NIGHT.
IF YOU NEED ANYTHING, DON'T HESITATE TO CALL.
THANK YOU.
GOOD NIGHT, SHAZAN.
SHUT
KNOCK KNOCK
?
DID YOU FORGET SOME-THING?

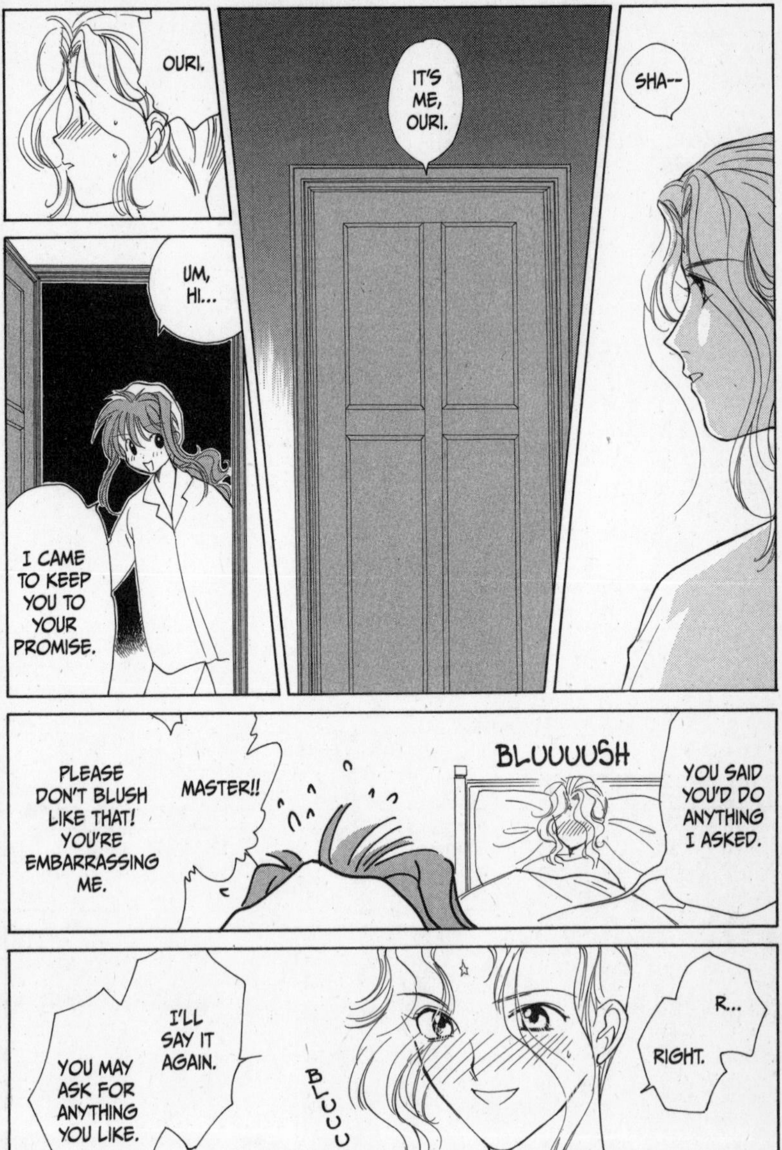
SHA--
IT'S ME, OURI.
OURI.
UM, HI...
I CAME TO KEEP YOU TO YOUR PROMISE.
YOU SAID YOU'D DO ANYTHING I ASKED.
BLUUUUSH
MASTER!!
PLEASE DON'T BLUSH LIKE THAT! YOU'RE EMBARRASSING ME.
R...
RIGHT.
BLUUUSH
I'LL SAY IT AGAIN.
YOU MAY ASK FOR ANYTHING YOU LIKE.

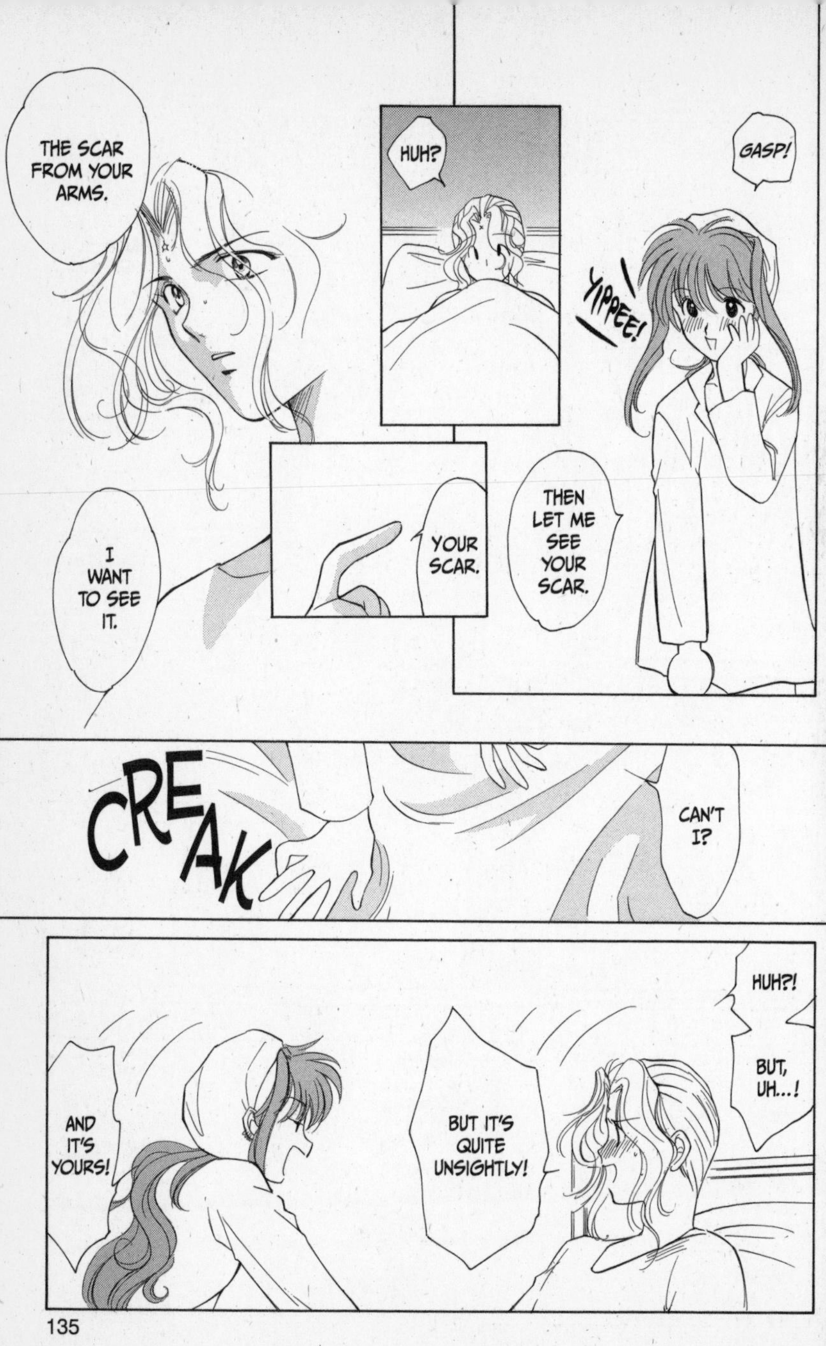
GASP!
YIPPEE!
THEN LET ME SEE YOUR SCAR.
HUH?
YOUR SCAR.
THE SCAR FROM YOUR ARMS.
I WANT TO SEE IT.
CAN'T I?
CREAK
HUH?!
BUT, UH...!
BUT IT'S QUITE UNSIGHTLY!
AND IT'S YOURS!

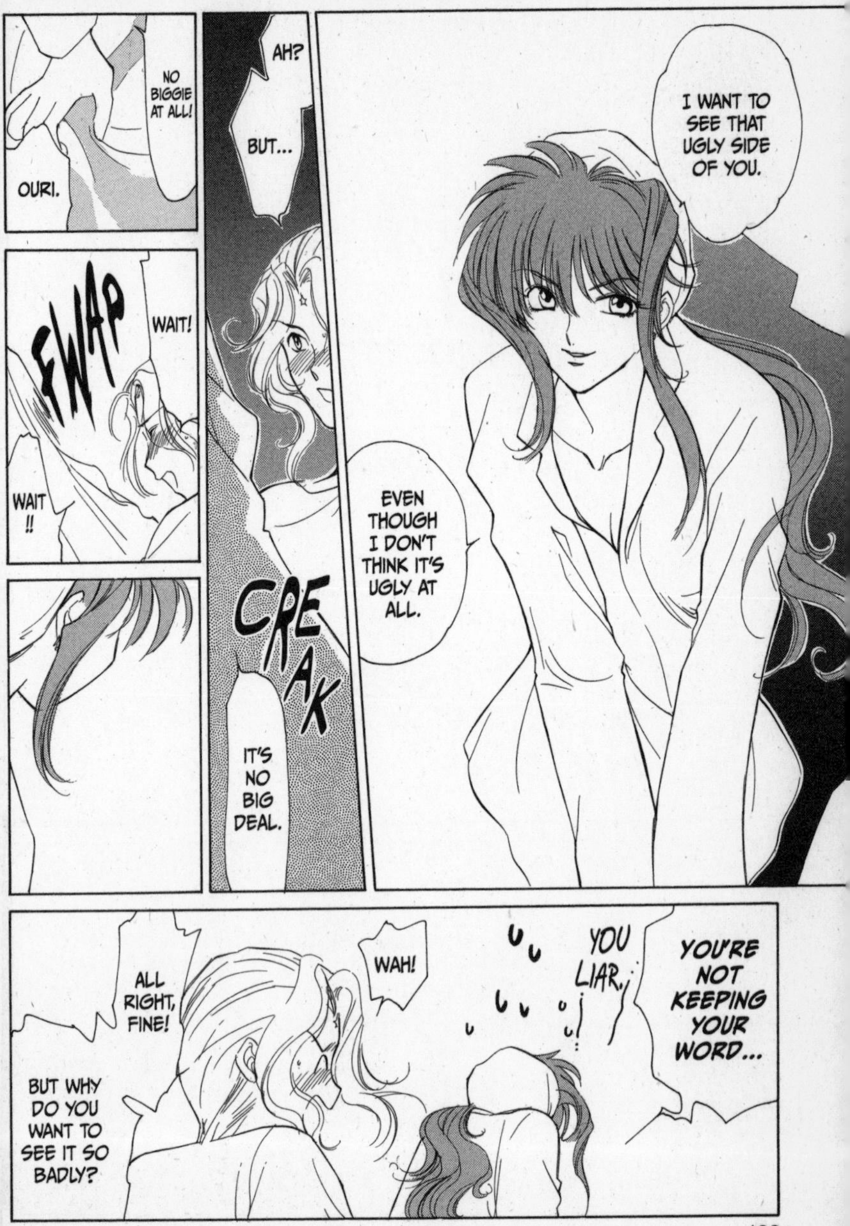
I WANT TO SEE THAT UGLY SIDE OF YOU.
EVEN THOUGH I DON'T THINK IT'S UGLY AT ALL.
AH?
BUT...
CREAK
IT'S NO BIG DEAL.
NO BIGGIE AT ALL!
OURI.
FWAP
WAIT!
WAIT !!
YOU'RE NOT KEEPING YOUR WORD...
YOU LIAR.
WAH!
ALL RIGHT, FINE!
BUT WHY DO YOU WANT TO SEE IT SO BADLY?

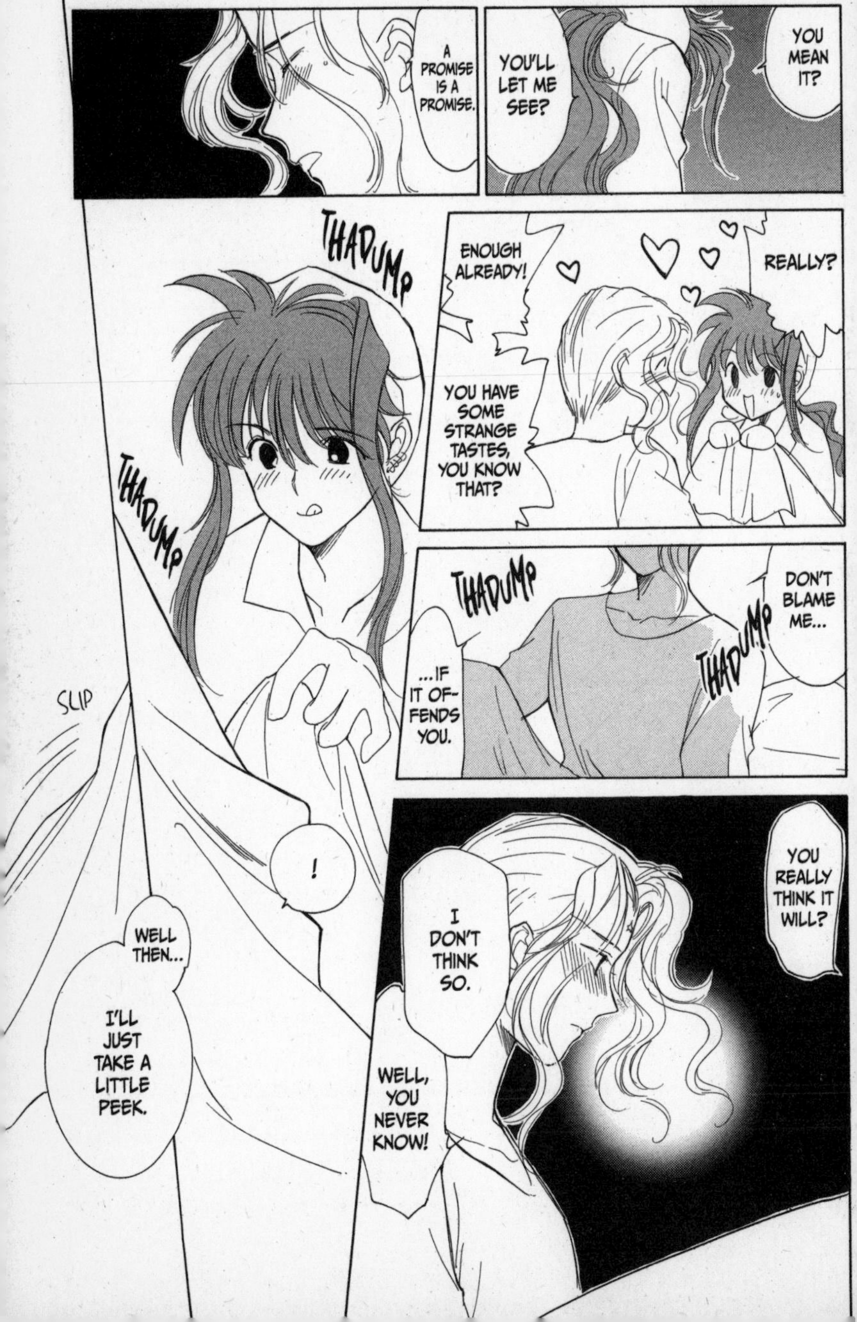
YOU MEAN IT?
YOU'LL LET ME SEE?
A PROMISE IS A PROMISE.
REALLY?
ENOUGH ALREADY!
YOU HAVE SOME STRANGE TASTES, YOU KNOW THAT?
DON'T BLAME ME...
THADUMP
THADUMP
...IF IT OF-FENDS YOU.
YOU REALLY THINK IT WILL?
I DON'T THINK SO.
WELL, YOU NEVER KNOW!
THADUMP
THADUMP
SLIP
!
WELL THEN...
I'LL JUST TAKE A LITTLE PEEK.

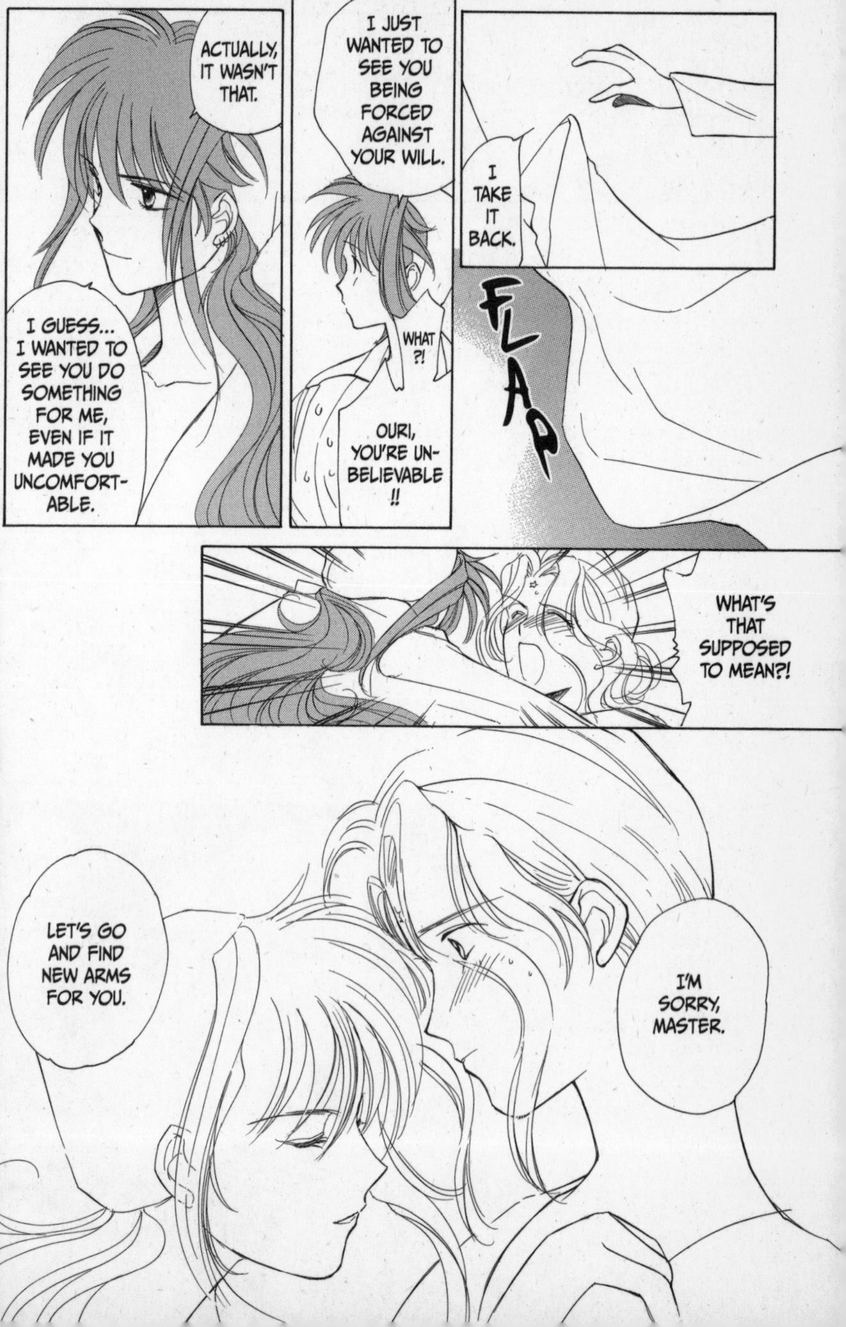
I TAKE IT BACK.
I JUST WANTED TO SEE YOU BEING FORCED AGAINST YOUR WILL.
WHAT ?!
OURI, YOU'RE UN-BELIEVABLE !!
ACTUALLY, IT WASN'T THAT.
I GUESS... I WANTED TO SEE YOU DO SOMETHING FOR ME, EVEN IF IT MADE YOU UNCOMFORT-ABLE.
FLAP
WHAT'S THAT SUPPOSED TO MEAN?!
I'M SORRY, MASTER.
LET'S GO AND FIND NEW ARMS FOR YOU.

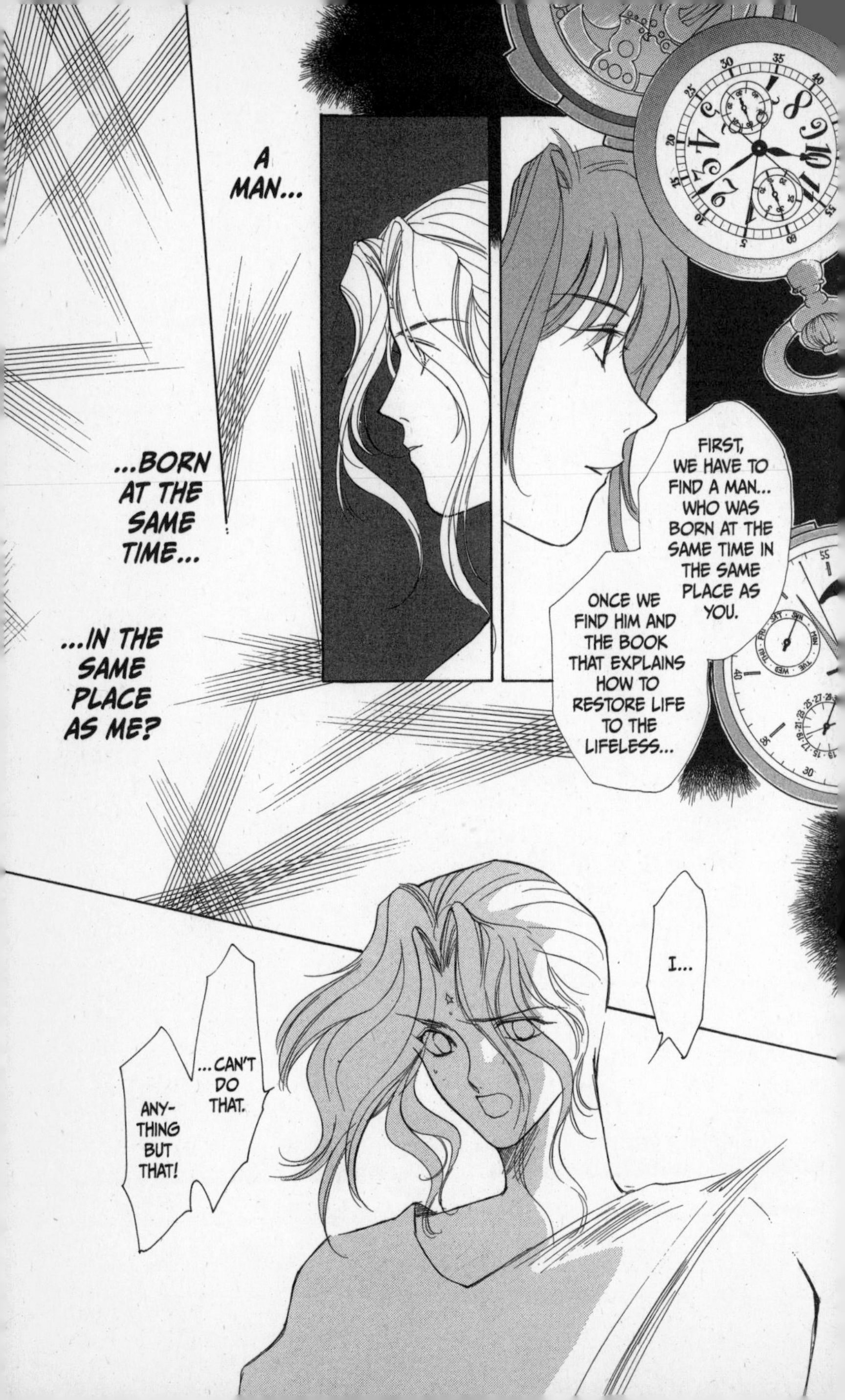
FIRST, WE HAVE TO FIND A MAN... WHO WAS BORN AT THE SAME TIME IN THE SAME PLACE AS YOU.
ONCE WE FIND HIM AND THE BOOK THAT EXPLAINS HOW TO RESTORE LIFE TO THE LIFELESS...
A MAN...
...BORN AT THE SAME TIME...
...IN THE SAME PLACE AS ME?
I...
...CAN'T DO THAT.
ANYTHING BUT THAT!

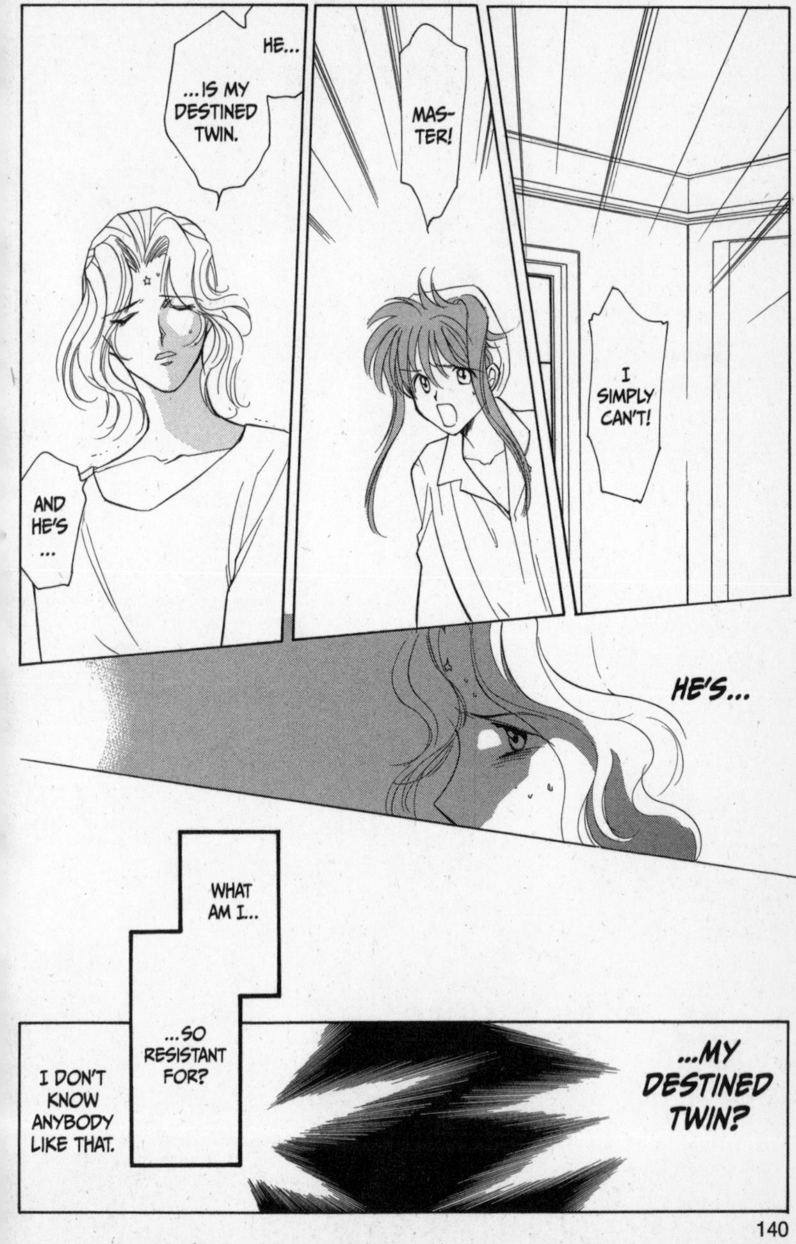
I SIMPLY CAN'T!
MAS-TER!
HE...
...IS MY DESTINED TWIN.
AND HE'S ...
HE'S...
...MY DESTINED TWIN?
WHAT AM I...
...SO RESISTANT FOR?
I DON'T KNOW ANYBODY LIKE THAT.

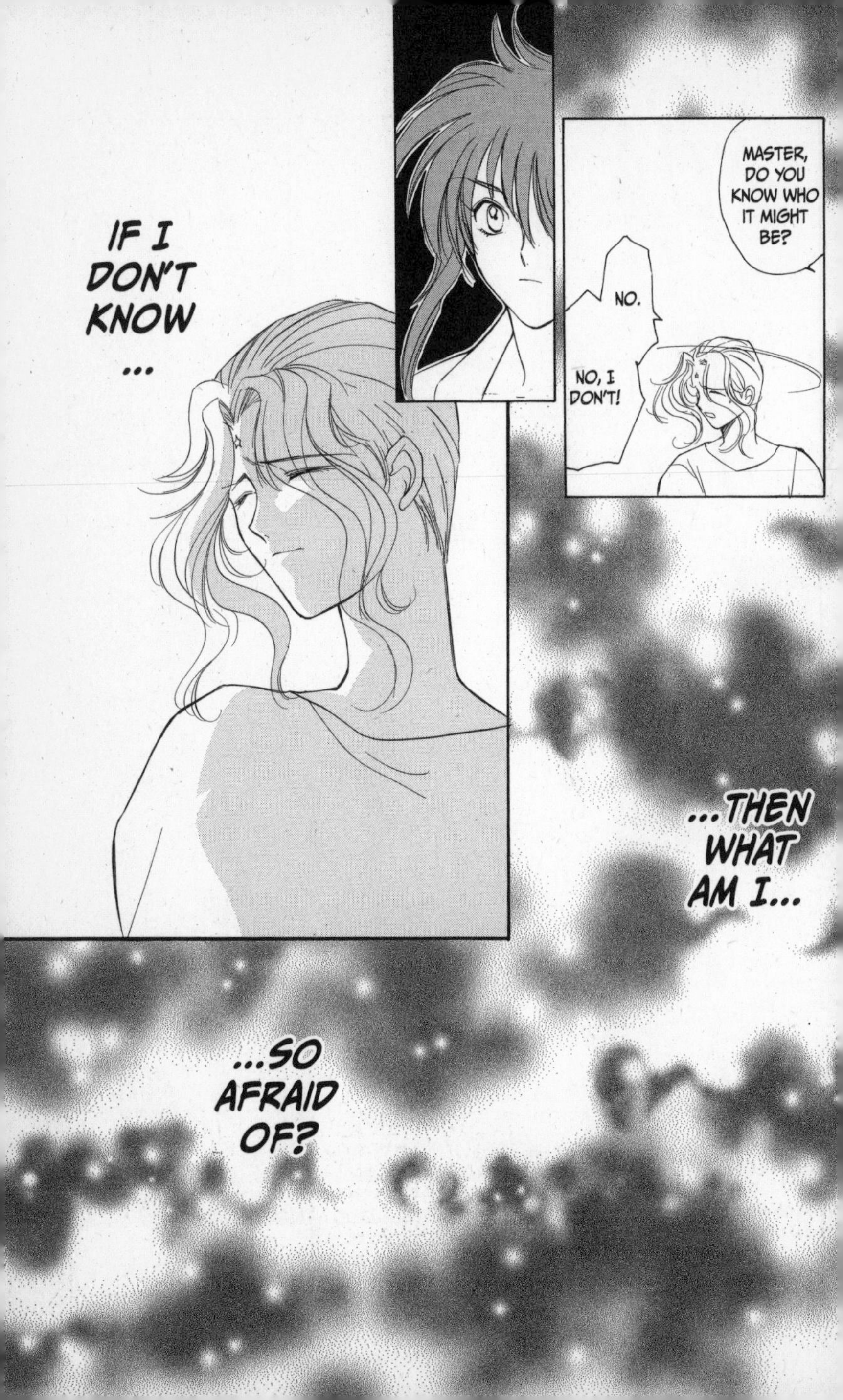
MASTER, DO YOU KNOW WHO IT MIGHT BE?
NO.
NO, I DON'T!
IF I DON'T KNOW ...
...THEN WHAT AM I...
...SO AFRAID OF?

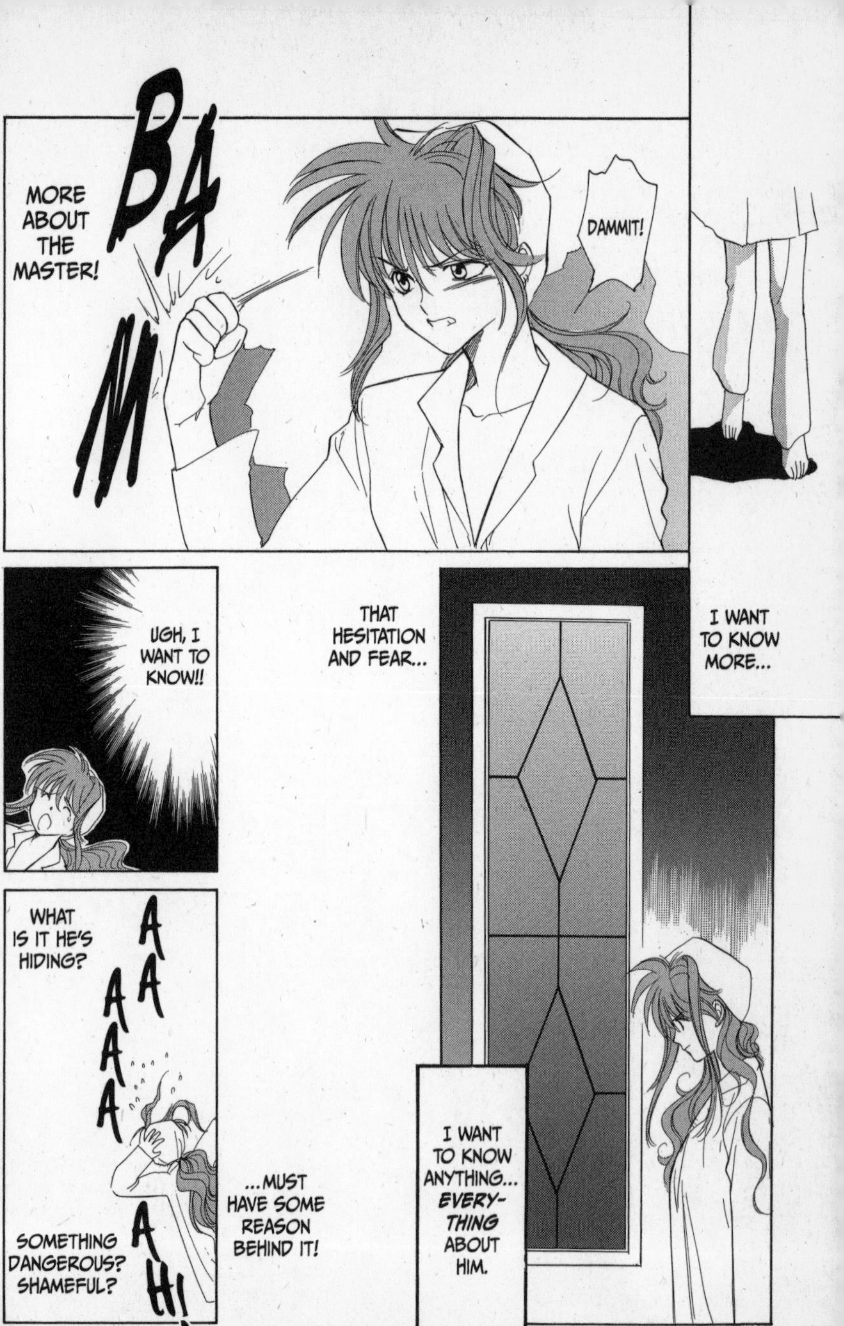
I WANT TO KNOW MORE...
DAMMIT!
BAM
MORE ABOUT THE MASTER!
THAT HESITATION AND FEAR...
...MUST HAVE SOME REASON BEHIND IT!
I WANT TO KNOW ANYTHING... *EVERYTHING* ABOUT HIM.
UGH, I WANT TO KNOW!!
WHAT IS IT HE'S HIDING?
AAAAAAH!
SOMETHING DANGEROUS? SHAMEFUL?

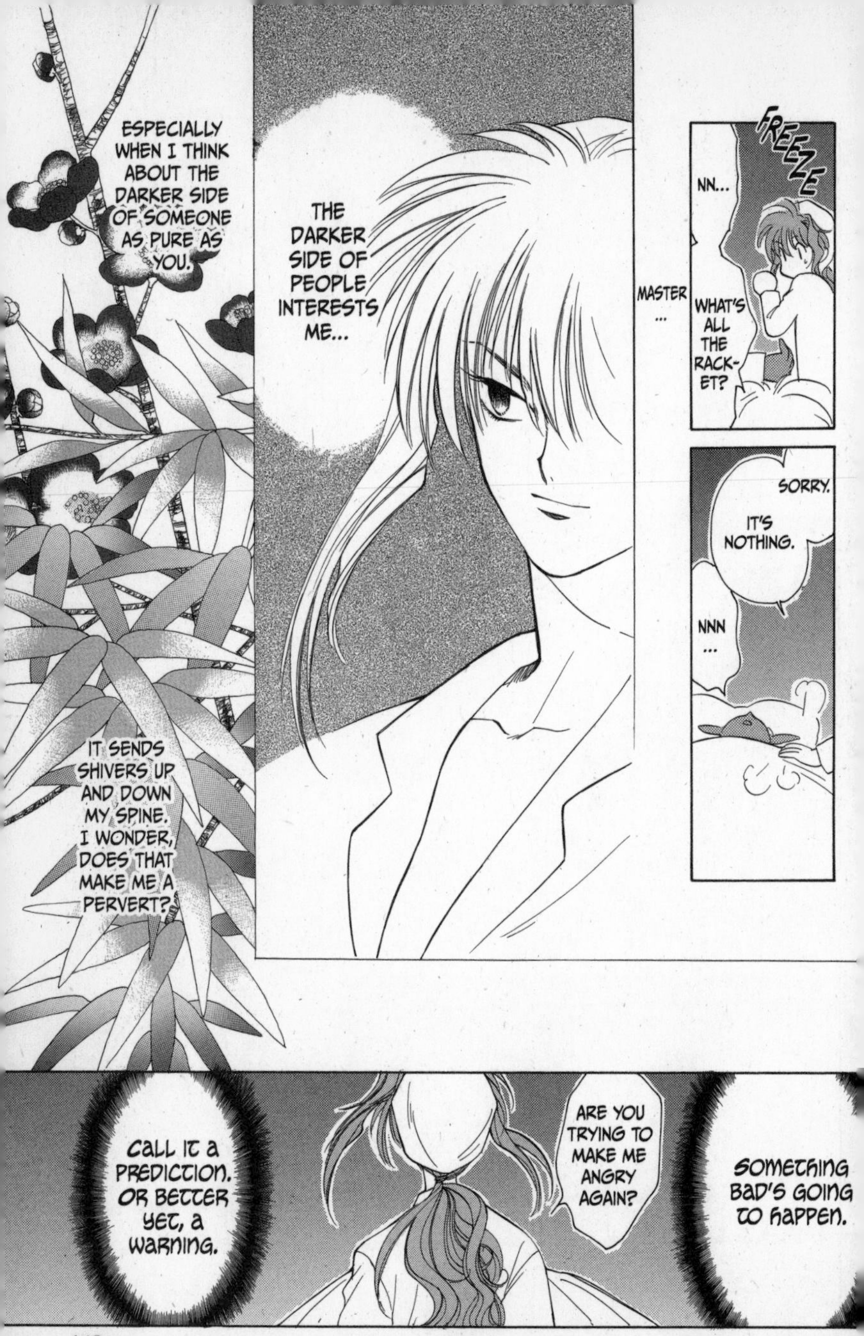
FREEZE
NN...
WHAT'S ALL THE RACK-ET?
MASTER ...
SORRY.
IT'S NOTHING.
NNN ...
THE DARKER SIDE OF PEOPLE INTERESTS ME...
ESPECIALLY WHEN I THINK ABOUT THE DARKER SIDE OF SOMEONE AS PURE AS YOU.
IT SENDS SHIVERS UP AND DOWN MY SPINE. I WONDER, DOES THAT MAKE ME A PERVERT?
SOMETHING BAD'S GOING TO HAPPEN.
ARE YOU TRYING TO MAKE ME ANGRY AGAIN?
CALL IT A PREDICTION. OR BETTER YET, A WARNING.

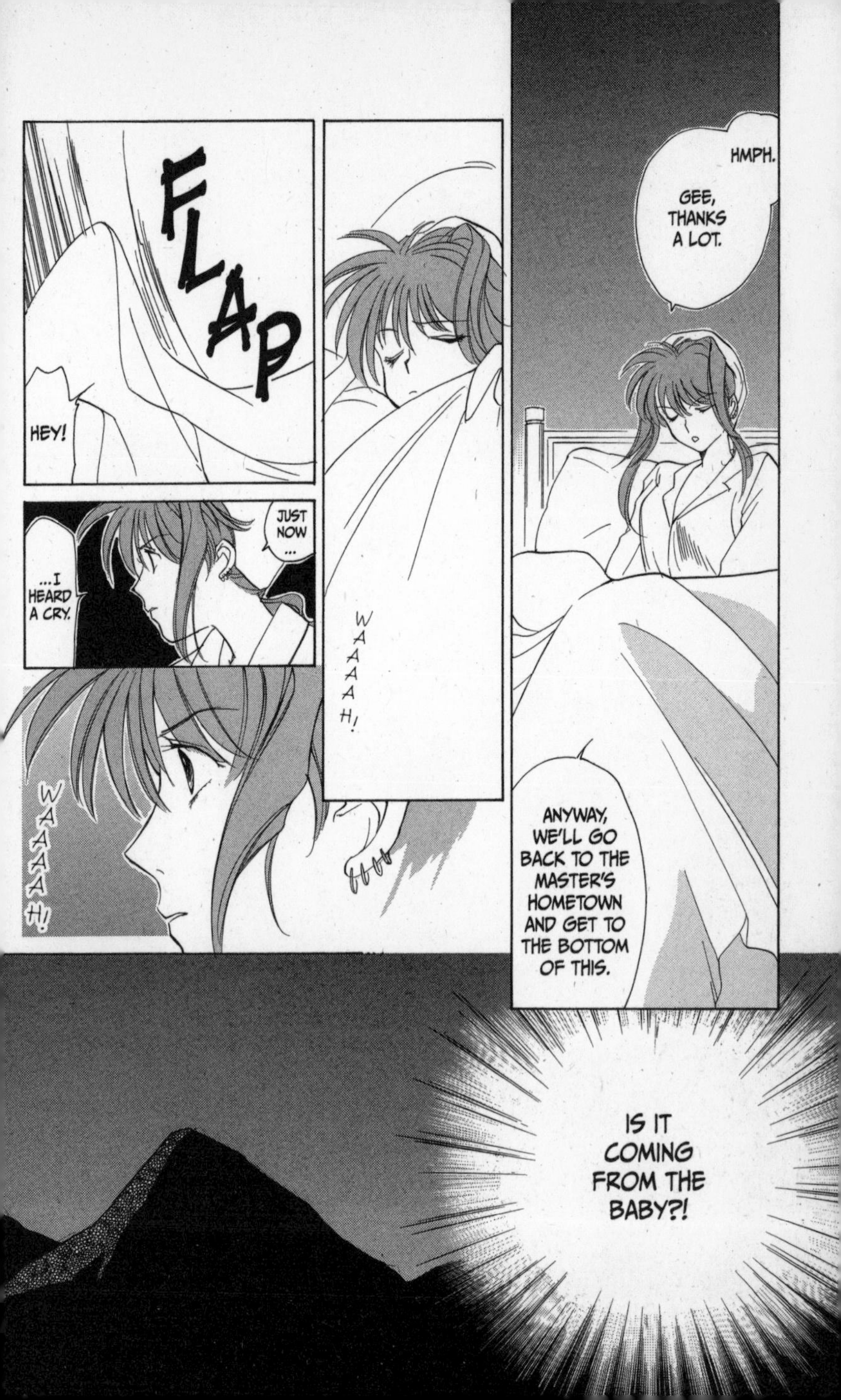
HMPH.
GEE, THANKS A LOT.
ANYWAY, WE'LL GO BACK TO THE MASTER'S HOMETOWN AND GET TO THE BOTTOM OF THIS.
WAAAAAH!
FLAP
HEY!
JUST NOW ...
...I HEARD A CRY.
WAAAAAH!
IS IT COMING FROM THE BABY?!

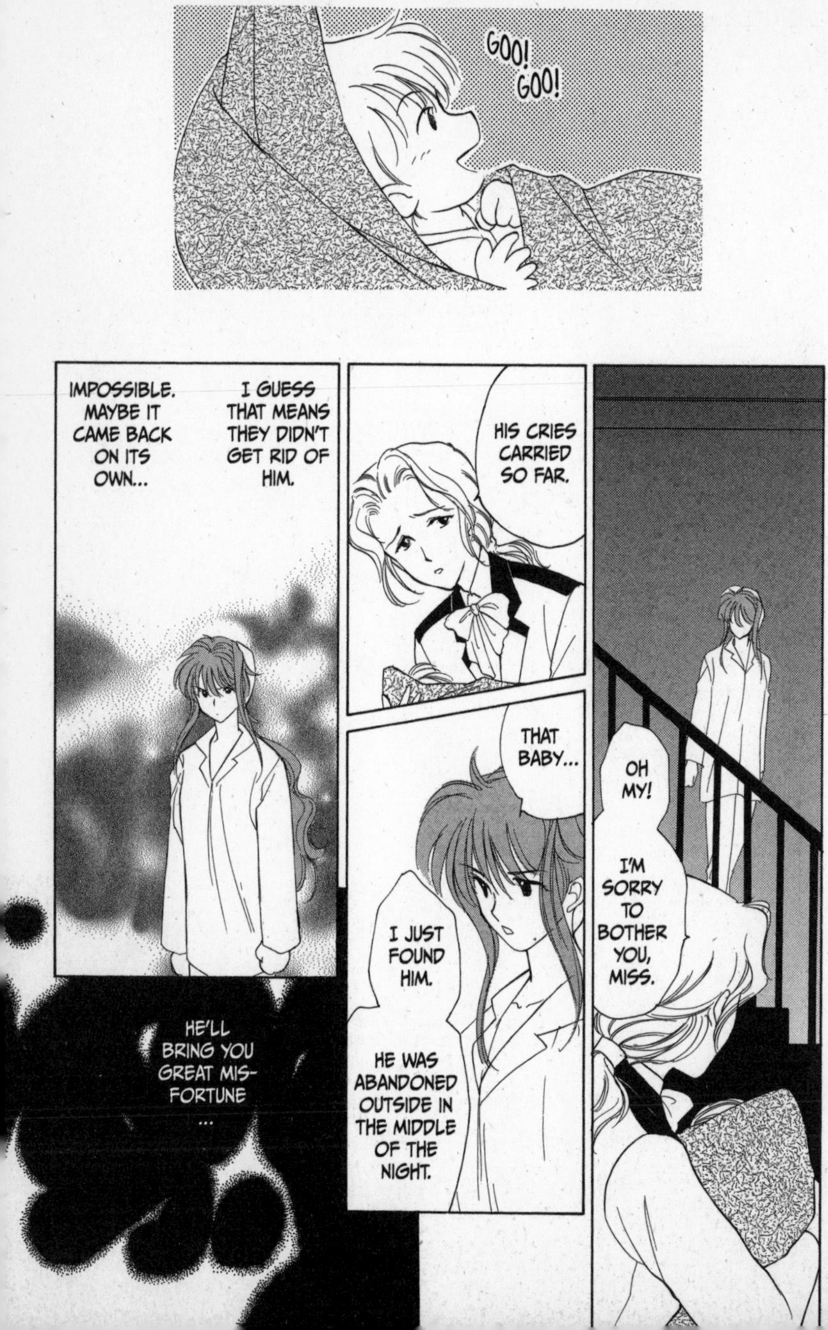
GOO! GOO!
OH MY!
I'M SORRY TO BOTHER YOU, MISS.
HIS CRIES CARRIED SO FAR.
THAT BABY...
I JUST FOUND HIM.
HE WAS ABANDONED OUTSIDE IN THE MIDDLE OF THE NIGHT.
I GUESS THAT MEANS THEY DIDN'T GET RID OF HIM.
IMPOSSIBLE. MAYBE IT CAME BACK ON ITS OWN...
HE'LL BRING YOU GREAT MIS-FORTUNE ...

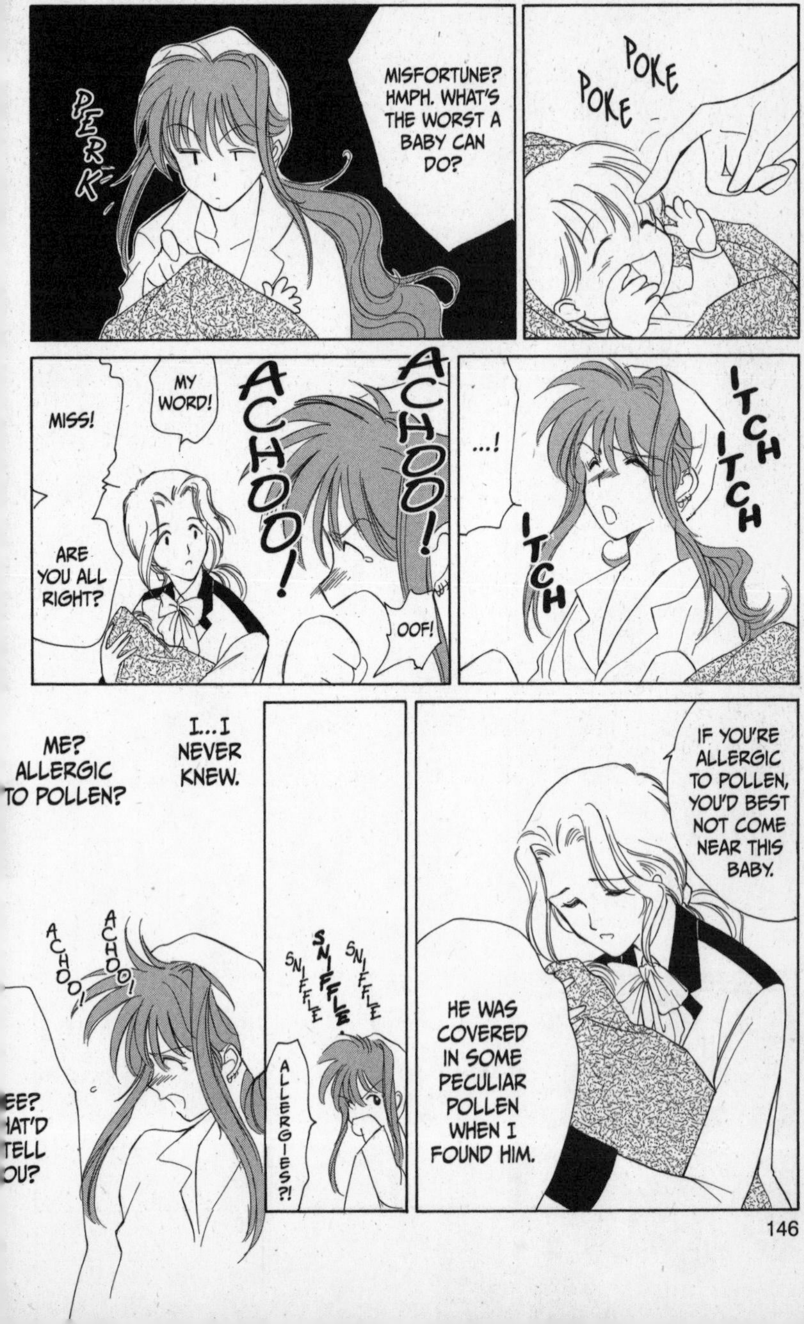
POKE POKE
PERK
MISFORTUNE? HMPH. WHAT'S THE WORST A BABY CAN DO?
ITCH ITCH
...!
ITCH
ACHOO!
ACHOO!
MY WORD!
MISS!
ARE YOU ALL RIGHT?
OOF!
IF YOU'RE ALLERGIC TO POLLEN, YOU'D BEST NOT COME NEAR THIS BABY.
HE WAS COVERED IN SOME PECULIAR POLLEN WHEN I FOUND HIM.
SNIFFLE SNIFFLE SNIFFLE
ALLERGIES?!
I...I NEVER KNEW.
ME? ALLERGIC TO POLLEN?
ACHOO! ACHOO!
EE? HAT'D TELL OU?

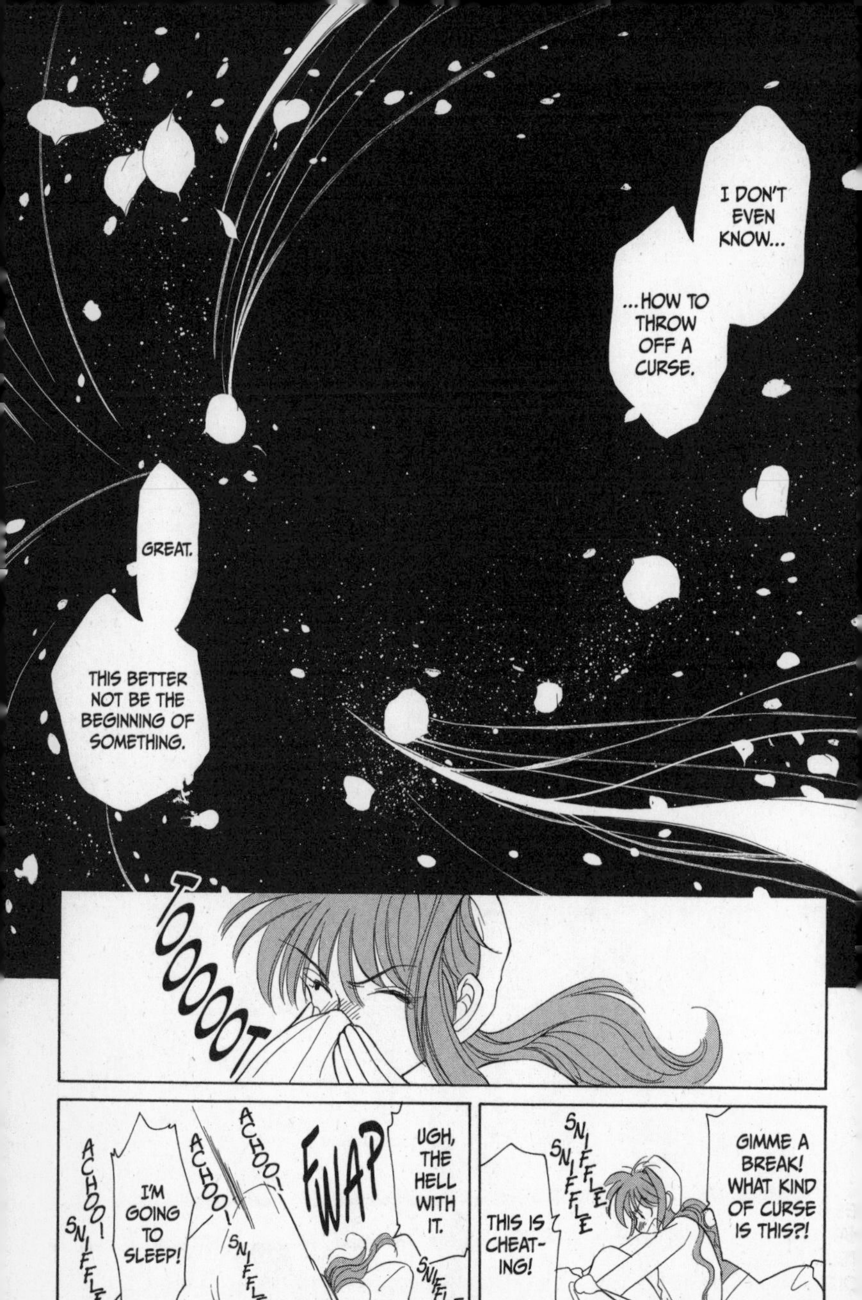
I DON'T EVEN KNOW...
...HOW TO THROW OFF A CURSE.
GREAT.
THIS BETTER NOT BE THE BEGINNING OF SOMETHING.
TOOOOOT
GIMME A BREAK! WHAT KIND OF CURSE IS THIS?!
SNIFFLE
SNIFFLE
THIS IS CHEAT-ING!
UGH, THE HELL WITH IT.
SNIFFLE
FWAP
ACHOO!
ACHOO!
SNIFFLE
I'M GOING TO SLEEP!
ACHOO!
SNIFFLE

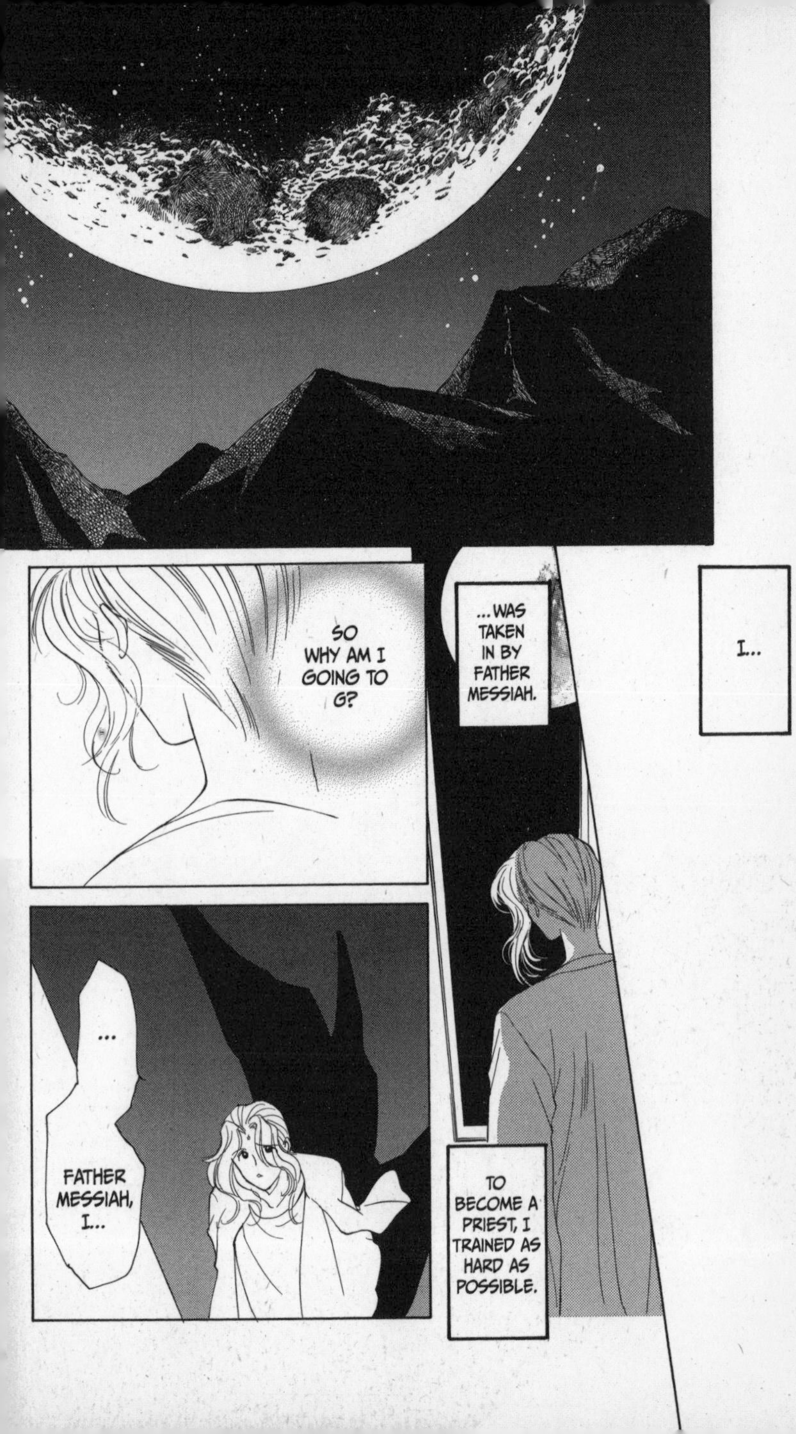
I...
...WAS TAKEN IN BY FATHER MESSIAH.
TO BECOME A PRIEST, I TRAINED AS HARD AS POSSIBLE.
SO WHY AM I GOING TO G?
...
FATHER MESSIAH, I...

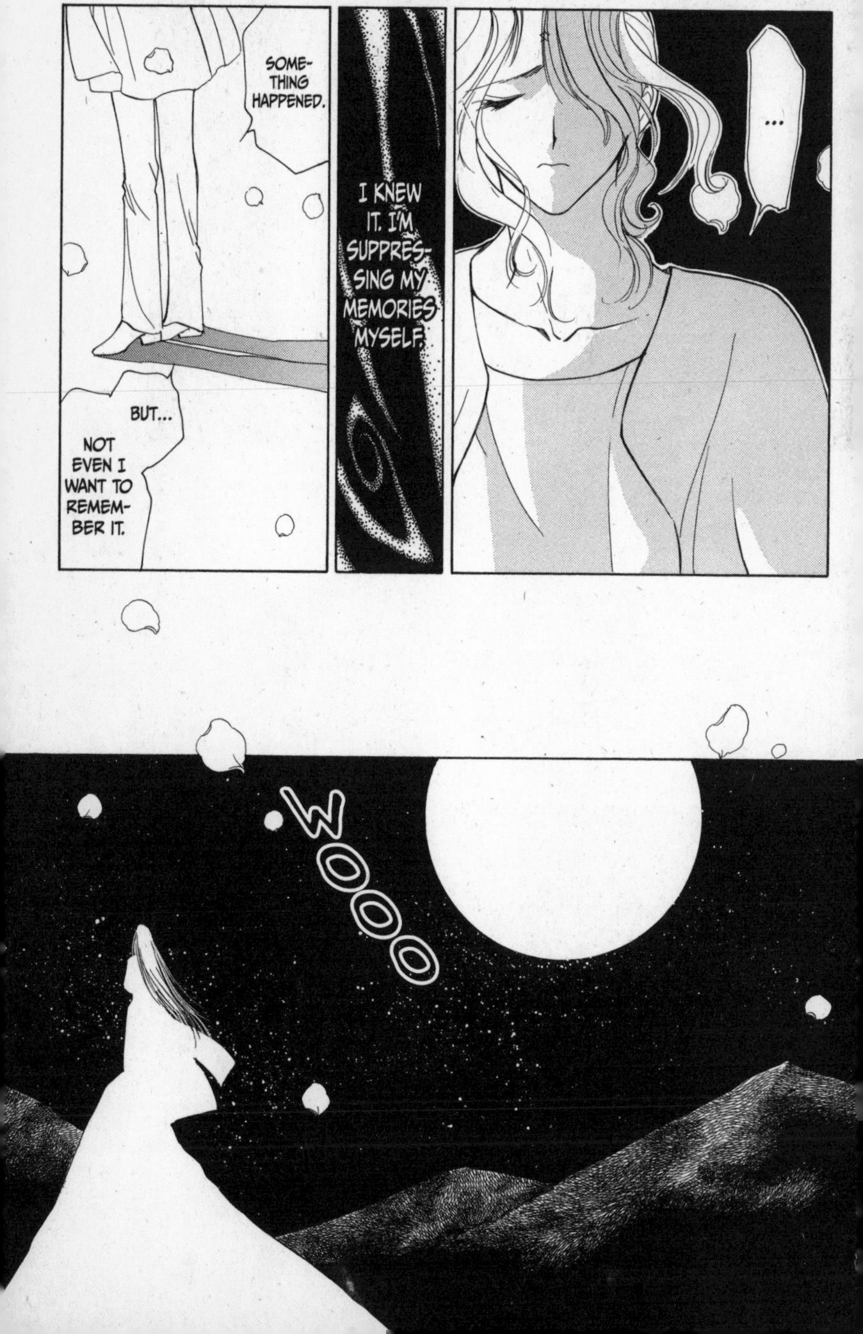

...
I KNEW IT. I'M SUPPRES-SING MY MEMORIES MYSELF.
SOME-THING HAPPENED.
BUT...
NOT EVEN I WANT TO REMEM-BER IT.
WOOOO

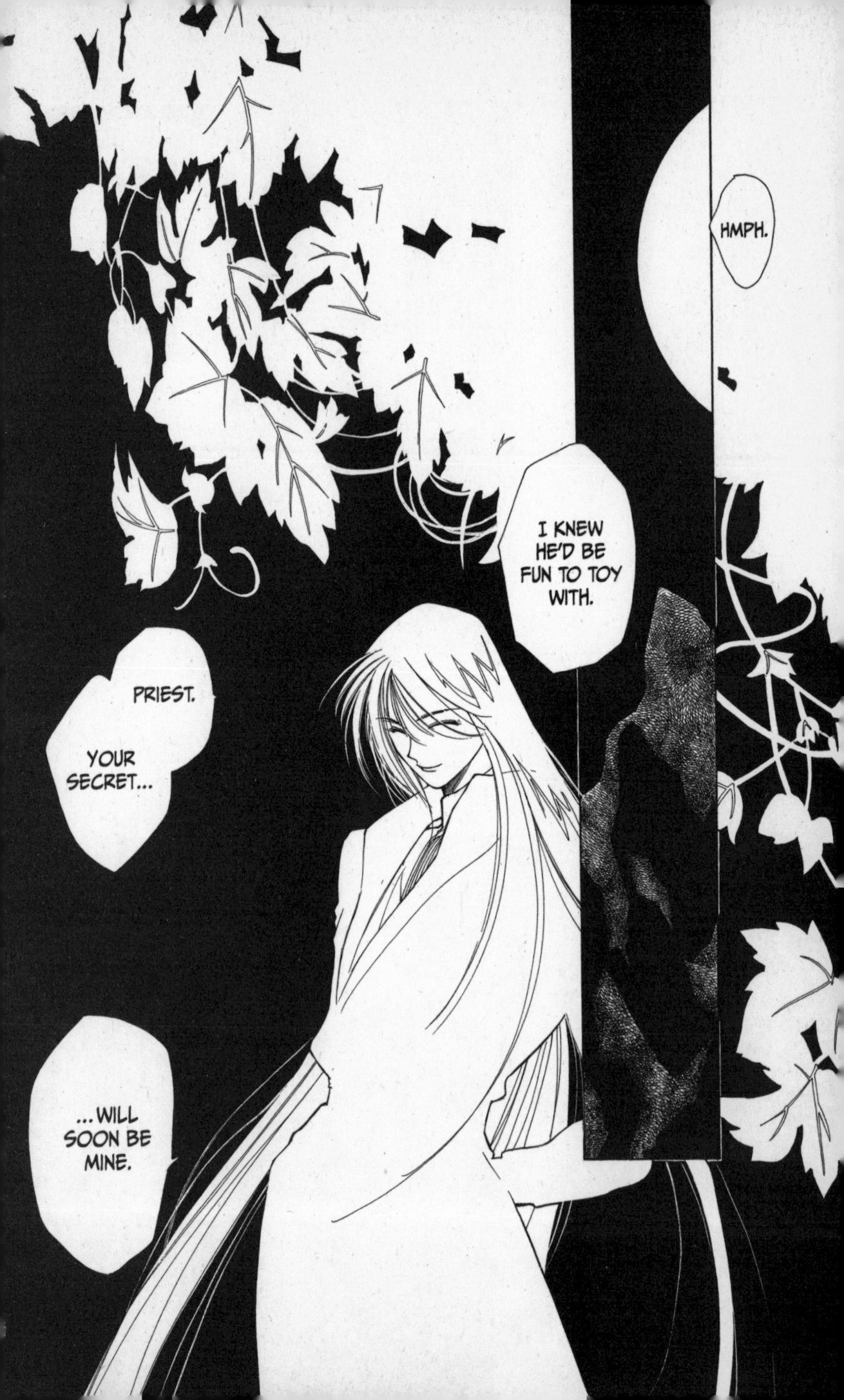
HMPH.
I KNEW HE'D BE FUN TO TOY WITH.
PRIEST.
YOUR SECRET...
...WILL SOON BE MINE.

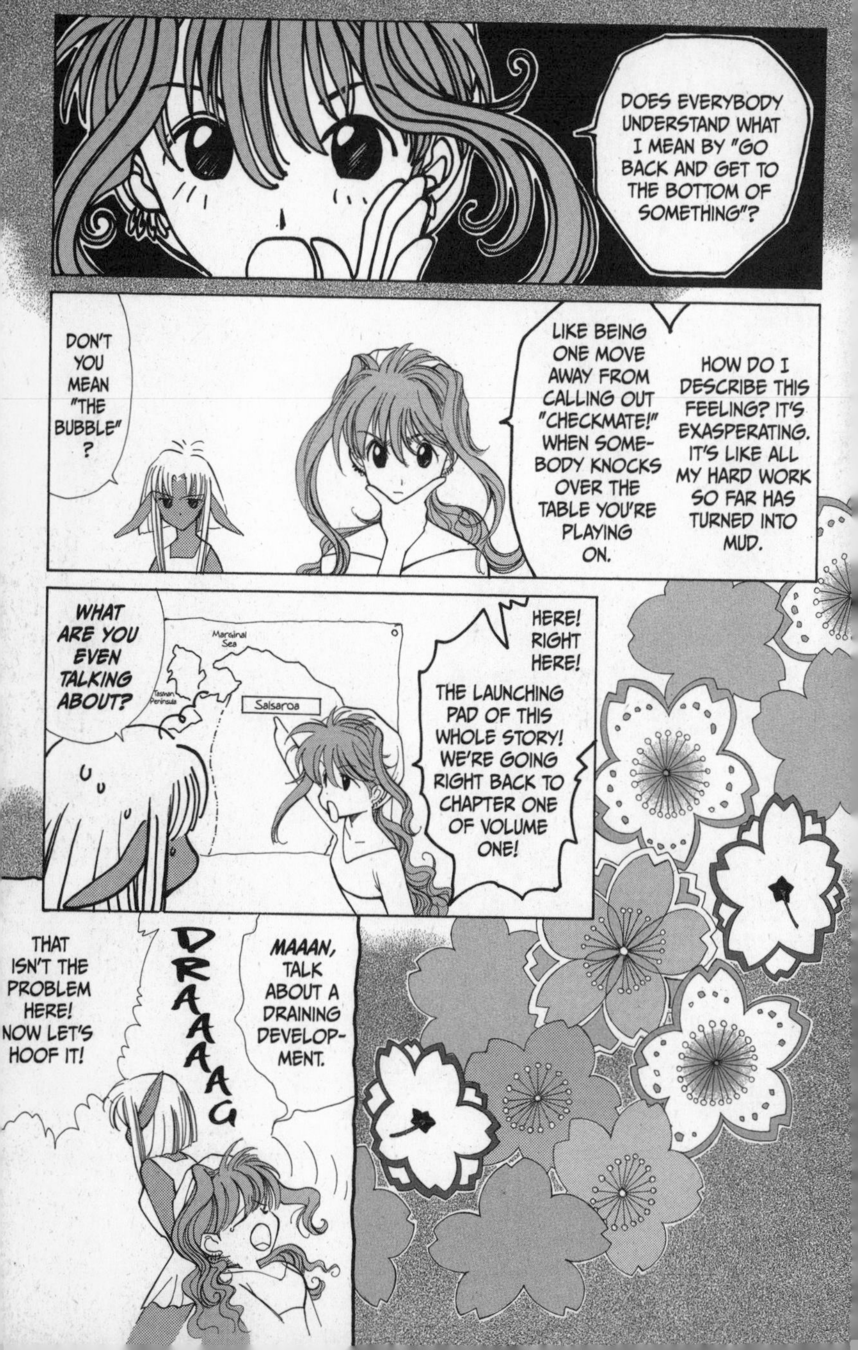
DOES EVERYBODY UNDERSTAND WHAT I MEAN BY "GO BACK AND GET TO THE BOTTOM OF SOMETHING"?
HOW DO I DESCRIBE THIS FEELING? IT'S EXASPERATING. IT'S LIKE ALL MY HARD WORK SO FAR HAS TURNED INTO MUD.
LIKE BEING ONE MOVE AWAY FROM CALLING OUT "CHECKMATE!" WHEN SOME-BODY KNOCKS OVER THE TABLE YOU'RE PLAYING ON.
DON'T YOU MEAN "THE BUBBLE" ?
HERE! RIGHT HERE!
THE LAUNCHING PAD OF THIS WHOLE STORY! WE'RE GOING RIGHT BACK TO CHAPTER ONE OF VOLUME ONE!
Marginal Sea
Salsaroa
Tasman Peninsula
WHAT ARE YOU EVEN TALKING ABOUT?
MAAAN, TALK ABOUT A DRAINING DEVELOP-MENT.
DRAAAAG
THAT ISN'T THE PROBLEM HERE! NOW LET'S HOOF IT!

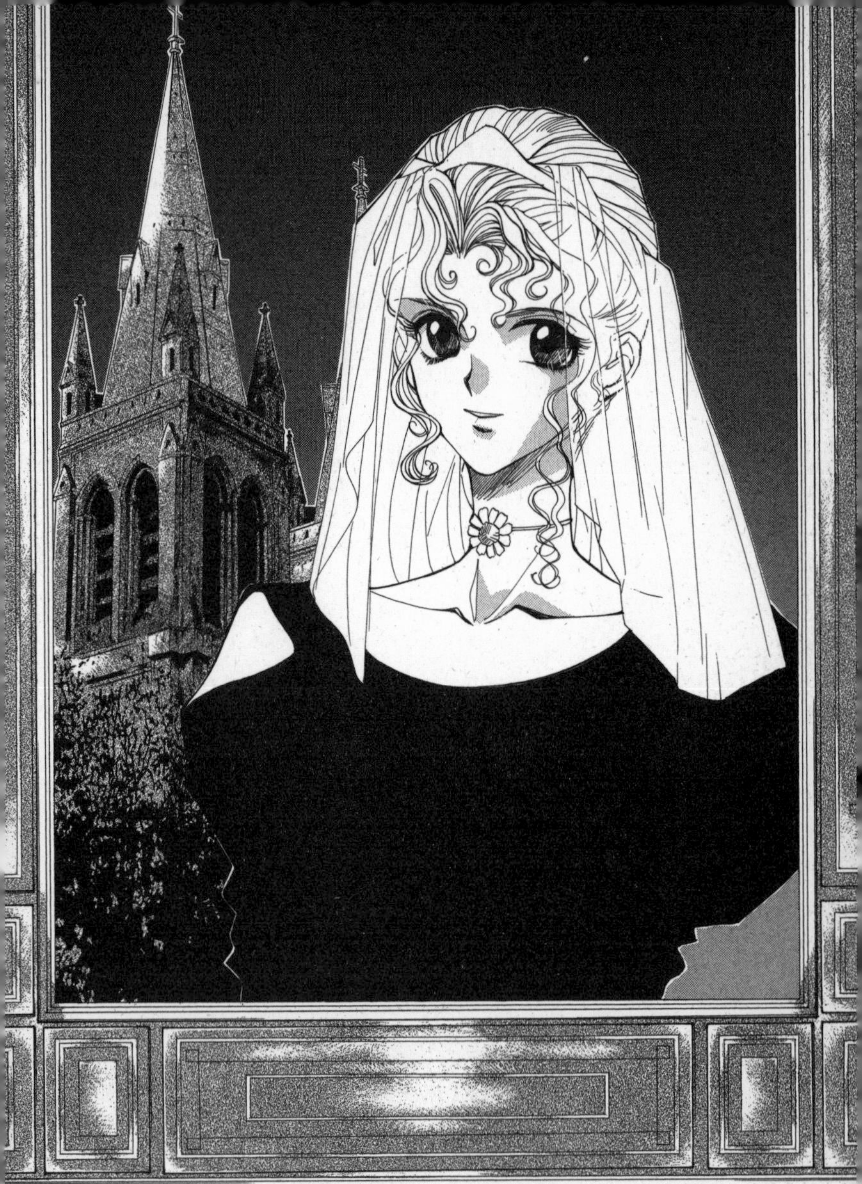

Chapter 21 "Joy," Book of W Pt. 1

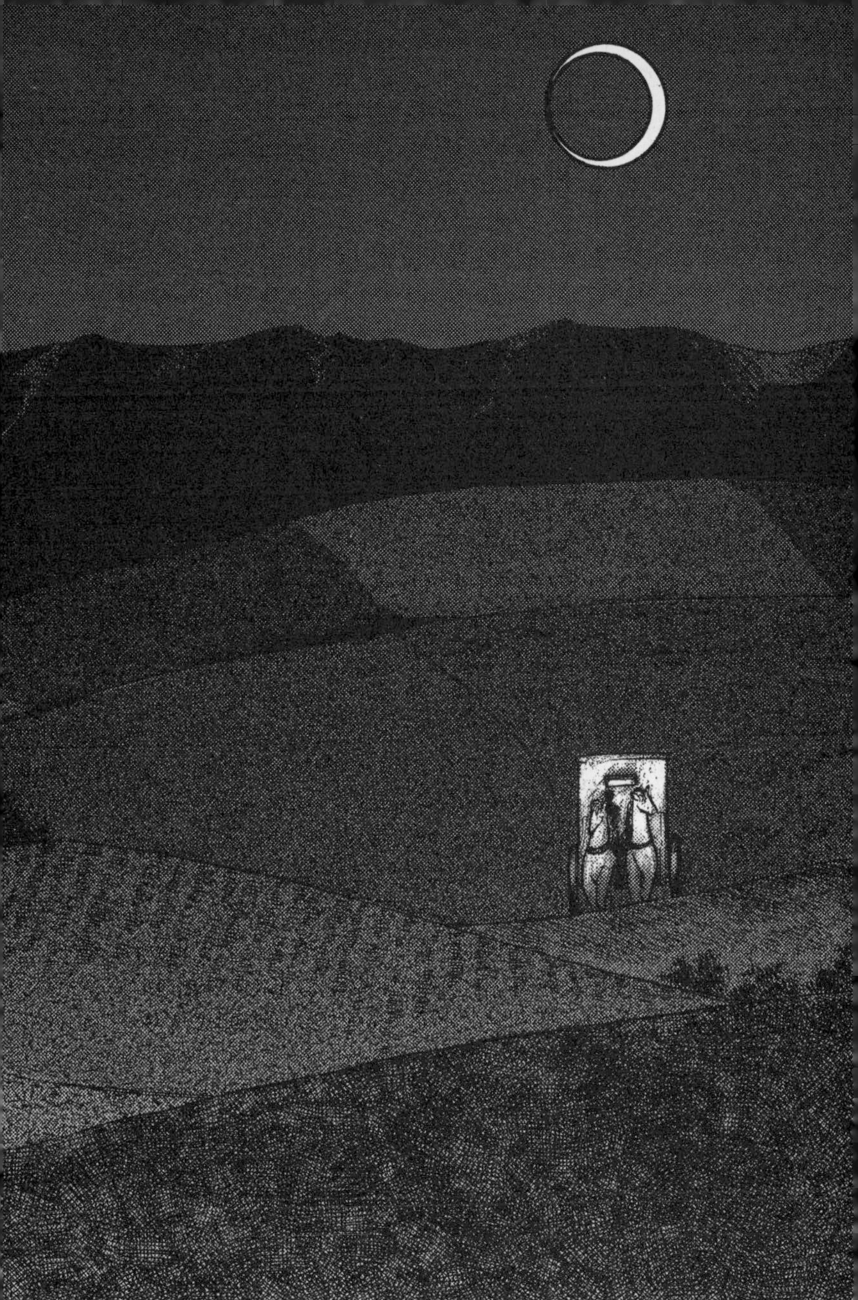

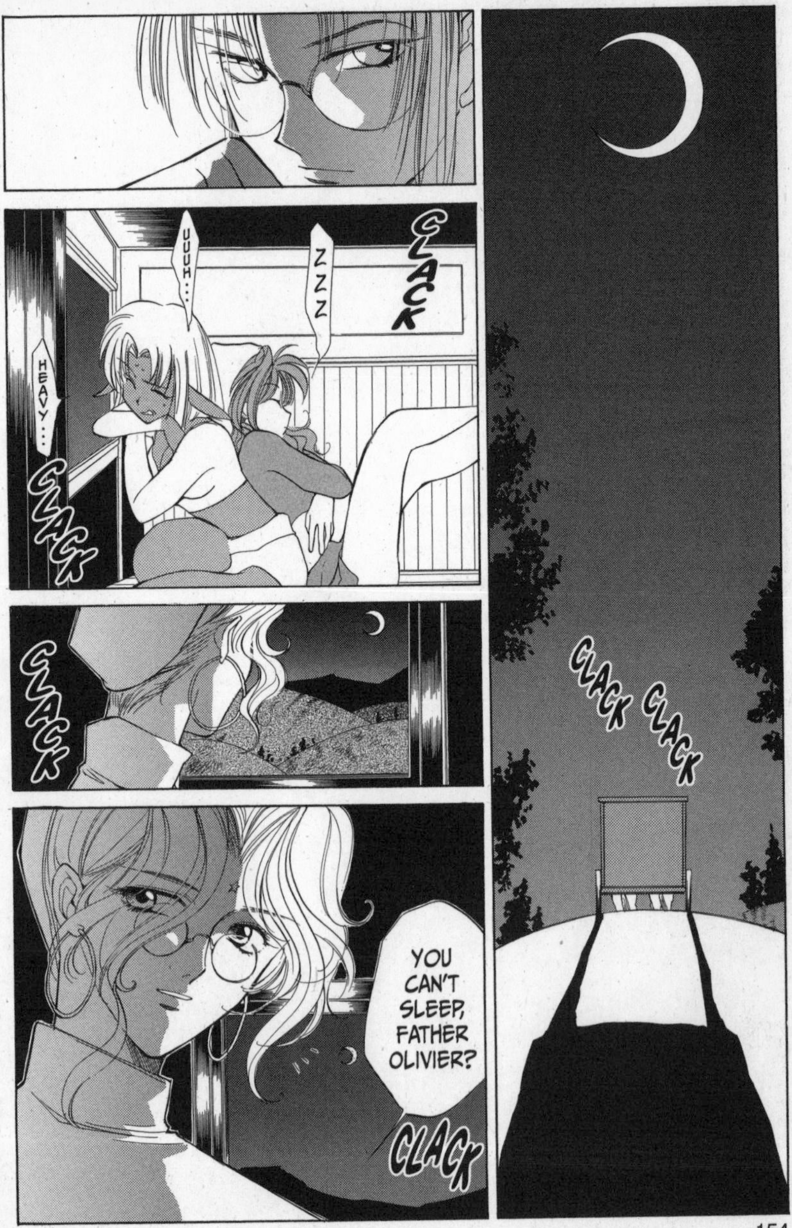
CLACK CLACK
CLACK
ZZZ
UUUH...
HEAVY...
CLACK
CLACK
YOU CAN'T SLEEP, FATHER OLIVIER?
CLACK

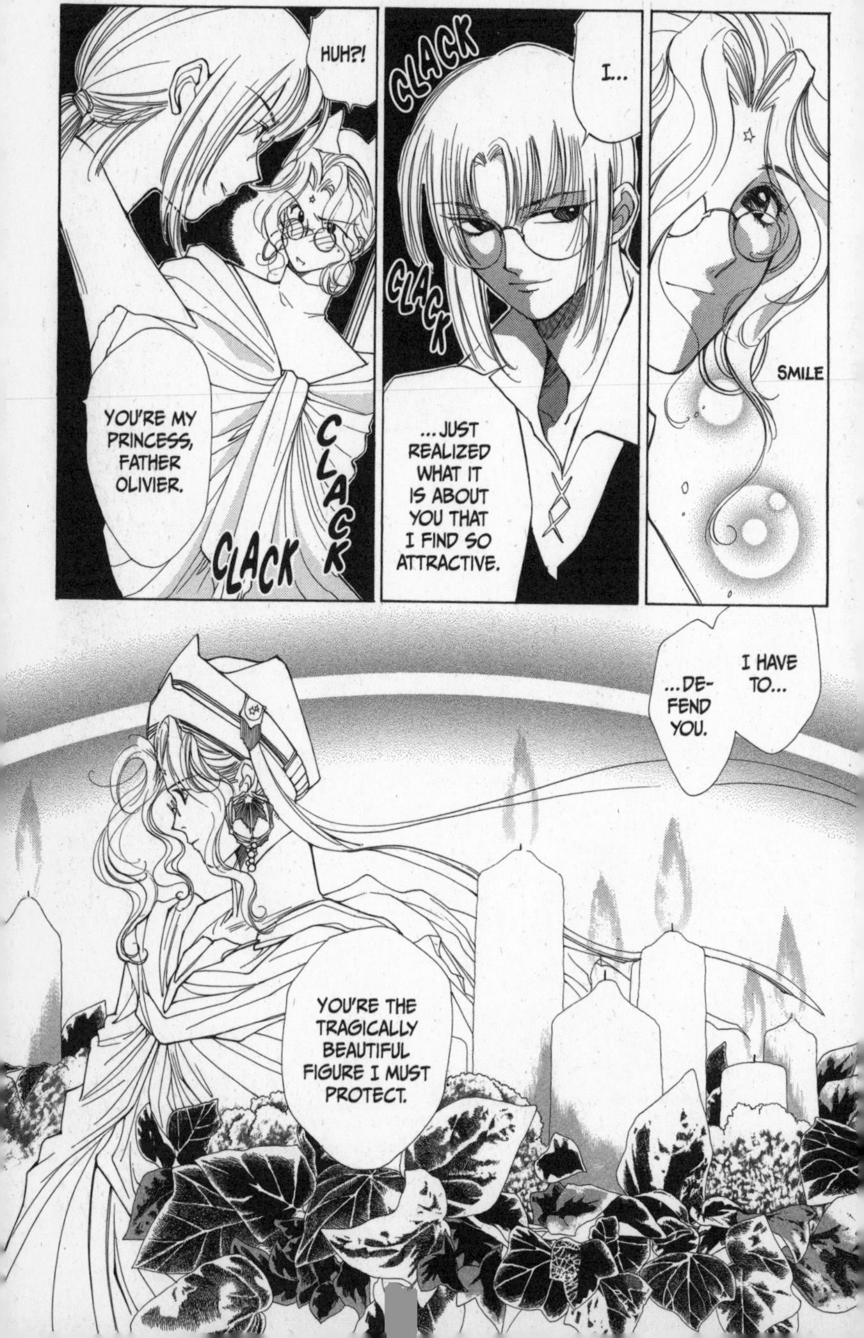
SMILE
I...
CLACK
CLACK
...JUST REALIZED WHAT IT IS ABOUT YOU THAT I FIND SO ATTRACTIVE.
HUH?!
YOU'RE MY PRINCESS, FATHER OLIVIER.
CLACK
CLACK
I HAVE TO...
...DE-FEND YOU.
YOU'RE THE TRAGICALLY BEAUTIFUL FIGURE I MUST PROTECT.

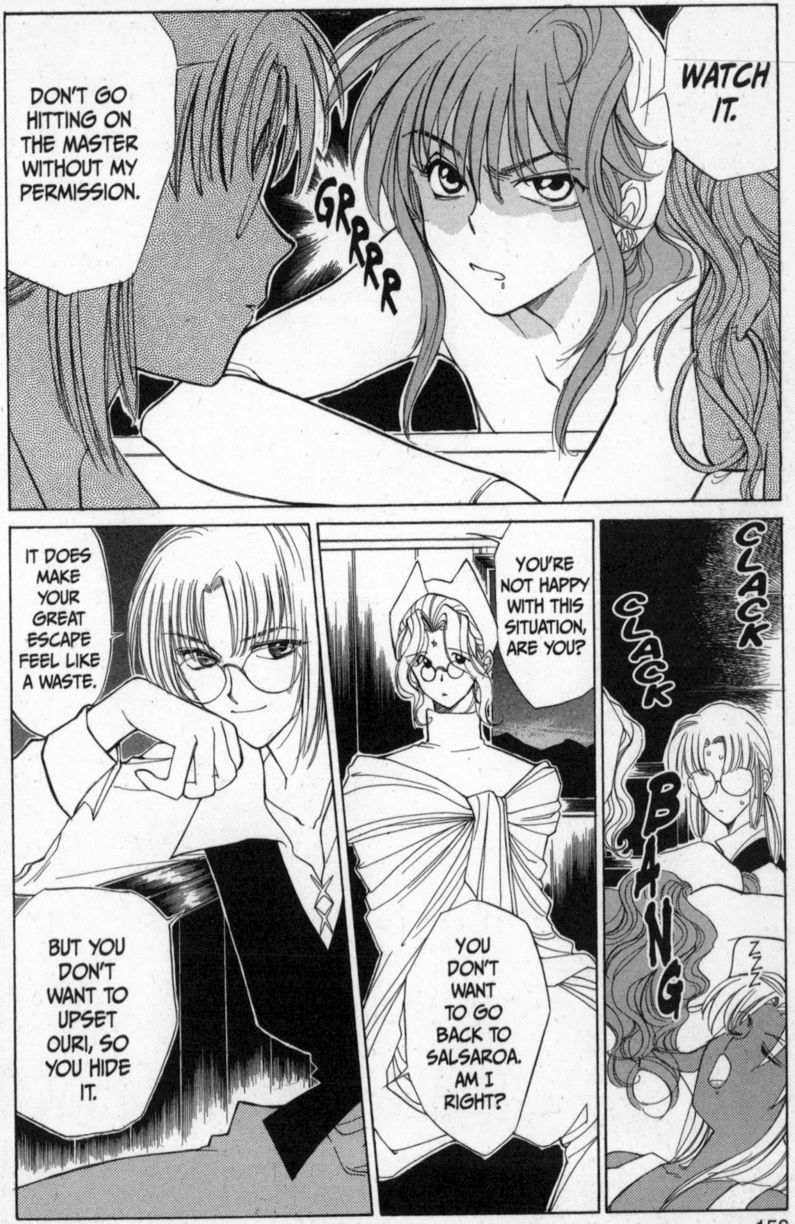
WATCH IT.
GRRRR
DON'T GO HITTING ON THE MASTER WITHOUT MY PERMISSION.
CLACK CLACK
BANG
ZZZ
YOU'RE NOT HAPPY WITH THIS SITUATION, ARE YOU?
YOU DON'T WANT TO GO BACK TO SALSAROA. AM I RIGHT?
IT DOES MAKE YOUR GREAT ESCAPE FEEL LIKE A WASTE.
BUT YOU DON'T WANT TO UPSET OURI, SO YOU HIDE IT.

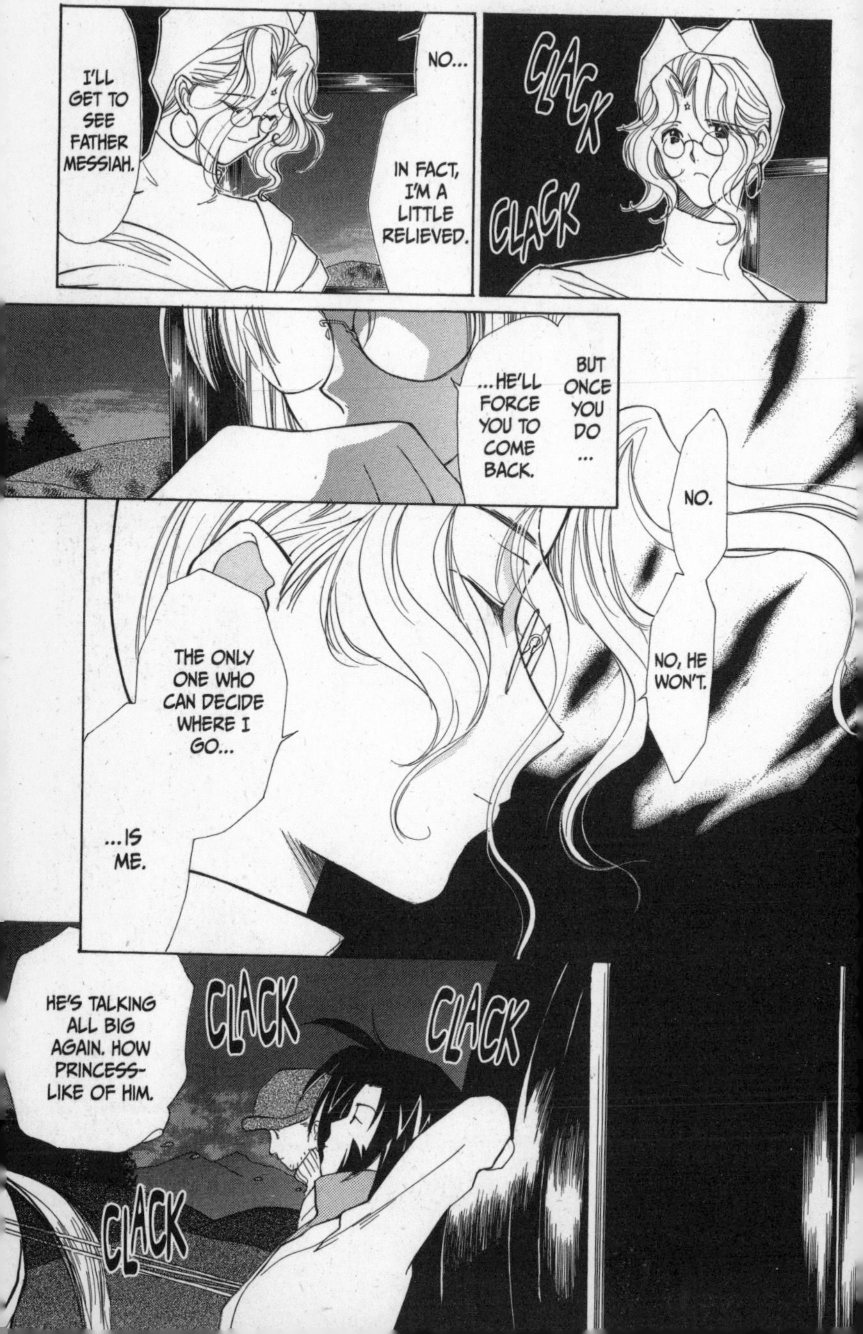
CLACK
CLACK
NO...
IN FACT, I'M A LITTLE RELIEVED.
I'LL GET TO SEE FATHER MESSIAH.
BUT ONCE YOU DO...
...HE'LL FORCE YOU TO COME BACK.
NO.
NO, HE WON'T.
THE ONLY ONE WHO CAN DECIDE WHERE I GO...
...IS ME.
CLACK
CLACK
HE'S TALKING ALL BIG AGAIN. HOW PRINCESS-LIKE OF HIM.
CLACK

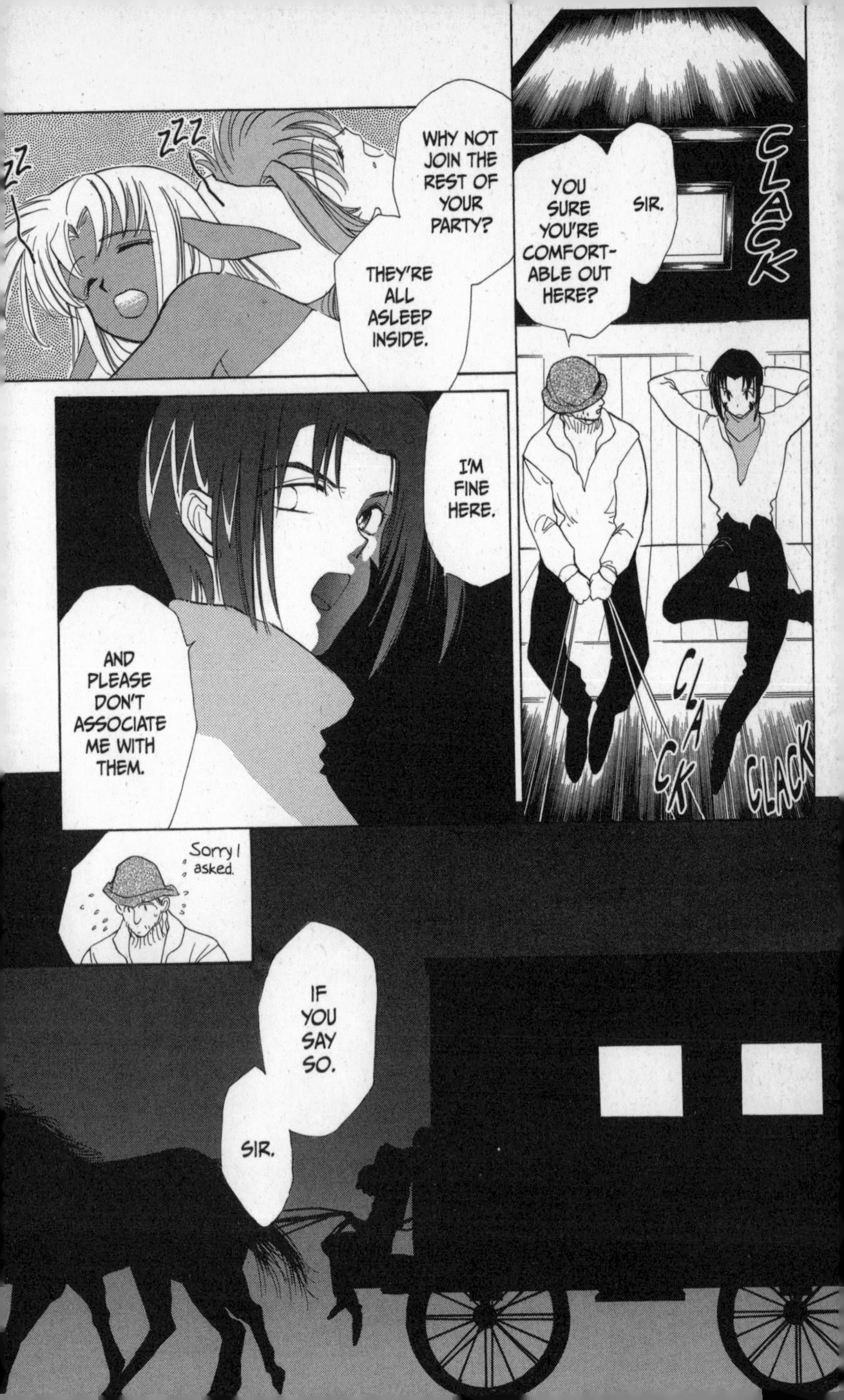
CLACK
SIR.
YOU SURE YOU'RE COMFORT-ABLE OUT HERE?
CLACK
CLACK
ZZZ
ZZ
WHY NOT JOIN THE REST OF YOUR PARTY?
THEY'RE ALL ASLEEP INSIDE.
I'M FINE HERE.
AND PLEASE DON'T ASSOCIATE ME WITH THEM.
Sorry I asked.
IF YOU SAY SO.
SIR.

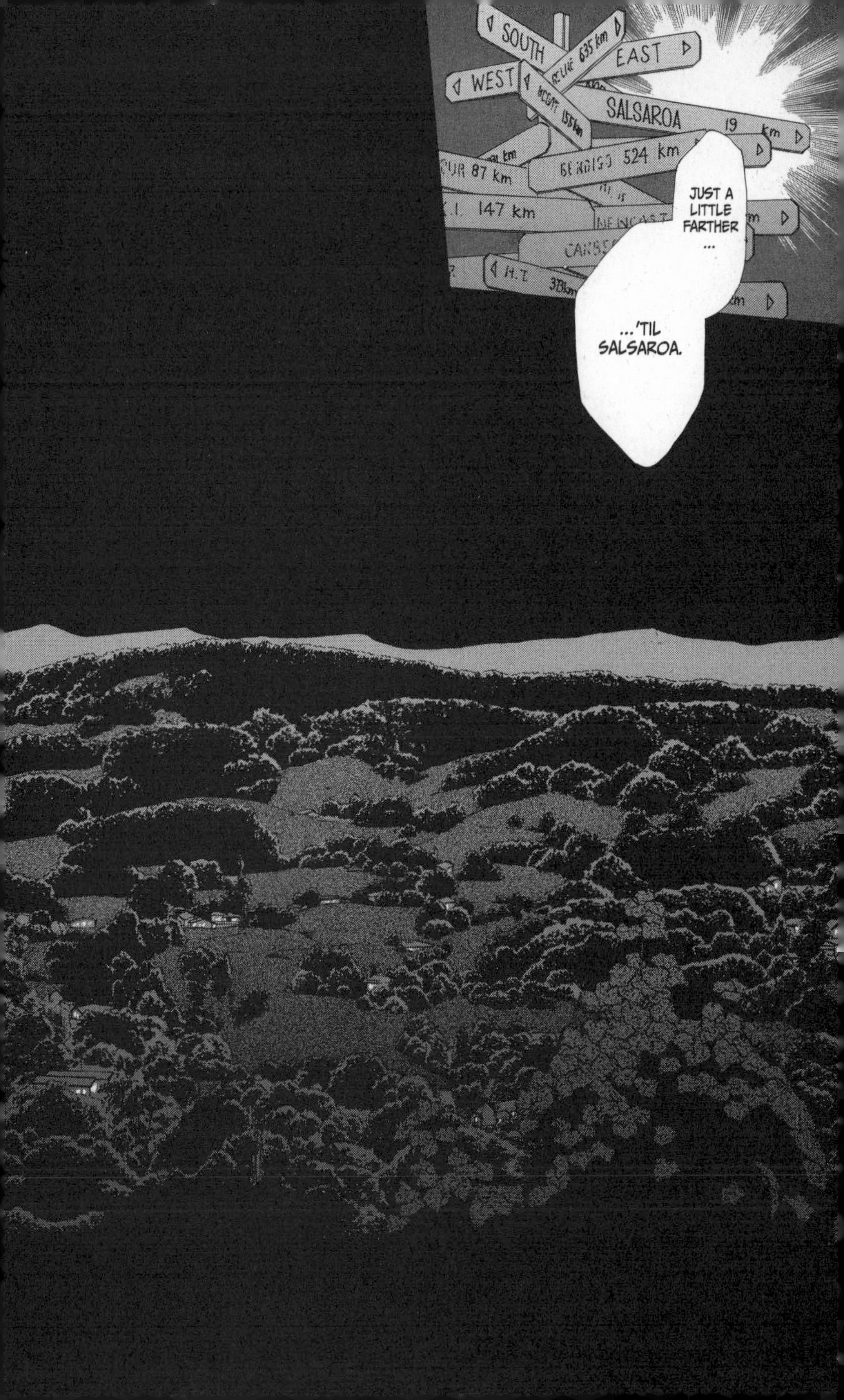
SOUTH
EAST
WEST
SALSAROA 19 km
524 km
147 km
JUST A LITTLE FARTHER ...
...'TIL SALSAROA.

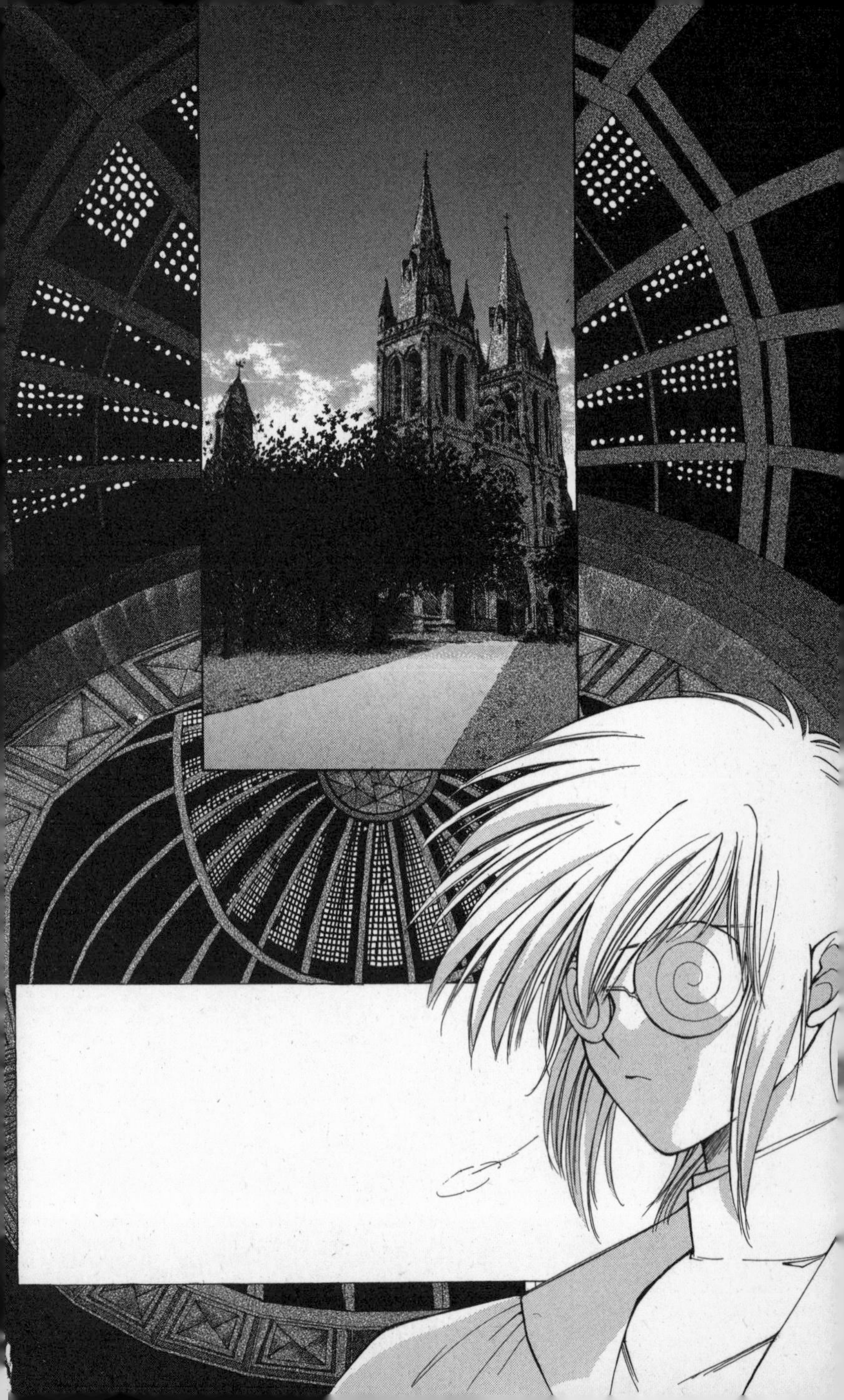

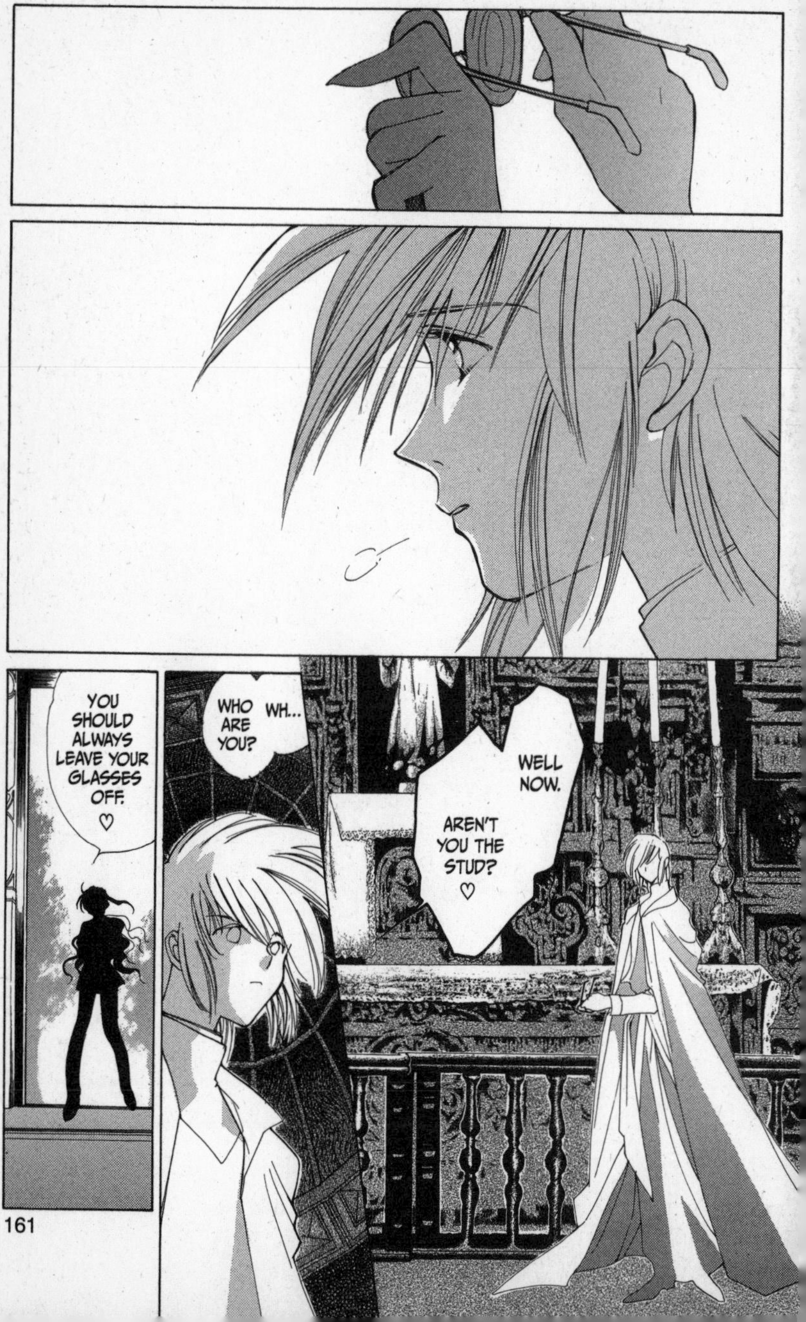
WELL NOW.
AREN'T YOU THE STUD? ♡
WH...
WHO ARE YOU?
YOU SHOULD ALWAYS LEAVE YOUR GLASSES OFF. ♡

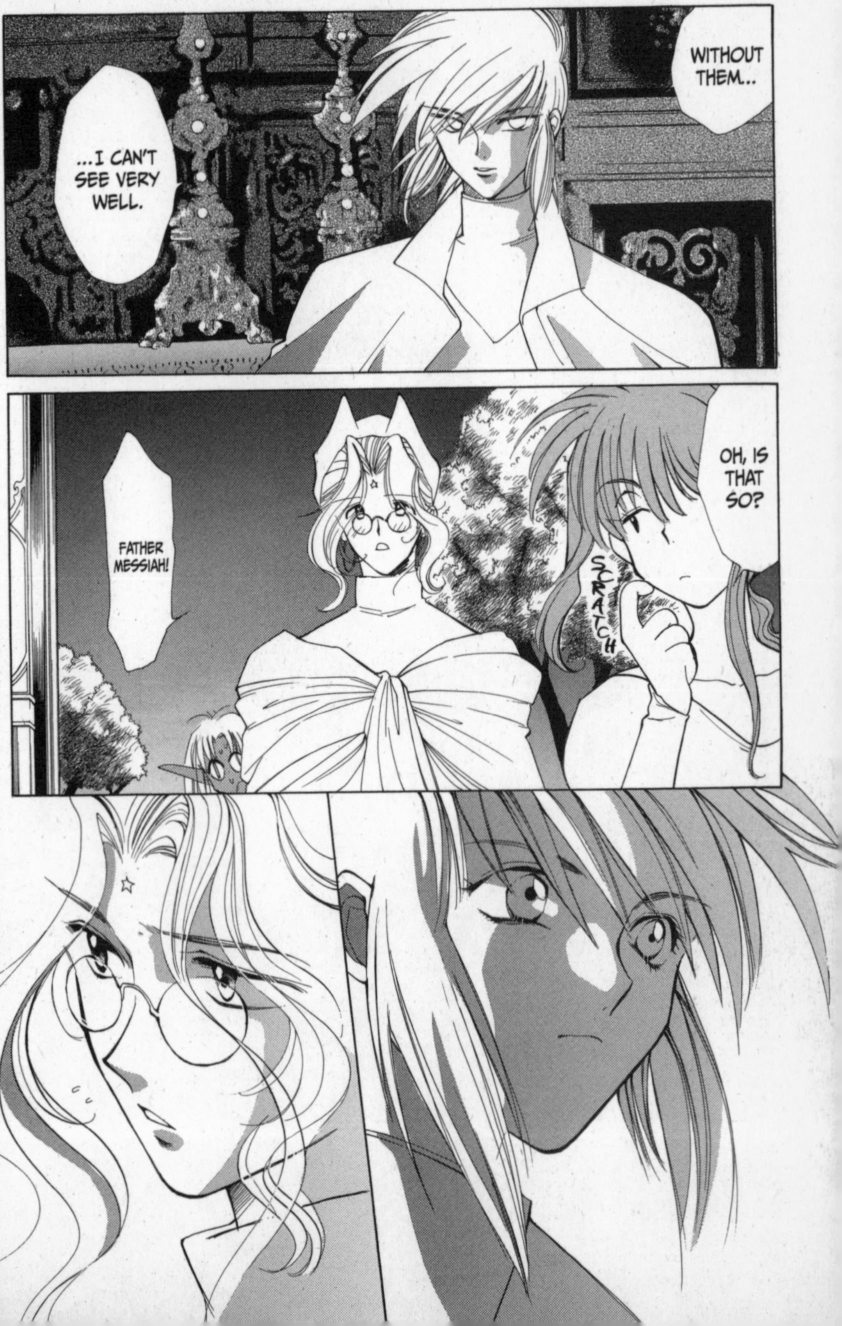
WITHOUT THEM...
...I CAN'T SEE VERY WELL.
OH, IS THAT SO?
SCRATCH
FATHER MESSIAH!

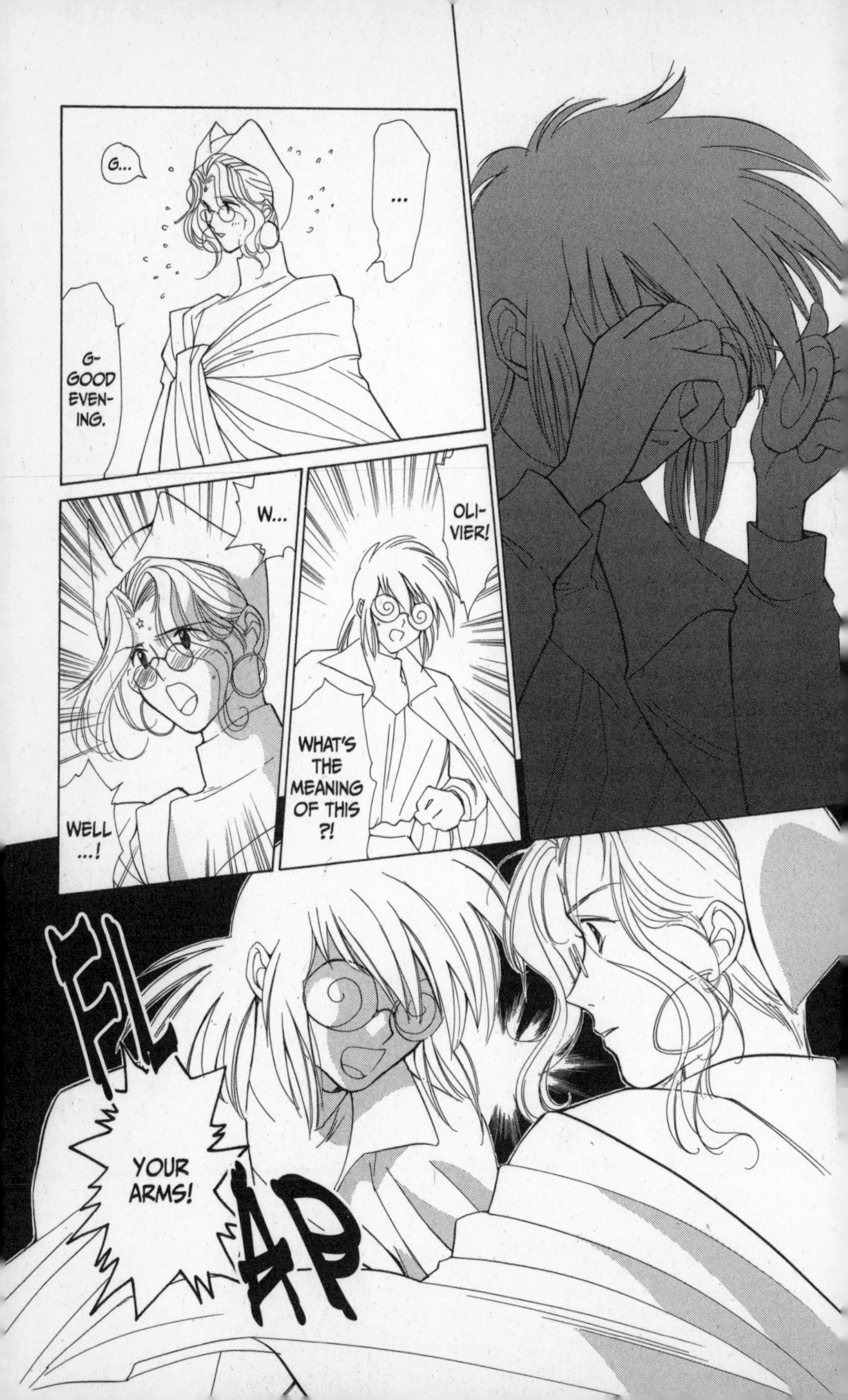
...
G...
G-GOOD EVENING.
OLIVIER!
WHAT'S THE MEANING OF THIS ?!
W...
WELL ...!
FLAP
YOUR ARMS!

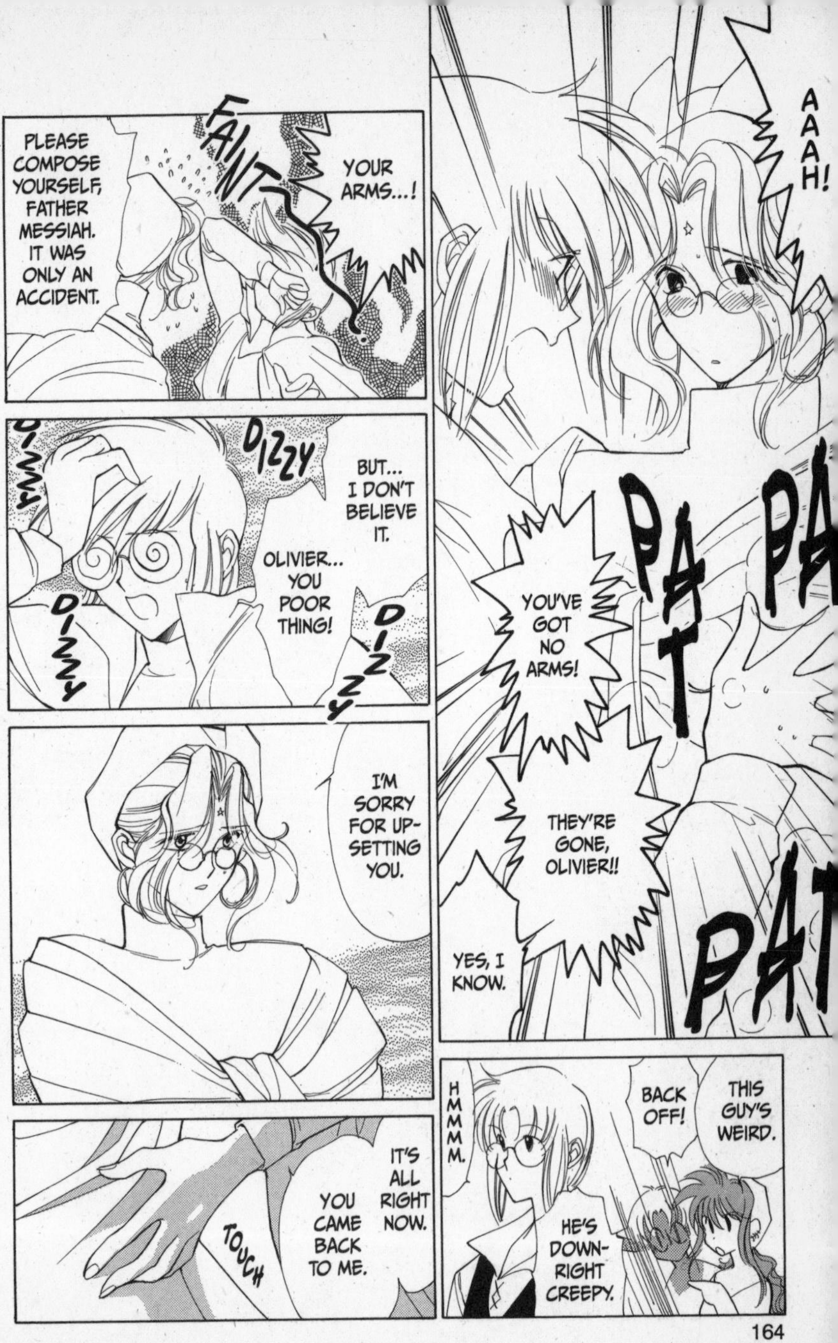
AAAAH!
PAT
PAT
PAT
YOU'VE GOT NO ARMS!
THEY'RE GONE, OLIVIER!!
YES, I KNOW.
THIS GUY'S WEIRD.
BACK OFF!
HMMMM.
HE'S DOWN-RIGHT CREEPY.
YOUR ARMS...!
FAINT
PLEASE COMPOSE YOURSELF, FATHER MESSIAH. IT WAS ONLY AN ACCIDENT.
BUT... I DON'T BELIEVE IT.
DIZZY
OLIVIER... YOU POOR THING!
DIZZY
DIZZY
DIZZY
I'M SORRY FOR UP-SETTING YOU.
IT'S ALL RIGHT NOW.
YOU CAME BACK TO ME.
TOUCH

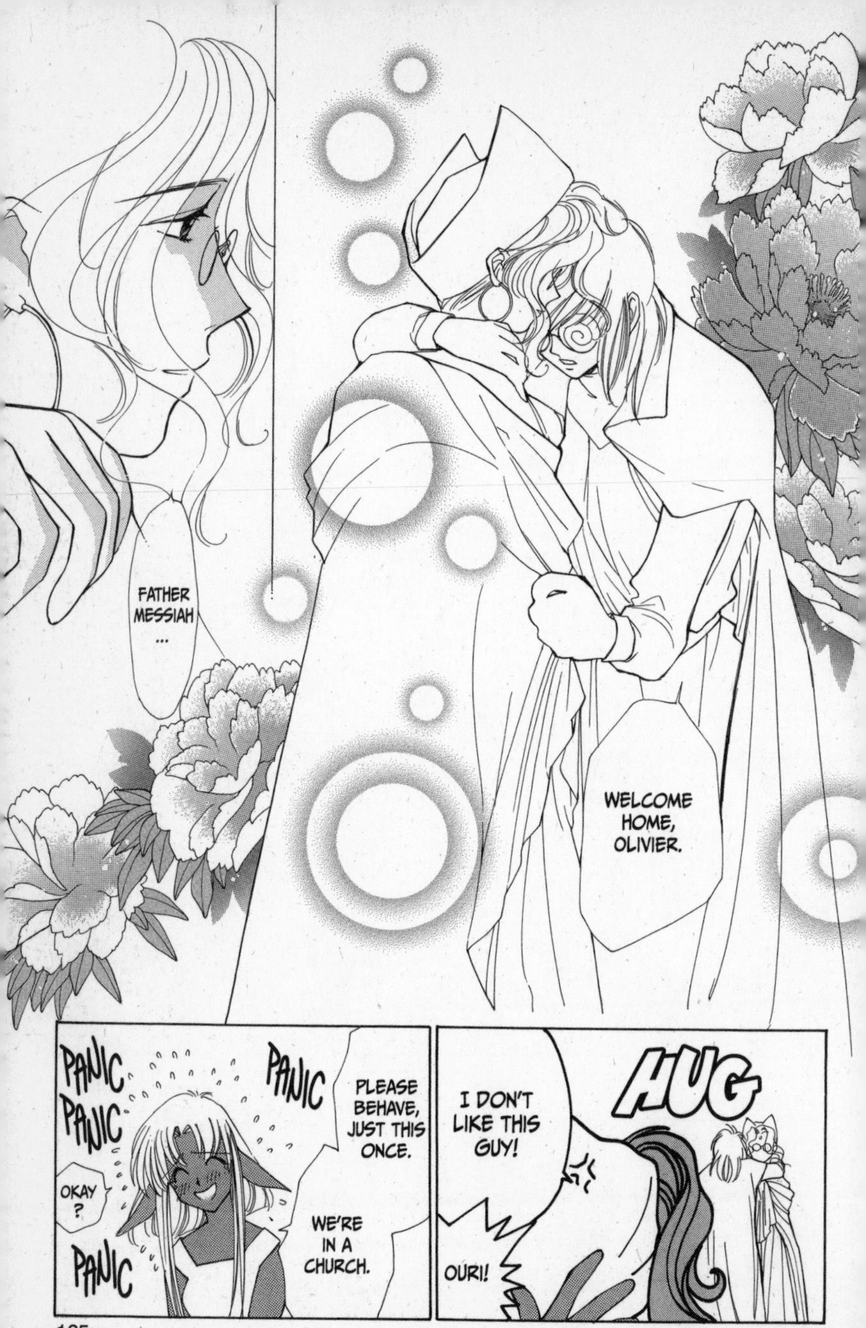
WELCOME HOME, OLIVIER.
FATHER MESSIAH ...
HUG
I DON'T LIKE THIS GUY!
OURI!
PANIC
PLEASE BEHAVE, JUST THIS ONCE.
PANIC PANIC
OKAY?
WE'RE IN A CHURCH.
PANIC

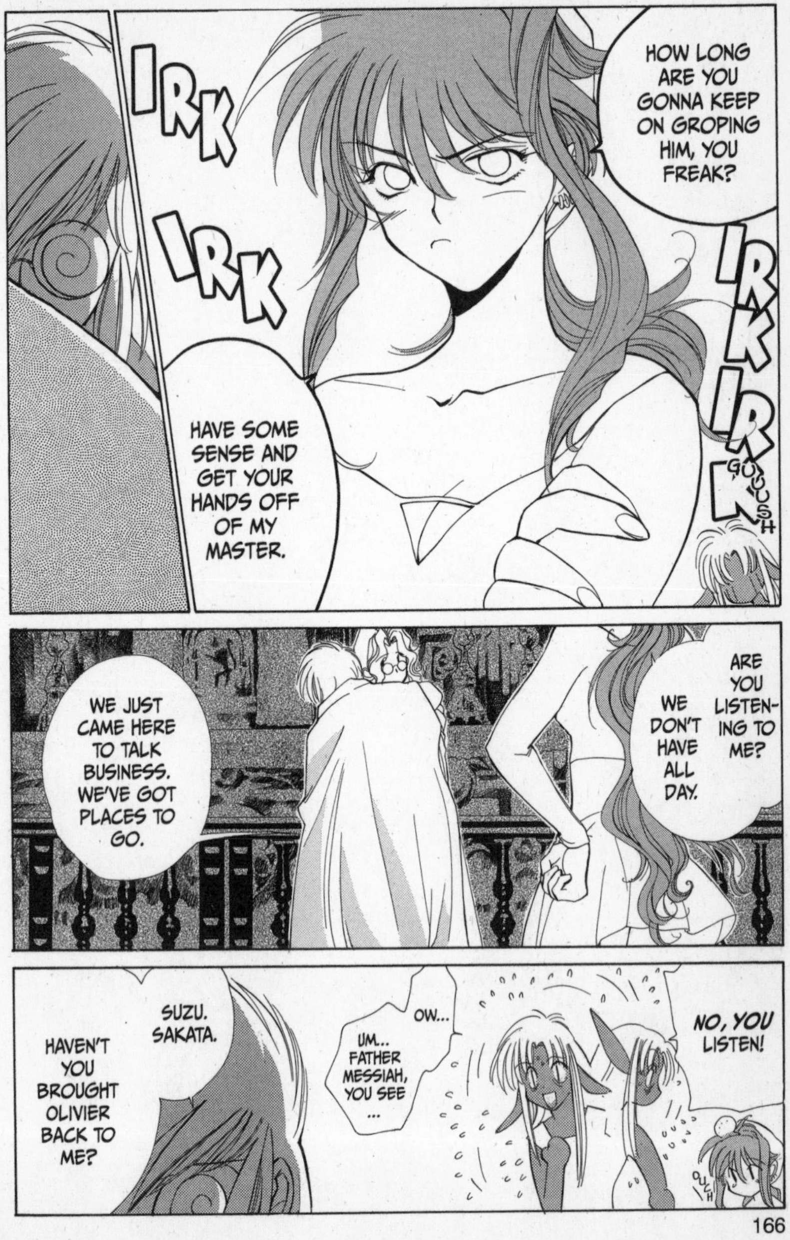

HOW LONG ARE YOU GONNA KEEP ON GROPING HIM, YOU FREAK?
IRK
IRK
GUUUSH
IRK
IRK
HAVE SOME SENSE AND GET YOUR HANDS OFF OF MY MASTER.
ARE YOU LISTENING TO ME?
WE DON'T HAVE ALL DAY.
WE JUST CAME HERE TO TALK BUSINESS. WE'VE GOT PLACES TO GO.
NO, YOU LISTEN!
OUCH
OW...
UM... FATHER MESSIAH, YOU SEE ...
SUZU. SAKATA.
HAVEN'T YOU BROUGHT OLIVIER BACK TO ME?

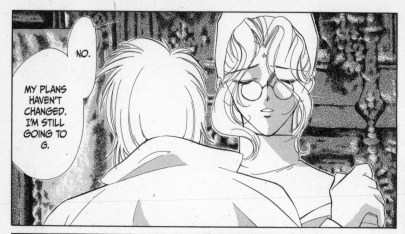

NO.
MY PLANS HAVEN'T CHANGED. I'M STILL GOING TO G.
WE ONLY CAME HERE TO HEAL THE MASTER'S ARMS!
FUME FUME
FUME
FUME FUME
WE'RE LOOKING FOR HIS "DESTINED TWIN."
AND WE FIGURED SINCE YOU RAISED HIM, YOU'D KNOW SOMETHING ABOUT IT...
SUZU. SAKATA.
WHAT'S THE MEANING OF THIS?
QUIT IG-NOR-ING ME!
GRRR!
WILL YOU BE QUIET?!
I DON'T KNOW.
I BROUGHT HIM HERE. THAT'S ALL.
FATHER MESSIAH.
PLEASE LISTEN TO WHAT FATHER OLIVIER HAS TO SAY.

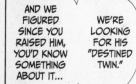

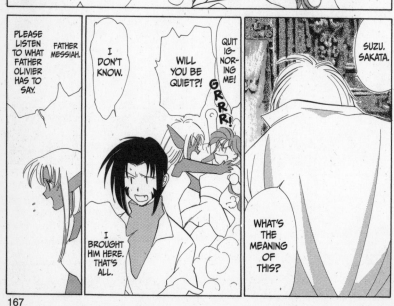

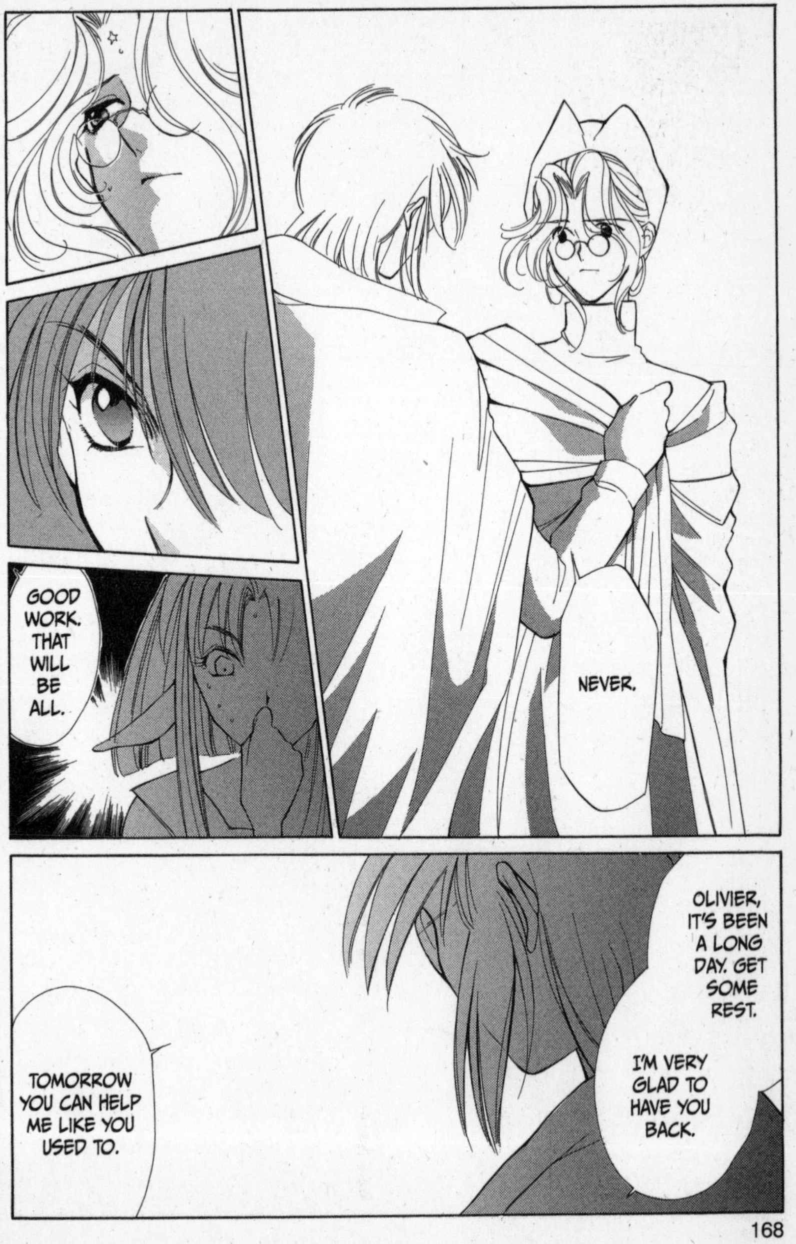
NEVER.
GOOD WORK. THAT WILL BE ALL.
OLIVIER, IT'S BEEN A LONG DAY. GET SOME REST.
I'M VERY GLAD TO HAVE YOU BACK.
TOMORROW YOU CAN HELP ME LIKE YOU USED TO.

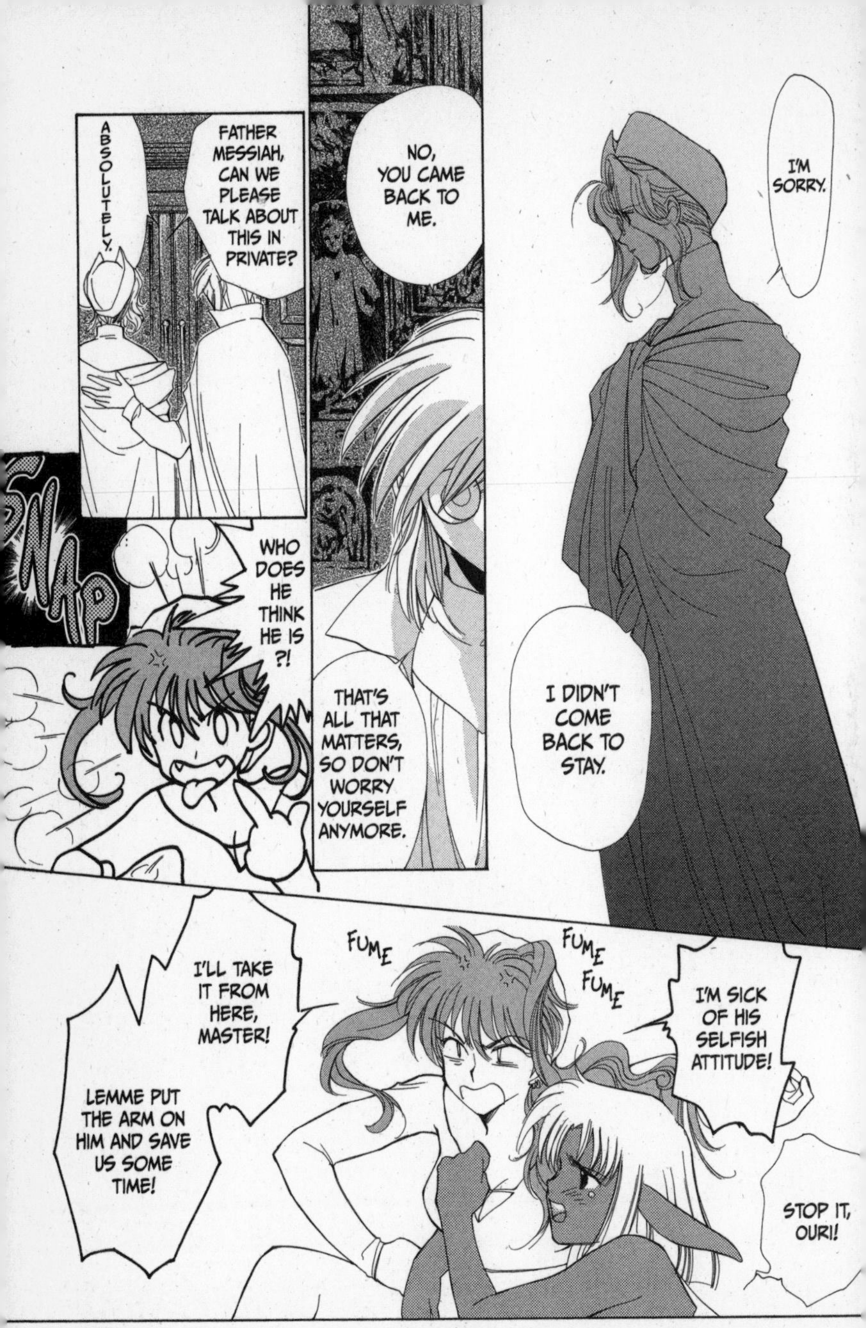
I'M SORRY.
I DIDN'T COME BACK TO STAY.
NO, YOU CAME BACK TO ME.
THAT'S ALL THAT MATTERS, SO DON'T WORRY YOURSELF ANYMORE.
FATHER MESSIAH, CAN WE PLEASE TALK ABOUT THIS IN PRIVATE?
ABSOLUTELY.
SNAP
WHO DOES HE THINK HE IS?!
I'M SICK OF HIS SELFISH ATTITUDE!
FUME FUME
FUME
STOP IT, OURI!
I'LL TAKE IT FROM HERE, MASTER!
LEMME PUT THE ARM ON HIM AND SAVE US SOME TIME!

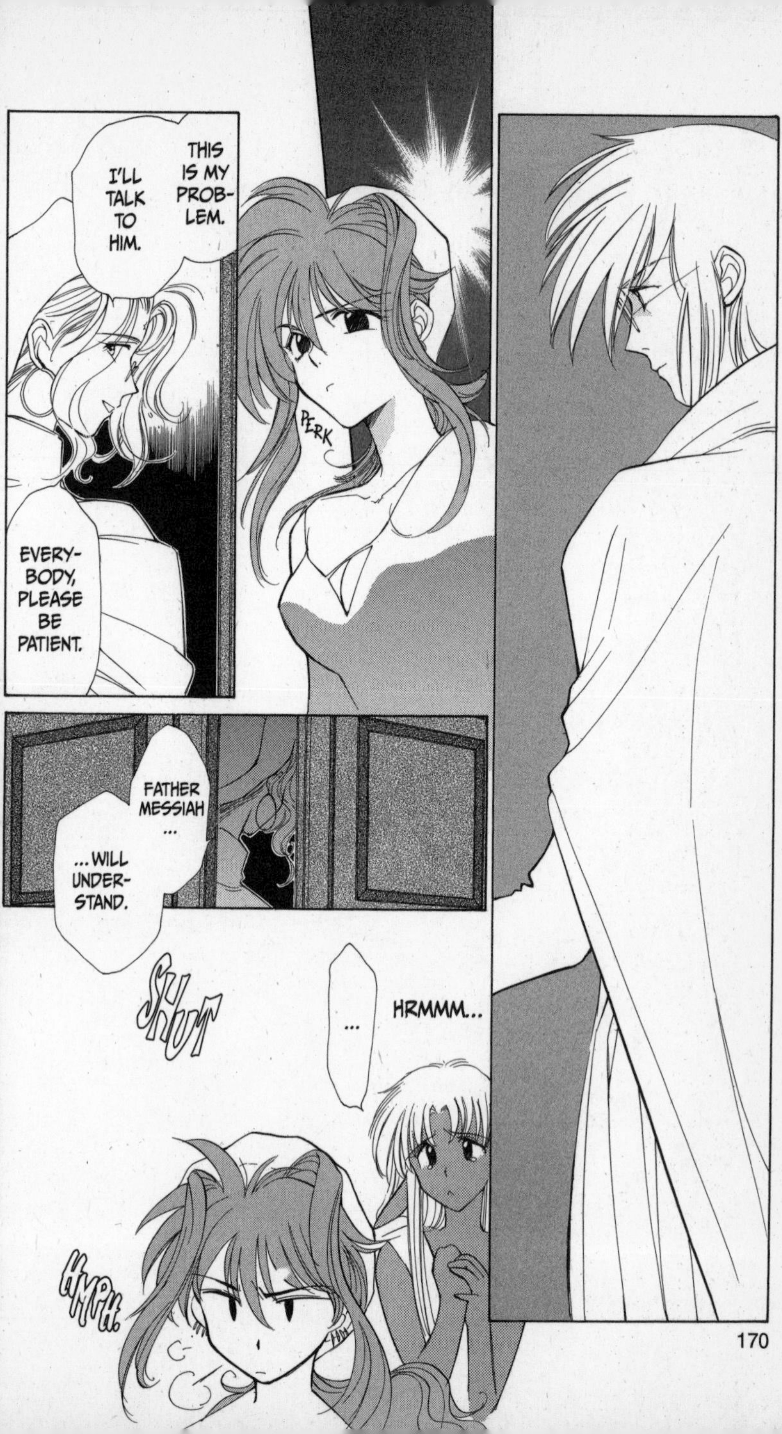
PERK
THIS IS MY PROBLEM.
I'LL TALK TO HIM.
EVERYBODY, PLEASE BE PATIENT.
FATHER MESSIAH ...
...WILL UNDERSTAND.
SHUT
HRMMM...
...
HMPH.

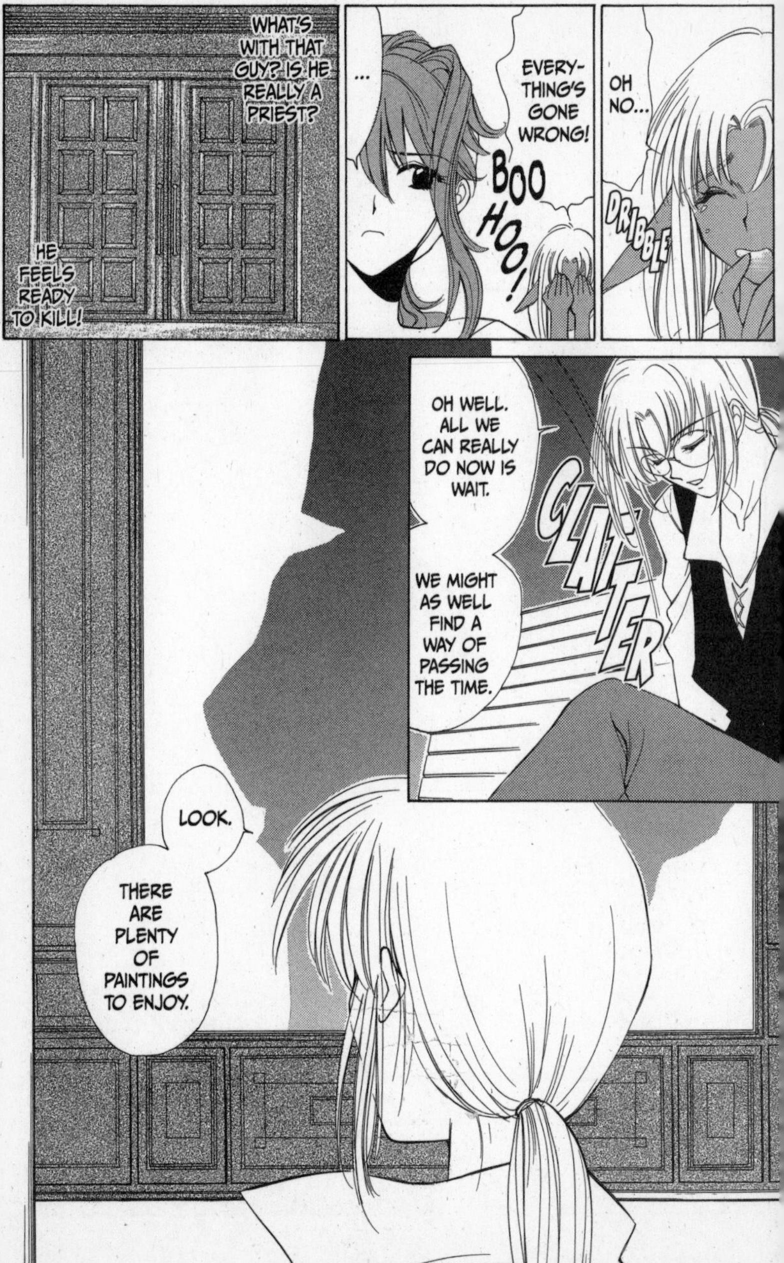

OH NO...
DRIBBLE
EVERY-THING'S GONE WRONG!
...
BOO HOO!
WHAT'S WITH THAT GUY? IS HE REALLY A PRIEST?
HE FEELS READY TO KILL!
OH WELL. ALL WE CAN REALLY DO NOW IS WAIT.
CLATTER
WE MIGHT AS WELL FIND A WAY OF PASSING THE TIME.
LOOK.
THERE ARE PLENTY OF PAINTINGS TO ENJOY.

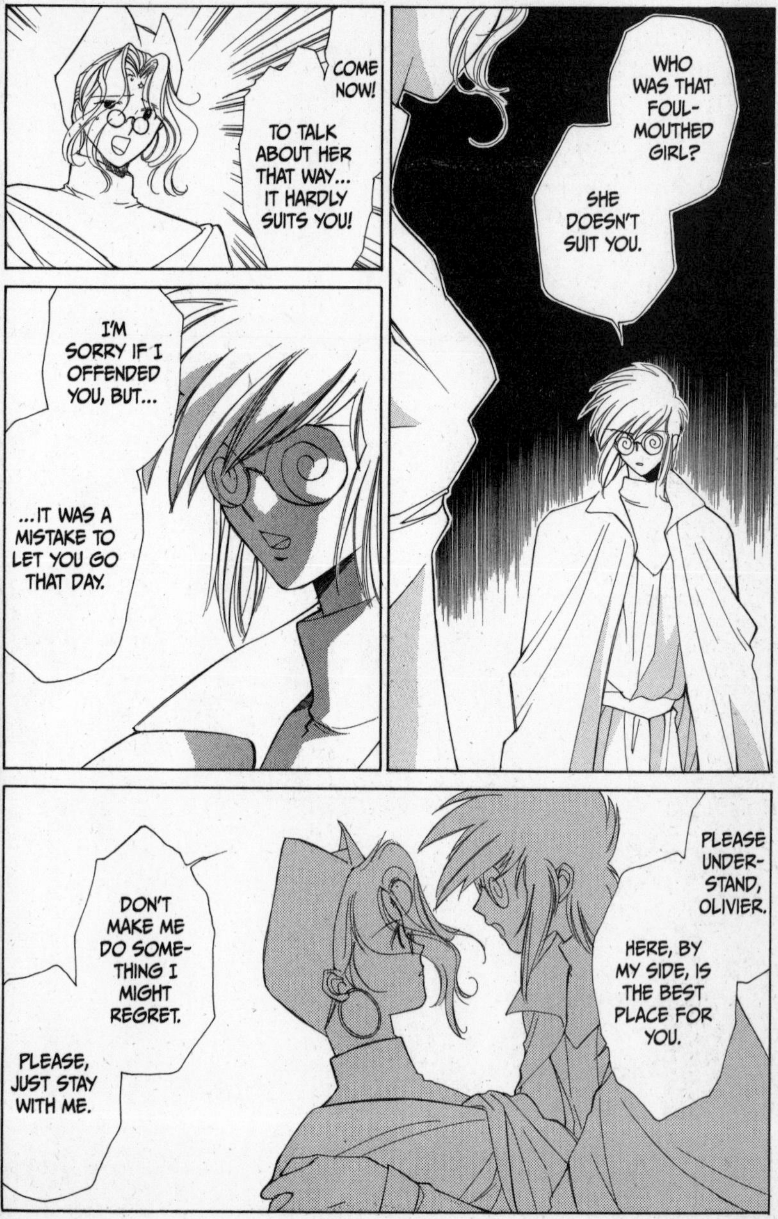
WHO WAS THAT FOUL-MOUTHED GIRL?
SHE DOESN'T SUIT YOU.
COME NOW!
TO TALK ABOUT HER THAT WAY... IT HARDLY SUITS YOU!
I'M SORRY IF I OFFENDED YOU, BUT...
...IT WAS A MISTAKE TO LET YOU GO THAT DAY.
PLEASE UNDER-STAND, OLIVIER.
HERE, BY MY SIDE, IS THE BEST PLACE FOR YOU.
DON'T MAKE ME DO SOME-THING I MIGHT REGRET.
PLEASE, JUST STAY WITH ME.

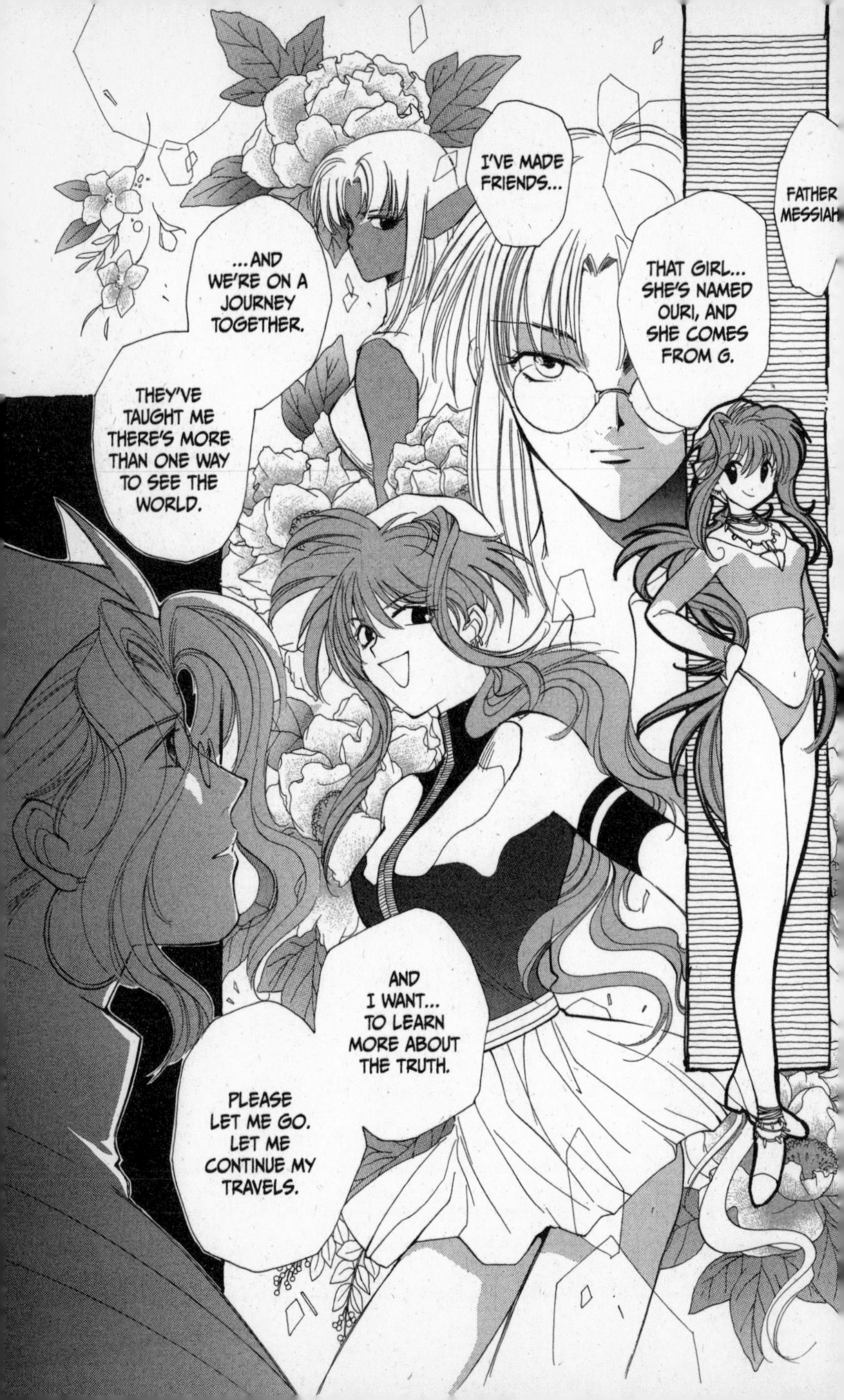
FATHER MESSIAH
THAT GIRL... SHE'S NAMED OURI, AND SHE COMES FROM G.
I'VE MADE FRIENDS...
...AND WE'RE ON A JOURNEY TOGETHER.
THEY'VE TAUGHT ME THERE'S MORE THAN ONE WAY TO SEE THE WORLD.
AND I WANT... TO LEARN MORE ABOUT THE TRUTH.
PLEASE LET ME GO. LET ME CONTINUE MY TRAVELS.

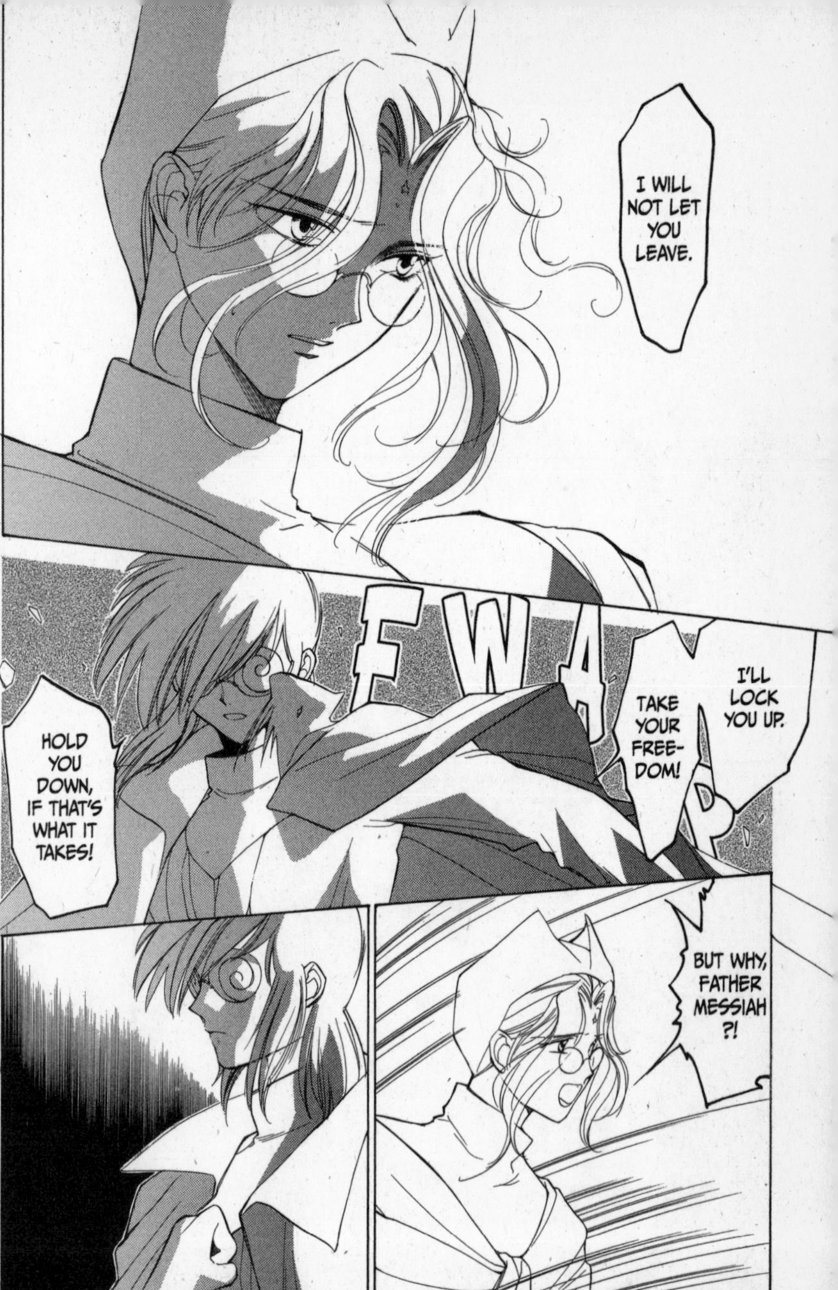
I WILL NOT LET YOU LEAVE.
I'LL LOCK YOU UP.
TAKE YOUR FREE-DOM!
FWAP
HOLD YOU DOWN, IF THAT'S WHAT IT TAKES!
BUT WHY, FATHER MESSIAH?!

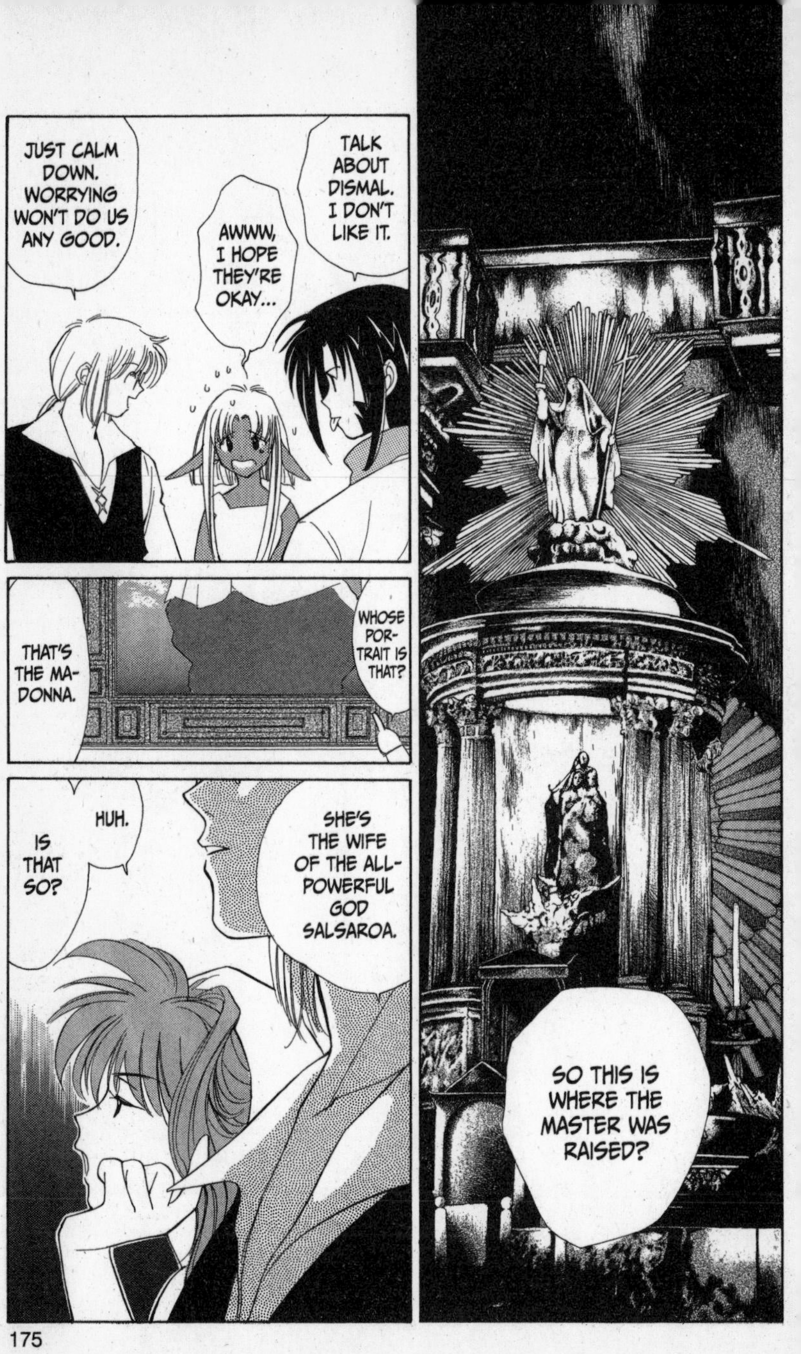
SO THIS IS WHERE THE MASTER WAS RAISED?
TALK ABOUT DISMAL. I DON'T LIKE IT.
AWWW, I HOPE THEY'RE OKAY...
JUST CALM DOWN. WORRYING WON'T DO US ANY GOOD.
WHOSE POR-TRAIT IS THAT?
THAT'S THE MA-DONNA.
SHE'S THE WIFE OF THE ALL-POWERFUL GOD SALSAROA.
HUH. IS THAT SO?

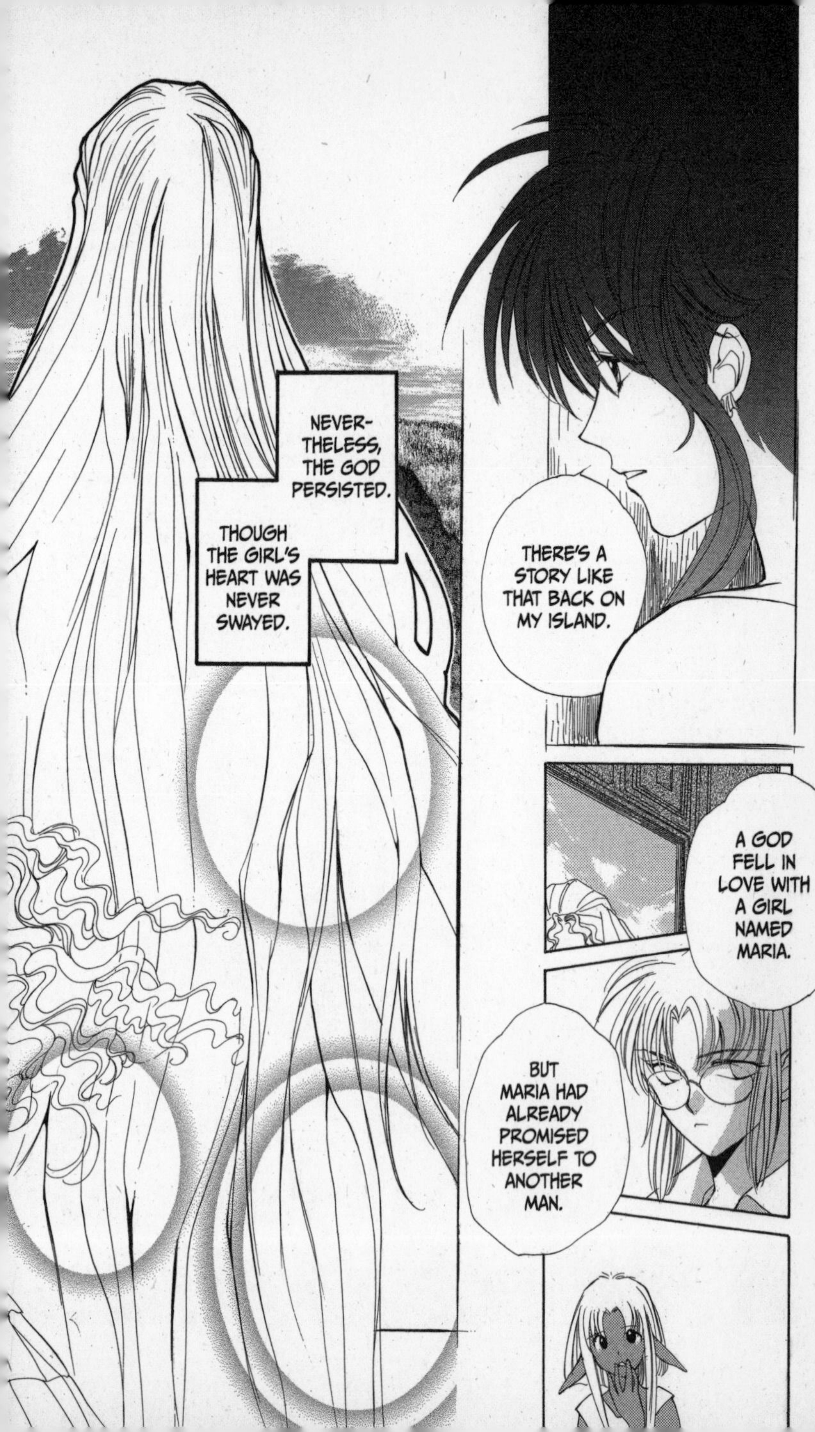
THERE'S A STORY LIKE THAT BACK ON MY ISLAND.
A GOD FELL IN LOVE WITH A GIRL NAMED MARIA.
BUT MARIA HAD ALREADY PROMISED HERSELF TO ANOTHER MAN.
NEVER-THELESS, THE GOD PERSISTED.
THOUGH THE GIRL'S HEART WAS NEVER SWAYED.

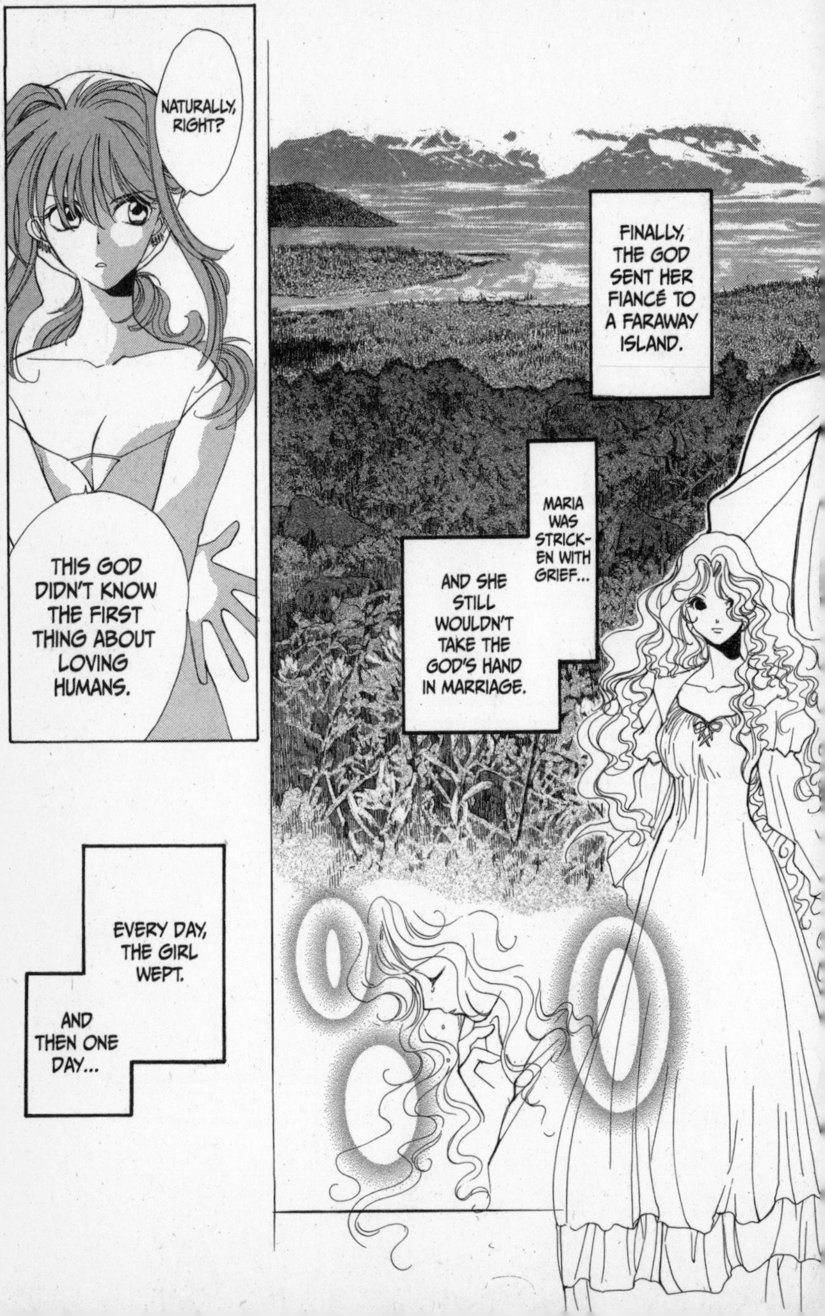
FINALLY, THE GOD SENT HER FIANCÉ TO A FARAWAY ISLAND.
MARIA WAS STRICK-EN WITH GRIEF...
AND SHE STILL WOULDN'T TAKE THE GOD'S HAND IN MARRIAGE.
NATURALLY, RIGHT?
THIS GOD DIDN'T KNOW THE FIRST THING ABOUT LOVING HUMANS.
EVERY DAY, THE GIRL WEPT.
AND THEN ONE DAY...

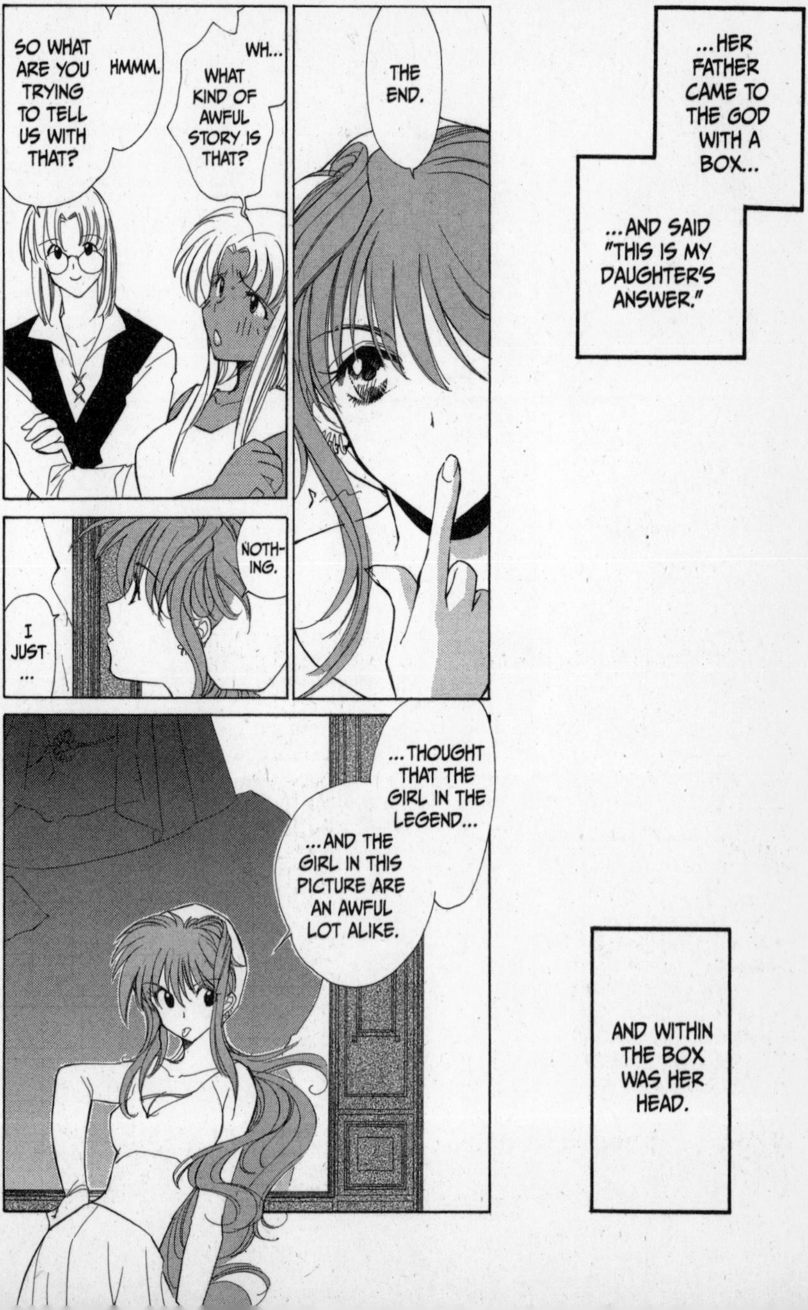
...HER FATHER CAME TO THE GOD WITH A BOX...
...AND SAID "THIS IS MY DAUGHTER'S ANSWER."
AND WITHIN THE BOX WAS HER HEAD.
THE END.
WH... WHAT KIND OF AWFUL STORY IS THAT?
HMMM.
SO WHAT ARE YOU TRYING TO TELL US WITH THAT?
NOTHING.
I JUST...
...THOUGHT THAT THE GIRL IN THE LEGEND...
...AND THE GIRL IN THIS PICTURE ARE AN AWFUL LOT ALIKE.

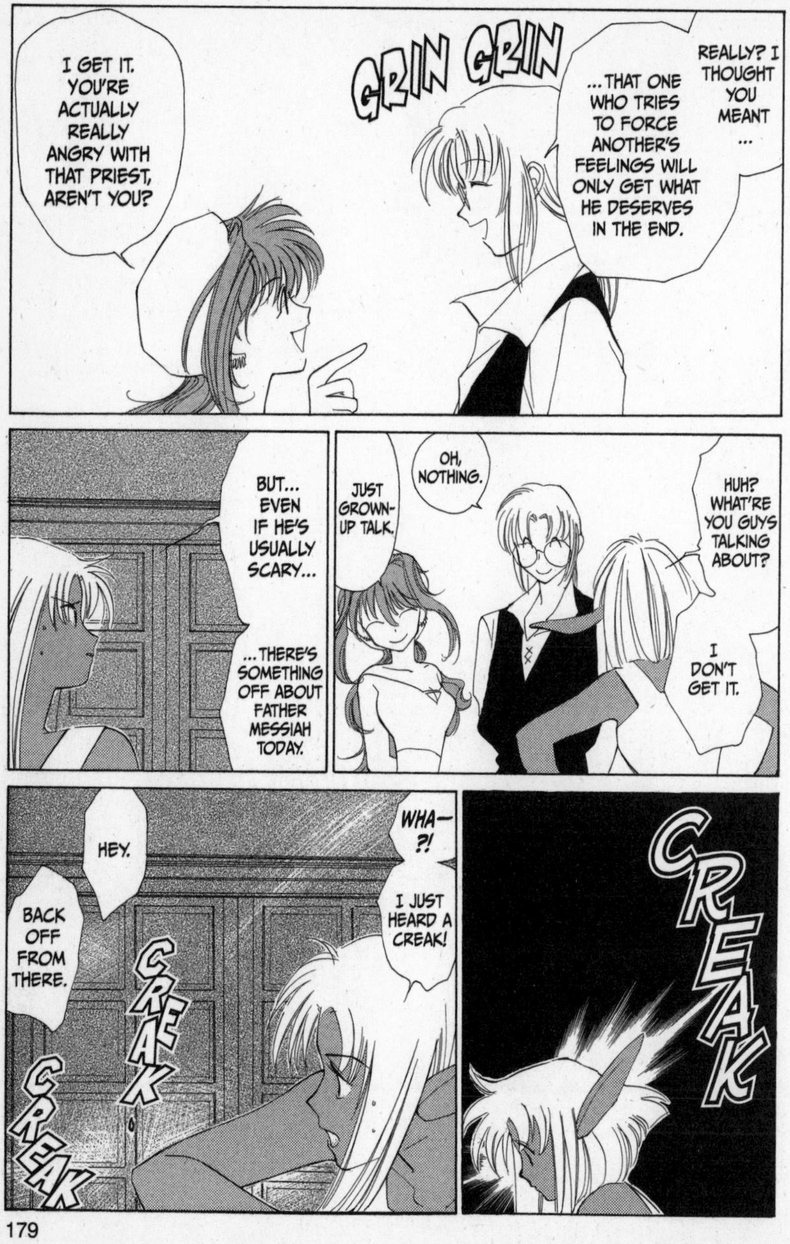
REALLY? I THOUGHT YOU MEANT ...
...THAT ONE WHO TRIES TO FORCE ANOTHER'S FEELINGS WILL ONLY GET WHAT HE DESERVES IN THE END.
GRIN GRIN
I GET IT. YOU'RE ACTUALLY REALLY ANGRY WITH THAT PRIEST, AREN'T YOU?
HUH? WHAT'RE YOU GUYS TALKING ABOUT?
I DON'T GET IT.
OH, NOTHING.
JUST GROWN-UP TALK.
BUT... EVEN IF HE'S USUALLY SCARY...
...THERE'S SOMETHING OFF ABOUT FATHER MESSIAH TODAY.
CREAK
WHA—?!
I JUST HEARD A CREAK!
HEY.
BACK OFF FROM THERE.
CREAK
CREAK

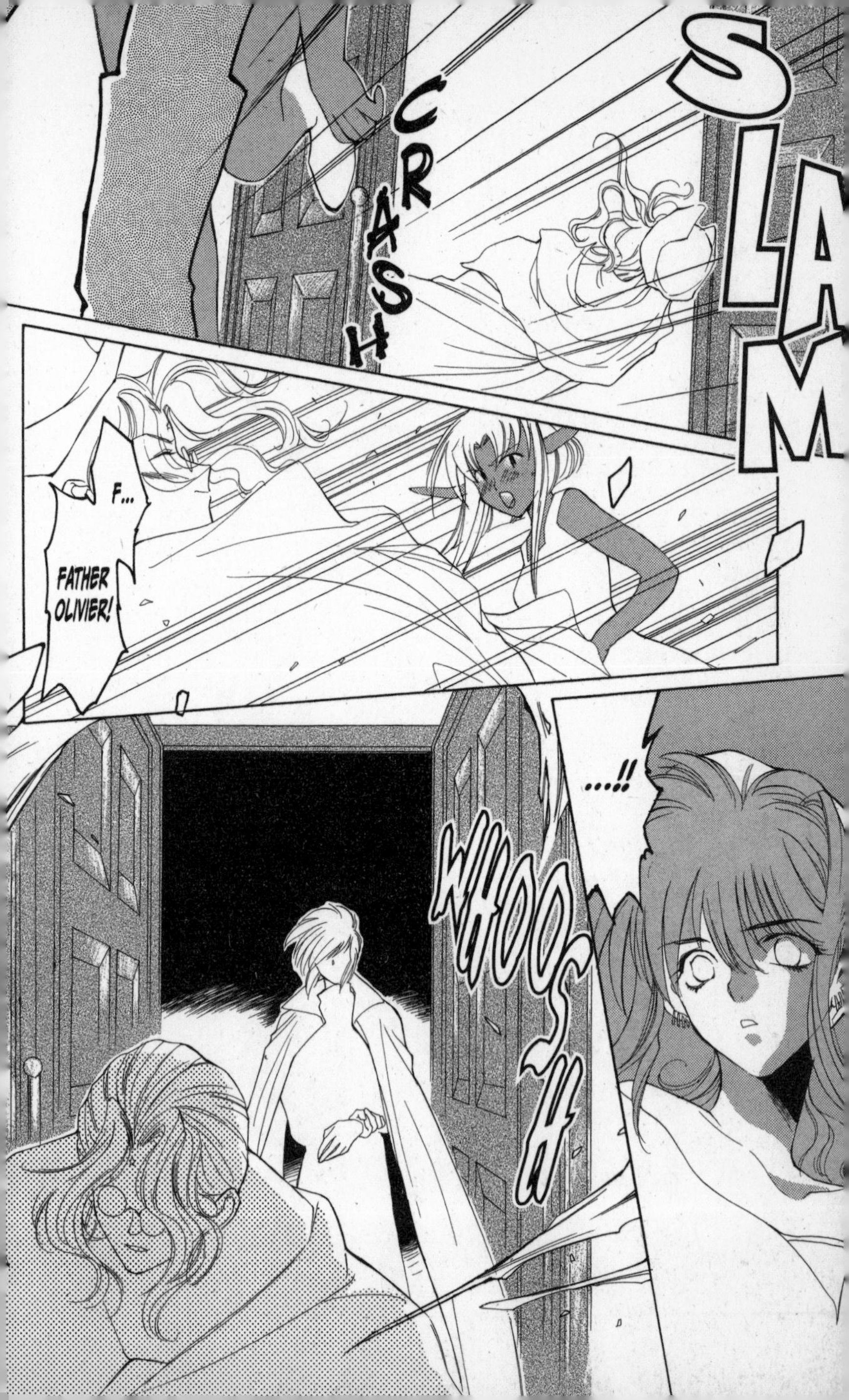
SLAM
CRASH
F...
FATHER OLIVIER!
...!!
WHOOSH

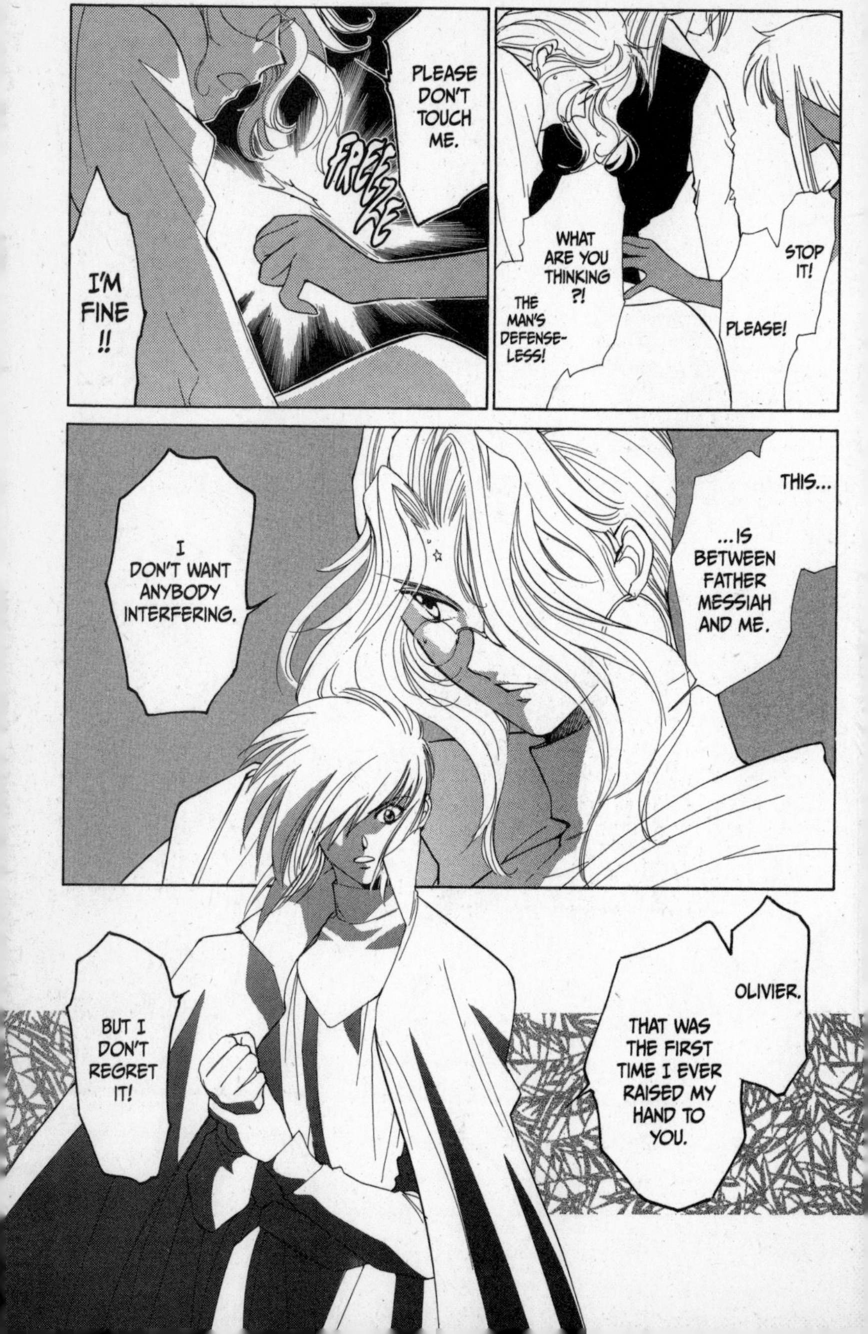
STOP IT!
PLEASE!
WHAT ARE YOU THINKING?!
THE MAN'S DEFENSELESS!
PLEASE DON'T TOUCH ME.
FREEZE
I'M FINE!!
THIS...
...IS BETWEEN FATHER MESSIAH AND ME.
I DON'T WANT ANYBODY INTERFERING.
OLIVIER.
THAT WAS THE FIRST TIME I EVER RAISED MY HAND TO YOU.
BUT I DON'T REGRET IT!

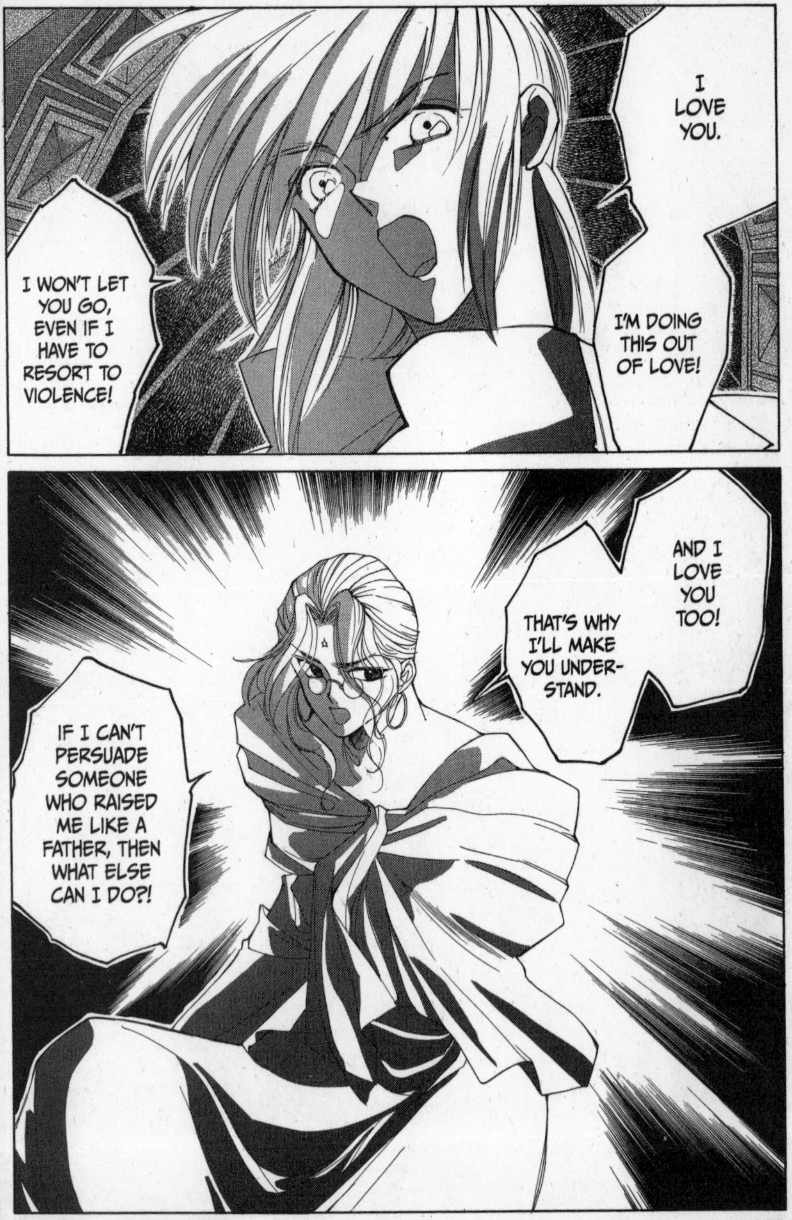
I LOVE YOU.
I'M DOING THIS OUT OF LOVE!
I WON'T LET YOU GO, EVEN IF I HAVE TO RESORT TO VIOLENCE!
AND I LOVE YOU TOO!
THAT'S WHY I'LL MAKE YOU UNDER-STAND.
IF I CAN'T PERSUADE SOMEONE WHO RAISED ME LIKE A FATHER, THEN WHAT ELSE CAN I DO?!

Gestalt 4 / THE END

ONCE AGAIN

THE GESTALT ROOM

☆WHAT IF YOU COULD CHANGE GENDERS?☆

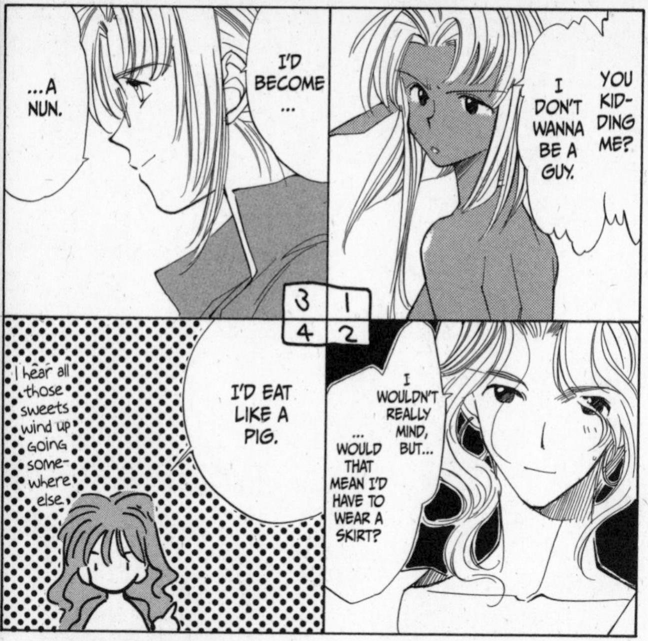
YOU KIDDING ME?
I DON'T WANNA BE A GUY.
I WOULDN'T REALLY MIND, BUT...
...WOULD THAT MEAN I'D HAVE TO WEAR A SKIRT?
I'D BECOME...
...A NUN.
I'D EAT LIKE A PIG.
I hear all those sweets wind up going somewhere else.

IT'S VOLUME 4! SO HELLO!

THANKS FOR BEING SO PATIENT! ♥

Then again, this volume seemed to come out even faster than previous ones, don't you agree? Volume 4 had scenes that are special favorites of mine, so I enjoyed writing it even more. I hope you all enjoyed it just as much as I did!

Sincerely, Kouga

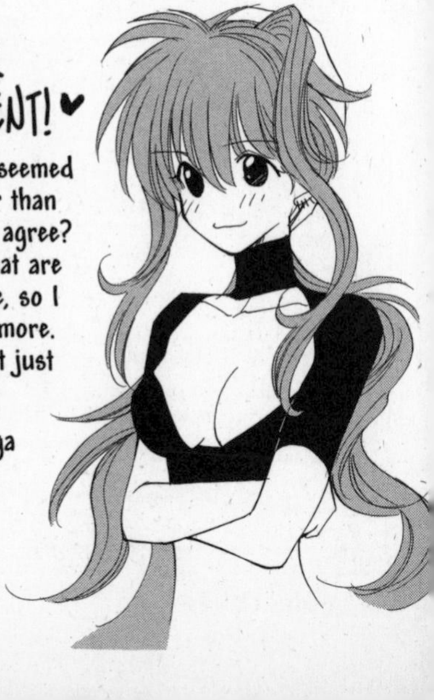

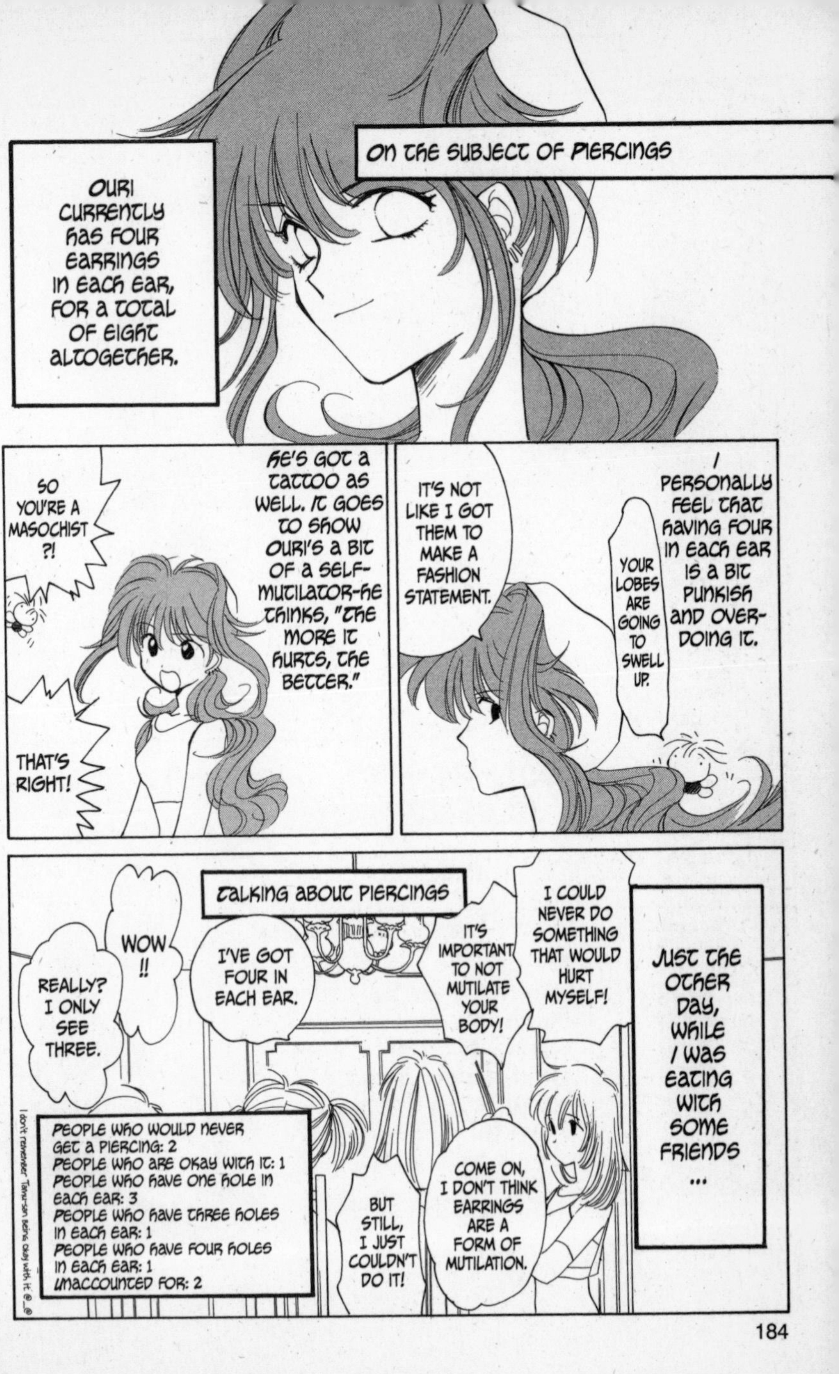
ON THE SUBJECT OF PIERCINGS
OURI CURRENTLY HAS FOUR EARRINGS IN EACH EAR, FOR A TOTAL OF EIGHT ALTOGETHER.
I PERSONALLY FEEL THAT HAVING FOUR IN EACH EAR IS A BIT PUNKISH AND OVER-DOING IT.
YOUR LOBES ARE GOING TO SWELL UP.
IT'S NOT LIKE I GOT THEM TO MAKE A FASHION STATEMENT.
HE'S GOT A TATTOO AS WELL. IT GOES TO SHOW OURI'S A BIT OF A SELF-MUTILATOR–HE THINKS, "THE MORE IT HURTS, THE BETTER."
SO YOU'RE A MASOCHIST?!
THAT'S RIGHT!
JUST THE OTHER DAY, WHILE I WAS EATING WITH SOME FRIENDS...
TALKING ABOUT PIERCINGS
I COULD NEVER DO SOMETHING THAT WOULD HURT MYSELF!
IT'S IMPORTANT TO NOT MUTILATE YOUR BODY!
I'VE GOT FOUR IN EACH EAR.
WOW!!
REALLY? I ONLY SEE THREE.
COME ON, I DON'T THINK EARRINGS ARE A FORM OF MUTILATION.
BUT STILL, I JUST COULDN'T DO IT!
PEOPLE WHO WOULD NEVER GET A PIERCING: 2
PEOPLE WHO ARE OKAY WITH IT: 1
PEOPLE WHO HAVE ONE HOLE IN EACH EAR: 3
PEOPLE WHO HAVE THREE HOLES IN EACH EAR: 1
PEOPLE WHO HAVE FOUR HOLES IN EACH EAR: 1
UNACCOUNTED FOR: 2
I don't remember Tamu-san being okay with it. @_@

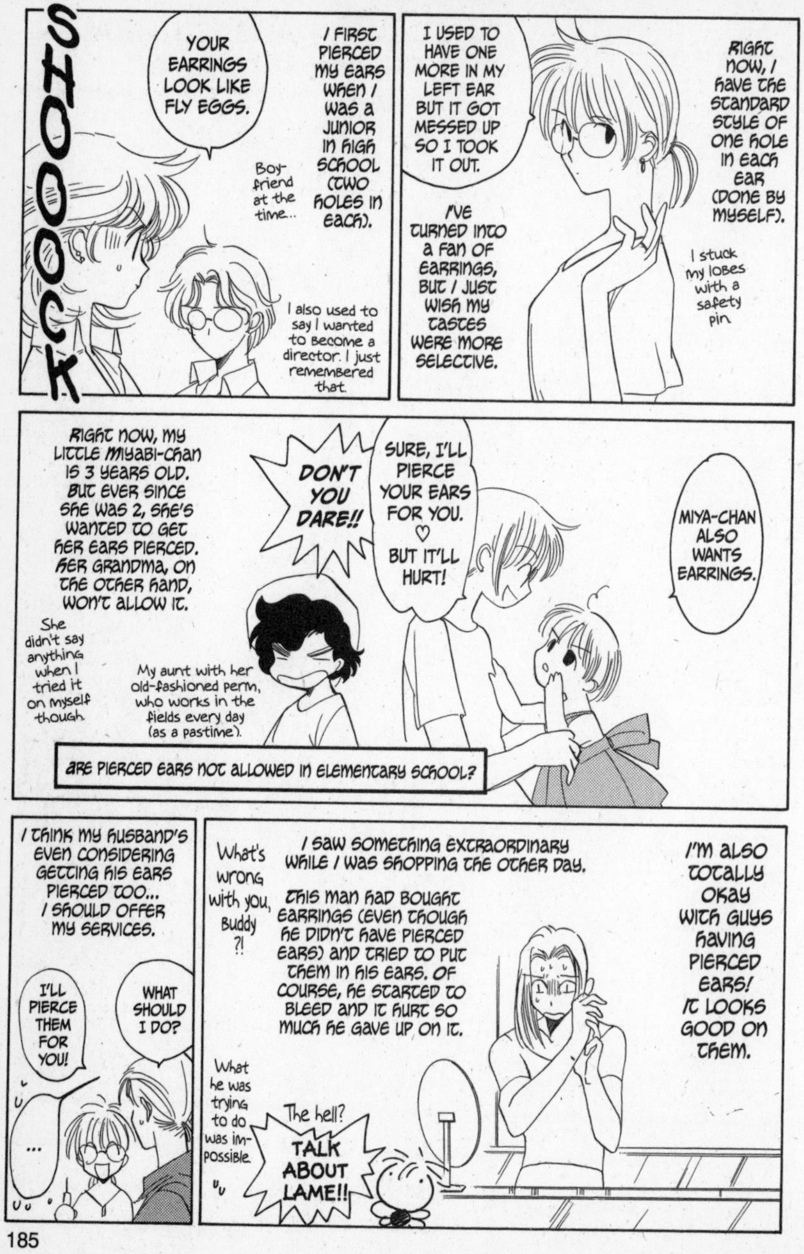
RIGHT NOW, I HAVE THE STANDARD STYLE OF ONE HOLE IN EACH EAR (DONE BY MYSELF).
I stuck my lobes with a safety pin.
I USED TO HAVE ONE MORE IN MY LEFT EAR BUT IT GOT MESSED UP SO I TOOK IT OUT.
I'VE TURNED INTO A FAN OF EARRINGS, BUT I JUST WISH MY TASTES WERE MORE SELECTIVE.
I FIRST PIERCED MY EARS WHEN I WAS A JUNIOR IN HIGH SCHOOL (TWO HOLES IN EACH).
Boy-friend at the time...
YOUR EARRINGS LOOK LIKE FLY EGGS.
SHOOOCK
I also used to say I wanted to become a director. I just remembered that.
MIYA-CHAN ALSO WANTS EARRINGS.
SURE, I'LL PIERCE YOUR EARS FOR YOU. ♡
BUT IT'LL HURT!
DON'T YOU DARE!!
RIGHT NOW, MY LITTLE MIYABI-CHAN IS 3 YEARS OLD. BUT EVER SINCE SHE WAS 2, SHE'S WANTED TO GET HER EARS PIERCED. HER GRANDMA, ON THE OTHER HAND, WON'T ALLOW IT.
She didn't say anything when I tried it on myself though.
My aunt with her old-fashioned perm, who works in the fields every day (as a pastime).
ARE PIERCED EARS NOT ALLOWED IN ELEMENTARY SCHOOL?
I'M ALSO TOTALLY OKAY WITH GUYS HAVING PIERCED EARS! IT LOOKS GOOD ON THEM.
I SAW SOMETHING EXTRAORDINARY WHILE I WAS SHOPPING THE OTHER DAY.
THIS MAN HAD BOUGHT EARRINGS (EVEN THOUGH HE DIDN'T HAVE PIERCED EARS) AND TRIED TO PUT THEM IN HIS EARS. OF COURSE, HE STARTED TO BLEED AND IT HURT SO MUCH HE GAVE UP ON IT.
What's wrong with you, Buddy?!
What he was trying to do was impossible.
The hell?
TALK ABOUT LAME!!
I THINK MY HUSBAND'S EVEN CONSIDERING GETTING HIS EARS PIERCED TOO... I SHOULD OFFER MY SERVICES.
WHAT SHOULD I DO?
I'LL PIERCE THEM FOR YOU!
...

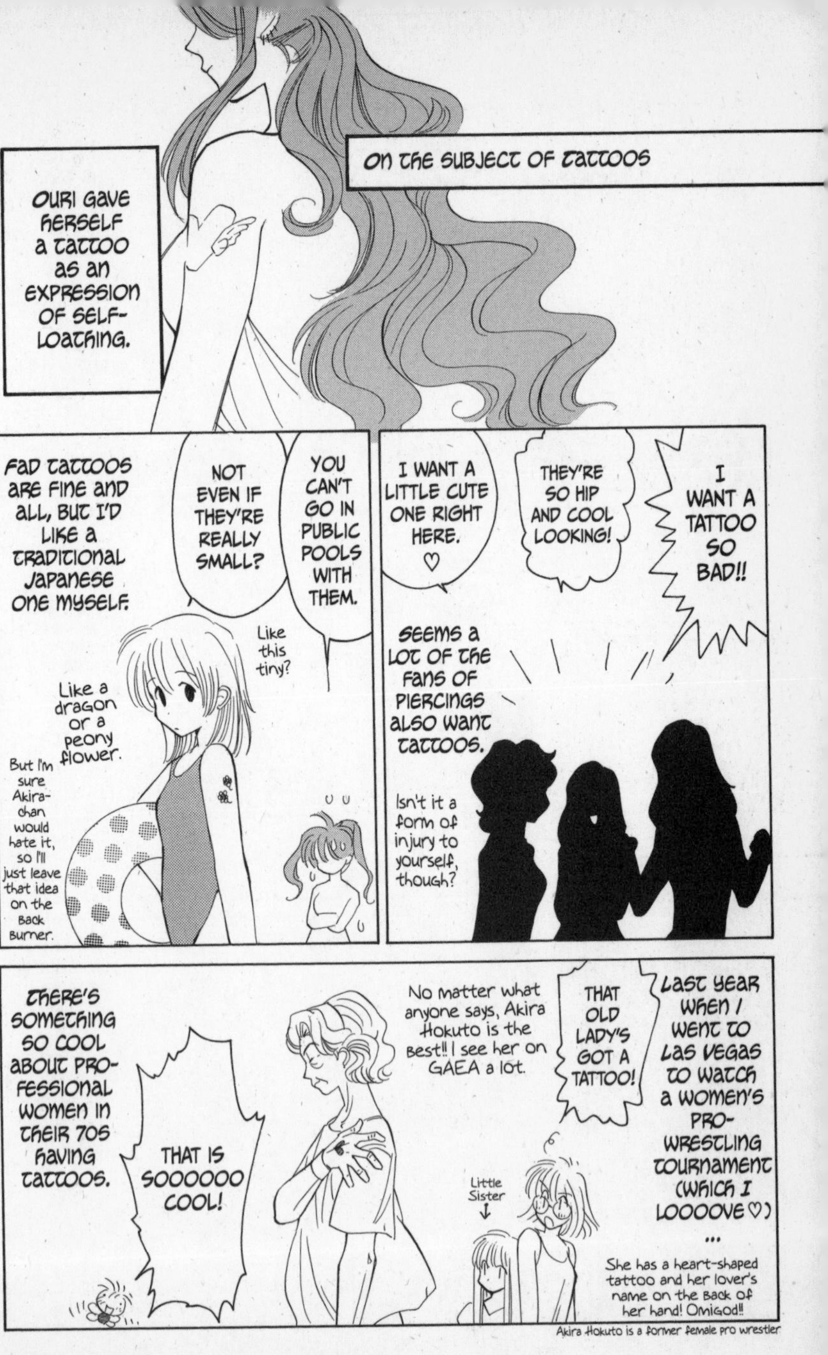
On the subject of tattoos
Ouri gave herself a tattoo as an expression of self-loathing.
I want a tattoo so bad!!
They're so hip and cool looking!
I want a little cute one right here. ♡
Seems a lot of the fans of piercings also want tattoos.
Isn't it a form of injury to yourself, though?
You can't go in public pools with them.
Not even if they're really small?
Fad tattoos are fine and all, but I'd like a traditional Japanese one myself.
Like this tiny?
Like a dragon or a peony flower.
But I'm sure Akira-chan would hate it, so I'll just leave that idea on the back burner.
Last year when I went to Las Vegas to watch a women's pro-wrestling tournament (which I loooove♡) ...
That old lady's got a tattoo!
No matter what anyone says, Akira Hokuto is the best!! I see her on GAEA a lot.
There's something so cool about pro-fessional women in their 70s having tattoos.
That is sooooooo cool!
Little Sister ↓
She has a heart-shaped tattoo and her lover's name on the back of her hand! Omigod!!

Akira Hokuto is a former female pro wrestler

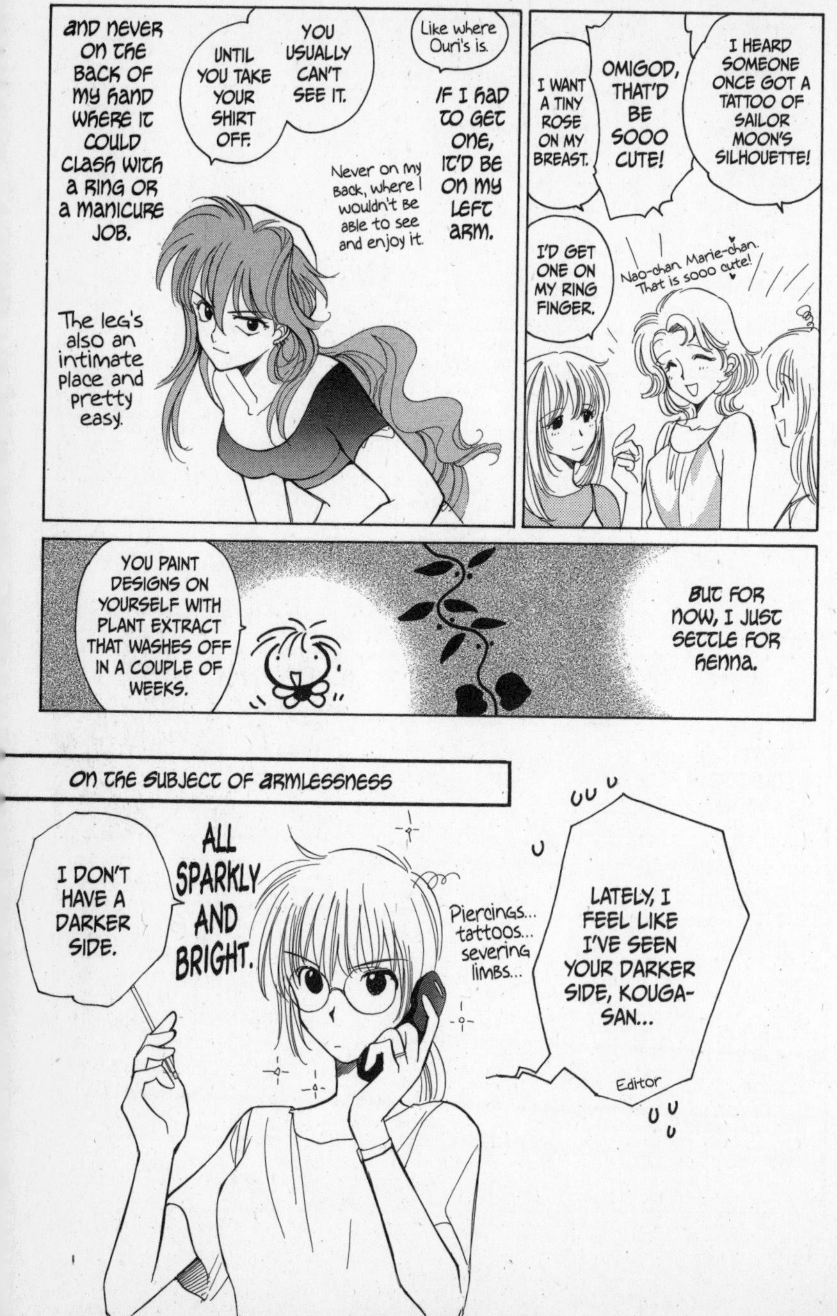
I HEARD SOMEONE ONCE GOT A TATTOO OF SAILOR MOON'S SILHOUETTE!
OMIGOD, THAT'D BE SOOO CUTE!
I WANT A TINY ROSE ON MY BREAST.
Nao-chan Marie-chan. That is sooo cute!
I'D GET ONE ON MY RING FINGER.
Like where Ouri's is.
IF I HAD TO GET ONE, IT'D BE ON MY LEFT ARM.
Never on my back, where I wouldn't be able to see and enjoy it.
YOU USUALLY CAN'T SEE IT.
UNTIL YOU TAKE YOUR SHIRT OFF.
AND NEVER ON THE BACK OF MY HAND WHERE IT COULD CLASH WITH A RING OR A MANICURE JOB.
The leg's also an intimate place and pretty easy.
BUT FOR NOW, I JUST SETTLE FOR HENNA.
YOU PAINT DESIGNS ON YOURSELF WITH PLANT EXTRACT THAT WASHES OFF IN A COUPLE OF WEEKS.
ON THE SUBJECT OF ARMLESSNESS
LATELY, I FEEL LIKE I'VE SEEN YOUR DARKER SIDE, KOUGA-SAN...
Editor
Piercings... tattoos... severing limbs...
ALL SPARKLY AND BRIGHT.
I DON'T HAVE A DARKER SIDE.

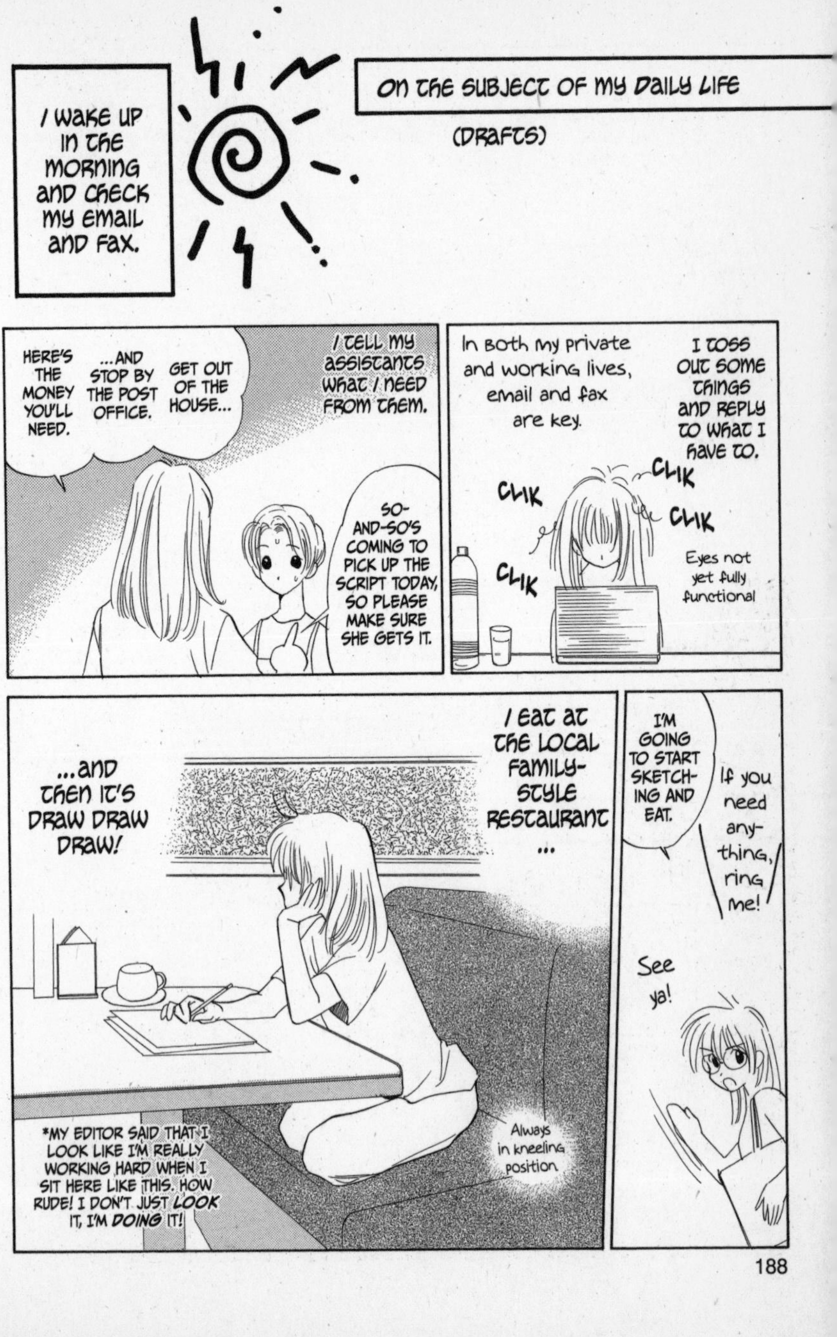
ON THE SUBJECT OF MY DAILY LIFE
(DRAFTS)
I WAKE UP IN THE MORNING AND CHECK MY EMAIL AND FAX.
I TOSS OUT SOME THINGS AND REPLY TO WHAT I HAVE TO.
In both my private and working lives, email and fax are key.
CLIK
CLIK
CLIK
CLIK
Eyes not yet fully functional
I TELL MY ASSISTANTS WHAT I NEED FROM THEM.
HERE'S THE MONEY YOU'LL NEED. ...AND STOP BY THE POST OFFICE. GET OUT OF THE HOUSE...
SO-AND-SO'S COMING TO PICK UP THE SCRIPT TODAY, SO PLEASE MAKE SURE SHE GETS IT.
I'M GOING TO START SKETCHING AND EAT.
If you need anything, ring me!
See ya!
I EAT AT THE LOCAL FAMILY-STYLE RESTAURANT...
...AND THEN IT'S DRAW DRAW DRAW!
Always in kneeling position
*MY EDITOR SAID THAT I LOOK LIKE I'M REALLY WORKING HARD WHEN I SIT HERE LIKE THIS. HOW RUDE! I DON'T JUST *LOOK* IT, I'M *DOING* IT!

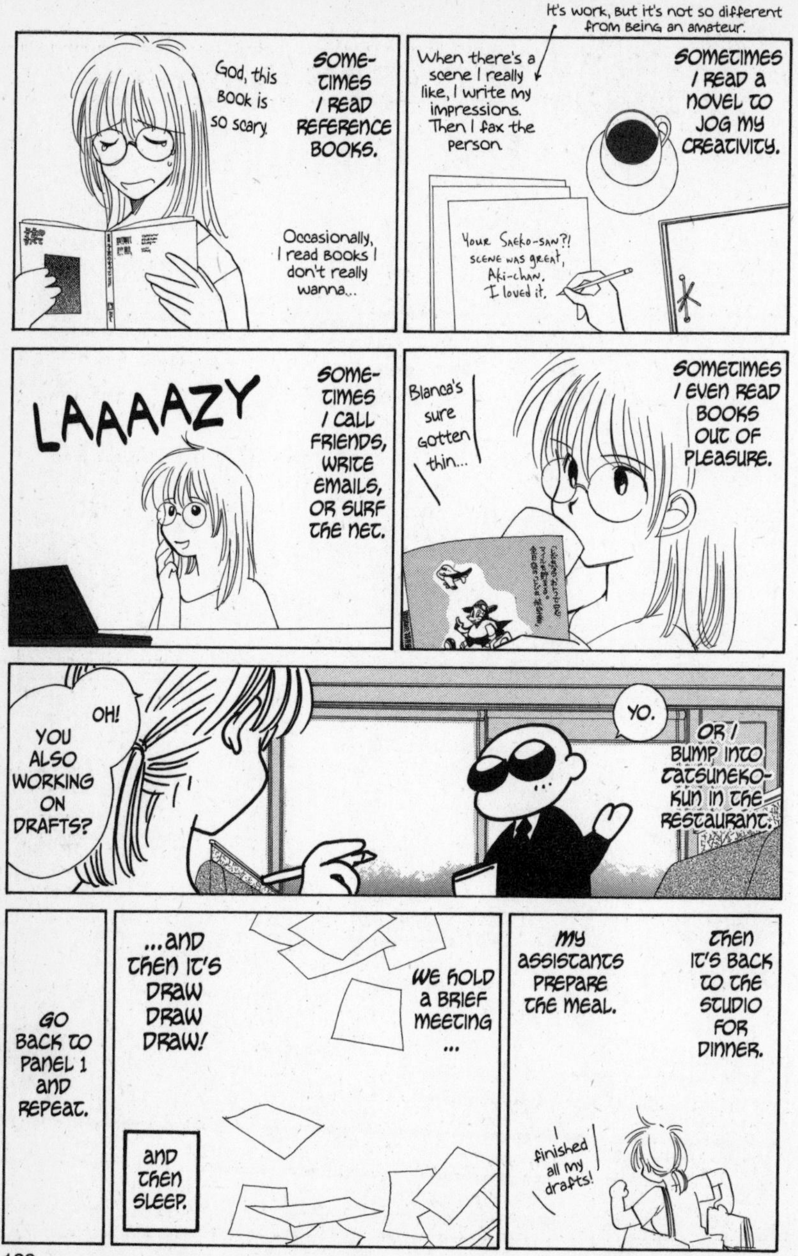
SOMETIMES I READ A NOVEL TO JOG MY CREATIVITY.
When there's a scene I really like, I write my impressions. Then I fax the person
It's work, but it's not so different from being an amateur.
Your Saeko-san?! scene was great, Aki-chan. I loved it.
SOME-TIMES I READ REFERENCE BOOKS.
God, this book is so scary.
Occasionally, I read books I don't really wanna...
SOMETIMES I EVEN READ BOOKS OUT OF PLEASURE.
Blanca's sure gotten thin...
SOME-TIMES I CALL FRIENDS, WRITE EMAILS, OR SURF THE NET.
LAAAAZY
OR I BUMP INTO TATSUNEKO-KUN IN THE RESTAURANT.
YO.
OH! YOU ALSO WORKING ON DRAFTS?
THEN IT'S BACK TO THE STUDIO FOR DINNER.
MY ASSISTANTS PREPARE THE MEAL.
I finished all my drafts!
WE HOLD A BRIEF MEETING...
...AND THEN IT'S DRAW DRAW DRAW!
AND THEN SLEEP.
GO BACK TO PANEL 1 AND REPEAT.

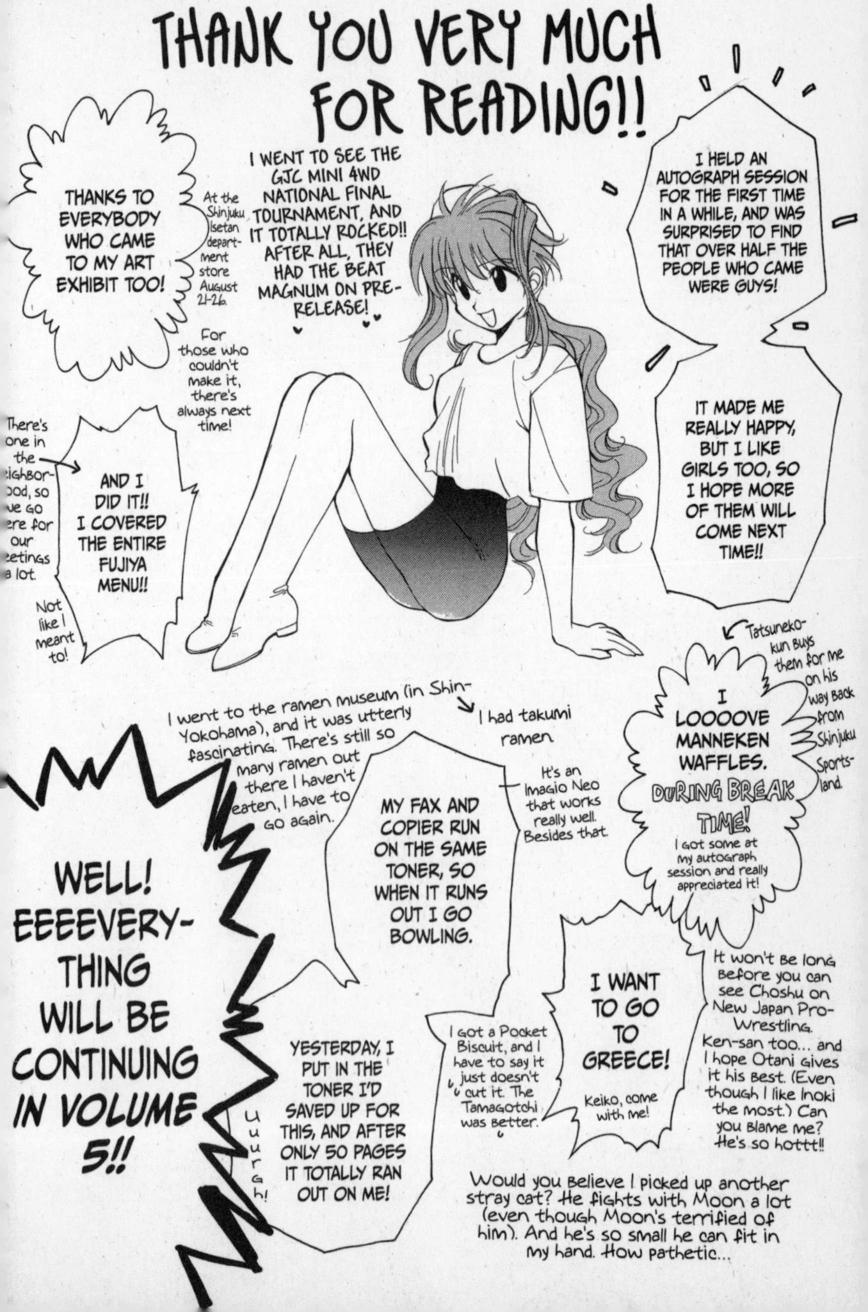
THANK YOU VERY MUCH FOR READING!!
I HELD AN AUTOGRAPH SESSION FOR THE FIRST TIME IN A WHILE, AND WAS SURPRISED TO FIND THAT OVER HALF THE PEOPLE WHO CAME WERE GUYS!
IT MADE ME REALLY HAPPY, BUT I LIKE GIRLS TOO, SO I HOPE MORE OF THEM WILL COME NEXT TIME!!
I WENT TO SEE THE GJC MINI 4WD NATIONAL FINAL TOURNAMENT, AND IT TOTALLY ROCKED!! AFTER ALL, THEY HAD THE BEAT MAGNUM ON PRE-RELEASE!
THANKS TO EVERYBODY WHO CAME TO MY ART EXHIBIT TOO!
At the Shinjuku Isetan department store August 21-26.
For those who couldn't make it, there's always next time!
AND I DID IT!! I COVERED THE ENTIRE FUJIYA MENU!!
There's one in the ighbor- ood, so we go ere for our etings a lot.
Not like I meant to!
Tatsuneko-kun Buys them for me on his way Back from Shinjuku Sports-land.
I LOOOOVE MANNEKEN WAFFLES.
DURING BREAK TIME!
I got some at my autograph session and really appreciated it!
I went to the ramen museum (in Shin-Yokohama), and it was utterly fascinating. There's still so many ramen out there I haven't eaten, I have to go again.
I had takumi ramen.
It's an Imagio Neo that works really well. Besides that.
MY FAX AND COPIER RUN ON THE SAME TONER, SO WHEN IT RUNS OUT I GO BOWLING.
It won't be long Before you can see Choshu on New Japan Pro-Wrestling. Ken-san too... and I hope Otani gives it his Best. (Even though I like Inoki the most.) Can you Blame me? He's so hottt!!
I WANT TO GO TO GREECE!
Keiko, come with me!
I got a Pocket Biscuit, and I have to say it just doesn't cut it. The Tamagotchi was Better.
YESTERDAY, I PUT IN THE TONER I'D SAVED UP FOR THIS, AND AFTER ONLY 50 PAGES IT TOTALLY RAN OUT ON ME!
Uuurgh!
WELL! EEEEVERY-THING WILL BE CONTINUING IN VOLUME 5!!
Would you Believe I picked up another stray cat? He fights with Moon a lot (even though Moon's terrified of him). And he's so small he can fit in my hand. How pathetic...

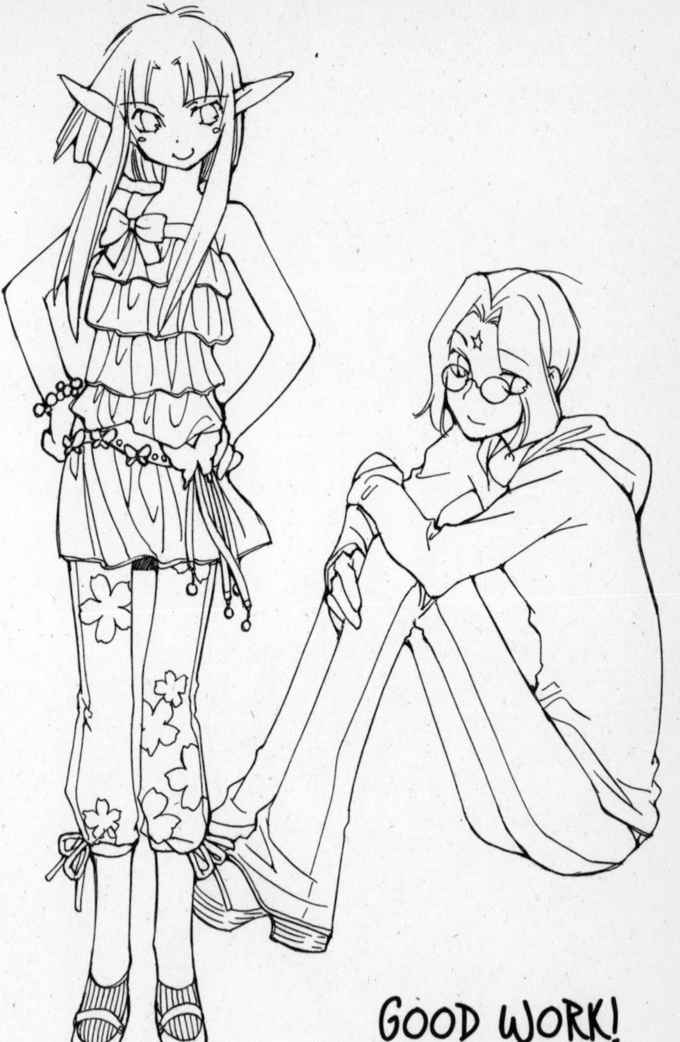

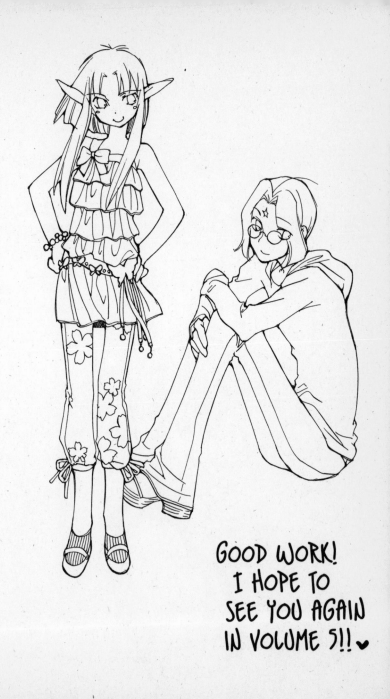

GOOD WORK!
I HOPE TO
SEE YOU AGAIN
IN VOLUME 5!! ♥

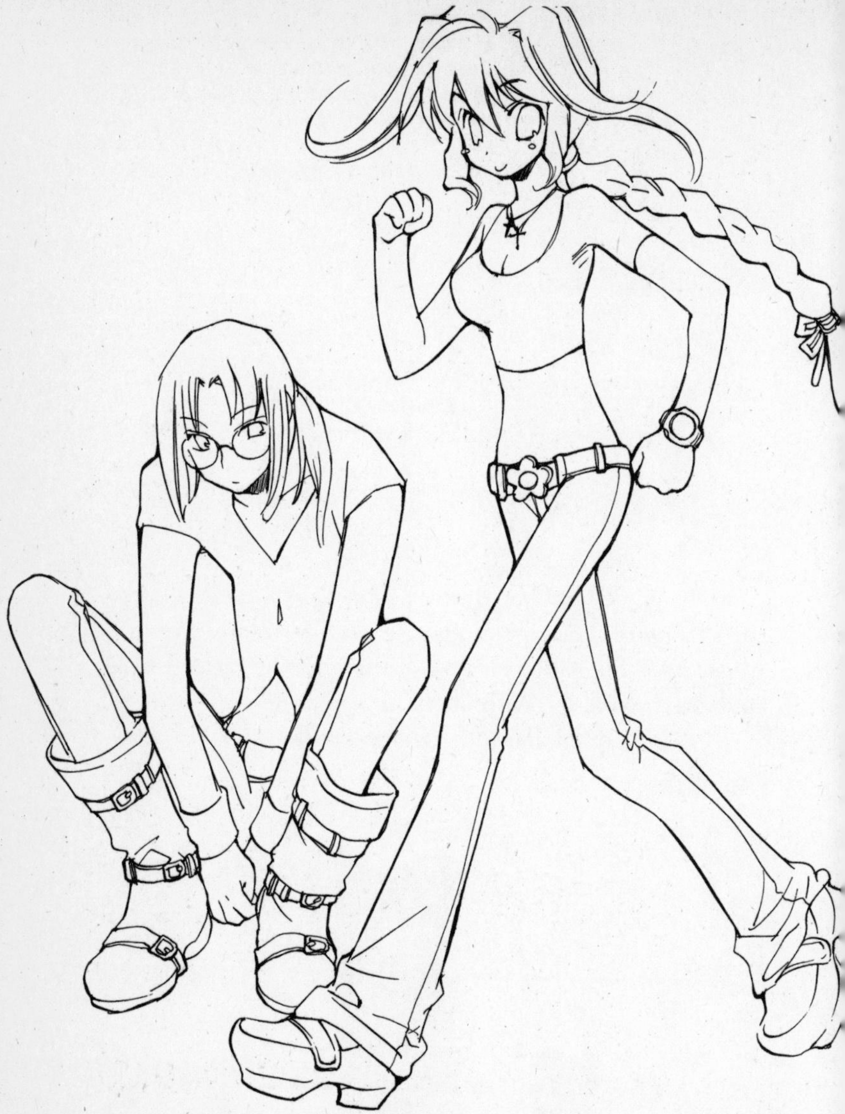

I want to go to the Aichi World's Fair!!
Signed, Yun Kouga
May 2005

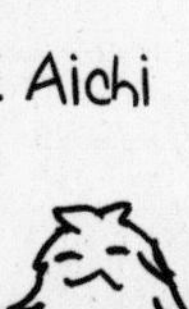

I keep thinking about this little guy.

Here we are at volume 4. It can feel like forever while the chapters are coming out one by one in the magazine, but then the finished volume hits the shelves before you know it! Whee!

To all the fans of *Loveless* out there, hi! ♡

Yun Kouga began her career as a doujinshi and debuted in 1986 with the original manga *Metal Heart*, serialized in *Comic VAL*. She is the creator of the popular series *Loveless* and *Earthian*, along with many manga and anime projects, including character design for *Gundam 00*.

Gestalt
Vol. 4
VIZ Media Edition

Story and Art by Yun Kouga

Translation & English Adaptation/Christine Schilling
Touch-up Art & Lettering/Evan Waldinger
Design/Sean Lee
Editor/Chris Mackenzie

VP, Production/Alvin Lu
VP, Publishing Licensing/Rika Inouye
VP, Sales & Product Marketing/Gonzalo Ferreyra
VP, Creative/ Linda Espinosa
Publisher/Hyoe Narita

CHOUJUU DENSETSU GESTALT © Yun Kouga / ICHIJINSHA

Printed in the U.S.A.

Published by VIZ Media, LLC
P.O. Box 77010
San Francisco, CA 94107

10 9 8 7 6 5 4 3 2 1
First printing, December 2009

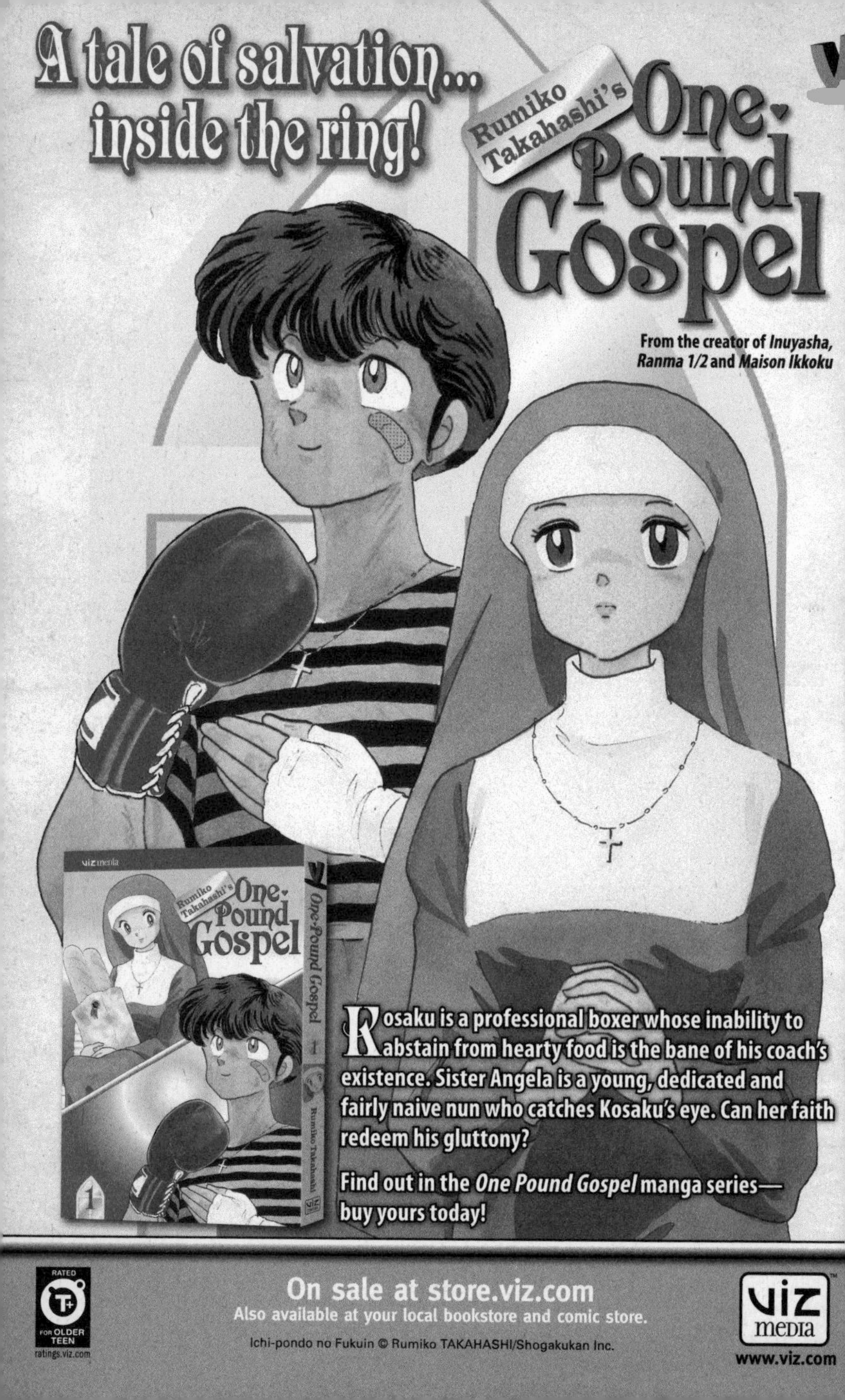

A tale of salvation... inside the ring!
Rumiko Takahashi's One-Pound Gospel
From the creator of Inuyasha, Ranma 1/2 and Maison Ikkoku
viz media
Rumiko Takahashi's One-Pound Gospel
One-Pound Gospel 1 Rumiko Takahashi
Kosaku is a professional boxer whose inability to abstain from hearty food is the bane of his coach's existence. Sister Angela is a young, dedicated and fairly naive nun who catches Kosaku's eye. Can her faith redeem his gluttony?
Find out in the One Pound Gospel manga series—buy yours today!
RATED T+ FOR OLDER TEEN ratings.viz.com
On sale at store.viz.com
Also available at your local bookstore and comic store.
Ichi-pondo no Fukuin © Rumiko TAKAHASHI/Shogakukan Inc.
viz media
www.viz.com